Competition Law of the UK and EC

Competition Law of the UK and EC

Third Edition

Mark Furse

OXFORD
UNIVERSITY PRESS

OXFORD
UNIVERSITY PRESS

Great Clarendon Street, Oxford OX2 6DP

Oxford University Press is a department of the University of Oxford.
It furthers the University's objective of excellence in research, scholarship,
and education by publishing worldwide in

Oxford New York

Auckland Bangkok Buenos Aires Cape Town Chennai
Dar es Salaam Delhi Hong Kong Istanbul Karachi Kolkata
Kuala Lumpur Madrid Melbourne Mexico City Mumbai Nairobi
São Paulo Shanghai Singapore Taipei Tokyo Toronto

Oxford is a registered trade mark of Oxford University Press
in the UK and in certain other countries

Published in the United States
by Oxford University Press Inc., New York

British Library Cataloguing in Publication Data

Data available

Library of Congress Cataloging in Publication Data

Data available

ISBN 0–19925–487–7

3 5 7 9 10 8 6 4 2

Typeset in ITC Stone Serif and ITC Stone Sans
by RefineCatch Limited, Bungay, Suffolk
Printed in Great Britain by
Antony Rowe Limited,
Chippenham, Wiltshire

OUTLINE CONTENTS

DETAILED CONTENTS

Appendix: The Enterprise Bill   327

PREFACE

Do you not play dirty when engaged in competition?
(Alanis Morrissette, *21 Things I want in a Lover*)

There has been unprecedented interest in, and activity relating to, competition law since the second edition of this book was published. At the time this third edition was prepared, in the spring of 2002, many further changes were in the offing, and I am very grateful to my publishers for their commitment to a fourth edition for the academic year 2003/4.

I have made substantial changes to this edition, affecting about one-quarter of the text in total, and thank OUP for their leniency in permitting me this indulgence. In the past two years the Competition Act 1998 has begun to bite in the UK. There have been a number of decisions taken by the OFT, and some private actions, albeit of limited success, all of which are dealt with here as appropriate, and the first fines have been imposed, and 'dawn raids' made. These have received much attention in the popular media, which have also been interested in the ongoing mire that has ensnared Microsoft Corporation on both sides of the Atlantic, and the prosecution of the Christie's/Sotheby's cartel by the US authorities. The Microsoft case formed an ill-disguised backdrop for the film *Antitrust* (2001, Peter Howitt—readers interested in competition law are recommended to watch this film, but not to base exam answers or client advice on it), and the latter led to an op-ed column in the London *Evening Standard* by its art critic, Brian Sewell, which was woefully ignorant of competition law, and would provide a fruitful source of exam and assignment questions ('[the auction houses] are perfectly entitled to agree a common scale of charges'—Critically discuss!).

In the EC there have been two new block exemption regulations, and the important horizontal restraint guidelines, as well as a new notice relating to *de minimis* agreements, and some significant case law. There have also been proposals to reform the operation of a large part of the procedure, and the merger regulation. I have as far as possible restricted discussion of these proposed changes to clearly demarked areas within the text so as to reduce the possibility of confusion between what is the law, and what is the anticipated law. I do not think that it is unreasonable to expect those interested in the area to read the original documentation relating to the reform processes.

In the UK further radical changes are expected across a range of areas, with the Government in its White Paper *Productivity and Enterprise: A world class competition regime* (Cm 5233, July 2001) announcing its commitment to changes to a substantial part of the domestic regime. Some of these changes, such as the removal of the political influence in the application of the merger regime, and the replacing of the public interest test of the Fair Trading Act 1973 with a competition test, are to be greatly welcomed. Others, such as the criminalization of cartel conduct, are, at least to me, of less obvious appeal.

This book continues to be aimed at those seeking an introductory-level text to the subject of competition law, and therefore deals with a wide range of material, although I hope in sufficient depth to satisfy the demands of most undergraduate courses. Special emphasis is placed in this text on some of the underlying economics, as I firmly believe that competition law cannot be understood without an understanding of the economic context in which it is being invoked. I have added, for this edition, a new Chapter 14 dealing briefly with the economics of mergers.

For me this edition of the book is particularly notable. It will be the first to be published following my departure from the University of Westminster, where until recently I was a Reader in Law, and where I had worked for nearly 16 years. While I am seeking pastures new, I would unhesitatingly recommend the law school and its staff to any prospective student, and I would like to take this opportunity to thank all the staff there with whom I have worked over the years. While it is invidious to single out any one person I will single out two—Susan, and Charlie, thank you, it's been fun.

This is the first edition of this book to be published by Oxford University Press, and I have been impressed by the professionalism of the team involved in its production. I owe particular thanks to students of the University of Westminster, the London School of Economics, and Lund University, who have continued to challenge my perceptions about this exciting subject, and whose company I have enjoyed in lectures and seminars. Verena Behnke in Germany provided useful up-to-date information relating to German competition law. Apologies are due to Victoria Elliott for the time I spent working on this edition on a break in Boston in March 2002—sorry.

As I expect to be working on a new edition of this book within a year of the publication of this one, I would remain grateful for any comments regarding its usefulness, or lack of usefulness, and particularly grateful if errors, for which I am solely responsible, are pointed out. I can be contacted either via Oxford University Press, or by email at mark@mfcompetitionlaw.com. Sadly no one has yet taken me up on this ongoing offer, but it is a sincere one.

The law in this text is intended to be up to date as at 1 May 2002.

Mark Furse
Ebrington, The Cotswolds
May 2002

TABLE OF CASES, DECISIONS, AND REPORTS

Numerical table of judgments of the CFI and ECJ

Numerical table of EC Commission decisions

TABLE OF STATUTES

UK Secondary Legislation

UK Bills

European Primary Legislation

LIST OF ABBREVIATIONS

ATC	Average total cost
AVC	Average variable cost
CBI	Confederation of British Industry
CC	Competition Commission
CCAT	Competition Commission Appeals Tribunal
CFI	Court of First Instance
DGFT	Director General of Fair Trading
DTI	Department of Trade and Industry
EAEC	European Atomic Energy Community (Euratom)
EC	European Community
ECHR	European Convention on Human Rights
ECJ	European Court of Justice
ECSC	European Coal and Steel Community
ECU	European Currency Unit (now replaced by the Euro)
EEA	European Economic Area
EEC	European Economic Community (now the EC)
EFTA	European Free Trade Area
EU	European Union
EUCAR	European Council for Automotive Research and Development
FTA	Fair Trading Act 1973
GATT	General Agreement on Tariffs and Trade
GISC	General Insurance Standards Council
ICPAC	International Competition Policy Advisory Committee
JV	Joint Venture
MMC	Monopolies and Mergers Commission
NCC	National Consumer Council
OECD	Organization for Economic Cooperation and Development
OFT	Office of Fair Trading
OPEC	Organization of Petroleum Exporting Countries
RPC	Restrictive Practices Court
RPM	Resale price maintenance
RTPA	Restrictive Trade Practices Act 1976
SCP	Structure-Conduct-Performance model
SSNIP	Small but significant non-transitory increase in price
TEU	Treaty on European Unity ('Maastricht Treaty')
WTO	World Trade Organization

STOP PRESS—AUTHOR NOTE

After this edition was prepared the Enterprise Bill was published. This is not due to complete its progress through Parliament until October 2002, and will not in its entirety take immediate effect at that point. It has not been possible, nor is it considered appropriate, given that debate on the Bill is continuing, to incorporate a full discussion of its provisions at each relevant point throughout the main body of the text, which continues to reflect the law as it stood at 1 May 2002. At some points in the text reference is made to the proposed changes as these have been informing the debate in the UK for some time.

However, in a final appendix to the text, the provisions of the Bill are discussed, and are cross-related to the appropriate chapter in the text. Readers should note in particular that the domestic law dealt with in the following chapters will be affected following the full entry into force of what is anticipated to become the Enterprise Act 2002:

The regime (Chapter 2)

Penalties (Chapter 4)

Third party rights (Chapter 5)

Agreements in the UK (Chapter 9)

Single-firm conduct in the UK (Chapter 12)

Merger control (Chapter 15)

1

Introduction to competition law

1.1 Introduction

The primary purpose of competition law is to remedy some of the situations in which the free market system breaks down. The point was well made in the House of Lords debate during the passage of the Competition Act 1998 that 'competition law provides the framework for competitive activity. It protects the process of competition. As such it is of vital importance' (Hansard (HL) 30 October 1997, col. 1156).

The 'invisible hand' that Adam Smith identified in 1776 ensures in most situations that free market economies left to their own devices will produce results more beneficial than can be realized by intervening in the markets. This conclusion has been supported by evidence put forward by economists over the last 200 years, and, since the collapse of East European planned economies, forms the basis for most of the world's economic systems. The process of competition is seen as being of value and meriting protection. In its White Paper *Productivity and Enterprise* (Cm. 5233, July 2001), the UK Government argued that

The importance of competition in an increasingly innovative and globalised economy is clear. Vigorous competition between firms is the lifeblood of strong and effective markets. Competition helps consumers get a good deal. It encourages firms to innovate by reducing slack, putting downward pressure on costs and providing incentives for the efficient organisation of production. As such, competition is a central driver for productivity growth in the economy, and hence the UK's international competitiveness.   (para. 1.1)

It is often said, however, that 'competition sows the seeds of its own destruction; encouraged to compete, successful entrepreneurs may achieve positions where they are able to prevent others from competing and thereby damage the process as a whole. A variant on this problem is that there may be some situations in which there is only room for a single firm in a market, and, unless steps are taken to regulate the conduct of this firm, it too may act to the detriment of the economy. The fact that in both the UK and the EC a competitor harmed by another's unlawful anti-competitive conduct may go to court to seek damages or another suitable remedy also serves to place stress on the right of business people to conduct their affairs in a fair and reasonable commercial environment. Competition law is not, directly, about consumer protection, or trading standards, although both may benefit from the application of competition law (see however, Averitt, N. W., and Lande, R. H., 'Consumer Sovereignty: A Unified Theory of Antitrust and Consumer Protection Law', (1997) *Antitrust Law Journal* 713).

In the United Kingdom there are two systems of competition law: domestic law and the law of the European Community (EC). With the passage of the Competition Act 1998 the domestic regime was strengthened and, following the demands of both the business community and consumer groups, brought into much closer alignment with EC law. An examination of these two regimes forms the basis of this book. Most of the law dealt with here is based on statutes or other public enactments. In both systems lawyers and regulators are likely to look for guidance to the operation of the antitrust law of the United States, which is briefly introduced later in this chapter, and then considered in relation to specific cases throughout the book. The common law of England and Wales remains applicable in a small class of cases, which are considered further in Chapter 17.

To the frustration of many lawyers competition law is heavily reliant on economics, and it is not only those new to the subject who may be hesitant when dealing with a different discipline with its own language and 'rules'. In practice lawyers handling the more complex cases are likely to rely on expert witnesses and documentation provided either by companies themselves or by firms of economic consultants. However, without some understanding of what questions should be raised, and what significance the answers then have, such communication becomes difficult and inefficient. It is for this reason that the reader of this book is faced with economics both later in this introduction, and in Chapters 6, and 14. It might be possible to pass these by, but the case law that is discussed elsewhere will be clearer if they are read, and then returned to as necessary. These sections are not intended to serve as a complete guide to the subject of industrial economics, and the interested reader is referred to specialist texts. Particularly useful is Bishop, S., and Walker, S., *The Economics of EC Competition Law*, London, Sweet & Maxwell (1999).

1.2 The development of competition law

The American Sherman Act 1890 is taken as the starting point of modern competition (or in America, 'antitrust') law but the roots of competition law lie much deeper. Senator Sherman himself told the Senate that his bill did 'not announce a new principle of law, but applies old and well-recognized principles of the common law to the complicated jurisdiction of our State and Federal Government'. It has even been suggested, unconvincingly, that the Act is based in part on the Constitution of Zeno, Emperor of the East from 474 to 491, promulgated in 483. Roman legislation dealing with some aspects of competition predates the Constitution by over 500 years.

In England competition law has developed in fits and starts since before legal memory, and only in the last half of the twentieth century was it subjected to rigorous economic analysis. At present there is no satisfactory single history of the early competition laws, and much of the best work has been done by those researching the circumstances surrounding the creation of the Sherman Act in 1890 (see, e.g., Thorelli, H. B., *The Federal Antitrust Policy*, Stockholm (1954); see also Lord Wilberforce, Campbell, A., and Elles, N., *The Law of Restrictive Trade Practices and Monopolies*, London, Sweet & Maxwell (2nd edn, 1966)). Various Saxon kings had taken action against a range of trading practices, including, for example, the purchase of commodities before they reached their designated market place in order to enhance the price, and make a profit on a later sale, known as the crime of foresteel, or forestalling, which is referred to in the Domesday Book (1086). Other laws set out punishments for ingrossers, who similarly obtained agricultural produce with the intention of reselling it at a profit; regrators, who purchased products in one market place to resell them in either the same or a neighbouring market at a higher price; and travelling salesmen, known as 'badgers', who dealt mainly in foodstuffs, purchasing in one place and reselling at a premium in another. At the time of the Magna Carta (1215) legislation provided that all monopolies were to be contrary to the law because of their pernicious effect on individual freedom.

The great plagues that swept across Europe in the late medieval period resulted in shortages of both labour and commodities. Although it is now believed that contemporary accounts tended to exaggerate the impact of the plagues, and of the Black Death in particular, there is no reason to doubt that 'there was such a scarcity of labourers that women and even small children could be seen at the plough and leading the waggons' (Keen, M., *Medieval Europe*, London, Penguin Books (1968), p. 234). The various statutes which aimed to fix both prices and wages at pre-plague levels in order to prevent labourers moving to seek better-paid employment, thereby damaging the interests of landowners, were a response in part to problems created by these shortages. The 1349 Statute of Labourers is notable by virtue of its introduction of the requirement that merchants overcharging should pay multiple damages to injured parties, which is followed today in the American treble-damages suit (see Chapter 4).

It has also been suggested that the common law doctrine of 'restraint of trade' (which is defined in Chapter 17) emerged in response to the pressures caused by labour shortages. *John Dyer's* case (1414) YB 2 Hen 5 (of. 5, pl. 26) appears to be the first recorded case of restraint of trade. John, the Dyer, had sought to enforce a writ against a colleague who had covenanted not to practise the craft of dyeing in the same town as John Dyer for half a year. Fortunately for Dyer he was not in court when the case was heard, for the judge held that the provision was against the common law 'and by God, if the plaintiff were here, he should go to prison'. The rule that covenants in restraint of trade were not enforceable remained in place until the beginning of the seventeenth century, at which time added flexibility was introduced to accommodate changing circumstances (see, e.g., *Rogers v Parrey* (1613) 80 ER 1012). By the middle of the nineteenth century the courts had introduced, and had begun to expand on, the relationship of the public interest to the operation of the doctrine. In *Horner* v *Graves* (1831) 131 ER 284, the judge brought the doctrine close to the modern day when he held that 'we do not see how a better test can be applied to the question whether reasonable or not, than by considering whether the restraint is not so large as to interfere with the interests of the public'. The extent to which restraint of trade was concerned with the issue of monopoly per se is a question that has not been fully resolved. It appears that judges were at least as swayed by arguments as to individual liberty, and as to the cost to the public purse of the support, however rudimentary, that might be available to the worker who was not able to secure employment because of the restraint's operation.

There was little the common law could do to combat arrangements between businesses, and this area was left largely to various statutes. However, the doctrine of conspiracy crept into the area of trade regulation from the seventeenth century onwards, particularly in relation to the attempts of working people to organize themselves. The doctrine was applied to business situations in the eighteenth century, but then fell into disuse. It was confirmed in *Mogul SS Co. Ltd* v *McGregor Gow & Co.* [1892] AC 25, that it would be applied only where the objective of the conspiracy was illegal, and that it was not illegal to seek to improve a business position.

1.2.1 Monopolies and the Crown

The word 'monopoly' was probably first used in England by Thomas More in *Utopia* (1516). It carried a specific meaning:

A Monopoly is an Institution, or allowance by the King, by His Grant, Commission, or otherwise, to any person or persons, bodies politic or corporate, of or for the sole buying, selling, making, working or using of any thing, whereby any person or persons, bodies politic or corporate are sought to be restrained of any freedom, or liberty that they had before or hindered in their lawful trade.   (The US Supreme Court in *Standard Oil Co. of New Jersey* v *US* (1911) 221 US 1, citing Sir Edward Coke, *Institutes*.)

Such monopolies were increasingly granted from the mid-1300s. In Elizabethan England (1558–1603) the system of Industrial Monopoly Licences was heavily abused as a mechanism for raising funds for the monarch without the inconvenience of consulting Parliament. Although Parliament protested, the Queen was able to persuade it to drop a Bill that would have curbed the practice. It was therefore left to the courts in 1602 to rule that a grant of a monopoly for the making of playing cards to one Darcy was illegal and void (*Darcy* v *Allin* (1602) 11 Co Rep 84b—also known as the *Case of the Monopolies*). Even at this time the arguments against monopoly practices were becoming well rehearsed, and the court found that there were inevitable and unwelcome consequences of all monopolies: an increase in price; a reduction in quality; and a reduction in the incentive to work. The position in the early 1600s was such that Ben Jonson, in *The Devil is an Ass* (1616), was able to satirize for his audiences the practice of granting monopolies and those who negotiated them: the character of Merecraft, 'The Great Projector', promoted and sold increasingly fantastical monopoly schemes, including an inventive scheme to monopolize the market in toothpicks.

The conflict between Crown and Parliament was resolved in 1623 with the passing of the Statute of Monopolies, which declared that 'All Monopolies . . . are altogether contrary to the Laws of this Realm, and so are and shall be utterly void and of none effect and in no wise to be put into use or execution'. In making an exception for patents for a period not exceeding 21 years save where these operated to raise prices or to damage trade, the statute also formed the basis for the modern law of patents. Monopolies could still be granted to trading corporations and guilds, a practice made much use of by Charles I. In the 'Great Case against Monopolies', *East India Company* v *Sandys* (1685) 10 St Tr 371; 'it was held that a distinction could be drawn between monopolies operating *within* the realm, and those established in order to compete *outside* the realm. In the latter situation it was accepted that only a firm in a strong position could trade successfully in the difficult conditions prevailing. This argument finds a modern counterpart in the debate on the relationship between competition and national industrial policy, in particular the promotion of 'national champions': 'Competition can be enormously beneficial in many cases, but where it involves the destruction of strong interests in a wider context, it could be weakening from UK PLC's point of view' (Graeme Odgers, MMC Chairman, *Evening Standard*, 5 May 1993).

In 1772, following a House of Commons committee report, most of the old laws were repealed, and by 1844 all earlier Acts were repealed, it then being considered that the prohibitions had effects contrary to that intended, and were partly responsible for inhibiting trade and raising prices. From that time till now monopolies have not been prevented in the United Kingdom, and the modern law of competition deals with issues of the *abuse* of monopoly power, not with its existence per se.

The United Kingdom, with a belief in the benefits of economic laissez-faire, did not return to competition law until after the Second World War, when in 1948 legislation was introduced that established a domestic structure for the examination and control of anti-competitive competitive conduct was largely, but not totally, replaced by the Competition Act 1998. This development and the current regimes in the UK and EC are examined in Chapter 2.

1.2.2 Competition law and the EC

According to the European Court of Justice the provisions of EC law dealing with competition constitute 'a fundamental provision . . . essential for the accomplishment of the tasks entrusted to the Community and, in particular, for the functioning of the internal market' (*Eco Swiss China Time Ltd* v *Benetton International NV* case C–126/97 [2000] 5 CMLR 816, para. 36).

Provisions relating to competition law were included in the Treaty of Rome of 1957, which formed the legal basis for the European Economic Community, from the outset. Thus:

From the inception of this process, there seems to have been little doubt that the Treaty would have to include provisions aimed at combating restraints on competition. Not only had such provisions been included in the ECSC treaty, but there seems to have been general agreement that the elimination of tariff barriers would not achieve its objectives if private agreements or economically powerful firms were permitted to be used to manipulate the flow of trade. (Gerber, D. J., *Law and Competition Policy in Twentieth Century Europe—Protecting Prometheus*, Oxford, Clarendon Press (1998), p. 343)

Articles 85 and 86 of the Treaty (now arts 81 and 82) related to the control of anti-competitive agreements and dominant firm abuses. Similar provisions had been placed in the earlier European Coal and Steel Community Treaty of 1951. There has been a substantial and interesting debate as to the policy pressures that underlay the inclusion of these provisions. David Gerber's seminal work, quoted above, deals in part with this question and the argument is made persuasively that rather than slavishly adopting an American-style model based on sections 1 and 2 of the Sherman Act (see below) the relevant Treaty provisions reflected a distinctly European approach to the issue of anti-competitive conduct. In particular the German ordo-liberals are cited as a key influence in the determination of the European policy. Some commentators have attacked Gerber's thesis, and it may be argued that whatever the roots of the policy, its operation in practice remains heavily influenced by American practices.

1.3 **The experience of the United States**

It is generally presumed that the Sherman Act, which ushered in the 'modern' era of competition law, was a response to irresistible pressures exerted from the agricultural heartland of the United States: prices and wages were rising, yet farmers, faced with disproportionately higher freight costs set by the railway companies which combined to set standard rates, were not benefiting from the trend.

Section 1 of the Sherman Act prohibits 'every contract, combination ... or conspiracy in restraint of trade' at a federal level (that is where inter-state trade would be affected). Decisions of the US Supreme Court have restricted these words, which would, if taken at face value, condemn nearly all business conduct to apply only to 'unreasonable' restraint of trade (*Standard Oil Co. of New Jersey* v *United States* (1911) 221 US 1). This 'rule of reason' is at the heart of American law, and there is intense debate as to the place of such a rule in EC law (see further Chapter 7, below). Section 2 of the Act is in the following terms: 'Every person who shall monopolize, or attempt to monopolize ... any part of the trade or commerce among the several States .... shall be guilty of a misdemeanor'. It is possible to argue that it is the legitimate goal of any businessman to 'monopolize' his industry, and in *United States* v *Grinnel Corp.* (1966) 384 US 563, a distinction was drawn between the 'wilful' acquisition of monopoly power, which fell to be condemned, and monopoly arising from better commercial practices which would escape the Act's application. Although it has been supplemented by other legislation over the last century, which is discussed elsewhere in this book as appropriate, the Sherman Act remains central to antitrust policy in the United States (see generally Sullivan, E. T. (ed.), *The Political Economy of the Sherman Act: The First One Hundred Years*, New York, OUP (1991)). Given that economic principles do not, unlike law, vary from country to country, there are often good reasons to look to the large body of American case law to illuminate competition cases brought elsewhere. There are, however, significant divergences in the underpinning philosophies of the American and European regimes, and principles from one regime should not be slavishly applied to the other without good justification:

Many valuable ideas for the interpretation of Community law can be derived from the discussions going on on the other side of the Atlantic and from the solutions found by the American courts. However, prudence must be counseled in transferring concepts and theories from one legal system to the other. There are substantial differences between the various elements going to make up US law and those going to make up Community law, with the result that not every problem confronting one of the two systems finds a counterpart in the other legal system.   (Advocate General Kirschner in *Tetra Pak Rausing SA* v *Commission* case T–51/89 [1991] 4 CMLR 334 at 343–4)

1.4 Economics and competition law

Economics can be employed in two main ways in relation to competition law. First, because competition law is aimed in part at remedying market failure a general macro-economic argument can be made as to the existence of such market failure and the costs imposed by it. Secondly, micro-economic arguments are likely to be relied upon in each individual case to justify intervention or to defend a company's position. Attempts to avoid the 'problem' of economics are likely to result in bad law—as was the case with the Restrictive Trade Practices Act 1976, which adopted an overly legalistic approach in an attempt to disregard economic issues. In Chapters 6 and 10 specific issues relating to collusion between firms and to actions by individual firms are considered in more detail and in Chapter 14 the economics of mergers is discussed. This section introduces the general argument advanced to support intervention and some standard economic terms.

For readers who are interested in developing their economic expertise further a good accessible text that deals with competition strategy is Besanko, D., Dranove, D., and Sharley, M., *Economics of Strategy*, New York, John Wiley & Sons (2000, 2nd edn). Specific references later in this text are given to Bishop and Walker *The Economics of EC Competition Law*, because of its direct connection to the subject-matter of this book.

1.4.1 **The problem of standards**

As was noted above, it is the presumed goal of entrepreneurs to maximize their profits, and to be as successful as possible. While Bill Gates probably did not envisage 20 years ago that Microsoft would become one of the largest and most profitable corporations in the world, if asked he would probably have said that he would like it to. Now that it has assumed such a strong position Microsoft's commercial practices have been scrutinized by competition authorities around the world, and practices that might be pursued legitimately by smaller firms may be condemned if followed by Microsoft. The managers of a business may determine a strategy for all the 'right' reasons as far as that business is concerned, and yet, on the basis of a test related to society's welfare, be attacked. To what standards then are businesses to conform? Competition law is often contrasted with environmental regulation. For any given standard in environmental law (e.g., 'mercury content to be no more than three parts per million') it is a relatively easy matter to test for any given sample whether the standard is indeed being broken. It is much harder to set similar tests in the area of competition law.

In the United States 'monopolization' is condemned (see above); in the European Community the standard of conduct for a monopolist is that it should not 'abuse' its 'dominant position' (see Chapter 12). It will be impossible to determine whether this standard is being breached without recourse to economic analysis. Amongst other things the regulator or plaintiff must consider: what the relevant market is (e.g., is the market for bananas discrete, or is it part of the market for soft fruit, or all fruit? — *United Brands Co.* v *Commission* case 27/76 [1978] 1 CMLR 429); is the firm a monopolist?; is the alleged 'abuse' in fact a legitimate business tactic?; what effect is the alleged abuse having?

The fact that some of these issues cannot always be resolved before the conduct in question is effected was used for many years to support the existence of a system in the United Kingdom which was based around investigation and conduct modification, instead of around rights and penalties. A further response in the UK was to rely on somewhat technical and formal legislation which, in light of the experience of the more effects-based Community law became, in the views of most commentators and practitioners, out of date and unsuitable to the task. In all save these formalistic areas an appreciation of the economic issues remains indispensable, and in regulatory agencies economists will be found working alongside lawyers.

1.4.2 **Industrial economics and markets**

The area of economics that is most important for competition law is industrial economics, which is the branch of the science that applies micro-economic tools, such as an individual's preferences for apples over pears, or the costs of making a chair instead of a table, to wider market situations. Markets are where producers and consumers interact, and in a theoretical world of 'perfect' competition a market will produce an efficient result. Efficiency has a particular meaning in economics. An efficient position is one in which the only way to make anyone better off is to make someone else worse off. This is to say it refers to a situation in which no more mutually advantageous bargains or contracts can be made. In any situation in which A can be made better off, with B being no worse off, it will be efficient for that transaction to take place. Such a situation is referred to as one of *pareto optimum*. This theoretical ideal permits an examination of the extent to which observed market structures diverge from 'perfect competition' and the resulting harm. The requirements of perfect competition are that there must be very large, tending to infinite, numbers of producers and of consumers. The product is homogenous so that there are no significant differences between one producer's product and the next. Both producers and consumers are perfectly informed about the market and are motivated by the desire to maximize profits and satisfaction. When added to various assumptions made about the costs of production, the result is that no consumer or producer is able to influence the price of the product, and that the price at which the item is sold exactly matches the cost of making it. In observed markets these assumptions break down: consumers and producers will be able to influence the price of products, which are not homogenous, and neither group is likely to have perfect information about the market place. The antithesis of perfect competition is monopoly, with 'monopolistic', or imperfect, competition lying somewhere between the two.

When an economist uses the term 'monopoly' it has a specific meaning, different from that put forward by Coke's *Institutes* (above). A monopoly market is one in which there is only one producer. It is frequently pointed out by those questioning the basis of much of competition regulation that the most common situation in which monopoly arises is where it is the product of government action (e.g., by legal controls limiting entry into an industry, in particular where the state regulates an industry). Empirical observation suggests, in particular, that monopolies, even where they do exist, are unable to remain monopolies in the long run unless they are protected by legislative barriers to entry.

A monopolist, unlike a firm in a perfectly competitive market, has the power to determine the price at which the product is sold. Adam Smith, whose *The Wealth of Nations* (1776) serves as the basis of modern economics, suggested that 'the price of monopoly is upon every occasion the highest which can be got'. The monopolist can achieve this by choosing how much of the product to supply.

1.4.2.1 *The adverse consequences of monopolies*

Ceteris paribus ('all other things being equal') prices are higher, and output less, in markets which are monopolistic than in markets which are perfectly competitive. A consequence of the steps taken to achieve this is that it results in a non-optimal allocation of resources, by sending the 'wrong' signals as to the value/cost of products. The monopolist, by raising prices above the production cost of an item, denies consumers who are in fact prepared to pay that cost the opportunity of doing so. The monopolist has, by raising the price of the product, sent the consumer a false signal about the true value of the product in relation to other products and less consumer demand is therefore satisfied under these conditions. Further, the money that would have been spent on the monopoly product is instead spent on other products thereby raising *their* prices and the market becomes distorted.

Another issue is that of 'consumer surplus'. If a monopolist can set only one price for a product, as is the usual case in competitive market conditions, a given number of consumers will buy the product. For one of these consumers the decision has been a marginal one, and had the price been any higher the purchase would not be made. Some of the other consumers might have been prepared to pay for more, and have, in effect, achieved savings on the purchase. Consider, for example, an item in a sale —one consumer might buy it only because it has been reduced in price, while another might have been quite happy to pay the full price and feel that they have got a bargain. The total amount of this 'saving' is known as the consumer surplus. If the monopolist could force each consumer to pay their maximum price the total revenue to the monopolist rises and the consumer surplus vanishes, which represents a transfer of income from the consumers to the monopolist. This issue is often dealt with in competition law under the heading of 'price discrimination' (see Chapter 13). It is not directly a matter that impinges upon the efficiency of the situation, but it is nevertheless of legitimate interest to a regulator concerned with the distribution of income.

In 1954, in an article which has assumed seminal importance but has led to a somewhat difficult and convoluted debate, Arnold Harberger attempted to quantify the total loss to American society from the monopolistic industries in the United States (Harberger, A. C., 'Monopoly and Resource Allocation', (1954) 44 *American Economic Review* 77). Harberger estimated the difference between the total consumer demand satisfied under competitive conditions, and the reduced demand satisfied under monopoly conditions (the 'welfare triangle', or 'Harberger triangle'). In fact Harberger's estimate was only 0.1 per cent of the national income. More recent studies, however, point to figures of between 4 per cent to 20 per cent, suggesting that Harberger's estimate is an understatement and may be seen as a lower boundary.

The strategic activity undertaken to achieve, or reinforce, a monopoly position ('rent seeking') may also represent a cost of monopolies. This might include excessive advertising that has no benefit in terms of increased sales, and aggressive competition that does not increase either consumer or producer welfare. The intense British Airways/Virgin Atlantic competition of the mid- to late 1990s is sometimes cited as an example of such conduct.

1.4.3 The policy debate—Harvard *v* Chicago, and the new industrial economics

Until the mid-1980s competition economists, regulators, and to a certain extent lawyers, could be placed into two broad camps: the Harvard school and the Chicago school. Although the crude divisions these labels suggest have largely broken down under the influence of more modern economic analysis, there remains some value in the distinction, and it is still common to find these labels applied either to personalities or to approaches. The debate is not an abstract one as the policy implications of the ideas advanced by each school are very different. As will be seen in Chapter 10, if the Chicago school adherents are correct there is no need for regulators to consider anti-competitive conduct such as 'predation'; if the Harvard school supporters are correct, it may be right for regulators to intervene in such situations.

The first major school of thought to develop emerged at Harvard University when, in the 1930s, researchers conducted analyses of specific industries. Their conclusions led to the Structure–Conduct–Performance model (SCP): performance is determined by firms' conduct, which is in turn determined by the market structure. Kaysen and Turner, for example, consistent with the general distrust of corporate America and large business that was widely shared at the time, argued that the limitation of market power should be the central focus of competition policy and that market power should be reduced wherever this could be done without a corresponding cost in the performance of the industry (Kaysen, C., and Turner, D. F., *Antitrust Policy: An Economic and Legal Analysis*, Cambridge, Mass., Harvard UP (1959)).

One of the first practices that the Chicago school and notably Stigler examined, was that of the welfare implications of the structure of an industry, and of barriers to entry into that industry. Where the Harvard economists had argued that higher barriers enabled incumbents to increase prices, and were therefore prima facie to be condemned, the Chicagoans are concerned to examine the nature of the barrier, tolerating those which are the result of efficiency considerations. The SCP, Harvard model is replaced by one in which performance dictates market structure—the 'reverse causation' argument. In other words, monopolistic industries are the result of efficiency and superior performance, and should not then be attacked precisely because the firms in them have succeeded. Thus Bork has argued that the real question for competition policy is whether 'artificial' barriers, not being the result of more efficient production or economies of scale, prevent the effective operation of the market (Bork, R. H., *The Antitrust Paradox*, New York, The Free Press (1993)). More generally it is the tendency of the Chicago school to accept that, in the real world, the model of perfect competition can be used to explain most business behaviour, which is to say that all companies are constrained by competition. Alongside this sits the general assumption of the school that the only concern of competition policy should be the attainment of efficiency, and that ancillary 'non-economic' goals such as the equitable distribution of income, or the socio-political problems of a concentration of economic power should not be a part of any competition policy.

The Chicagoan assumption that real-world behaviour will tend to match that forecast by the perfect competition model is now being subject to increasingly rigorous challenges with the emergence of the new (or 'modern') industrial economics, which is informed in part by the empirical evidence provided in various antitrust actions. It appears to be now well established that the competitive assumptions made by some of the more extreme Chicagoans are incorrect, and are not supported by evidence. The standard-bearers of the Chicagoan viewpoint in America over more recent years have been R. H. Bork and R. A. Posner, both of whom were appointed to the bench under the Republican presidencies, and who remain in a position to exercise some considerable influence over the debate in America. Bork's *The Antitrust Paradox* (above) is a highly entertaining polemic, and provokes much debate, although it now lags behind contemporary economic argument. Posner's record in adjudicating antitrust actions in his time on the bench has been examined by American commentators and found lacking. Again it has been noted that he has disregarded strong evidence, characterized by some economists as incontrovertible, to the effect that concentration in any industry is almost inevitably damaging to consumer welfare.

The more pragmatic line taken by the new industrial economics is that in a monopolistic market, where the expected benefits outweigh the likely costs, a profit-maximizing firm will engage in strategic behaviour. For adherents to the new industrial economics one of the roles of competition policy is to make the expected costs of such strategic behaviour sufficiently great to outweigh the expected benefits, thereby deterring such conduct.

Broadly, the aims of competition policy are in line with the new industrial economics, although generalizations as to the aims of the various regimes are dangerous (see further Chapter 2). As was noted above, the aim of competition policy is not to achieve perfect competition as an alternative to monopoly. The definition of competition more usually accepted by regulatory authorities is that of the 'workable competition' first discussed by J. M. Clark in 1940 (30 *American Economic Review* 241). Workable competition accepts that there are elements of monopoly in virtually all markets, and has, as its goal, making such structures compatible with strong competition. It therefore contains an element of pragmatism that courts find more attractive than more rigorous economic models (see, e.g., *Metro-SB-Grossmärkte GmbH & Co. KG* v *Commission* case 26/76 [1978] 2 CMLR 1).

It should be noted, too, that an increasing emphasis on the impact of technology on industrial development is leading to some new approaches to markets and industry being developed (see, e.g., Sutton, J., *Technology and Market Structure*, Boston, MIT Press (1999)).

1.4.4 Basic tools of economic analysis

There is less controversy surrounding the basic tools of economics than there is about the policy implications of different market structures. The Harvard and Chicago schools alike are in agreement as to these components. Markets represent the aggregation of individual elements, and there will be situations in competition law where these individual elements become important in determining the existence of anti-competitive behaviour, and in resolving other economic issues, such as the ability of a monopolist to raise prices, or the existence of other products that restrict the monopolist's power.

1.4.4.1 *Demand, supply, and price*

In a free market economy the price of any product is set by the relationship between the demand for the product and the supply of the product. *Ceteris paribus*, the greater the supply, and the less the demand, the less the price of the product will be. The demand for a product is the sum of the demand of individual consumers. In all save a few cases a consumer's individual demand for a product will be inversely related to its price, and can be represented diagrammatically as a 'curve' that slopes downwards from left to right (see Figure 1.1). The 'elasticity of demand', references to which are often encountered in competition cases, is the extent to which demand is sensitive to price. An inelastic demand curve denotes that consumers are unresponsive to changes in price: if price rises by 10 per cent demand falls by *less* than 10 per cent. The more inelastic demand is, therefore, the more a monopolist will be able to raise prices and still increase their income. It may be presumed that petrol has an inelastic demand. If the demand for petrol was in fact elastic the government would not be able to raise significant revenue by taxation on petrol, for any increase in tax would be more than matched by a drop in sales. An elastic demand curve denotes that consumers are very responsive to changes in price: if price rises by 10 per cent demand falls by *more* than 10 per cent, and in such a situation a monopolist raising prices will find that income will fall. Any product that has many substitutes is likely to have an elastic demand. The demand for compact discs is probably inelastic, but the demand for any individual disc will be more elastic. Thus if the price of all discs were to rise by 10 per cent, sales would probably not fall by as much as 10 per cent, but if The Spice Girls' new CD was

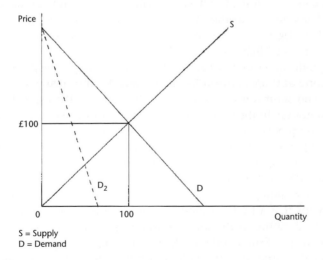

Figure 1.1 Demand and supply curves

Note: The price at which the product is sold, and the quantity sold, will be that where the demand and supply curves intersect. Demand curve D_2 is less elastic than D; if these two curves are looked at in isolation it will be seen that a change in price (from, e.g., £100 to £150) will have a bigger effect on D than on D_2.

priced at 20 per cent more than any other disc, consumers might prefer to purchase an alternative from the wide range stocked by any music store. Supply curves slope upwards left to right, showing that the relationship between supply and price is that, *ceteris paribus*, the higher the price the greater the level of supply. The price of the product, the quantity supplied, and the quantity bought will be that set where demand and supply curves intersect.

As suggested above, the demand for a product will also be affected by the prices of *other* products, which is termed 'cross-elasticity of demand' or 'substitutability'. An examination of substitutability is almost essential in determining the boundaries of any given product market. If demand for one product is highly sensitive to the price of another (e.g., clementines and mandarins) it is probably unwise to treat the market for clementines as being a separate one distinct from the market for mandarins. Producers and retailers of clementines will have to be always considering what is happening in the market for mandarins. Analysis of substitutability accordingly features prominently in many competition cases. This is just one area in which the language of business may differ from the language of competition law. The sales or marketing director of any business may have a very clear view of the market that is being targeted by that business, but, if subject to a competition investigation, a very different definition of the market (often but not always a wider one) may be adopted.

1.4.4.2 *Costs*

Certain competition law issues cannot properly be resolved without an analysis of the costs faced by the company concerned. This is true of allegations of predation, where the charge is that the business is making losses or acting primarily with the intention of driving a competitor out of the market, or of preventing entry into the market, and of allegations of 'profiteering' where the company is accused of making too much profit (see Chapters 10 and 13).

Costs of production can be separated out in various ways. The primary divisions made by economists are between fixed and variable costs; marginal, average, and total costs; and short-run and long-run costs. Consider the example of a mass-produced motor car. In the short run fixed costs are those that stay constant whatever the level of production (e.g., the rent on the factories and perhaps research and development); variable costs alter according to the level of production (e.g., the cost of steel, plastics, and labour). Marginal costs are those of the additional unit of production (the cost of making one extra car). Generally marginal costs fall as production rises through the operation of 'economies of scale'. Economies of scale are the benefits that arise from producing more of any item. It is, for example, cheaper to produce the tenth motor car in a mass-production plant than it is to produce the first, and the 10,000th will be considerably cheaper still. Where there are economies of scale, the average cost, which is the total cost divided by the quantity produced, will fall as output rises. In the long run there may be significant differences and the concept of fixed costs in particular becomes less definite, for even factories can be disposed of. The various cost curves are shown in Figure 1.2.

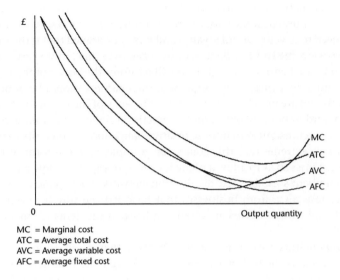

MC = Marginal cost
ATC = Average total cost
AVC = Average variable cost
AFC = Average fixed cost

Figure 1.2 Cost curves
Note: This figure assumes that there are economies of scale, so marginal and variable cost fall first. Once these economies are exhausted costs will begin to rise again.

Supply of a product will be determined by the costs of production and the demand for the product.

1.4.5 **Barriers to entry**

The implications of barriers to entry are that their existence reinforces monopolistic tendencies in a market. Theoretical models of market structure focus only on *actual* competition facing producers, and make no reference to *potential* competition. It has long been recognized that potential competition serves as a restraint on the conduct of incumbents (those already in the market) in just the same way as does the actual competition faced. The higher the barriers that exist, the greater is the ability of the incumbent to ignore the potential competition.

While the existence of barriers to entry in any given situation may be a matter of some concern to those investigating the market, there is intense debate between the Harvard and Chicago schools as to the policy implications of barriers to entry, and even as to what a barrier to entry is. The issue is of such importance that it should be dealt with at this early stage. At its very broadest, a barrier to entry is any factor that operates as a cost of a new entrant into a market. By this definition it might include such factors as: lack of knowledge about the market; any premium rate paid for capital to compensate for the risk this lack of knowledge results in; the cost of acquiring the necessary physical capacity (plant and raw materials); the cost of establishing brand recognition with consumers, and a distribution system, etc.

Whether all barriers to entry should be a matter of concern to competition regulation is contested. Some barriers are the result of the success of the incumbent (e.g., the need to develop brand loyalty) and it may be argued that if the incumbent has had to overcome this hurdle it is, or has been over time, in no better a position than any potential entrant. In fact these still reinforce the power of the incumbent, but some (notably 'Chicagoans') argue that such barriers should be of no concern to regulators and are merely evidence of the efficiency of the incumbent. Adherents of the 'Harvard' school would permit competition policy to examine *any* barrier, and in some circumstances to impose positive obligations on incumbents to reduce barriers. In an extreme case this could, for example, take the form of restricting their product lines so as to allow a niche for the entrant, or to allow entrants access to the incumbent's established distribution network. Such policies are likely to face severe resistance from businesses that have led the way into a market and succeeded, and whose officers are often perplexed at the demands made on them by the law.

All commentators would accept that barriers that result from governmental action are a source of legitimate concern, although such barriers will often be justified on the grounds of health and safety, or may be accompanied by ongoing industry regulation that will ameliorate the consequence of the market power granted to the incumbent.

1.4.6 Conclusion

Unfortunately the analysis conducted by the various regulatory authorities is often somewhat lacking in formal rigour, and the EC Commission decisions have in particular been criticized for lacking in-depth economic analysis. In its *Green Paper on Vertical Restraints* (see Chapter 7) the EC Commission argued that

economic theory is just one of the sources of policy. In practice, the application of economic theory must take place in the context of the existing legal texts and jurisprudence. Secondly, economic theories are necessarily based on simplifying assumptions often obtained in the context of stylised theoretical models that cannot take into account all the complexities of real life cases.   (para. 86)

It might plausibly be argued that, if an economic theory based on simplifying assumptions has been tested and refined against empirical data, that theory could serve as a legal test and is at least as likely to produce reliable results as is a pragmatic individual analysis of each case.

Care should be taken over the way in which economic 'evidence' is used in competition cases. While economic consultants will regularly be employed to advance arguments in competition cases, and in many cases their evidence will be determinative of the issues, there are some dangers with constructing elaborate economic 'stories' to explain observed conduct. An illustration of the problems may be found in the UK case of *Napp Pharmaceutical Holdings Ltd* v *The Director General of Fair Trading* [2002] CompAR 13. Napp was condemned for discriminatory predatory pricing in one sector of its market (the case is discussed in full in Chapter

13). Its economic consultants, Nera, produced an argument to the effect that the undertaking was rationally pricing low in one sector as this ensured follow-through sales in another sector, and that this 'portfolio' pricing was a legitimate and profitable strategy that was available to all its competitors as well. The Competition Commission Appeals Tribunal, which heard the case, found no suggestion in the documents produced by Napp that it had in fact been consciously following such a strategy. The Tribunal noted that 'Napp does not strike us as a naïve or badly managed company', and argued that 'if its pricing policy had in fact been seen by Napp in the way that its economic consultants suggest, we would have expected the company's internal documents to demonstrate that' (para. 252).

2

....

The European Community and United Kingdom regulatory regimes

2.1 Introduction

The enactment of the Sherman Act in the United States of America in 1890 was a major development in competition law, and the American regime has had a pervasive influence on the development of the law elsewhere. In part this is because the success of the American economy was attributed, amongst other factors, to the efficacy of the US antitrust law. The domestic and Community regimes arose independently and the idiosyncratic approach originally taken by the UK stands alone, and the story since the UK's accession to the EC on 1 January 1973 has been that of pressure on the domestic regime to adapt to the dominant EC system. The impetus for change has come largely from industry in the UK whose interests would be likely to be served by a 'one-stop' shop. This pressure culminated in the introduction of the Competition Act 1998 which introduced radical reforms to the domestic structure. This Act, and the changes it effects, are dealt with in some detail below, and throughout this book. The aim of this chapter is to introduce the reader to the structure of each of the regimes. The substantive rules and the rules of procedure are dealt with as appropriate in later chapters.

2.2 Undertakings—the subjects of competition law

Throughout this chapter, and throughout the rest of this book, references are made to undertakings. The word is taken from the Treaty and from the secondary legislation, neither of which refers to the more familiar rubrics of 'companies', 'businesses', or 'enterprises'. In the French texts the word '*entreprise*' is used, which has no exact equivalent in United Kingdom commercial law. Commentators who came early to EC competition law made attempts to provide definitions of 'undertaking' where none exists, and as a result such definitions were rarely satisfactory. The better course is to argue by analogy with past decisions and cases, and to look to the intent underlying the legislation itself. For the domestic company lawyer it must be made clear above all that the concept of the 'corporate veil' has only the most oblique relationship with EC competition law. A broad understanding of the concept may be clear from the words used by the ECJ in *Hofner and Elser* v *Macrotron GmbH* case C–41/90 [1993] 4 CMLR 306, where the Court held that 'the concept of an undertaking encompasses every entity engaged in economic activity, regardless of the legal status of the entity and the way in which it is financed' (para. 21).

In defining the undertaking in any particular circumstance the Commission will look to the economic and factual reality of the situation, and not to legal structure. A single individual may be an undertaking in circumstances where he has an impact on the market in a capacity other than that of a consumer. Thus in *Reuter/ BASF* 76/743/EEC (1976) OJ L254/40, an inventor was held to be an undertaking and therefore subject to art. 81. In *UNITEL* 78/516/EEC (1978) OJ L157/39 opera singers were brought within the scope of the law. Parent and subsidiary companies may be held to be part of the same undertaking, and not to be their separate legal constituents. This can have the benefit of removing arrangements between them from the provisions of art. 81(1), which require that 'two or more undertakings' be implicated in the practice (see, e.g., *Re Christiani & Nielsen* 69/165/EEC [1969] CMLR D36 and more recently, *Viho Europe BV* v *Commission* case T–102/92 [1995] 4 CMLR 299; and see further Chapter 7). Undertakings do not have to be making profits, as was once suggested, nor even be engaged in profit-making activity: in the course of a proceeding relating to the 1990 football World Cup, the Commission expressly stated that organizations did not have to be profit-making as long as they were engaged in economic activity (*Distribution of Package Tours During the 1990 World Cup* 92/521/EEC (1992) OJ L326/31). In restricted circumstances commercial activities carried out by arms of the state may not fall within the definition of 'undertaking', although this cannot serve as a broad exemption. For example, in the case of *Coapi* 95/188 (1995) OJ L122/37, the Commission condemned a decision of an association of industrial property agents in Spain. Coapi argued that as it was responsible for the discharge of functions assigned to it by virtue of Spanish law (Law No. 2/1974), and was governed by public law, it could not be regarded as an undertaking for the purposes of Community competition law. The Commission, relying on the definition given by the Court in *Hofner* (above), held that these facts did not prevent Coapi from being regarded as an undertaking subject to the provisions of art. 81.

Apart from providing a test as to the application of art. 81(1), the limits of the undertaking can be relevant to the fact-finding procedure of Regulation 17 of 1962 (see Chapter 3), and to the penalties imposed under that Regulation. The 10 per cent of turnover that is provided for in art. 15 of Regulation 17 can mean the turnover of the entire undertaking, and not merely of the specific arm or division of the undertaking that has infringed the law, although the trend is towards focusing the fine in relation to the relevant infringing activity (see Chapter 4).

For the purposes of United Kingdom law the same approach is to be taken under the terms of the Competition Act 1998 as is taken under Community law. In the case of *The Institute of Independent Insurance Brokers* v *The Director General of Fair Trading* [2001] CompAR 62 the CCAT held that the OFT had been incorrect to dismiss a complaint on the grounds that the entity the activity of which formed the basis of the complaint was not an undertaking. The Director was called upon to look at various rules relating to insurance set by the General Insurance Standards Council (GISC). This described itself as 'an independent, non-profit making organisation, funded entirely by membership fees, whose main purpose is to make sure that general insurance customers are treated fairly'. In the decision the Director concluded that 'in light of European case law' GISC's regulatory function 'does not constitute an economic activity' (*Application by the Institute of Insurance Brokers ('IIB') under s. 47(1)* [2001] UKCLR 838, para. 18). Considering all the facts, including the fact that GISC was set up as a private company, existing solely by contract, and was run by a board of directors, the CCAT found that it could see 'no compelling reason why GISC should not be regarded itself as an undertaking' (para. 258).

The OFT has also held that a health care trust purchasing social care services is not acting as an undertaking (*The North & West Belfast Health and Social Services Trust* CA/98/11/2002). This decision, made in the form of a series of published letters, is as of May 2002, subject to appeal.

2.3 The European Community

The Community legal order is governed by the primary legislation of the treaties, to which all 15 Member States have acceded. The three core treaties are those of the European Coal and Steel Community (ECSC); the European Atomic Energy Community (EAEC, or Euratom); and, primarily, the European Community (EC) (formerly the European Economic Community (EEC)). These treaties have been amended on several occasions since their inception, both in response to the accession of new Member States, and in response to pressures for institutional reform. Secondary legislation may be enacted under the authority of these treaties, in particular by way of art. 249 EC. European Community competition law is often enforced by way of decisions, which are a form of secondary legislation. Article 249 provides that: 'A decision shall be binding in its entirety upon those to whom it is addressed'. Case law of the European Court of Justice more recently supported by the Court of First Instance (CFI) forms the third plank of Community law.

Competition law featured as part of the Community regime from its inception by way of arts 4, 65, and 66 of the ECSC Treaty which was signed in 1951 and entered into force on 1 January 1952. Operating in the context of a well-regulated market, in accordance with aims set out in part in art. 4 art. 65 prohibited agreements, decisions, and concerted practices that would tend to restrict or distort competition in the relevant market. Article 66 dealt with transactions likely to bring about a concentration in the market. The inclusion of these provisions arose in part from the 'absence of, or at least the major imperfections of, competition readily visible in the [relevant] markets' (Goyder, D. G., *EC Competition Law*, Oxford, OUP (1993), p. 19) and in part from the example of the USA whose economic success was perceived to be based partly on its free competition policies (for a challenging and distinctive view of the impact of US law on the development of EC competition policy, see Gerber, D. J., *Law and Competition in Twentieth Century Europe: Protecting Prometheus*, Oxford, Clarendon Press (1998)). The 1957 Treaty of Rome (entry into force 1 January 1958), which created the European Economic Community, provided the blueprint for a much greater economic integration than that envisaged in the ECSC Treaty, and the various amendments to the Treaty since then have left its competition regime intact. One of the effects of the Treaty on European Union (Maastricht; TEU) 1992 (entry into force 1 November 1994) was to so amend the EEC Treaty as for it to become the European Community Treaty, and all references in this book will be to articles of the EC Treaty unless a clearly historical context is being adopted. Those seeking a fuller discussion of the nature of Community law and of the 'new legal order' that is the Community (*NV Algemene Transport-en Expeditie Onderneming Van Gend en Loos* v *Nederlandse Belastingadministratie* case 26/62 [1963] 1 CMLR 105) should refer to a current edition of a specialist Community law textbook, such as Steiner, J., and Woods, L., *Textbook on EC Law*, Oxford, OUP (7th edn, 2000).

Article 3(g) EC provides, as one of the aims of the Community, 'a system ensuring that competition in the internal market is not distorted'. Article 81 introduces a prohibition against 'agreements, decisions by associations of undertakings and concerted practices which may affect trade between Member States and which have as their object or effect the prevention, restriction or distortion of competition within the common market' (and see Chapter 7). Article 82 prohibits the 'abuse by one or more undertakings of a dominant position within the common market or a substantial part of it . . . in so far as it may affect trade between Member States' (and see Chapter 11). Conduct falling within the scope of the prohibitions is prohibited without the need for further investigation. Article 83 made provision for the enactment of 'any appropriate regulations or directives to give effect to the principles set out in Articles [81] and [82]'. The major regulation made under this authority is Regulation 17 of 1962, which is discussed in detail in the next chapter. Various other procedural regulations and, in particular, block exemptions have been enacted: the former are largely dealt with in Chapter 4, the latter in Chapter 10. Although not expressly provided for in the Treaty, the Community has also introduced a regime to control large merger situations in the EC. Regulation 4064/89 was enacted following cases in which it was established that arts 81 and 82 could, in the appropriate circumstances, apply to mergers or other concentrative actions. This aspect of the regime is considered in Chapter 15.

Outside of arts 81 and 82, other aspects of Community policy have an impact upon competition regulation. Most obviously art. 86 applies to public undertakings and undertakings 'to which Member States grant special or exclusive rights'. The requirement of the article is that 'Member States shall neither enact nor maintain in force any measure contrary to the rules contained in this Treaty', which is to say that state-owned or state-established or regulated undertakings are in no better position in relation to EC competition law than their private sector, market-regulated counterparts. However, undertakings falling within para. 2 of art. 86 may be placed in a more favourable position, being given the leeway to operate outside of the usual rules where these rules would 'obstruct the performance, in law or in fact, of the particular tasks assigned to them'.

Articles 87–89 EC relate to the control of state aids. Article 87(1) sets out the primary rule that

any aid granted by a Member State or through state resources in any form whatsoever which distorts or threatens to distort competition by favouring certain undertakings or the production of certain goods shall, in so far as it affects trade between Member States, be incompatible with the common market.

The Competition Directorate of the EC Commission has as one of its central tasks the review and control of state aids. This is an area that brings its staff into frequent conflict with the Member States. State aids are not dealt with in this book, and the interested reader is referred instead to one of the specialist texts dealing with the area.

Provisions of the Treaty relating to the free movement of goods (arts 28–30), and of services (arts 49–55) may also have a secondary effect upon competition and the carrying out of business in the Community. These provisions, however, do not fall within the ambit of the Competition Directorate's remit and lie outside the scope of this work.

2.3.1 The function of Community competition law

As is the case with UK law, the aims of Community policy are nowhere encapsulated in its legislative provisions. Limited guidance only may be obtained from the words of the Treaty, a primary aim of which is to ensure 'a harmonious and balanced development of economic activities' (art. 2 EC). Article 3(g) then refers to the non-distortion requirement; art. 81 emphasizes that consumers' interests are to be taken into account in deciding whether to grant an exemption under art. 81(3) and that consumers must be allowed 'a fair share of the resulting benefit'; and art. 82 is silent, save in its pejorative reference to 'abuse'. Valentine Korah has written that, in the EC, 'there is no agreement as to what objectives should be pursued by competition policy' ('EEC Competition Policy—Legal Form or Economic Efficiency' (1986) *Current Legal Problems* 85). The ECJ and the Commission have both indicated what the primary objectives of Community competition policy *might* be. In *Metro-SB-Grossmärkte GmbH & Co. KG v Commission* case 26/76 [1978] 2 CMLR 1 at 2, the ECJ held that

The requirement contained in Articles 3 and [81] EEC that competition shall not be distorted implies the existence on the market of workable competition, i.e., the degree of competition necessary to ensure the observance of the basic requirements and attainment of the objectives of the Treaty, in particular the creation of a single market achieving conditions similar to those of a domestic market.

Thus the position appears to be that competition policy is just one area that will be balanced alongside other objectives of Community policy as the need requires, and is not, exclusively, a tool to achieve efficiency maximization. It is the case therefore that, as other policy requirements change over time, so too might the application of competition law.

The Commission has made various claims for the operation of the law in its annual reports. The widest are those made in the 1972 Report which places stress on the general benefits of the policy:

Competition is the best stimulant of economic activity since it guarantees the widest possible freedom of action to all. An active competition policy ... makes it easier for the supply and demand structures continually to adjust to technological development ... Through the interplay of decentralised decision-making machinery, competition enables enterprises continuously to improve their efficiency ... competition is an essential means for satisfying ... the individual and collective needs of our society.   (p. 11)

In the same report the Commission also emphasized the importance of consumer interests—'Such a policy encourages the best possible use of productive resources for the greater possible benefit of the economy as a whole and for the benefit, in particular, of the consumer' (p. 12)—and the effects of anti-competitive actions on individual undertakings. In its ninth report the Commission set out its goals at the time with some clarity:

The first fundamental objective is to keep the common market open and unified ... There is ... a continuing need—and this is the primary task of the Community's competition policy— to forestall and suppress restrictive or abusive practices of firms attempting to divide up the market again so as to apply artificial price differences or impose unfair terms on their consumers ...

It is an established fact that competition carries within it the seeds of its own destruction. An excessive concentration of economic, financial and commercial power can produce such far-reaching structural changes that free competition is no longer able to fulfil its role as an effective regulator of economic activity. Consequently, the second fundamental objective of the Community's competition policy must be to ensure that at all stages of the common market's development there exists the right amount of competition in order for the Treaty's requirements to be met and its aims attained. The desire to maintain a competitive structure dictates the Commission's constant vigilance over abuses by dominant firms ...

Thirdly, the competition system instituted by the Treaty requires that the conditions under which competition takes place remain subject to the principle of fairness in the market place [these principles are] ...

First, equality of opportunity must be preserved for all commercial operators in the common market.

A second aspect of the principle of fairness in the market place is the need to have regard to the great variety of situations in which firms carry on business ... this factor makes it necessary to adapt the Community competition rules so as to pay special regard in particular to small and medium [size] firms that lack strength.

Finally, equity demands that the Commission's competition policy takes account of the legitimate interests of workers, users and consumers.   (*Ninth Report on Competition Policy* (1980), pp. 9–11)

The fact that one of the fundamental aims of the Community is to integrate the economies of the Member States has been crucial in shaping the policy, but may be less so in the future as the internal market coalesces.

This dominant concern has been continually restated in decisions and cases, and is evidenced in the continuing rule that territorial protection in distribution agreements is not permitted where parallel imports are excluded. The ECJ has held, in *Etablissements Consten SA RL and Grundig-Verkaufs-GmbH* v *Commission* cases 56 and 58/64 [1966] 1 CMLR 418 at 471, that

> an agreement between a producer and a distributor which might tend to restore the national divisions in trade between member-states might be such as to thwart the most basic objects of the Community. The Treaty, whose preamble and text aim at suppressing the barriers between States . . . could not allow undertakings to restore such barriers.

It is clearly the case that changes in the EU are affecting the approach taken to competition law. Thus, in its *White Paper on Modernisation of the Rules Implementing Articles [81] and [82]* (1999) OJ C132/1, hereinafter cited as the *Modernisation White Paper*, the Commission recognizes that

> Economic and monetary union is certain to have major consequences for competition policy. It will first entail further economic integration and, in the long term, will strengthen the effects of the internal market by helping to remove the last economic barriers between Member States. It also will help to cut the overall costs of intra-Community trade by reducing transaction costs. Such factors will encourage undertakings to develop trade and thus increase competition throughout the Union. A single currency will also increase price transparency and thus highlight price differences still existing between Member States. Economic operators may, when faced with stronger competition, be tempted to take a protectionist attitude to avoid the constraints of adapting to the new conditions, thereby compensating for their lack of competitiveness in a new environment. Lastly, the fact that some member states are, at least for the time being, not part of the monetary union may encourage undertakings to partition markets (para. 6).

2.3.2 The regulatory organs

A clear outline of the relationship between the two primary bodies, the EC Commission and the ECJ, in relation to the application of Community competition law, is given in Figure 2.1.

2.3.2.1 *The EC Commission*

The EC Commission has the primary role in the enforcement of Community competition law, and in certain areas has exclusive competence. This is consistent with the broad function of the Commission as 'guardian of the Treaty', or 'watchdog of the Community'. Rules relating to the Commission are set out in the Treaty at arts 211–19, art. 211 providing that the Commission should ensure compliance with EC law, and exercise specific powers given to it by the Council of Ministers, as is the case with competition law. The Commission consists of 20 Commissioners, nominated by the Member States, and accepted en masse by the European Parliament. Administratively the Commission is divided into Directorates General, with one Directorate General having responsibility for competition policy, which includes the contentious area of state aids, and merger policy. A list of the Directorate's personnel and their areas of responsibility is set out at the Commission's web site.

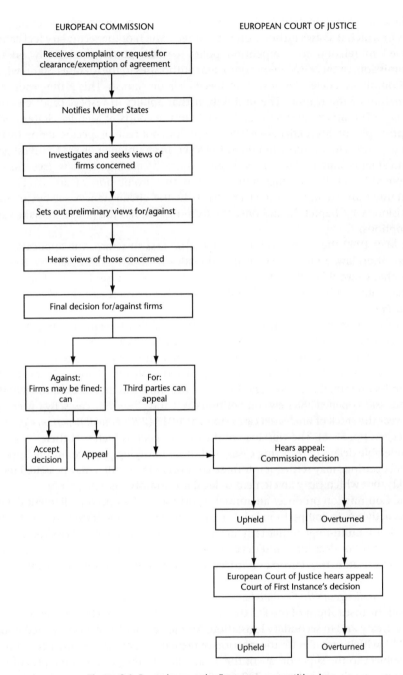

EUROPEAN COMMISSION

EUROPEAN COURT OF JUSTICE

Receives complaint or request for clearance/exemption of agreement

Notifies Member States

Investigates and seeks views of firms concerned

Sets out preliminary views for/against

Hears views of those concerned

Final decision for/against firms

Against:
Firms may be fined: can

For:
Third parties can appeal

Accept decision

Appeal

Hears appeal:
Commission decision

Upheld

Overturned

European Court of Justice hears appeal:
Court of First Instance's decision

Upheld

Overturned

Figure 2.1 Procedures under European competition law

There are areas in which the Commission has exclusive competence, and areas in which it shares jurisdiction with others. Much of the secondary legislation enacted in relation to competition policy confers powers exclusively on the Commission, or on occasion on competent authorities in the Member States where the Commission delegates powers in specific circumstances. This is the product of the nature of the regime. The prohibition that applies in respect of all conduct falling within arts 81 and 82 is enforceable in the courts of Member States under the principles of direct effect (see below) and does not require specific action by the Commission. The Commission does, however, have unique powers to investigate infringements and to levy fines against those breaching the law (see further Chapters 3 and 4). Conduct falling within the prohibition of art. 81(1) may be granted an exemption under art. 81(3) in the circumstances set out in that provision (see Chapter 7), and only the Commission has the power to make such exemptions.

In May 1999 the Commission initiated a process to reform the application of competition law, a process which it optimistically hoped to complete by 2002. A large change would be the introduction of the direct effect (see below) of art. 81(3), so that courts in Member States could apply this provision (see the *Modernisation White Paper*).

The Commission is also the only body with the ability to grant a formal decision of negative clearance under art. 2 of Regulation 17 (see Chapter 3). Commentators and national authorities involved in this area frequently suggest that these exclusive powers should in some way be shared with the Member States, as the Commission is unable to manage effectively the workload that faces it. In 1999 the Commission opened 388 new competition cases and closed 582 cases. By the end of that year the stock of uncleared cases stood at 1,013 (*29th Annual Report on Competition Policy*, pp. 57–8). The workload of the Commission is such that there are often considerable delays in resolving cases, and those notifying practices in the hope of formal decisions may settle for informal 'comfort letters' which may be issued more quickly, but which carry an element of legal uncertainty (see Chapter 3).

The Commission produces an annual report for the European Parliament detailing its activities in competition law over the year. The Competition Directorate also publishes a multi-lingual quarterly newsletter (*Competition Policy Newsletter*). Press releases, current decisions, and developments may be found on the Commission's Internet site at: **http://europa.eu.int/comm/competition/index_en.html**

2.3.2.1.1 *Challenges to the Commission—arts 230, 232, and 288 EC*
Like all the institutions of the EC, the Commission is governed by the law as set out in the Treaty and in secondary legislation. Any secondary legislation enacted under art. 249, which provides for the creation of regulations, directives, and decisions, is also subject to the superior law of the Treaty, and to the general principles of law developed by the ECJ. Articles 230 and 232 provide a procedure akin to domestic judicial review: under the former, acts of the institutions which produce legal effects may be challenged; under the latter, the failure to act may be challenged.

Article 288 sets out rules relating to a quasi-tortious liability of the Community for the acts of its servants.

Article 230 provides in part that:

The Court of Justice shall review the legality of acts . . . of the Commission, other than recommendations and opinions . . .

It shall for this purpose have jurisdiction . . . on grounds of lack of competence, infringement of an essential procedural requirement, infringement of this Treaty or of any rule of law relating to its application, or misuse of powers.
. . .

Any natural or legal person may . . . institute proceedings against a decision addressed to that person or against a decision which, although in the form of a regulation or decision addressed to another person, is of direct and individual concern to the former.

The proceedings provided for in this article shall be instituted within two months of the publication of the measure, or of its notification to the plaintiff . . .

While the protection of the article obviously extends to the decisions with which the Commission imposes penalty payments, which also fall within art. 229, and otherwise enforces the law under Regulation 17 (see Chapter 3), the ECJ has held that the article will also apply to a range of other actions relating to competition policy, and can be invoked in circumstances other than where a formal decision has been made. Thus the ECJ, in *IBM* v *Commission* case 60/81 [1981] 3 CMLR 635, held that an act is open to review where 'it is a measure definitively laying down the position of the Commission . . . and not a provisional measure intended to pave the way for a final decision'. It has held, therefore, that the rejection of a complaint may be reviewed (*CICCE* v *Commission* case 298/83 [1986] 1 CMLR 486), as may a decision to allow a party to proceedings to examine documents obtained by the Commission (*AKZO Chemie BV* v *Commission* case 53/85 [1987] 1 CMLR 231). It appears, following the perfumes case (*Procureur de la République* v *Bruno Giry and Guerlain SA* case 253/78 [1981] 2 CMLR 99), that 'comfort letters' cannot be so challenged, although the position may have changed after the tightening up of the procedure in respect of such letters by the Commission (see Chapter 3).

While it might be difficult for parties other than those to whom the decisions are addressed to establish the necessary *locus standi* to mount a challenge under the article it would appear that any party fulfilling the requirements of art. 3(2)(b) of Regulation 17 will be able to mount a challenge. Article 3 of Regulation 17 provides that the Commission may consider applications relating to infringements of competition law from 'natural or legal persons who claim a legitimate interest'. Such an expansive approach to *locus standi* follows from the analogous case of *Timex Corporation* v *EC Council and Commission* case 264/82 [1985] 3 CMLR 550, an anti-dumping case where the applicant had been the source of the initial complaint to which the Commission responded. However, the Court has held that the Commission is not required to respond to all complaints by launching a full investigation, and is allowed to determine its own priorities (*Automec srl* v *Commission* case T–24/90 [1992] 5 CMLR 431).

The most fruitful grounds for challenge tend to be that an essential procedural requirement has been breached, and both the ECJ and the CFI would appear now to require scrupulous observance of the correct procedures on the part of the Commission. Thus in *BASF AG v Commission* cases T–80/89, etc. [1995] ECR II-729, the Court of First Instance reacted against a decision which had not been correctly transposed into all official Community languages.

The ECJ will not inquire into the matters of economic fact on which the Commission has based its decision, but will

limit its review . . . to verifying whether the relevant procedural rules have been complied with, whether the statement of the reasons for the decision is adequate, whether the facts have been accurately stated and whether there has been any manifest error of appraisal or a misuse of powers.   (*Remia BV v Commission* case 42/84 [1987] 1 CMLR 1, at para. 34)

However, it will be noted that this formula leaves significant room for the Court to go over the factual grounds relied on by the Commission, and in practice the distinction between a review of the application of the law, and of the factual evidence, can become blurred. In the 'wood pulp' cases (*A Ahlström oy v Commission* cases C–89/85, etc. [1993] 4 CMLR 407) the CFI, for example, relied heavily upon economic evidence in rejecting a Commission decision (see further Chapter 7). It does in fact appear to be the case that the CFI is more prepared to consider the detail of the facts of the case than is the ECJ, which is required to take a somewhat more formal legal approach.

The effect of a successful challenge under art. 230 is, according to art. 231, to render the decision, or the affected parts of it, void. Article 231 does not give the court the power to order the Commission, or any other party, to take any positive action following such a case, although there may be an obligation on the Commission arising under the pertinent legislation, to reinstitute proceedings.

Article 232 provides in part that

Should the . . . Commission, in infringement of this Treaty, fail to act, the Member States and the other institutions of the Community may bring an action before the Court of Justice to have the infringement established.

The action shall be admissible only if the institution concerned has first been called upon to act. If, within two months of being so called upon, the institution concerned has not defined its position, the action may be brought within a further period of two months.

Any natural or legal person may, under the conditions laid down in the preceding paragraphs, complain to the Court of Justice that an institution of the Community has failed to address to that person any act other than a recommendation or an opinion.

Article 232 is less likely to form the basis of successful applications to the ECJ. In part this is because there are fewer situations in which it is likely to be invoked in practice, and in part because the obligation on the Commission is only to define its position. The Commission may define its position by an action that falls some way short of a decision reviewable under art. 230 (see, e.g., *Spijker Kwasten v Commission* case 231/82 [1984] 2 CMLR 284). The Court has held that the Commission does not owe a complainant the duty to take a final decision (*GEMA v Commission* case 125/78 [1980] 2 CMLR 177). The effect of a successful action is to require the Commission to, take the necessary steps to define its position, not to compel the Commission to take a decision to any particular effect (see further Chapter 5).

Article 288 provides in part that

In the case of non-contractual liability, the Community shall, in accordance with the principles common to the laws of the Member States, make good any damage caused by its institutions or by its servants in the performance of their duties.

Although this provision is rarely invoked it would cover, for example, the situation in which Commission officials exceeded their powers in the process of carrying out any investigations authorized by Regulation 17 and caused damage in the process. Article 235 provides that any disputes founded on art. 288(2) shall be heard by the ECJ. One case in which the applicant was successful was that of *Adams* v *Commission* case 145/83 [1986] 1 CMLR 506. This arose from a notorious incident in which Stanley Adams, an Englishman working in Switzerland, had provided to the Commission evidence of infringements of competition law by his employer. When the Commission returned documents to the undertaking they were so labelled as to reveal the identity of the informant, who subsequently faced prosecution under Swiss domestic law. The Court held that the Commission was liable to Mr Adams for its negligence in revealing the source of the complaint. The case became famous following the broadcast of a TV film, *A Song For Europe*, starring David Suchet as Stanley Adams.

2.3.2.2 *The Advisory Committee*

Article 10 of Regulation 17 makes provision for an 'Advisory Committee on Restrictive Practices and Monopolies', which must be consulted before the Commission takes various decisions, in particular decisions which have an adverse affect on those to whom they are addressed. The Committee would also automatically be consulted on draft or proposed legislation in the area of competition policy. The Committee 'shall be composed of officials competent in the matter of restrictive practices and monopolies. Each Member State shall appoint an official to represent it' (art. 10(4)), and the Committee therefore serves as an important link between the Commission and the Member States. The Committee will deliver its opinion on the basis of a preliminary draft decision, and 'should therefore be consulted concerning a case after the inquiry in that case has been completed' (Regulation 2842/98, recital 13). The hearings provided for in Regulation 17 (art. 19(1), see Chapter 3), are to be held prior to the opinion of the Committee being sought. Committee opinions are not acts that may be reviewed by the ECJ. However, the failure by the Commission to consult the Committee, or to take its opinion into account, might, in the view of Advocate General Warner, provide grounds for an art. 230 review (*Distillers Co. Ltd* v *Commission* case 30/78 [1980] 3 CMLR 121; and see also *ACF Chemiefarma NV* v *Commission* case 41/69 [1970] ECR 661). The views of the Committee do not have to be transmitted to the undertakings involved in the procedure (*Musique Diffusion Française SA* v *Commission* cases 100–103/80 [1983] 3 CMLR 221), a rule which does not assist the appellant concerned that the views of the Committee have not been taken into account.

2.3.2.3 *The European Court of Justice and the Court of First Instance*

Article 220 EC provides that the 'Court of Justice shall ensure that in the interpretation and application of this Treaty the law is observed'. Recognizing that the ECJ was overstretched, with cases frequently taking two years or more to be heard, the Court of First Instance (CFI) was created by Council Decision 88/591, following amendments made to the Treaty by the Single European Act 1986 (entry into force 1 July 1987). The CFI is now governed by art. 225 EC, which provides in part that the court has 'jurisdiction to hear and determine at first instance, subject to a right of appeal to the Court of Justice on points of law only . . . certain classes of action'. Cases brought under art. 230 are included in the CFI's jurisdiction, and it is consequently heavily involved in determining matters of competition law, and has insisted in particular that the Commission respect the rights of undertakings against which it brings proceedings.

The numbers of judges to be appointed to each of the courts, and the qualifications they are required to possess, are set out in the EC Treaty. The ECJ consists of 15 judges, one from each Member State, assisted by nine advocates general, all of whom are required to be eligible for the highest judicial appointments in the Member State from which they come. The 15 judges of the CFI are required to be eligible only for judicial office in their respective Member States. Both courts function by way of chambers which must contain at least three judges, thus giving the courts the ability to hear several cases simultaneously. The role of the Advocate General, who has no direct equivalent in domestic law, is to 'assist the court' (art. 220). This function is fulfilled by way of the opinions delivered to the court at the penultimate stage of the proceedings. The opinion is not binding on the court, which delivers only a single unanimous judgment, but is very often followed, and may be of interest as it is likely to be both more wide-ranging and more speculative than the final judgment, which is often terse and focused directly to the point at issue.

As well as its specific roles in relation to arts 230, 232, and 288 (see above) the ECJ has, in accordance with art. 229 EC, 'unlimited jurisdiction . . . to review decisions whereby the Commission has fixed a fine or periodic penalty payment', and 'may cancel, reduce or increase the fine or periodic penalty payment imposed' (Regulation 17, art. 17). At the time of writing there have been no cases in which the ECJ has increased the fine imposed by the Commission, but many in which it has reduced the fine (see Chapter 4).

Appeals from the CFI to the ECJ can only be made on points of law, within two months of the CFI notifying the parties of its decision. Three specific grounds are set out in the Protocol on the Statute of the ECJ (art. 51):

(a) lack of competence of the CFI;

(b) breach of procedure before the CFI; and

(c) breach of Community law by the CFI.

The ECJ will not, therefore, review the CFI's own review of the facts of the case (*Hilti AG* v *Commission* case C–53/92P [1994] 4 CMLR 614, and *Deutsche Bahn AG* v *Commission* case C–436/97P [1999] 5 CMLR 775) and neither will it interfere in the CFI's assessment of fines where the latter has in turn considered the penalties imposed by the Commission (*BPB Industries plc and British Gypsum Ltd* v *Commission* case C–310/93P [1997] 4 CMLR 238). Were such a further review permitted the benefit of a quicker process offered by the creation of the CFI would be lost, with the effect being merely that of adding yet another judicial stage to an already drawn-out process.

2.3.3 Subsidiarity, the duties of the Member States, and conflicts between domestic and Community law

Article 10 EC provides that Member States shall

take all appropriate measures, whether general or particular, to ensure fulfilment of the obligations arising out of this Treaty or resulting from action taken by the institutions of the Community. They shall facilitate the achievement of the Community's tasks.

They shall abstain from any measure which could jeopardise the attainment of the objectives of this Treaty.

This provision applies equally to the measures relating to competition law as to any other obligation.

Article 5 of the EC Treaty, introduced by the TEU, provides that

In areas which do not fall within its exclusive competence, the Community shall take action, in accordance with the principle of subsidiarity, only if and in so far as the objectives of the proposed action cannot be sufficiently achieved by the Member States and can therefore, by reason of the scale or effects of the proposed action, be better achieved by the Community.

When the concept of subsidiarity, the definition of which is uncertain at best, was introduced many commentators pointed out that, at least with respect to competition law, the principle had been in operation from the inception of the Treaty. Community jurisdiction is established only where trade between Member States is likely to be affected by the conduct in question, which, although the test is in practice generous on the side of the Community (see, e.g., *La Technique Minière* v *Maschinenbau Ulm GmbH* case 56/65 [1966] 1 CMLR 357), serves to curtail greatly the circumstances in which the Commission is able to act, and leaves a large measure of discretion to national governments in the structure and operation of their domestic competition law regimes.

Where Community law exists it is supreme in relation to national law (*Costa* v *ENEL* case 6/64 [1964] CMLR 425), and will prevail in the event of there being any conflict. This fundamental principle of the Treaty, which has been consistently emphasized by the ECJ, extends even to provisions of national constitutions (*Internationale Handelsgesellschaft mbH* case 11/70 [1972] 1 CMLR 255; and in relation to Acts of Parliament see, for example, *R* v *Secretary of State for Transport ex parte Factortame Ltd* case C–213/89 [1990] 3 CMLR 1). The ECJ has ruled on the matter specifically in relation to competition law in *Wilhelm* v *Bundeskartellamt* case 14/68 [1969] CMLR 100, holding that where the German cartel laws conflicted with Community law the latter must take precedence. There is unlikely to be conflict in situations where a practice is condemned under arts 81(1) or 82, as the principles of direct effect alone would ensure that any domestic action purporting to permit such a practice would be likely to be frustrated by private claims. The position would be less certain were domestic authorities seeking to prohibit action that is permitted under Community law, particularly if a specific individual exemption granted under art. 81(3) is in place. The matter has yet to be ruled on directly at Community level, but it has been suggested that such a conflict would be outside the spirit of Community law. The Commission is of the view that stricter national standards should not be allowed to prevail over a more permissive Community regime. However, this proposition sits uneasily with the principle of subsidiarity, and does not take into account the fact that national policies might pursue different goals from that of the Community. It would be unfortunate were practices with a purely domestic impact, and thus falling outside the ambit of the operation of Community law, condemned by national authorities in situations where an identical practice having an effect on trade between Member States would be permitted, purely on the grounds that the Commission had granted an art. 81(3) exemption precluding the national authority from taking action. Member States would certainly be expected to be allowed to condemn practices that fell outside the ambit of Community law altogether (*Procureur de la République* v *Bruno Giry and Guerlain SA* case 253/78 [1981] 2 CMLR 99).

The general attitude of the UK authorities appeared, even prior to the enactment of the Competition Act 1998, to give paramountcy to Community law, and there were provisions of the pre-1998 statutes which appear to give effect to this principle (see, e.g., Restrictive Trade Practices Act 1976, s. 5(2)). Frequent reference to Community law is made in Competition Commission reports, with relevant EC Commission decisions being reproduced. The Competition Act 1998 greatly reinforced this general position, and to a significant degree aligned national law with Community law.

2.3.4 **Direct effect**

It was established by the ECJ, in the landmark case of *NV Algemene Transport-en Expeditie Onderneming Van Gend en Loos* v *Nederlandse Belastingadministratie* case 26/62 [1963] 1 CMLR 105, that where articles of the Treaty are clear, precise and unconditional they are capable of creating rights vested in individuals which can be enforced against Member States ('vertical direct effect'). In *Defrenne* v *Sabena (No. 2)* case 43/75 [1976] 2 CMLR 98, the principle was extended to allow such rights to be enforced against other persons not being part of the state ('horizontal direct effect'). The principle applies equally to regulations, which are, by the wording of art. 249 'binding in [their] entirety and directly applicable in all Member States'. Both the prohibitions set out in arts 81 and 82 meet the criteria set out in *Van Gend*, although art. 81(3), at present, does not, and an undertaking engaging in conduct that falls within the prohibitions may therefore face actions before national courts by those harmed by that action (see, e.g., *Belgische Radio en Televisie (BRT)* v *Société Belge des Auteurs, Compositeurs et Editeurs (SABAM)* case 127/73 [1974] 2 CMLR 238). However, victims of anti-competitive action appear reluctant to take such steps, and there are very few occasions on which courts in the United Kingdom have been called upon to rule on matters of Community competition law, although the House of Lords has suggested that damages may be available to those so injured. This matter was first discussed by Lord Diplock in *Garden Cottage Foods Ltd* v *Milk Marketing Board* [1983] 2 All ER 770, HL, where he suggested that a breach of EC law may give rise to a remedy for damages for breach of statutory duty. It has been suggested that the judgment of the ECJ in the case of *Francovich* v *Italian Republic* cases C 6 and 9/90 [1993] 2 CMLR 66, in which it was established that a Member State becomes liable for its breaches of Community law to those who can show harm as a result of the breach where an identifiable right has been infringed, further increases the pressure for national courts to find remedies for those injured by breaches of directly effective competition provisions. While some commentators have called for the Commission to promulgate a directive on remedies, introducing a welcome level of harmonization and certainty, this proposal has been resisted by the Competition Directorate.

In the *Modernisation White Paper* the Commission recognizes that the lack of private litigation is a problem, and is looking at ways to further encourage private parties to enter into proceedings (see, e.g., para. 39).

If more actions were brought directly by injured parties in the Member States the workload on the Commission would be reduced. Alexander Schaub, responding to a question from *In Competition* which suggested that businesses find it unattractive to take such steps, responded that 'it should be interesting to use national courts, maybe it is not well enough known. They should play a much bigger role. I don't think it is in [the Commission's] interest to systematically centralise decision-making'. National courts are encouraged to apply competition law themselves in the *Notice on Cooperation between National Courts and the Commission* in applying Articles [81] and [82] of the EEC Treaty ((1993) OJ C39/6), in which the Commission makes clear its view that there are strong advantages to claimants in taking this course. In particular the Commission points out that: it is unable to award damages to injured parties; national courts can order interim measures; national and EC-based claims may be combined before national courts; and the national court may be able to award costs to the successful plaintiff. The Commission recognizes that it, in turn, 'has a duty of sincere cooperation vis-à-vis judicial authorities of the Member States' (para. 33) and that if national courts require assistance from the Commission they may, to the extent that national law permits, ask the Commission for certain information in order to assist the court (para. 37).

National courts ruling on directly effective Community law may also have recourse to the procedure set out in art. 234 EC. This provides a formal link between any court or tribunal in a Member State and the ECJ, giving the latter the ability to 'give preliminary rulings concerning', *inter alia*, '(a) the interpretation of this Treaty'; and '(b) the validity and interpretation of acts of the institutions of the Community—'. The purpose of the article is to restrict the scope for divergence in the application of EC law by national courts. To that end, national courts or tribunals 'against whose decision there is no judicial remedy . . . shall bring the matter before the Court of Justice' (art. 234(3)), whereas lower courts or tribunals have discretion to refer (art. 234(2)). The article does not serve as an appeal process—questions must be asked in the abstract and the answers provided by the ECJ are unlikely to be such as to determine the outcome of the case on the facts, although they may often be conclusive on the point of law in question. The jurisdiction of the CFI does not extend to art. 234 references (art. 225(1)), and all references must therefore be made directly to the ECJ. Although national courts may be reluctant to involve themselves in areas of law in which they have little expertise, such as is the case with competition issues and the United Kingdom courts, the reference procedure should assist them with such matters. The relationship between national courts and the EC Commission was explored in the case of *Masterfoods Ltd* v *H B Ice Cream Ltd; HB Ice Cream Ltd* v *Masterfoods Ltd* case C–344/98 [2001] 4 CMLR 14, discussed is more detail in Chapter 16.

The UK Competition Commission (see below), constituted under the Competition Act 1998, is classed, in the exercise of some of its powers, as a tribunal, and is competent to make references to the Community courts by way of the art. 234 reference procedure (see, in this respect, The Competition Commission Appeal Tribunal Rules 2000, SI 2000/261, Part IX). The Director General of Fair Trading will *not* be able to make such references.

2.4 The United Kingdom

2.4.1 The control of monopolies and restrictive trade practices

There is a clean historical break between earlier competition laws and the system of public regulation introduced shortly after the end of the Second World War, the only legacy of the earlier law being in those areas of common law which remain relevant to competition issues (these are discussed in Chapter 17). The post-war regime has itself been largely replaced by the Competition Act 1998, although this does not mark a total break with older practice. It repeals the majority of the old law, but the bulk of the Fair Trading Act 1973, with its provisions for monopoly references and for merger control, has been left in place, although the operation of the former will change as a result of the new Act and the Government has begun the process of reforming the law of merger control. Changes made to the organizational structures were not as radical as many commentators and lawyers expected, and the three bodies at the heart of the domestic system—the Director General of Fair Trading, the Monopolies and Mergers Commission (MMC), and the Secretary of State for Trade and Industry—continue to have a role to play, although the MMC's functions have been subsumed into a new Competition Commission (CC).

Discussion of the adverse impact on the economy and employment of restrictive practices in the 1944 White Paper on *Employment Policy* (Cmd. 6527) played a dominant role in shaping the post-war regime until the introduction of the Competition Act 1998, and its effects continue to be seen in the system of monopoly references that will still be applied under the Fair Trading Act 1973. The White Paper dealt only peripherally with restrictive practices and monopoly control, but the threat posed to government policy by combinations of businesses seeking, for example, to raise prices was recognized. It was then noted that

There has in recent years been a growing tendency towards combines and towards agreements, both national and international, by which manufacturers have sought to control prices and output, to divide markets and to fix conditions of sale. Such agreements or combines do not necessarily operate against the public interest; but the power to do so is there. The Government will therefore seek power to inform themselves of the extent and effect of restrictive agreements, and of the activities of combines; and to take appropriate action to check practices which may bring advantages to sectional producing interests but work to the detriment of the country as a whole.

The White Paper was accepted by the government and was reflected in competition legislation relating to the control of monopoly conduct through to the Fair Trading Act 1973. The 'public interest' test lay at the heart of the earlier legislation, and continues to exist in the Fair Trading Act (although the Government has announced its intention to replace the public interest test with a competition-based test). The lack of definition of 'public interest'—which is not elaborated on significantly in the Act, although a range of factors to be considered is given—was subject to severe criticism by the House of Commons Select Committee on Trade and Industry in *UK Policy on Monopolies* ((1995) HC 249) which reported that

The DGFT defined the public interest as 'consumer well-being' but admitted that 'I do not think anybody could possibly pretend that they could sit down and do some sums and have an answer they can defend against all comers at the end of the day'. The Chairman of the MMC said that it was impossible to define the public interest in a general context, and the Minister simply referred to the criteria set out in the [Fair Trading Act]. These criteria, however, are extremely broad and lack an indication of priorities . . . Since the 'public interest' judgment lies at the heart of UK policy on monopolies, this ambiguity is a matter of concern.   (HC 249–1, para. 20)

In referring to 'public interest', in s. 84, the Fair Trading Act gives indications of those factors that may fall to be considered, in as much as it makes mention of 'the desirability of maintaining and promoting effective competition' (s. 84(1)(a)), but does not expand much on this.

Under the public interest test, in each case the important factor was the circumstance in which any particular practice operated, rather than the nature of the practice itself. Common pricing systems, for instance, were condemned in *The Supply of Insulated Electric Cable and Wires* (25 April 1953) but exonerated in *Standard Metal Windows and Doors* (8 January 1957). The basic principle, whereby practices that *might* be anti-competitive will be banned only if they are shown *in a specific case* to be contrary to the public interest, was largely, but not totally, abandoned only with the entry into force of the Competition Act 1998.

However, the Fair Trading Act 1973 remains in force even following the entry into force of the Competition Act 1998. The Act sets a threshold at which monopoly investigations can be launched of 25 per cent of market share, and introduced the office of the Director General of Fair Trading, appointed by the Secretary of State. The relevant provisions of the Fair Trading Act are discussed throughout this book as appropriate, and in particular in Chapter 12.

Specific legislation was created to deal with anti-competitive agreements, as the control of these fell outside the regime created to deal with monopoly conduct. A 1956 Restrictive Trade Practices Act was replaced by the Restrictive Trade Practices Act 1976 (RTPA). This established a system under which agreements falling within the scope of the Act were to be registered. The RTPA took an overly legalistic and technical approach to matters that were being better dealt with under art. 81 EC. For a good example of how this approach could fail in practice, reference should be made to the 'Premier League' cases (*In the matter of the RTPA 1976 and In the matter of an agreement between the Football Association Premier League Ltd and the Football Association Ltd and the Football League Ltd and their respective member clubs, etc.* [1999] UKCLR 258). The judgment runs to some 150 pages, and although the Court agreed that the rules under attack resulted in restrictions on competition it had no power to prescribe any alternative (see also the Office of Fair Trading (OFT) *Statement on the Premier League case*, 28 July 1999).

The possibility remains that provisions of the RTPA could still be raised in the context of litigation until limitation periods are exceeded, but this Act is not dealt with any further in this book.

2.4.2 **The Competition Act 1998**

If evidence was needed that the 'old' regime had fallen into disrepute it was provided by the inclusion of a reference to a competition Bill in the first Queen's Speech of the new Labour government in 1997. This followed a long-running discussion under the previous Conservative government, which had early on introduced the Competition Act 1980 designed to supplement the Fair Trading Act 1973, but of limited practical application, and then followed various Green and White Papers with only minor reforms to the administrative processes in the Deregulation and Contracting Out Act 1994, although its own draft Bill had been introduced in 1996. The 1997 Bill, which bore little relation to the 1996 Conservative version, was brought before the House of Lords in October 1997 following a relatively short consultation process, and completed its progress through both Houses of Parliament in October 1998. Royal Assent was granted on 9 November 1998.

Since the case of *Pepper (Inspector of Taxes)* v *Hart* [1993] AC 593, comments made during the passage of an Act have become a useful means of resolving ambiguities or clarifying the legislation where necessary, and frequent references are made to 'Pepper-amendments', so designed that if the amendment itself is rejected the government will nevertheless confirm in the process its clear intention in drafting the legislation. This clearly influences Parliamentary proceedings, as was shown during the Committee stage of the Bill's progress in the House of Lords (Hansard (HL) 17 November 1997, col. 426). Accordingly the sources for the debates are given here. House of Lords: 2nd Reading, 30 October 1997, coll. 1144–95; Committee stage, 13 November 1997, coll. 256–314, 325–55, 17 November 1997, coll. 367–427, 432–55, 25 November 1997, coll. 868–77, 897–932, 946–89; Report stage, 9 February 1998, coll. 873–935, 955–90, 19 February 1998, coll. 327–82, 23 February 1998, coll. 453–77, 491–538; 3rd Reading, 5 March 1998, coll. 1301–84. House of Commons: 2nd Reading, 11 May 1998, coll. 23–127; Standing Committee G, 21 May 1998, 2 June 1998, 4 June 1998, 9 June 1998, 11 June 1998, 16 June 1998, 18 June 1998, 23 June 1998, 25 June 1998; 3rd Reading, 8 July 1998, coll. 1100–1212; House of Lords: Consideration of Commons Amendments, 20 October 1998, coll. 1336–1409. Frequent reference is made to these debates throughout this book.

In bringing forward the Bill, Lord Simon for the Government explained that it showed the Government's 'commitment to ensuring effective and fair competition' and that 'it would benefit both consumers and business' (Hansard (HL) 30 October 1997, col. 1144). The Bill was praised by Lord Borrie, a former Director General of Fair Trading who had been a harsh critic of the regime under which he was expected to operate, but was condemned as 'half-baked and ill thought out' by the Opposition (Lord Fraser, ibid., col. 1149). The majority of comments received during the consultation exercise had been positive, however, and the Act has been broadly welcomed as reducing the uncertainties of the old regime. Consumer groups and smaller competitors who have suffered as a result of anti-competitive activity have also welcomed the increased deterrent effect of the 1998 Act.

The Act repealed much of the then existing competition legislation—the Restrictive Trade Practices Acts 1976 and 1977, the Resale Prices Act 1976, the Restrictive Practices Court Act 1976, and those parts of the Competition Act 1980 dealing with anti-competitive conduct. It thus completely replaced the domestic law dealing with anti-competitive agreements, and introduced in its place a prohibition based on art. 81 EC (the 'Chapter I' prohibition). Similarly, art. 82 is reproduced in a second prohibition (the 'Chapter II' prohibition). The prohibitions became operative from 1 March 2000 although transitional periods applied in relation to agreements made before the starting date (see the OFT technical guideline *Transitional Arrangements* [1999] UKCLR 47).

The Government made clear that its overriding objective was to reduce the burdens on industry by aligning domestic law with Community law:

To ensure smooth interaction between the EC legal and business environment and the UK prohibitions, we intend that the UK prohibitions would be interpreted in a manner consistent with the equivalent provisions under EC law. Clause 58 of the Bill [s. 60] has this effect. Such consistency would be of great benefit to so many of our businesses that currently have to worry about two different approaches to competition policy. It delivers a level playing field for our business community in the UK as firms become more and more engaged in European home markets.   (Lord Simon, Hansard (HL) 30 October 1997, col. 1145)

However, the Government chose to retain the monopoly investigation system of the Fair Trading Act as an additional power operating alongside, and in conjunction with, the Chapter II prohibition. The retention of this power in relation to single firm situations ('scale monopolies') is a contentious one as these are equally well covered by the prohibition. The explanation given in the introduction to the original draft of the Bill is unsatisfactory. The Department of Trade and Industry's (DTI's) position was set out at para. 6.22 of the Consultation Document:

A prohibition based approach is, however, less able to deal with the situation where, for example, an individual abuse has been tackled but where there is a prospect that other abuses by the dominant company may continue in the future. In such a situation, structural remedies to reduce the dominant position of the firm concerned may be more appropriate than relying on the prohibition alone to deter future abuse.

Given that both the prohibitions in the Act are backed up with strong investigative powers and substantial penalties, the justification for supplementing these provisions with yet another mechanism appears thin. A stronger case may be made for the retention of complex monopoly investigations under the Fair Trading Act. In the White Paper *Productivity and Enterprise* (Cm. 5233, July 2001), the DTI noted that a 'peer review' of the UK competition regime showed that 'the complex monopoly provisions of the Fair Trading Act 1973 are particularly well regarded' (Box 3.2, p. 11). The situations in which such investigations may be held, and the definition of a complex monopoly, are dealt with in Chapter 12. While such situations may be considered under art. 82 EC, and therefore by implication under the Chapter II prohibition, these have not been adequately tackled at Community level, and the apparent success of the Fair Trading Act in such markets has been one of the more obvious successes of the domestic regime over the years. The procedure to be adopted under the Competition Act 1998 is shown in Figure 2.2.

As with Community law, the primary focus of the Act is on 'competition', and the tests for the application of the prohibitions and exemptions are to be broadly the same. An Opposition initiative to introduce into the Office of Fair Trading a 'consumer representative' officer was defeated during the Bill's passage. The National Consumer Council (NCC), for example, argued that while it may well be the case that consumers will be presumed to benefit from the application of a competition law regime, an explicit recognition of their role should be made. The Government maintained that consumer interests lay at the heart of the legislation and did not need to be specifically incorporated (see generally Hansard (HL) 25 November 1997, coll. 870–5).

The substantive provisions of the Act are dealt with as necessary throughout this book. The Office of Fair Trading (OFT) has published a number of 'technical guidelines' relating to various aspects of the new regime. While these are referred to throughout this book as appropriate they are best read in their entirety, and all are

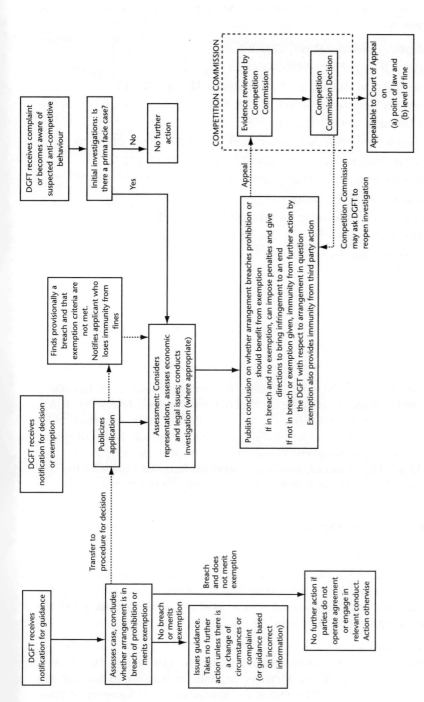

Figure 2.2 The decision-making process

Notes: 1. Exemption procedure and immunity from fines on notification only apply to prohibition of anti-competitive agreements.

2. 'Arrangement' means an agreement or relevant conduct.

3. Immunity ceases if decision is based on incorrect information, or circumstances have changed materially.

4. Sector regulators will also apply the prohibitions in the same manner as the DGFT.

available from the OFT's web site. The list of relevant guidelines at the end of May 2002 is as follows:

- *The Chapter I Prohibition* [1999] UKCLR 1
- *The Chapter II Prohibition* [1999] UKCLR 23
- *Assessment of Individual Agreements and Conduct* [2000] UKCLR 1
- *Assessment of Market Power* [2000] UKCLR 40
- *Market Definition* [2000] UKCLR 61
- *Trade Associations, Professions and Self-Regulating Bodies* [2000] UKCLR 163
- *Exclusion for Mergers and Ancillary Restraints* [2000] UKCLR 178
- *Vertical Agreements and Restraints* [2000] UKCLR 405
- *Land Agreements* [2000] UKCLR 418
- *Guidance Notes on Completing Form N* [2000] UKCLR 391
- *Transitional Arrangements* [1999] UKCLR 47
- *Early Guidance Directions* [1999] UKCLR 71
- *Form EG* [1999] UKCLR 76
- *Powers of Investigation* [1999] UKCLR 195
- *Enforcement* [1999] UKCLR 217
- *Director General of Fair Trading's Guidance as to the Appropriate Amount of a Penalty* [2000] UKCLR 431
- *Concurrent Application to Regulated Industries* [2001] UKCLR 1015

Further guidelines are likely to be published (there is, for example, in the *Chapter I Prohibition* guideline a reference to the *General Economic Interest* guideline, which has not yet been published). The various industry regulators, whose ambit and powers are not discussed specifically in this book, have also issued their own guidelines in relation to their powers under the Competition Act 1998.

As of 1 May 2002, 10 formal, numbered, decisions have been made by the OFT under the Act. These are dealt with as appropriate throughout this text.

2.4.3 **The regulatory organs**

2.4.3.1 *Secretary of State*

The Secretary of State leading the DTI has a number of powers in relation to the application of the domestic competition regime. However, it should be noted that these are gradually being curtailed in an attempt to take politics out of the application of competition law.

2.4.3.1.1 *Fair Trading Act 1973*

The Secretary of State has various powers under the Fair Trading Act. Section 12 sets out the powers of the Secretary of State in relation to the Director General of Fair Trading (DGFT), who is the appointee of the Secretary of State.

In particular the Secretary of State may determine the priorities which the DGFT is to give to certain matters, and may establish the consideration that the DGFT should have in mind in determining whether to make a monopoly reference to the CC. The Secretary of State may also, although this power is rarely used, block monopoly references made by the DGFT: the Director is obliged to send a copy of any reference he makes to the Secretary of State, who may order the Commission not to proceed to consider the reference if he acts within 14 days of the publication of the reference (s. 50(6)). The Secretary of State, or certain other ministers acting jointly with the Secretary of State, may make monopoly references under s. 51 of the Act (and see also Competition Act 1980, s. 21).

CC reports are addressed to the Secretary of State, and it is for the Secretary of State, bearing in mind any advice given by the DGFT, to act on these reports. Under s. 56(2), the Minister may 'by order made by statutory instrument exercise [such of his powers] as he considers it requisite to exercise for the purpose of remedying or preventing the adverse effect specified in the report'. The Secretary of State is not obliged to act upon the receipt of a report, even where both the CC and the DGFT recommend that action be taken. It is also for the Secretary of State to decide whether undertakings should be sought from companies as an alternative to a reference to the CC.

More generally the Secretary of State has the power, under various sections of the Act, to lay before Parliament the necessary regulations relating to the Act. These relate, for example, to classes of goods or services that may be excluded from the operation of the Act (see, e.g., Sch. 7). The Secretary of State also has a role under this Act in relation to merger control, having the final decision in this area (see further Chapter 15). Reforms of the merger control system brought forward in 2001 will reduce this role to a vestigial one.

2.4.3.1.2 *Competition Act 1998*

The Secretary of State has a greatly restricted role under the Competition Act 1998 and is not to be directly involved in the operation of the prohibitions. In this respect the Act is far less political in its operation than is the Fair Trading Act, a development consistent with the application of a more tightly defined standard. The role of the Secretary of State under the Act is largely limited to the making of regulations under the Act. Notably these will include, on recommendations from the DGFT, the making of block exemptions which will limit the effect of the Chapter I prohibition (s. 6).

2.4.3.2 *Director General of Fair Trading*

Section 1(1) of the Fair Trading Act 1973 provides that 'The Secretary of State shall appoint an officer to be known as the Director General of Fair Trading'. These appointments are for five-year terms and may be renewable (s. 1(2)). At May 2002 the DGFT was John Vickers, whose background lay in economics and commerce.

The DGFT has various roles, not all of which stem from the operation of the competition Acts. The general functions of the Director under the Fair Trading Act are set out in s. 2 of the Act. Section 2(a) is in the following terms:

[the Director shall] keep under review the carrying on of commercial activities in the United Kingdom which relate to goods supplied to consumers in the United Kingdom or produced with a view to their being so supplied, or which relate to services supplied for consumers in the United Kingdom, and to collect information with respect to such activities, and the persons by whom they are carried on, with a view to his becoming aware of, and ascertaining the circumstances relating to, practices which may adversely affect the economic interests of consumers in the United Kingdom.

2.4.3.2.1 *Fair Trading Act 1973*

The Director's annual reports focus on the broad role in relation to competition policy: 'Section 2 of the Fair Trading Act 1973 requires the Director General to keep commercial activities in the United Kingdom under review in order to detect monopoly situations (as defined in ss. 6–11) and uncompetitive practices'. The DGFT is further required to extend to the Secretary of State any information or assistance that the latter requires relating to commercial activities in the UK, and to make any recommendations to the Secretary of State relating to this that the DGFT considers necessary.

The main responsibilities of the DGFT under the 1973 Act are to make, where appropriate, monopoly references to the CC, and at ss. 44 and 45 the Director is given the power to obtain the necessary information 'for the purpose of assisting him in determining whether to ... make a monopoly reference'. The two types of monopoly references, s. 48 references limited to the facts and s. 49 full public interest references, are dealt with more fully in Chapter 12. Copies of subsequent CC reports must be sent to the DGFT, save in situations where a reference has been made by the Secretary of State and could not have been made by the DGFT, and the Secretary of State is to take into account any advice made by the DGFT (s. 86). Where the CC recommends that action be taken following its examination of the situation it is for the DGFT to consult with the relevant parties regarding any undertakings that might be offered by them where the Secretary of State indicates that such action be taken (s. 88). Once undertakings are in place the DGFT has the further task of reviewing their operation and of taking appropriate action where the undertaking is not being met. In the alternative, where circumstances have changed and the undertaking is no longer appropriate, for example, where it acts to a firm's disadvantage and market conditions have changed, the DGFT may recommend to the Secretary of State that it be withdrawn (s. 88(3)–(4)).

As a consequence of amendments made by the Deregulation and Contracting Out Act 1994, the Director may, in lieu of a reference, make recommendations to the Secretary of State regarding the acceptance of undertakings by those who might have been subject to such a reference (Fair Trading Act 1973, s. 56A).

The role of the DGFT in relation to merger control is set out in Chapter 15.

2.4.3.2.2 *Competition Act 1998*

The Director's role under the Competition Act 1998 is a significant one, and is elaborated on in more detail as appropriate throughout this book. The Director, or officers appointed by the Director, is responsible for investigating infringements of the Act, for issuing guidance to companies and ruling on the status of notified practices and agreements under both the Chapter I and Chapter II prohibitions, and for determining the level of any penalties that may be imposed or remedial measures that may be required where breaches of the Act have occurred.

2.4.3.2.3 *Information*

One of the duties of the DGFT is to provide information about competition policy. Thus, s. 124 of the Fair Trading Act provides that 'he may arrange for the publication, in such form and in such manner as he may consider appropriate, of such information and advice as it may appear to him to be expedient to give to consumers in the UK'. Section 125 of the Fair Trading Act provides that the DGFT shall, at the end of each year, 'make to the Secretary of State a report on his activities . . . during that year'. These reports are then published and are highly informative'. Various documents and explanatory booklets are also available (some of which will be referred to from time to time in this book); in particular research and discussion papers commissioned by the OFT are a very valuable resource, although to date they have concentrated on economic issues. The OFT has a site on the Internet which is linked to the open government initiative, and can be found at **www.oft.gov.uk**. This site includes links to other competition resources on the Internet. The OFT is required under the Competition Act 1998 to issue guidance as to the operation of the Act's prohibitions and procedures (the list of guidelines published as at May 2002 is given above). The Director 'is working to ensure that the documents are business-friendly and aimed at those likely to be affected by the provisions of the [Act] rather than legal specialists' (Hansard (HL) 19 February 1998, col. 361).

2.4.3.2.4 *Community competition law in the UK*

For the purposes of EC law the DGFT, supported by the OFT, is the 'competent authority' of the Member State in the UK. Thus the DGFT serves as the link between the operation of EC law by the EC Commission and the operation of that law in the UK by the EC Commission or by the OFT at the Commission's behest (see Chapter 3). Sections 61–5 of the Competition Act 1998 give the Director specific powers in relation to investigations conducted on behalf of the EC Commission.

2.4.3.3 *Office of Fair Trading*

The DGFT has the power, under the Fair Trading Act 1973, s. 1(5), to 'appoint such staff as he may think fit, subject to the approval of the Minister for the Civil Service as to numbers and as to terms and conditions of service'. The OFT is the support office to the DGFT, assisting him to carry out his designated roles. In relation to competition policy the bulk of the OFT's work under the old regime lay in conducting preliminary investigations to assess whether action needed to be taken in respect of particular practices. Where such preliminary investigations were followed by a full reference to the CC there was much duplication of effort, notwithstanding the fact that the DGFT is required to make available to the CC relevant information, although the CC's brief will be wider, and this is criticized by those subject to the procedure.

2.4.3.4 *The Competition Commission*

The Competition Commission (CC) is a creation of the Competition Act 1998, and supersedes the MMC (s. 45, and see also schs 7 and 8). All roles of the MMC that continue to be applicable to the new regime are to be performed by the CC (s. 45(3)). The CC will fulfil two distinct functions. First, it is the body to which appeals against decisions of the DGFT relating to the application of the Competition Act 1998 are to be made (s. 46). For this purpose an appeals tribunal has been created which is part of the CC (s. 48). Secondly, it will continue to investigate and report on those matters which were considered by the MMC under the Fair Trading Act (see below) and other regulatory measures. The relationship between the appeals tribunal and the rest of the CC's work is not a comfortable one, although a system of Chinese walls will keep the two divisions separate. The problems can be seen in the hypothetical situation where a company is made subject to a monopoly investigation under the terms of the Fair Trading Act, at the same time as appealing against an adverse decision taken against it by the DGFT under one of the prohibitions of the Competition Act 1998. The same body, albeit in different guises and with different personnel involved in each case, will be expected both to investigate the company's affairs thoroughly, and at the same time to act as an impartial tribunal passing judgment on the DGFT's decision. A chairman of the CC and a president of the appeals tribunal have been appointed.

The hearing of appeals against decisions of the DGFT will be the most contentious role of the CC. The appeals tribunal is headed by a legally qualified president, and, similar to other tribunals, each case is dealt with either by the president, or another legally qualified chairman appointed by the president, and two lay members with relevant expertise in business and competition matters who are members of the CC appeals tribunal panel. The tribunal is able to take appeals on both points of law and matters of fact, and third parties with the requisite *locus standi* (s. 47) as well as those to whom the DGFT's decisions are directed are able to appeal. The tribunal has the power to refer matters back to the DGFT, as it did in *Aberdeen Journals ltd v The Director General of Fair Trading* ([2002] CompAR 167), to overturn the DGFT's decision altogether, or to vary the fine or penalty imposed in any particular case. The Tribunal has a wide discretion in its power to award costs (see, e.g., *Institute of Independent Insurance Brokers v The Director General of Fair Trading* [2002] compAR 141, at paras 57–60). The primary role of the tribunal is to re-examine evidence presented by the Director, and it is not anticipated that it will often initiate its own investigations.

Appeals from decisions of the appeals tribunal, which may be made only on points of law and in relation to the levels of penalty imposed, are to the Court of Appeal (s. 49). In *Napp Pharmaceutical Holdings Ltd and subsidiaries v The Director*

General of Fair Trading [2002] compAR 160 the CCAT derived the appellant company's application for leave to appeal following its upholding of an adverse decision.

2.4.3.4.1 *Fair Trading Act 1973*

The CC's principal functions are set out at s. 5. It is the duty of the Commission 'to investigate and report on any question which may be referred to the Commission under this Act' (s. 5(1)). Those references may be '(a) with respect to the existence, or possible existence, of a monopoly situation, or (b) with respect to a transfer of a newspaper or of newspaper assets . . ., or (c) with respect to the creation, or possible creation, of a merger situation qualifying for investigation'. The questions which the CC is required to consider depend upon the type of monopoly reference made to it by the DGFT or by a relevant minister. References may relate either to an examination of the factual situation (s. 48) or, as is most often the case, to an evaluation of the impact of such a factual situation on the public interest (s. 49). The nature of the references and the circumstances surrounding them are dealt with in more detail in Chapter 12. Following such a reference it is the duty of the CC to make a report, and to

include in it definite conclusions on the questions comprised in the reference, together with (a) such an account of their reasons for those conclusions, and (b) such a survey of the general position with respect to the subject-matter of the reference, and of the developments which have led to that position, as in their opinion are expedient for facilitating a proper understanding of those questions and of their conclusions.   (s. 54)

Further, the Commission is required to consider what actions might be taken to remedy the situation if it finds that the public interest is being harmed (s. 54(3)). For administrative convenience and in order to streamline the process, the Chairman of the CC will designate individual Commission members to serve on panels when each inquiry is initiated. Each panel, which usually consists of around five to seven members, is chaired by one of the part-time deputy chairmen or by the Chairman himself. Once the CC has made its report its role in the process is over. The decision as to what action is to be taken, is, as noted above, for the Secretary of State bearing in mind any advice given him by the DGFT.

2.5 **The internationalization of competition law**

Increasingly the operation of competition law affects companies based in more than one state, or activities taking place in more than one state. International organizations such as the Organization for Economic Cooperation and Development (OECD) and the World Trade Organization (WTO), as well as regional groupings, are turning towards the consideration of competition law matters. The problems and challenges raised by these developments are considered more thoroughly in Chapter 18.

3

Investigation

3.1 **Introduction**

In neither the European Community nor the United Kingdom can competition law be characterized as part of the body of criminal law. This in turn means that the process of investigation is less contentious than is the case in criminal law, and is surrounded with fewer safeguards, as the outcome may be viewed as less serious. Nevertheless, the consequences for a firm found in breach can be severe (see Chapter 4 for a discussion of penalties), and there may well be disputes as to whether the powers available to the authorities have been exercised appropriately. It has been accepted that for the purposes of the human rights guarantees enshrined in the European Convention of Human Rights (see below) the law should be treated *as if* it were criminal. The Competition Act 1998 significantly expanded the powers available to the UK authorities, and these were largely modelled on, but are not identical to, those available to the EC Commission.

3.2 **The European Community**

The body responsible for ensuring the observance of EC competition law is, as we have seen in Chapter 2, the EC Commission. Where its acts produce legal effects it may in turn be overseen by the CFI, under the review powers conferred by way of art. 230 EC, with the possibility of further appeal to the ECJ. Articles 81 and 82 do not, in their own words, establish the necessary mechanism for enforcement of the proscriptions contained therein; the Commission's powers are set out in Regulation 17 of 1962. This Regulation, which is now criticized as being outdated in its approach, in particular in the imbalance it establishes between the Commission and those undertakings subject to investigation, sets out the procedures to be adopted by the Commission when pursuing possible breaches, or when considering granting exemptions from the general prohibition of art. 81, and the penalties that may be imposed where undertakings are found to have breached the law. The Commission may, in this respect, be characterized as investigator, prosecutor, and decision-maker. For the remainder of this section the structure of the Regulation will be followed. The section will conclude with an examination of the limited rights that undertakings have in the investigation process.

As of May 2002 the process of reforming this Regulation was well under way, and the Commission in September 2000 Published a new draft regulation ([2000] 5 CMLR 1182). It is too early, however, to base the text in this book on the proposal.

3.2.1 **Regulation 17**

3.2.1.1 *The purpose of the Regulation*

Regulation 17 was enacted under the ambit of art. 83 EC. The preamble to the Regulation sets out some of the hopes of the Community in enacting the law. The following are, *inter alia*, referred to: 'the need to ensure effective supervision'; a recognition of the need to balance the general principle under which it would be obligatory for undertakings formally to seek the benefit of art. 81(3) with the fact that the numbers of arrangements to be affected 'are probably very numerous' necessitating a flexible approach; the benefit of 'uniform application', which would be achieved by the Commission acting in 'close and constant liaison with the competent authorities of the Member States'; the need to compel undertakings to provide necessary information relating to potential breaches of the rules; and the rights of undertakings and third parties to be heard by the Commission where they are affected by the application of the law.

3.2.1.2 *Notification, complaints, and the Commission's own initiative*

The Commission is likely to receive information about potential breaches of the competition rules from two main classes: those who are party to such practices; and those objecting to such practices, who will most likely be competing businesses alleging that they have in some way been harmed by another's anti-competitive conduct (for the position of complainants generally see Chapter 5). There is a strong incentive for parties to potentially illegal practices to notify them to the Commission. The general prohibition of arts 81 and 82 is confirmed by art. 1 of the Regulation, and as is made clear, 'no prior decision to that effect' is required. Although many undertakings could, as many evidently did, choose to keep in place illegal agreements or maintain abusive conduct, the better course, in the eyes of the Commission at least, would be to seek a formal exemption from the application of the law.

Article 2 of the Regulation therefore opens up the possibility of what is termed 'negative clearance'. This is a formal decision under which 'the Commission may certify that, on the basis of the facts in its possession, there are no grounds [under arts 81 or 82] for action on its part'. Article 4 of the Regulation provides that no decision can be taken in respect of negative clearance until such time as the parties to the agreement have notified the Commission as to its contents. Certain classes of agreements are exempted from the need to notify, and the Commission has extended and redefined these classes by the issuance of 'block exemptions' in the light of its experience and consultation with industry and other affected groups (see Chapter 8). The Commission has been so overwhelmed by the numbers of notifications that, along with the block exemptions, it has introduced a less formal resolution, the 'comfort letter' (see below). Notification also has the, strictly temporary, benefit of providing immunity from fines in tightly defined circumstances (Regulation 17, art. 15(5)). Notifications are to be made on form A/B, which is attached to Commission Regulation 3385/94 (1994) OJ L377/28. This is a searching process, and the Commission requires that the information must be correct and complete' (art. 3(2)). Applicants are required to submit 17 copies of each application and notification.

The Commission may also act 'upon application or by its own initiative' (art. 3). Those entitled to make applications to the Commission are:

(a) Member States; and

(b) 'natural or legal persons who claim a legitimate interest'.

The latter will be the case particularly where one undertaking alleges that it is being harmed by another's anti-competitive acts, or is being excluded from participating in the market, for example by being denied entry into a distribution system (see further Chapter 5). The Commission is not, however, required to investigate fully all complaints received, even where these are made by parties falling within art. 3. This would be too onerous a burden in the light of the Commission's resources, and the ECJ held, in *Automec srl v Commission* case T–24/90 [1992] 5 CMLR 431, that the Commission is entitled to prioritize its workload. In this respect note should be taken also of *Guerin Automobiles v Commission* case C–282/95P [1997] 5 CMLR 447, discussed further in Chapter 5. In particular, the Commission may have regard to whether national authorities are in a position to deal with the matter effectively, or whether principles of direct effect apply. This is consistent with the principle of subsidiarity now enshrined in art. 5 EC, and the Notice on Cooperation between National Courts and the Commission (see Chapter 16). The Commission will not, therefore, be subject to a plethora of successful actions brought under art. 232 EC, relating to the power of the ECJ to review situations in which the institutions fail to act, if it fails to initiate formal proceedings in response to all complaints received. It is a political inevitability that complaints received from Member States are likely to be accorded higher priority than those taken from other concerned parties.

In the *Modernisation White Paper* the Commission gave the following breakdown of its actions between 1988 and 1998.

Own-initiative proceedings	13%
Notifications	58%
Complaints	29%

In its view these show that too much of its time is taken up in reactive, rather than proactive, investigation (para. 44). The OFT has introduced a fee system for

exemptions and notifications that is designed to discourage speculative notifications, and is attempting to encourage complainants to come forward in an effort
to direct the domestic regime more towards dealing with harms, rather than
confirming that conduct is lawful.

3.2.1.3 *Fact finding*

Once the Commission has become aware of potential breaches of the rules, either
following notification or complaint, or following its own ongoing reviews of markets and industry, the Commission may choose to take no action. In the alternative
it may carry out the necessary investigations to establish that the Treaty is indeed
being breached. Its powers in this area, which are considerable, are derived from
arts 10–14 of Regulation 17, and primarily from arts 11 and 14.

The Commission is required to maintain 'close and constant liaison with the
competent authorities of the Member States' (art. 10). This is facilitated by the
operation of the Advisory Committee on Restrictive Practices and Monopolies (see
Chapter 2). A primary duty of the Commission is to 'transmit to the competent
authorities of the Member States a copy of the applications and notifications
together with copies of the most important documents lodged with the Commission for the purpose of establishing the existence of infringements' of the Treaty
(art. 10(1)). The competent authorities may subsequently become involved in the
investigative process, either by acting at the request of the Commission pursuant to
art. 13(1), or by assisting and accompanying Commission officials pursuant to art.
13(2). If the competent authority acts alone its officials must produce, in writing,
authorization which 'shall specify the subject matter and purpose of the
investigation'.

By virtue of art. 11 the Commission is empowered to make 'requests for information'. Article 14 gives it the right to carry out investigations, that is, to attend
premises and conduct on-the-spot searches for material, etc. The Commission does
not have to try to gather information under art. 11 before using its art. 14 powers.
Article 14 will most often be used where the Commission has reason to believe that
an undertaking may be obstructive and attempt to conceal information, or destroy
evidence if it is given due warning of the Commission's interest in its actions. In
both cases the Commission can act only against 'undertakings' (see Chapter 2),
although there may well be circumstances in which, for the purposes of EC
competition law, an individual is treated as an undertaking.

3.2.1.3.1 *Article 11*

Paragraph (1) of art. 11 of Regulation 17 sets out the broad power available to the
Commission, which may 'obtain all necessary information from the governments
and competent authorities of the Member States and from undertakings and
associations of undertakings'. 'Necessary information' is anything which has a
relationship with possible infringements of arts 81 and 82 (see *SEP* v *Commission*
case T–39/90 [1992] 5 CMLR 33). The general duty of cooperation between the
Commission and the Member States is reinforced in para. (2) which requires

the Commission to send a copy of any request for information it makes to an undertaking to the competent authority in the Member State in which that undertaking has its seat. The request shall both state the legal basis on which it is made and also set out the penalties provided for supplying incorrect information (art. 11(3)). If the Commission has acted only by way of an art. 11(1) request there is no obligation on the undertaking to supply any information, but if it chooses to comply it is expected to do so fully and truthfully. The penalties provided for breaching this obligation are set out below but are not in themselves significant. The undertaking's officials, however, should be aware that the Commission is unlikely to respond favourably to obstruction at this phase, and is likely to pursue the investigation more forcefully, and to take into account the lack of cooperation when considering any mitigating factors before setting the fines following the establishment of any breach of the substantive rules of arts 81 or 82.

If the undertaking does not respond to an art. 11(1) request within the time limit set out, the Commission may avail itself of art. 11(5). Here it 'shall by decision require the information to be supplied'. The decision 'shall specify what information is required, fix an appropriate time limit within which it is to be supplied and indicate the penalties provided for [elsewhere in the Regulation] and the right to have the decision reviewed by the Court of Justice'. As with a request, the Commission must forward a copy of the decision to the competent authority of the relevant Member State. The Commission cannot avail itself of this power unless it has first made a request under art. 11(1).

3.2.1.3.2 *Article 14*

The Commission can turn straight away to the powers conferred by virtue of art. 14 of Regulation 17 without first seeking information under art. 11. The broad power is set out in para. (1), which provides that 'the Commission may undertake all necessary investigations into undertakings and associations of undertakings'. Commission officials are empowered: '(a) to examine the books and other business records; (b) to take copies of or extracts from the books and business records; (c) to ask for oral explanations on the spot; (d) to enter any premises, land and means of transport of undertakings'. The structure of the article is similar to that of art. 11, in that the Commission may request that an undertaking comply with an investigation, or may issue a formal decision under art. 14(3). As with art. 11, the Commission is required to inform the competent authority of the Member State in which the investigation is to be conducted.

Under art. 14(3), which the Commission may proceed to directly without first giving the undertaking the chance to cooperate under para. (1), undertakings 'shall submit to investigations ordered by decision'. The competent authority of the Member State shall be consulted before the decision is taken, and the relevant officials conducting the investigation shall provide a copy of the decision to the undertaking under investigation. The decision 'shall specify the subject matter and purpose of the investigation, appoint the date on which it is to begin', which may be the date on which the Commission's officials arrive at the relevant premises, 'and indicate the penalties provided for [elsewhere in the Regulation] and the right to have the decision reviewed by the Court of Justice'. An explanatory note that the Commission officials pass on to the relevant undertaking is nothing more than a simplified restatement of the terms of the relevant parts of Regulation 17.

Once the Commission's officials have started the investigation the undertaking is under a duty to cooperate fully. It is not sufficient for an undertaking merely to give the officials unfettered access to all files and records, and employees must actively help the Commission find the material that it seeks (see, e.g., *Fabbrica Pisana* 80/334 (1980) OJ L75/30, in which the undertaking had made all its files available but had not assisted the Commission's officials in finding the relevant documents). An undertaking is not entitled to have a lawyer present while the investigation is in progress, although the Commission has indicated in its 12th Report on Competition Policy that it may be prepared to wait for one to arrive as long as this does not unduly delay matters.

A contentious area has been that of legal professional privilege. This was first dealt with in *AM&S Europe* v *Commission* case 155/79 [1982] 2 CMLR 264, in which the undertaking had applied to the ECJ to strike down the Commission action after it had seized material held by the undertaking's in-house lawyers. The Advocate General conducted a thorough review of the law relating to legal privilege in the Member States and the Court held that only in recognizing the privilege attaching to documents emanating from independent lawyers relating to the client's right of defence did the laws of the Member States converge to the extent necessary for a common protection to be recognized. Thus the Court affirmed that Regulation 17 was to be interpreted so as to protect such communications only. Internal lawyers are most unlikely to be covered by the protection, although the Court indicated in *Hilti AG* v *Commission* case T–30/89A [1990] 4 CMLR 602 that, in certain highly restricted circumstances, the protection might apply (see also *VW* 98/273 (1998) OJ L124/61, paras 198–9). It may be argued that this general approach is consistent with the treatment of the undertaking as an economic whole: the in-house lawyer is part of the undertaking and it cannot be logical that any one part of the undertaking should be more privileged than another.

There is debate as to the extent to which the Commission is able to exploit its power to ask for oral explanations (art. 14(1)(c)). While the Regulation does not restrict the article so as to apply it only to specific officers of the undertaking, or to specific subject-matter, it would appear that the Commission is not able to ask any employee of the undertaking any question. In *National Panasonic (UK) Ltd* v *Commission* case 136/79 [1980] 3 CMLR 169, Advocate General Warner suggested that the power related to 'specific questions arising from the books and business records which [the Commission officials] examine' in the course of the investigation. If this is a comprehensive statement of the Commission's power, which has been doubted, it would rule out 'fishing trips' by the Commission officials. The Commission has stated elsewhere that it is for the undertaking to nominate the appropriate persons to answer questions, as the Commission is not in the position to judge the competence or knowledge of individual employees (*Fabbrica Pisana* 80/334 (1980) OJ L75/30).

There have been many occasions on which undertakings have challenged the way in which the Commission has conducted its investigation. *National Panasonic* is one of the most significant cases. Commission officials arrived at the sales offices of Panasonic in Slough at about 10 a.m. on 27 June 1979. The officials notified the undertaking's directors of a decision taken on 22 June authorizing an on-the-spot investigation under art. 14(3). The directors asked if the investigation could be delayed while the undertaking's solicitor travelled to the scene from Norwich and the officials stated that their authorization entitled them to act immediately. The inspection, which lasted until 5.30 p.m., began at 10.45 a.m. and the undertaking's solicitor did not arrive until 1.45 p.m. Panasonic subsequently appealed against the art. 14(3) decision and, *inter alia*, asked the ECJ to order that the Commission return or destroy all documents seized by it. Panasonic argued that this was the first time that the Commission had proceeded to a formal investigation by way of decision without first affording the undertaking the opportunity to submit of its own vol- ition to an informal investigation. In fact since 1973 there had been 24 other cases in which the Commission had so acted, and the Commission contended that there was too great a risk that, if both stages of the procedure were followed, documents would be destroyed or removed. The Commission claimed that, even if only the one-stage procedure were followed, there were sufficient safeguards for the undertaking concerned. In doing so it pointed to eight factors:

(a) the need for written authorization;

(b) the need for a formal decision taken by the Commission;

(c) the fact that only 'necessary' investigations could be carried out;

(d) the requirement that the decision be adequately reasoned;

(e) the requirement that the Commission consult the competent authority of the Member State concerned;

(f) the fact that the decision must state within it the right to challenge under art. 230 EC;

(g) the fact that a successful challenge would deprive the Commission of the right to use any materials obtained; and

(h) the availability of a remedy under art. 288 EC were the Commission officials to exceed their authority.

The Court rejected the general arguments made by Panasonic, and in doing so affirmed that Regulation 17 did not infringe the rights invoked, unsuccessfully, by the applicant.

The Commission officials may not use force in carrying out their investigation (*Hoechst AG v Commission* cases 46/87 and 227/88 [1991] 4 CMLR 410, para. 31), although they may be able to fall back on the assistance of national authorities where this is necessary to compel an undertaking to comply with an investigation (see below).

3.2.1.3.3 *Fines*

As well as the penalties imposed for breaches of the substantive rules (see Chapter 4) the Commission can impose fines where undertakings obstruct investigations or supply misleading information. Article 15(1) of the Regulation makes provision for fines of from €100 to €5,000 where undertakings: supply incorrect or misleading information when making an art. 2 application or a notification under arts 4 or 5; and supply incorrect information in response to an art. 11(3) request, or do not comply within the time limit to an art. 11(5) demand. Periodic penalty payments of from €50 to €1,000 per day may be imposed on undertakings in order to compel them to supply information required by an art. 11(5) decision; and to submit to an investigation ordered under art. 14(3). The ECJ has unlimited jurisdiction within the meaning of art. 229 EC to review any fines or periodic penalty payments imposed by the Commission under these provisions.

3.2.1.4 *The hearing*

Once the Commission has conducted its enquiries it must, before making any decision, give the undertaking(s) concerned the chance to be heard (art. 19, Regulation 17). It may also hear applications from other natural or legal persons who can 'show a sufficient interest' (para. 2). However, far from providing a well-developed system of checks and balances, this system is subject to criticism as it is the Commission itself that is responsible for the process.

The general procedure for these hearings is set out in Commission Regulation 2842/98 (1998), OJ L354/18. This Regulation, which entered into force on 1 February 1999, makes provision for the hearing of those to whom objections are addressed (arts 2–5), applicants and complainants (arts 6–8), and other third parties (art. 9). In its final decisions the Commission will 'deal only with objections in respect of which the parties have been afforded the opportunity of making their views known' (art. 2(2)). The Regulation does not apply to hearings in merger cases, which are covered by Regulation 447/98 (1998) OJ L61/1. The main guarantees are those provided for in art. 9 of the Regulation.

Hearings are conducted by persons appointed by the Commission, 'the Hearing Officer' (art. 10, whose terms of reference are set out in Commission Decision 2001/462 (2001) OJ L162/21).

The role of the Hearing Officer has changed substantially since the post was first introduced in 1982. Changes were made in 1994, and then again in 2001. This reflects in part the difficult role the Commission has had to play both as the guarantor of the rights of undertakings involved in competition proceedings, and as the agency charged with pursuing those in breach of the law. The essence of the role of the Hearing Officer is set out in Commission Press Release IP/01/736 (23 May 2001), which states in part that

This new Mandate of the Hearing Officer will substantially improve the overall accountability of the Commission's decision-making process in merger and antitrust proceedings, ensuring that all fundamental rights of parties and economic operators involved in its procedures are respected.

The key function which ensures that this aim is met is set out in Commission Decision 2001/462, art. 1, which provides that the 'Commission shall appoint one or more hearing officers . . . who shall ensure that the effective exercise of the right to be heard is respected in competition proceedings before the Commission'. This role extends to proceedings brought under arts 81 and 82 EC, the comparable provisions in the ECSC to the extent that these may still be invoked, and to proceedings brought in relation to merger control under Regulation 4064/89 (dealt with in more detail in Chapter 15).

The first significant change from the earlier practice introduced in the 2001 Decision is that the Hearing Officer is no longer part of the mainstream of the Competition Division of the Commission, a practice which had been previously criticized. The Hearing Officer is now attached directly to the office of 'the member of the Commission with special responsibility for competition' (art. 2(2)). During the hearings which take place the Hearing Officer 'shall ensure that the hearing is properly conducted and contributes to the objectivity of the hearing itself and of any decision taken subsequently' (art. 5).

Those who want to be heard at hearings, and who are not the primary parties to the action, may make applications to be heard setting out their reasons for wanting to participate. Where it is found that such an applicant does not have sufficient interest in the proceedings to be permitted to participate the applicant shall be informed of this in writing, and will have the opportunity to make further representations (art. 6).

Article 7(2) sets out three classes of documents the communication of which to an applicant may be grounds for the applicant to apply to be heard orally in a hearing. These are: (a) a statement of objections; (b) an invitation to third parties to submit comments once these have shown a sufficient interest to be heard; and (c) informing a complainant that there are insufficient grounds for finding an infringement and inviting that complainant to submit further comments. Where any person or undertaking has received any of these letters,

and has reason to believe that the Commission has in its possession documents which have not been disclosed to it and those documents are necessary for the proper exercise of the right to be heard, access to those documents may be sought by means of a reasoned request (art. 8(1)).

Any decision taken in relation to such a request shall be communicated to all relevant parties (art. 8(2)). In situations in which it is intended to disclose information which may be regarded as a business secret the undertaking from which the information comes shall be given the opportunity to contest this decision by way of written comments (art. 9). In situations in which an undertaking objects to the disclosure of information, but the Commission determines that the information in question is not secret and therefore not protected, a reasoned decision will again be issued.

As regards the hearings themselves the Hearing Officer may, in order to clarify the proceedings, supply to the parties concerned a list of questions in advance (art. 11). It should be recognized that these hearings may deal with very complex questions of fact, and that much better information may be presented if the parties concerned know which issues are likely to be raised at the hearings. The Hearing Officer 'shall determine the date, the duration and the place of the hearing' (art. 12(1)), and is 'fully responsible for the conduct of the hearing' (art. 12(2)). In addition the Hearing Officer 'shall decide whether fresh documents should be admitted during the hearing, what persons should be heard on behalf of a party and whether the persons concerned should be heard separately or in the presence of other persons attending the hearing' (art. 12(3)). Where it is considered appropriate to do so the Hearing Officer may give parties who attended the hearing the opportunity to submit further written comments after the date of the oral hearing. In doing so a deadline may be set, and if documents are submitted after that point the Commission is not required to take these into account (art. 12(4)).

Once the hearing has taken place the Hearing Officer shall make a report on the hearing, commenting on 'procedural issues, including disclosure of documents and access to the file, time limits for replying to the statement of objections and the proper conduct of the oral hearing' (art. 13(1)). When the Commission prepares its draft decision on the case following the hearing, which is then submitted to the Advisory Committee, the Hearing Officer shall prepare a final report dealing with the extent to which this draft decision deals with issues which the parties concerned have had the opportunity to comment on. This final report shall be presented to the relevant Commissioner, and also to the relevant authorities in the Member States, as well as being attached to the draft decision when the Commission comes to make its final decision. It shall also be published in the Official Journal alongside the final decision. These steps go a long way to increase the transparency in the proceedings, a matter which had been criticized on a number of occasions, particularly by the House of Lords Select Committee on the European Communities in 1993.

3.2.1.5 Access to file

A difficult and contentious issue is that of the extent to which undertaking should have access to documents held by the Commission relevant to the case, some of which may well have been obtained from the undertaking's commercial rivals. This matter is dealt with in part in Commission Decision 2001/462, arts 8–9 (see above). The Commission recognized in its *23rd Annual Report* that 'the disclosure to the parties of any relevant information is an essential part of the procedure' (citing *Hoffmann-La Roche & Co. AG* v *Commission* case 85/76 [1979] 3 CMLR 211, (1993) *Annual Report*, point 199). In *Hoffmann* the ECJ held that any undertaking must be able to have its views heard and, in particular, must be able to comment 'on the documents used by the Commission to support its claim that there has been an infringement' (at para. 11). The matter is complicated, as was recognized in *Hoffmann-La Roche*, by the obligation of secrecy imposed on the Commission by way of art. 20 of Regulation 17, and by art. 13 which provides that information, including documents, shall not be communicated, or made accessible in so far as it contains business secrets of any party ... the Commission shall make appropriate arrangements for allowing access to the file, taking due account of the need to protect business secrets, internal commission documents and other confidential information.

Decision 2001/462 in effect enshrines what became known as the '*AKZO* procedure' (*AKZO Chemie BV* v *Commission* case 53/85 [1987] 1 CMLR 231). Under this procedure the Commission will notify the undertaking from which the document has been taken that it intends to allow a third party to inspect the document. The first undertaking will then have the opportunity to contest the decision before the court prior to the release of the document. In the *Soda Ash* series of cases (cases T 30–32/91 and T 36–37/91 [1996] 5 CMLR 57 ff.) the CFI annulled decisions of the Commission in part because they had violated the rights of the appellants in denying them access to various files held by the Commission. In particular the Court held that 'it is not for the Commission alone to decide which documents are useful to the defence and the advisors of the company must have the opportunity to examine documents which may be relevant'.

The Court in *Soda Ash* suggested that the Commission should either allow the undertaking's lawyers unfettered access to the documents held by it prior to the hearing, or make available a list of *all* documents in its possession. This judgment will make life difficult for the Commission, and has been criticized as imposing impractical demands in operation (see, e.g., Ehlermann, C. D. and Drijber, B. J., 'Legal Protection of Enterprises: Administrative Procedure, in particular Access to Files and Confidentiality' [1996] *ECLR* 375). The response of the Commission has been to issue a notice in 1997 'on the internal rules of procedure for processing requests for access to the file' in competition cases (1997) OJ C25/3.

It is clear from the terms of the notice that it is difficult to reconcile the opposing obligations of safeguarding the rights of the defence and protecting confidential information (see below). The notice recognizes the obligation on the Commission to provide access to all the documents making up its file, with the exception of those identified by the CFI in *Hercules Chemicals NV* v *Commission* case T–7/89 [1992] 4 CMLR 84 as being reserved, that is, business secrets, internal Commission documents which do not form part of the investigation and are not placed in the main investigation file, and any other confidential information. The Commission therefore has expressly made clear that it will not, in future, itself select which documents an undertaking may have access to and which it may not (see also *Cimenteries CBR SA* v *Commission* cases T 25–26/95, etc. [2000] 5 CMLR 204).

The failure to disclose information, such as trade-press extracts, which is in the public domain, was found not to invalidate a Decision in *Limburgse Vinyl Maatschappij NV* v *Commission* cases T 305–307/94, etc. [1999] 5 CMLR 303, at para. 496.

3.2.1.6 *Secrecy*

Any information obtained by the Commission in the course of its investigations must be treated carefully by the Commission and can 'be used only for the purpose of the relevant request or investigation'. The concern of undertakings is that the power given to the Commission to examine business records is sufficiently wide as to extend to all information held by the company, with the exception of independent legal advice. The Commission has held that 'business secrecy cannot be invoked against Commission officials acting pursuant to [Regulation 17] since article 20 of the same Regulation provides that they shall not disclose information' (*Fides* 79/253 (1979) OJ L57/33). Thus undertakings may be required to surrender to the Commission highly sensitive information relating both to industrial processes and to marketing. The Commission has repeatedly relied on its obligation under art. 20 to deny the undertaking concerned the opportunity to withhold information. The point was made forcefully in *FNIC* (*Fédération nationale de l'industrie de la chaussure de France* 82/756 (1982) OJ L319/12) where the company refused to hand to the Commission certain 'confidential documents' which, the company argued, went 'far beyond the investigators' terms of reference'. The Commission reiterated its long-held view that undertakings 'may invoke the confidentiality of such documents only within the framework of [art. 20]'.

The requirement of art. 20 is that the Commission and competent authorities shall not disclose any information gained under the Regulation and 'of the kind covered by the obligation of professional secrecy'. This article is itself based on art. 214 EC, which provides a more general guarantee that Community institutions and officials shall not disclose 'information of the kind covered by the obligation of professional secrecy, in particular information about undertakings, their business relations or their cost components'. The ECJ has held that this requirement is crucial as regards the rights of the undertakings in the process (*Dow Benelux NV v Commission* case 85/87 [1991] 4 CMLR 410), and in *AKZO* (case 53/85 [1987] 1 CMLR 231) the ECJ held that '[b]usiness secrets are thus afforded a *very special* protection' (para. 28, emphasis added). However, as the Commission notes in its notice on access to the file (see above), this remains a problem if for no other reason than that there has been no case in which the criteria for determining that any particular piece of information is a business secret have been fully discussed. In the event that any information is shared between the Commission and the competent authorities in the Member States, the obligation in Regulation 17 is binding on all bodies.

Article 21 of Regulation 17 provides a further guarantee in that when the Commission publishes, as it is required to do, any formal decision that it takes in relation to a particular proceeding 'the publication ... shall have regard to the legitimate interest of undertakings in the protection of their business secrets'.

The tension between the requirement of secrecy and confidentiality and the right of undertakings to have access to pertinent information in order to ensure that their rights are observed is a very clear one. The very strict position taken by the Court in *AKZO* was largely determined by the fact that the undertaking seeking access to the confidential information was the complainant, and a competitor of AKZO.

3.2.1.7 *Sectoral enquiries*

The Commission usually makes investigations into specific undertakings and specific practices. However, it has a more general power under art. 12 of Regulation 17 to conduct general enquiries into any economic sector if factors suggest that, in the sector concerned, competition is restricted or distorted. The Commission may obtain all necessary information from undertakings in the relevant sector. This provision has fallen into desuetude, and appears to have been used only on two occasions; in relation to margarine, and in relation to the market for beer. While the Commission has looked at markets in general, it has done so without recourse to art. 12.

3.2.1.8 *Subsequent action*

Several results are possible following the Commission's fact finding. First, it may decide that there has been no breach of the law and terminate proceedings at that point. In the alternative, where an undertaking has itself notified the Commission about the practice, it may issue either formal negative clearance (art. 2) or a less formal comfort letter, or it may hold that there has been a breach of art. 81(1) but that the conditions are in place to issue a formal exemption under art. 81(3) EC. Where the Commission is of the view that the law is being or has been breached it may order remedial action (art. 3) or impose fines for the past conduct (art. 15, and see Chapter 4) or indeed determine on a combination of the two.

3.2.1.8.1 *Negative clearance/art. 81(3) exemptions*

A formal decision taken under art. 2 of Regulation 17 is a relatively straightforward matter. The decision merely affirms that the practice in question does not fall within the general prohibitions of arts 81 and 82 EC. The Commission is, at present, the only body in the Community with the power to grant negative clearance (art. 9) and the benefit of the formal decision is inestimable. In particular, because decisions are binding law, the decision will serve as a defence in actions brought before national courts by third parties on the basis of the direct effect of EC law (see Chapter 2) where the action is founded on the subject-matter of the decision. Such decisions bear one qualification, in that they are taken 'on the basis of the facts in [the Commission's] possession'. If the circumstances materially change, or if the undertakings have held back or misrepresented the truth, the decision may be revoked.

Article 81(3) exemptions are also valuable, and may, at present, be issued only by the Commission. Advocates of reform of the centralized approach to competition law have suggested that national authorities should also be given some powers in respect of this area, although there would be inevitable dangers of divergence in practice. Article 6 of the Regulation provides that, whenever an art. 81(3) exemption is granted, the Commission 'shall specify the date from which the decision shall take effect' and that '[s]uch date shall not be earlier than the notification'. That is to say that, generally, an art. 81(3) exemption cannot be granted so as to have retroactive effect. Vertical agreements, however, may have exemptions backdated to the inception of the agreement, following an amendment made to Regulation 17 by Regulation 1216/1999.

While there is little prospect of an undertaking being penalized in respect of a practice for which an exemption has subsequently been granted, the formal benefits to exemption should encourage undertakings to notify practices to the Commission at the earliest possible date. In particular, as has been noted above, an art. 81(3) exemption is a total defence to a civil action brought in a Member State based on an alleged breach of art. 81(1) EC.

Exemptions are issued only for a specific period, and may have conditions attached to them (Regulation 17, art. 8(1)). This was the case in, for example, *Transocean Marine Paint Association* 88/635 (1988) OJ L351/40, where the undertaking was required to notify to the Commission any alterations to the agreement in respect of which the exemption was granted. Obligations most often relate to mechanisms whereby the Commission is to be able to review the operation of the exempted agreement in practice. In an earlier case, *Transocean Marine Paint Association* v *Commission* case 17/74 [1974] 2 CMLR 459, the Advocate General argued that there should be two limits to the power of the Commission to attach conditions to exemptions: that the condition should relate directly to competition policy; and that it should not be unduly onerous.

Exemptions may be renewed 'if the requirements of article 81(3) of the Treaty continue to be satisfied' (art. 8(2)). There are four circumstances in which the benefit of the exemption may be withdrawn. These are:

(a) where there is a change in the facts;
(b) where the parties breach any obligation or condition attached to the exemption;
(c) where the parties misled the Commission when making the application; and
(d) where the exemption is abused.

In the last three circumstances the withdrawal of the exemption may have retroactive effect. The conditions under which art. 81(3) exemptions may be granted are discussed in Chapter 7.

3.2.1.8.2 *Comfort letters*
Form A/B (Commission Regulation 3385/94 (1994) OJ L377/28) makes it clear that applications 'will normally be dealt with by way of a comfort letter' although the undertaking may state its preference for a formal decision. Thus, a typical comfort letter would include a paragraph in the following terms: 'You have indicated that you can agree to the notification under consideration being dealt with by means of an administrative letter closing the file.' In its *Modernisation White Paper* the Commission indicated that 'over 90 per cent of notifications are closed informally', with some 150–200 comfort letters issued a year (para. 34).

A comfort letter may be issued much more quickly than a formal art. 2 decision. There are, however, disadvantages to comfort letters in that the protection they afford to the recipient is less than is the case with a formal decision. The matter came before the ECJ in *Procureur de la République* v *Bruno Giry and Guerlain SA* (*'Perfumes'* case 253/78 [1981] 2 CMLR 99), which arose by way of an art. 234 EC reference in the course of proceedings taken relating to the agreements in the national court. The ECJ was asked by the national court to advise it as to the status of the comfort letters issued by the Commission. Significantly the ECJ held that the letters amounted to no more than a statement of the Commission's opinion and that the national court, albeit it should have regard to the comfort letter, was entitled to reach a different opinion on the merits of the case. It was suggested by the Advocate General, however, that the issuance of a comfort letter would bind the Commission itself. This is a practice now accepted and followed by the Commission. Following the case the Commission stated that it would revise its policy with regard to comfort letters in an attempt to increase the legal certainty surrounding them (see *11th Report on Competition Policy*, para. 15). In particular, in some cases, advance notice of the issue is published and comments are invited. Further, the Advisory Committee is also consulted before the letter is issued. It is uncertain whether these moves have significantly altered the legal position from that set out by the ECJ in the *Perfumes* case and, in the view of the Commission, comfort letters, following *L'Oreal NV and L'Oreal SA* v *De Nieuwe AMCIT PVBA* case 31/80 [1981] 2 CMLR 235 'constitute an element of fact which the national courts and authorities may take into account' (*Modernisation White Paper*, para. 35).

The position in the United Kingdom is that comfort letters are not considered to be binding on either the courts or the competition authorities, although they are highly persuasive. Moves to introduce an exemption into the Competition Act 1998 for those in possession of a comfort letter failed, although it was indicated that the EC and UK 'will be applying a consistent prohibition test and therefore a European comfort letter will be of persuasive authority'. However, the fact that such a letter might, for example, conclude that a practice was exempt from the application of Community law on the grounds that there was no Community dimension, would not mean that it was appropriate to bind the Director General in relation to the application of law in the UK (Hansard (HL) 13 November 1997, col. 351).

The approach to be taken to comfort letters is set out, *inter alia*, in the OFT guideline, *The Chapter 1 Prohibition*. The relevant section is as follows:

7.11 Many agreements notified to the European Commission receive an informal indication of the European Commission's likely assessment by means of a comfort letter rather than a formal decision. EC comfort letters are not legally binding but it is clear that the European Commission will re-open the file only in certain limited circumstances. The Act does not make provision for the informal procedures of the European Commission.

7.12 As a general policy, the Director General will not depart from the European Commission's assessment of an agreement as set out in an EC comfort letter, but the following exceptions to this policy should be noted:

— an agreement may raise particular concerns in relation to competition in the United Kingdom;

— the European Commission may indicate that there is an infringement of art. 81 which would not qualify for exemption, but that as a matter of its internal priorities it will not consider the matter further (a discomfort letter);

— the European Commission may indicate that the agreement in question does not have an appreciable effect on inter-state trade for the purposes of the application of art. 81(1).

In these circumstances, the parties will need to consider the application of the Chapter 1 prohibition and, if the agreement is subject to the prohibition, whether notification to the Director General is appropriate.

3.2.1.9 *Rights of the parties and fundamental protections*

At face value the power accorded to the Commission by way of arts 11 and 14 is substantial, and appears to be largely unfettered. Undertakings have frequently protested about the imbalance in the process, and the ECJ has interpreted parts of the articles restrictively so as to accord them some better protection than is apparent from an immediate reading of the words. The Commission, however, remains concerned about its ability to police large and well-prepared organizations. In a press release (IP (95) 1355 of 13/12/95 [1996] 4 CMLR 120) the Commission noted that '[o]btaining irrefutable proof of a cartel remains a well-nigh impossible task . . . since a number of firms do not hesitate to organise "red alert" exercises to instruct their staff in how to make life difficult for European inspectors on unannounced visits'.

The extent to which legal persons, as distinct from natural persons, should be accorded fundamental rights is a matter of intense debate: the question is one of whether it is 'appropriate to extend a privilege, which began as a protection for individuals, to an artificial entity such as a corporation' (*Environment Protection Authority* v *Caltex Refining Co. Pty Ltd* (1993) 118 ALR 392, at 553 *per* McHugh J). More pithily Lord Denning has said that a company has 'no body to be kicked or soul to be damned' (*BSC* v *Granada TV* [1981] AC 1096).

In the EC there is a further complication in that there is no clear standard of 'fundamental rights' set out in the founding treaties. Instead the ECJ has developed, at first slowly and then with greater force, a jurisprudence of general principles of law, drawing in part on international instruments in which the Member States have participated. The ECJ confirmed in *Firma J Nold KG* v *Commission* case 4/73 [1974] 2 CMLR 338, that the European Convention on Human Rights (ECHR) is of particular importance in this regard, and all Member States of the European Community are bound equally by its provisions, although the two regimes are legally and politically distinct. This judicial activity received belated support by the Member States in the Treaty on European Union, art. 6(2) of which provides, in part, that 'the Union shall respect fundamental rights, as guaranteed by the European Convention'. This declaration notwithstanding, the EC cannot become a state party to the Convention, lacking the legal capacity to do so (Opinion of ECJ 2/94 [1996] ECR 1–1759). The application of fundamental rights jurisprudence in relation to the competition procedures has caused problems for the Court, which remains bound by the words of the legislation. The procedural rules set out in Regulation 17/62 are very much a product of the 1960s, and predate the case law of the European Court of Human Rights.

In *National Panasonic (UK) Ltd* v *Commission* case 136/79 [1980] 3 CMLR 169, the applicant's contention that its fundamental rights had been infringed was rejected, but the ECJ left open the possibility that fundamental rights could be relied upon where the Commission's actions could be shown to be disproportionate. In *AM & S Europe* v *Commission* case 155/79 [1982] 2 CMLR 264, at 322, the Court concluded that EC law 'must take into account the principles and concepts common to the laws of (the Member States)' and a similar position was reached in *Hoechst AG* v *Commission* cases 46/87 and 227/88 [1991] 4 CMLR 410, in which the Court held that 'in interpreting article 14 of Regulation No. 17, regard must be had in particular to the rights of the defence' (at 465); and in *Soda Ash* cases T–30–32/91 and T–36–37/91 [1996] 5 CMLR 57ff., the CFI referred to the need to achieve the general requirement of 'equality of arms'. The most substantial arguments relating to fundamental rights made to date are those in *Orkem SA* v *Commission* case 374/87 [1991] 4 CMLR 502. Here the Commission had made an art. 11(5) decision demanding information in respect of which an earlier art. 11 request had been largely ignored. The undertaking's argument was that the documents requested were potentially self-incriminating. Advocate General Darmon recognized that 'exploitation to the full of any latitude allowed by the legal rules and efforts to ensure [that the] broadest interpretation of that latitude is acknowledged to constitute a positive right are the very essence of defence' (art. 513). The Advocate General focused on the distinction between the *investigative* stage of the Commission's proceedings, the purpose of which is to allow the Commission to check the existence of 'a given factual and legal situation', and the *statement of objections* wherein 'there is a much greater protection' afforded to the undertaking. As regards the alleged right of the undertaking not to incriminate itself, the Advocate General argued that, on an inspection of the text of the Regulation, it was clear that the Council which enacted the Regulation 'did not intend to give undertakings to which a request for information was addressed the right not to incriminate themselves'. More strongly, he stated that the machinery of Regulation 17 appeared to him 'to be intellectually incompatible with the right to silence'. In giving judgment the Court allowed greater protection to the individual than the Advocate General had suggested. The Court drew a somewhat uneasy distinction between documentary evidence and oral explanations. The Court held that the Commission could compel an undertaking to provide documents in its possession, but that it 'may not compel an undertaking to provide it with answers which might involve an admission on its part of the existence of an infringement which it is incumbent upon the Commission to prove'. Only purely factual answers may be required (*Mannesmannrohren–Werke AG* v *Commission* Case T–112/98 [2001] 5 CMCR 1).

The case of *Orkem* was further discussed in *Otto* v *Postbank* case C–60/92 [1993] ECR 1–5683, which came before the ECJ as an art. 234 reference from the Dutch courts. The defendant in domestic proceedings had argued that national law was incompatible with Community law because it was obliged to produce incriminatory evidence. One of the arguments made by the defendant before the ECJ was that this evidence could, and probably would, come to the attention of the Commission which might use it as part of its own enforcement procedure. The Court held that the Commission would not be able to use any such evidence in order to establish an infringement of the relevant parts of the Treaty, but that in the case in question it would not interfere as the matter was strictly one between private parties and did not involve the possibility of a penalty imposed by a public authority.

In its *Modernisation White Paper* the Commission itself recognizes that there remains controversy in this area, and suggests an amendment to art. 14 of Regulation 17, 'to make it quite clear that in the course of an investigation the authorised Commission officials are empowered to ask the undertakings representatives or staff any questions that are justified by and related to the purpose of the investigation, and to demand a full and precise answer' (para. 113).

The relationship in particular between the law of the Human Rights Convention and the treatment of these rights under Community law remains a complex and not altogether satisfactory one. In *Funke v France* (1993) 16 EHRR 297, the European Court of Human Rights emphasized that the Convention's provisions apply to commercial matters as well as to personal rights, and that special provisions of law could not justify the restriction of such rights. This is in conflict with the view of the Advocate General in *Orkem* and suggests that the ECJ may need to reconsider this area if it intends to stay in line with Convention law. In *Stichting Certificatie Kraanverhuurbedrijf (SCK) and Federatie van Nederlandse Kraanver-huurbedrijven (FNK) v Commission* joined cases T–213/95 and T–18/96 [1998] 4 CMLR 259, the CFI considered claims founded on the contention that the EC Commission had failed to comply with art. 6(1) of the Convention in the proceedings. Article 6(1) makes reference to the entitlement 'to a fair and public hearing within a reasonable time'. In this case, which related to the market for the hire of cranes in The Netherlands, the proceedings were commenced on 15 January 1992 when the two undertakings notified their statutes to the EC Commission with a request for either negative clearance or an exemption under art. 81(3). The applicants first requested a hearing in early 1993, and later, in an attempt to speed matters up, waived their rights to a formal hearing prior to the taking of any decision. However, the final decision was not made until 29 November 1995, at which point fines were imposed on the undertakings (*Stichting Certificatie Kraanverhuurbedrijf and the Federatie van Nederlandse Kraanverhuurbedrijven* 95/551 (1995) OJ L312/79).

Although the CFI started from the position that 'it is settled case-law that fundamental rights form an integral part of the general principles of law whose observance the Community judicature ensures', and accepted that 'the [Convention] has special significance in that respect' (para. 53), it avoided any substantive discussion relating to the application of Convention law directly to competition proceedings. It did this by noting instead that 'it is a general principle *of Community law* that the Commission must act within a reasonable time in adopting decisions following administrative proceedings relating to competition policy' (emphasis added). Because the Court held that the matter fell directly within Community law, which would ensure adequate safeguards, any discussion of the Convention became unnecessary. The Court then relied on *Automec Srl* v *Commission* case T–24/90 [1992] 5 CMLR 431, which already made it clear that the Commission is allowed within reasonable constraints to prioritize matters as it sees fit. In its analysis of the chain of events, which took in total just under four years, the CFI found that the Commission had acted reasonably, and that the fundamental rights of the parties had not been breached. However, the fact that it did so without expressly applying that part of Convention law relied on by the applicants undermines the argument, and will not encourage parties to rely on Convention-based arguments.

The CFI itself was found by the ECJ, in another case, to have acted too slowly in delivering judgment. In *Baustahlgewebe GmbH* v *Commission* case T–145/89 [1995] ECR II–987, on appeal C–185/95P [1999] 4 CMLR 1203, the appellant relied on art. 6(1) of the Convention in seeking an annulment of the CFI judgment, and of the earlier Commission Decision in *Welded Steel Mesh* 89/515 (1989) OJ L260/1. The appeal against the Decision was lodged in October 1989, and it was five years and six months before judgment was delivered, and 22 months passed between the close of the hearing and the delivering of the judgment. The ECJ held, notwithstanding the fact that 'the procedure called for a detailed examination of relatively voluminous documents and points of fact and law of some complexity' (para. 36), that 'the proceedings before the [CFI] did not satisfy the requirements concerning completion within a reasonable time' (para. 47). The ECJ found, however, that this breach was insufficient to annul the proceedings in their entirety, and in the alternative the applicant was awarded a sum of €50,000 (the appellant, having lost on some of the heads of its appeal, was also obliged to pay all its own costs, as well as three-quarters of those of the Commission).

If the EC courts demonstrate a continuing reluctance to accord to the Human Rights Convention the status that it merits, there remains the theoretical possibility of another route for an undertaking that is penalized by the Commission. In *Société Stenuit* v *France* (1992) 14 EHRR 509, the European Commission on Human Rights considered a case brought on the basis of French competition law that was purely an internal matter and not related to Community law. The Commission suggested, in declaring the application admissible, that the imposition of penalties in relation to proceedings under French competition law could be reviewed under the architecture of the Convention. In doing so it affirmed the long-held position of the Court of Human Rights that it is for the Court and not for the states to determine the nature of the proceedings taken against the injured party. Although the relationship between the three legal orders—EC, the Convention, and states—is a very complex one, the EC Commission, when it imposes a fine under Community law, is reliant upon the judicial architecture of the host state of the undertaking to recover the fine should the undertaking refuse to pay. Such cooperation on the part of the state is a Community law obligation and will be taken for granted. However, should the undertaking resist before the national courts, and base its argument on the obligation of that state to comply with the Convention, one of the possible options would be for the national court either to apply Convention law directly where it had the power to do so, or to refer the matter to the Convention authorities. *Société Stenuit* would appear to suggest that the Convention bodies would consider such a reference; and although Regulation 17, art. 15(4) provides that the fines imposed under the Regulation shall not be of a criminal law nature, the possibility of a challenge to the Commission and Court of Human Rights is open, and at such time it could be held that guarantees afforded to undertakings under Community law are not in fact the same as should be available in the light of Convention obligations imposed on the Member States.

3.2.2 National law and Regulation 17

As has been seen, the competent authorities of the Member States have a role to play in the enforcement of EC competition law. *Inter alia*, officials of the competent authority may, at the request of the Commission, assist officials of the Commission in carrying out their duties. Generally officials of the OFT accompany Commission officials on their inspections in the UK. More strongly, where an undertaking opposes an investigation the Member State is required to 'afford the necessary assistance to the officials authorised by the Commission to enable them to make their investigation' (art. 14(6)). In *Hoechst AG* v *Commission* cases 46/87 and 227/88 [1991] 4 CMLR 410, the court held that the national authorities are not permitted to question the need for the investigation itself, as only the ECJ has power to review the acts of the Commission, but that national authorities can decide on the procedure by which the required assistance will be given. However, the assistance must be sufficient, within the law, to achieve the aims of the lawful investigation.

In the United Kingdom the Competition Act 1998 introduced specific measures relating to the power of the EC Commission to conduct investigations in relation to arts 81 and 82 EC, and created specific offences relating to the obstruction of such investigations. This is in accordance with the general obligation of art. 10 EC, which requires Member States to take appropriate steps to ensure that the objectives of the Community are fulfilled, and is an improvement on the previous position where an *ex parte* injunction would be sought in the High Court. Where any properly authorized Commission investigation is being obstructed, the Director may request that a judge of the High Court issue a warrant to give effect to that investigation (s. 62(1)). The warrant will authorize the Director, or an officer appointed by the Director, and any Commission official, 'to enter the premises specified in the warrant, and search for books and records which the official has power to examine, using such force as is reasonably necessary for the purpose' (s. 62(5)). This is a substantial power, which is in accordance with the established law of the Court of Justice and past Commission practice. It is not unusual for the powers of search and seizure conferred on any appropriate authority in the United Kingdom to be strong ones, and there may be situations in which the Commission will be able to act more vigorously in the United Kingdom than it will in some other Member States, although any such actions will remain subject to the scrutiny of the Court of Justice notwithstanding the fact that they are authorized under a domestic statute. Any person who obstructs an investigation authorized under a warrant may, on conviction, be fined or subject to imprisonment (s. 65).

3.2.3 **Reform of Regulation 17**

In September 2000 the EC published the *Draft Council Regulation on the implementation of the rules on competition laid down in Articles 81 and 82 of the Treaty and amending Regulations 1017/68, 4056/86 and 3975/87* ([2000] 5 CMLR 1148). A substantial explanatory memorandum was published alongside the proposal which the Commission aimed at bringing into force in 2002. A major thrust of the proposed new regime would be to eliminate the exclusive competence held by the Commission to apply art. 81(3) EC which the Commission argued 'is a significant obstacle to the effective application of rules by national competition authorities and courts'. Some controversy has surrounded the view of the Commission and the Council that art. 81(3) can be applied directly by the courts and authorities in Member States without the need for revisions of the Treaty to provide for this. The view of the Commission is that the Treaty does not exclude the possibility that art. 81(3) could be applied in this way, and that the fact that there is some margin of appreciation in the interpretation of art. 81(3) does also not serve as a bar. The explanatory memorandum clearly sets out the principles underpinning the draft Regulation, and those seeking a discussion of this issue are therefore encouraged to turn to the primary source until such time as the Regulation is adopted. See also Bourgeois, J. H. J., and Humpe, C., 'The Commission's Draft "New Regulation 17"' [2002] ECLR 43.

3.3 **The United Kingdom**

The Competition Act 1998 made substantial amendments to the investigative powers set out in the Fair Trading Act 1973. It was an obvious and much discussed anomaly that the investigative domestic regime contained within it so few powers of investigation. In relation to the Fair Trading Act in particular, it was difficult to draw a distinction between the investigation in any particular case and the entire process of assessment of the practice under consideration. However, a distinction could be drawn between the initial process of fact finding prior to a full reference being made, and the fuller assessment of those and additional facts at the reference stage.

It remains the case under the Fair Trading Act that the division of responsibility and powers between the DGFT and the Competition Commission (CC) is at its most apparent at the fact-finding stage. Broadly, it is the responsibility of the DGFT, under the Fair Trading Act and the Competition Act, to establish that, on the basis of the evidence available to him, a reference to the CC is in order. The CC then investigates the position more fully and produces its report, on the basis of which recommendations are made to the Minister (see Chapter 12). There has been much criticism from all sides of the duplication of effort, the relatively weak powers of the DGFT to assess the initial concerns, and the cost imposed on firms subject to the process.

The two key guidelines published by the OFT in this area are *Powers of Investigation*, and *Enforcement*.

3.3.1 The Competition Act 1998

The Competition Act 1998 amended the powers of enforcement and investigation available under the Fair Trading Act 1973, and, in Chapter III, introduced substantial powers in relation to the enforcement of the two prohibitions set out in Chapter I (see Chapter 9) and Chapter II (see Chapter 12). Under the Act the Competition Commission (see Chapter 2) does not have an investigative role, and so the powers of investigation it confers are bestowed exclusively on the Director. In the *11B* case the CCAT noted that the Act has endowed 'the Director, in the public interest, with wide ranging and draconian powers, exercised on behalf of the State, which may substantially affect the civil rights and obligations of those concerned' (*Institute of Independent Insurance Brokers v The Director General of Fair Trading* [2002] compAR 141, para 57).

The Director has the power to conduct any investigation where he has 'reasonable grounds for suspecting' that either of the two prohibitions are being infringed (s. 25). Upon the presentation of a written notice to that effect the Director may require 'any person to produce to him a specified document, or to provide him with specified information which he considers relates to any matter relevant to the investigation' (s. 26(1)). This is the provision that, according to the guideline *Powers of Investigation*, will be most frequently used. In line with the powers conferred on the EC Commission under arts 11 and 14 of Regulation 17, the Director is able to take copies of the document or of extracts from it, and to require 'any person who is a present or past officer of [the person], or is or was at any time employed by him, to provide an explanation of the document' (s. 27(6)(a)(i)–(ii)). This latter ability to require an explanation of the documents from 'any person' who has been an employee or officer of the undertaking is a substantial one, and may conflict with obligations arising under the European Convention on Human Rights (see above, in relation to EC law). It is inevitable that there will be disputes over the meaning of 'explanation', with undertakings insisting that they are not required to incriminate themselves when giving an 'explanation' of any particular document. Concern was expressed in the House of Lords that this provision would allow for the possibility of 'an investigating officer shimmying up to the cleaning lady and extracting from her the skeleton key' (Hansard (HL) 17 November 1997, col. 388), and the Confederation of British Industry (CBI) pressed very strongly for changes to these provisions. The Government's view, however, was that 'the statutory investigatory powers must be able to cater for the very worst case of unscrupulous concealment of evidence of a cartel or other anti-competitive behaviour', although generally 'full use of the powers provided in the [Act] should . . . be unnecessary' (col. 391). There was specific recognition that it might often be the case that secretaries and younger assistants could have a great deal of knowledge about practices referred to in documents or under investigation, whereas a more senior manager might lack the 'hands-on' involvement in a practice. The question of the extent to which there is a right to silence is to be resolved by reference to EC case law (see above).

Investigations of undertakings' premises may be conducted either with or without notice being given to the undertaking. Section 27 of the Act gives the Director, or an 'investigating officer' appointed by the Director, power to 'enter any premises'. Although it is not expressly stated in the Act, homes may be entered only if they are also business premises, but it is envisaged that there will be situations where this is the case (see generally Hansard (HL) 25 November 1997, coll. 957–961). This point was reasonably dealt with by Nigel Griffiths for the Government, in Committee, when he pointed out that 'domestic premises may be entered only if they are used in connection with the affairs of an undertaking . . . the Director General's actions are subject to judicial review if he exceeds his powers' (Committee G, 16 June 1998, col. 421).

In relation to many of the investigations which will be carried out under this section the investigating officer is required to give two working days' notice before the power of entry is enforced (s. 27(2)). Section 27(3), however, provides that in situations where there is a 'reasonable suspicion' that the premises are being occupied by a party to an agreement or conduct under investigation, the two-day notice period may be waived. The period may also be waived when 'the investigating officer has taken all such steps as are reasonably practicable to give notice but has not been able to do so' (s. 27(3)(b)). The powers that relate to such an investigation are similar to those found in Regulation 17. Thus the investigating officer may take any necessary equipment with him, which might include, for example, portable photocopiers, and computer disks (s. 27(5)(a)). Any person on the premises may be required 'to produce any document which [the officer] considers relates to any matter relevant to the investigation' and 'to provide an explanation of it' (s. 27(5)(b)). Any person on the premises may further be required to 'state to the best of his knowledge and belief, where any such document is to be found' (s. 27(5)(c)).

As well as permitting the officer to take copies of, or extracts from, any document (s. 27(5)(d)), a special provision relates to material held in computer systems. Where this is 'accessible from the premises' and is relevant to the investigation, this must be produced in a form 'in which it can be taken away' and in which it is 'visible and legible', which presumably means that a print-out must be provided (s. 27(5)(e)). The reference to material which is 'accessible from the premises' is an interesting one, and it appears to extend to material held on computer systems outside of the premises under investigation, but which can be accessed over a network from the site. This would mean that where the internal information system of the company under investigation was so set up, international records from a multinational company could all be accessed through a single site investigation in the UK, thus avoiding the complexities of establishing jurisdiction and enforcing warrants elsewhere. This conclusion follows if the company is using the information itself as part of its management system. Information held in hard copy at the premises and relied upon on that basis would not be protected and the undertaking should not be able to deny the investigating officers access to the information simply on the basis of which part of their computer system the material is stored on.

While investigations conducted under s. 27 of the Act require that two days' written notice be given, the Director may use powers under s. 28 of the Act to conduct an investigation without warning following the issuing of a warrant to that effect by a judge. A warrant may be sought either where documents required to be produced under s. 26 or s. 27 have not been produced, or where there is a reasonable ground for believing that if the notice required by s. 27 was given the documents would be destroyed, removed, or concealed (s. 28(b)). A warrant may also be requested where an investigating officer acting under the powers in s. 27 has been unable to gain access to the site. Once the warrant has been issued the powers are the same as for s. 27, with the notable exception that the officer may enter the premises 'using such force as is reasonably necessary for the purpose' (s. 28(2)(a)). Although the introduction of the right to enter by force was criticized by the Opposition the Government clung to it, with Lord Simon being 'thoroughly of the view that the right to entry using reasonable force is a necessary part of ensuring that the process of investigation goes forward. It is a key element of our strategy' (Hansard (HL) 17 November 1997, col. 406). These powers are to be exercised only at 'the very limits of investigation' in 'exceptional cases in which we know that the rogues have thus far repelled all boarders' ibid, col. 409). Later the Government confirmed that force would not be used against persons, but that, if the circumstances were to arise, force could be used inside premises to gain entry to specific parts of the premises: 'every subsequent door, if closed, could be broken down to enter the premises' (Hansard (HL) 19 February 1998, col. 339).

Section 28 powers were used for the first time, although the use of force does not appear to have been necessary, in the course of the OFT investigation leading to the decision *Market Sharing by Arriva plc and FirstGroup plc* CA 98/9/2002, 30 January 2002. Here the Director

applied to the High Court and the Court of Session for warrants to enter premises of the two undertakings in England and Scotland, and exercise powers under s. 28 of the Act. Warrants were issued on 4 and 6 October 2000. Unannounced visits to the premises took place on 10 and 11 October 2000 and copies of documents were taken. (para. 7)

The *Powers of Investigation* guideline follows the approach of the EC Commission in relation to the legal advice to which an undertaking may have access during the course of an investigation (paras 4.10–4.11). Thus it is made clear that an undertaking may contact its legal advisers, and that 'the investigating officer will grant a request to wait a short time for legal advisers to arrive at the premises before the investigation continues if he considers that it is reasonable to do so in the circumstances'. This provision is also set out in The Competition Act 1998 (Director's Rules) Order, SI 2000/293, para. 13. There is no definition of what constitutes 'a reasonable time' and the Order simply provides that this means 'such period of time as the officer considers is reasonable in the circumstances'.

Any person who does not comply with a requirement imposed under ss. 26, 27, or 28 is guilty of an offence, and may be liable to a fine. Where the offence has been the obstruction of an officer acting under a warrant issued under s. 28 the person may, on conviction, be fined, or imprisoned for a maximum of two years (s. 42). Fines and/or imprisonment may similarly be imposed where any person destroys or disposes of a document that they have been required to produce under ss. 26, 27, or 28 (s. 45), or where any person gives information to the Director which is materially false or misleading when that person knows it to be so, or is reckless as to its status (s. 44).

It is perhaps in recognition of the problems caused by the *AM&S* judgment (*AM&S Europe* v *Commission* case 155/79 (1982) 2 CMLR 264) that specific provisions in s. 30 of the Act relate to privileged communications. 'Privileged communication' is defined in s. 30 as being a communication 'between a professional legal advisor and his client' or 'made in connection with, or in contemplation of, legal proceedings and for the purposes of those proceedings'. No person shall be required to produce any material under any provision in the Act that falls within this definition. This is one area in which the Act explicitly is out of step with Community law, and where UK practice will not be affected by future developments in EC case law. As was clearly stated in the debates:

it is the government's intention that the Director should *not* be able to require, under his investigative powers, the production of legal advice and other material enjoying legal professional privilege, whether the lawyer concerned is an external lawyer or an 'in-house' lawyer. (Hansard (HL) 17 November 1997, col. 416)

This is consistent with the approach adopted by the House of Lords in *Alfred Compton Amusement Machines Ltd* v *Customs and Excise Comrs (No. 2)* [1974] AC 405, where the Court held that no distinction could be made between the two groups.

It will be clear that these powers are very substantial, and at least match those held by the Commission. In fact, given that the ECJ has made moves towards increasing the protections afforded to undertakings with reference to 'general principles of law' and the European Convention on Human Rights, the powers given to the Director may be greater than those arising under Regulation 17. Considerable debate surrounded the passing of these provisions, with members of the House on the Conservative benches showing particular hostility to the powers of search and seizure. Some of the amendments brought forward would, if accepted, have largely emasculated the Act (see, e.g., Lord Kingsland, Hansard (HL) 17 November 1997, col. 377), and the Government was able to carry through its original intentions. Some mention should be made here of the fact that the Human Rights Act 1998 was progressing through Parliament at the same time as the Competition Act 1998, and that the former requires courts and tribunals, where possible, to interpret domestic legislation so as to conform to the international obligations set out in the Human

Rights Convention. It is likely that, as has been the case in the EC, cases will be brought challenging the application of the investigation powers, particularly where investigations are followed by the imposition of substantial penalties. Section 60 of the Competition Act 1998 does not apply to the investigative process, as there are relevant differences between the provisions of the Act and those of Regulation 17 (see, e.g., Pertetz, G., 'Detection and Deterrence of Secret Cartels Under the UK Competition Bill' [1998] *ECLR* 145). However, the effect of s. 60 is to import into UK law the so-called high-level principles of EC law, such as fairness, due legal process, etc., and in these respects jurisprudence in the UK should take into account the development of these principles in the EC.

It is recognized in the *Powers of Investigation* guideline, for example, that the approach to be taken to self-incrimination is the same as under Community jurisprudence. Thus 'the Director General may compel an undertaking to provide specified documents or specified information but cannot compel the provision of answers which might involve an admission on its part of the existence of an infringement' (para. 6.4).

3.3.1.1 *Interim measures*

Under s. 35 the Director has the power to impose interim measures on those suspected of infringing either of the prohibitions where a reasonable suspicion to that effect exists. These powers may be exercised, and indeed are likely to be exercised, notwithstanding that an investigation is in progress. Such interim measures may be taken in order to prevent serious and irreparable harm to any person, or general damage to the public interest.

The procedures relating to interim measures are dealt with in the guideline *Enforcement* (paras 3.1–3.14). Herein lies a difference between the Community regime, and that intended under the Act. It is noted that the EC Commission has not used its powers to apply interim measures very often (see above), and that this may be because it first has to establish a prima facie case that arts 81 or 82 are being breached. The 'reasonable suspicion' standard is a lower one. Once interim measures are in place they continue to have effect for as long as the reasonable suspicion is held, and until such time as the investigation is complete.

3.3.1.2 *Secrecy*

Safeguards have been provided in the Act to protect the information which must be surrendered to the Director (s. 55). It is an act subject to criminal penalty for the Director unlawfully to disclose any information. Information may, in appropriate circumstances, be disclosed to the EC Commission, which will remain bound by its obligation under Regulation 17, art. 20 (see above). Section 56 of the Act provides further that the Director and Secretary of State are to have regard 'to the need for excluding, so far as is practicable, information the disclosure of which would . . . be contrary to the public interest'. This applies to situations in which information might be published, as for example would be the case where a formal decision is being published. In particular, this provision excludes the publication of information which, if made available, would significantly harm the party's commercial interests (see paras 6.5–6.10 of the guideline).

3.3.1.3 *The right to be heard before a decision is taken*

Wherever the Director intends, following any investigation permitted under s. 25, to make a decision to the effect that either the Chapter I or Chapter II prohibitions have been infringed, he must give written notice of that to the appropriate person, and give that person an opportunity to make representations (s. 31).

3.3.2 **The Fair Trading Act 1973**

3.3.2.1 *The DGFT and the OFT*

The general duties of the DGFT are set out in the Fair Trading Act 1973, s. 2. Amongst other things, the Director is to 'keep under review the carrying on of commercial activities in the United Kingdom' with a view to his becoming aware of, and ascertaining the circumstances relating to, practices which may adversely affect the economic interests of consumers'.

The Annual Report of the DGFT usually states the broad investigative framework as follows:

> The OFT carries out this function in two ways. First, it monitors the economic performance of industries to identify areas where there may be monopolies and abuses of monopoly situations. . . . Secondly, it takes note of complaints and other representations it receives from business and the public. (see, e.g., *1995 Annual Report*, p. 29.)

A great many complaints are dealt with through informal enquiries outside the statutory framework. At this stage the OFT will contact both the complainant and the companies whose actions may be considered. These enquiries are often very focused, and may involve as few as two parties. In its *Code of Practice of Enforcement* the OFT set itself the target of completing 75 per cent of informal investigations within six months from the date of their starting.

The formal powers made available to the DGFT for the purpose of investigating monopoly situations were amended by the operation of the Competition Act 1998. The core provisions of the Fair Trading Act relating to the power of the Director to gather information under its auspices are ss. 44–46. Section 44 provides the general power for the Director to require information, s. 45 provides special powers in relation to complex monopoly situations, and s. 46 sets out the penalties for failure to comply with ss. 44 and 45. Section 44 was largely replaced by the Competition Act 1998, s. 66.

Under the powers of s. 44 the Director may conduct an investigation where he believes that a monopoly situation exists and where he would be able to make a reference to the CC in relation to that situation, or where he would be inclined to propose that in lieu of a reference the Secretary of State should accept an undertaking from the monopolist(s). In these situations the Director may require the production of documents (s. 44(2)(a)), or may require any person 'to give the Director specified estimates, returns, or other information' (s. 44(2)(b)). This latter obligation extends not only to the monopolist(s), but also to any person who produces or supplies the relevant goods or services in the UK (s. 44(3)). This obligation on those who cannot be subject to the application of the substantive provisions of the Act reflects the fact that the determination as to whether a monopoly position exists cannot be made without reference to a wide range of market information, which will come not only from the company under investigation, but also from other companies in the same market. The Director may also enter any premises and require the production of documents which are held there, and be provided with explanations of the documents. As with the powers conferred on the Commission under Regulation 17, the Director may take copies of or extracts from the documents produced. Where a required document is not produced in the course of an investigation the person may be obliged to state, to the best of their knowledge, where the document is being held. 'Document' means any information however it is recorded; and where it is not recorded in written form, for example where it is held as a computer record, a legible copy of it must be supplied. Following the full entry into force of the Competition Act 1998 it is likely that this provision will be rarely used. As scale monopoly investigations under the Fair Trading Act will be held only where a company has already been found to be in breach of one of the prohibitions of the Competition Act 1998 and appears likely to reoffend, they are unlikely to play a prominent role in domestic competition law.

Section 45 of the Fair Trading Act was left untouched by the Competition Act 1998. This section grants the Director wide discretion in formulating investigations into complex monopoly situations (see Chapter 12), which may present particular problems for the investigator. Thus the Director is given the power to 'formulate proposals for requiring specified persons to furnish information to him' (s. 45(1)). Any such proposals may be submitted to the Secretary of State for approval or for modification. As complex monopoly investigations will continue to play an active role in the new regime these provisions are more likely to have an ongoing relevance than the s. 44 powers. Although s. 56A of the Act gives the Director the power to accept undertakings in lieu of making a reference, in practice the role of the Director in relation to monopoly investigations is less significant than that of the CC (see further Chapter 12).

Section 46 was largely rewritten by the Competition Act 1998 (s. 67), and provides that any person who 'refuses or willfully neglects' to comply with an obligation imposed under s. 44(2) shall be guilty of an offence. The penalty for such a breach may be either a fine or a term of imprisonment not exceeding two years. Obstruction of the Director in the course of a s. 44 investigation may result in the imposition of a fine, and the destruction or alteration of any document which has been required under s. 44(2) is an offence carrying either a fine and/or imprisonment.

3.3.2.2 *The CC*

When carrying out any investigation under the Fair Trading Act the CC is required to take into account representations made by persons with a substantial interest in the matter, or by bodies representing substantial numbers of persons who have such an interest. In practice the CC will advertise publicly the fact of an enquiry, the placing of the advertisements to depend on the subject-matter of the enquiry, and announce its launch by way of press releases, and accept all submissions subsequently made to it. A consequence of this is that the CC may have to consider the views of a great many people: it is not uncommon for over 5,000 parties to be in some way involved in investigations. Apart from this broad obligation to accept the input of interested parties the CC is largely free to establish its own procedure. In order to further its powers, however, and in recognition of the fact that it may face obstruction, it has been given specific powers to compel the production of evidence and the attendance of witnesses. Section 85 of the Fair Trading Act gives the CC the power to require persons to give evidence to it, and to compel the production of documents 'relating to any matter relevant to the investigation' and to require 'such estimates, forecasts, returns or other information as may be specified'. Evidence may be taken under oath (s. 85(2)) and any person who 'willfully alters, suppresses or destroys any document which he has been required by any such notice to produce . . . shall be guilty of an offence' (s. 85(6)). Where any person does not comply with these requirements the matter may be referred to the High Court, which may punish the defaulter as if they had been guilty of contempt of court (s. 85(7)). Section 93B of the Act relates to the provision of false or misleading information, in relation to both the 1973 and the 1980 Acts. A person is guilty of an offence, and may on conviction be imprisoned for a term of not more than two years, or fined, where that person furnishes any information knowing it to be false or misleading, or is reckless as to whether that information is false or misleading.

In practice companies are likely to cooperate with the CC: there is little to be gained by not doing so, and the most onerous part of the burden of compliance with CC requirements is usually the cost. A solicitor specializing in this area noted at a conference in 1996 that 'clients frequently comment favourably on the admirable efforts which the CC devote to understanding their business'.

Broadly, the process of investigation is the same in each case. The CC may, at an early stage (and particularly in the case of complicated investigations), arrange informal meetings with the major parties in order to establish a groundwork understanding, and to make clear the hoped-for timetable. It will then distribute to the parties an initial fact sheet, the completion of which will let the CC officials know some of the parameters of the enquiry, and will outline the industry and the relationships of those in it. It will then issue a much more detailed industry questionnaire, the completion of which will be time-consuming (questionnaires can run to over 100 pages requiring detailed production, costs, and accounting information). It is also likely that the CC officials will ask to make industry visits, although these are not in the nature of investigative 'raids'. These will allow the CC to widen its understanding of the industry and to clarify aspects of the information submitted to it. Following this initial fact finding the CC will issue a 'public interest letter' which offers a tentative analysis of the situation, and possible findings. This will be followed some time later by a public interest hearing, which may in turn be followed by a further hearing to consider any likely remedies if it is established that there is a monopoly position which is acting against the public interest. Lastly, the CC will produce its report, having first given the parties named in it the opportunity to review it for material that they feel should be excluded on confidentiality grounds.

The DGFT is required to assist the CC in its investigations, and has an obligation to give it 'any information which is in his possession and which relates to matters falling within the scope of the investigation' (Fair Trading Act 1973, s. 5(2)).

The CC is required to present its reports to the Secretary of State with a copy sent to the DGFT. Neither the DGFT nor the CC can be sued for defamation on the basis of reports published under the relevant provisions of the 1973 Act, there being absolute privilege in relation to these (Fair Trading Act 1973, s. 82(2)). However under the Act there are provisions relating to the exclusion of confidential material. Material will be excluded from the final report where its publication would 'seriously and prejudicially affect the interests of that individual', or of the body corporate (Fair Trading Act 1973, s. 82(1)). Information obtained under the Acts shall not be disclosed without the consent of the relevant person, save in the circumstances outlined in the Act. Notwithstanding these conditions, the fact remains that reports of the OFT and in particular of the CC are often very detailed, and may be read avidly by competitors seeking useful market information.

The important role of the CC under the Fair Trading Act has been left intact, even following the full implementation of the Competition Act 1998.

3.3.3 Judicial review

In principle the acts of the domestic competition authorities are subject, in accordance with the Supreme Court Act 1981 and Order 53 of the Rules of the Supreme Court, to judicial review. This is an area of law in which there has been rapid growth in recent years, and for a detailed analysis a specialist text should be referred to (and for an interesting discussion of some of the aspects of this area, see Black, J., et al, *Commercial Regulation and Judicial Review*, Oxford, Hart Publishing (1998). Generally the greater the discretion available to any authority to act the less likely is a judicial review application to be successful. This is certainly the case where the competition authorities are concerned, both the DGFT and the CC having very wide discretion in the exercise of their powers, and there is little prospect of *Wednesbury* unreasonableness (*Associated Provincial Picture Houses Ltd* v *Wednesbury Corpn* [1948] 1 KB 223) applying to a formal decision made by either body. This is particularly so when the final views of these bodies are conditioned by detailed analyses of economic principles which the courts are unlikely to review (see Sir Gordon Borrie QC, 'The Regulation of Public and Private Power' [1989] *PL* 552). The majority of the very few reported judicial review cases in this area arise out of challenges to decisions taken by the CC or Secretary of State in relation to merger control. However, it has been established that the law of judicial review relates to the operation of the bodies responsible for competition law at the investigative stage. In *Secretary of State for Trade and Industry* v *Hoffmann-La Roche & Co. AG* [1975] AC 295, at 368, Lord Diplock held that

it is the duty of the Commissioners to observe the rules of natural justice in the course of their investigation—which means no more than that they must act fairly by giving to the person whose activities are being investigated a reasonable opportunity to put forward facts and arguments in justification of its conduct.

And in *R* v *MMC, ex parte Matthew Brown Plc* [1987] 1 WLR 1235, Macpherson J held that 'provided each party has its mind brought to bear on the relevant issues it is not in my judgment for the court to lay down rules as to how each group should act in a particular enquiry'. As has been noted above, the CC's reports tend to be very detailed and densely argued. While one might take issue with the conclusions drawn, there is only a remote possibility that an action could be founded on the basis that the CC did not bring its mind to bear on the relevant issues. A partially successful judicial review was mounted on behalf of Thomson Holidays against the Foreign Package Holidays (Tour Operators and Travel Agents) Order 1998, SI 1998/1945, which followed the MMC report into the supply of foreign package holidays (Cm. 3813, 1998) (*R* v *Secretary of State for Trade and Industry, ex parte Thomson Holidays* [2000] UKCLR 189). In part the Order was struck down because it would prohibit restrictions that were not found by the MMC to operate against the public interest. A further partial success arose in *Interbrew SA and Interbrew UK Holdings Ltd* v *The Competition Commission and the Secretary of State for Trade and Industry* [2001] UKCLR 954 in which it was found that a remedy required following a merger report was unreasonable in the light of the lack of opportunity the undertaking concerned had had to comment on the proposed remedy in the course of the inquiry. However, the CC's substantive findings regarding the public interest were left largely intact (see CC press release 20/01, 23 May 2001, [2001] UKCLR 734).

It is likely that there will be more challenges made under the new regime, with its tighter and more formal structure, than there have been in the past, and the normal rules of judicial review apply to the 1998 Competition Act.

4

Penalties

4.1 **Introduction**

The issue of how best to compel corporate compliance within a system designed to modify corporate conduct is a difficult one. Whereas individual unlawful acts may be presumed to be committed for the immediate gain of the perpetrator, the decision-making process within complex organizations, such as the modern company, is less focused and harder to direct externally. There is a substantial body of literature which considers the decision-making process within companies and the methods by which this may be affected. A large amount of this is American, and differences in corporate and legal cultures mean that such material may not necessarily relate to the situation in Europe. An interesting survey conducted into compliance and deterrence in relation to UK and EC competition law was carried out by Frazer in 1994 and is reported on at (1995) 58 *MLR* 847. Frazer found that respondents in UK-registered companies with a turnover of at least £200 million were 'motivated more by questions of legitimacy than by the desire to avoid penalties' (p. 855).

In industrial economics a general presumption is that companies have as their main goal profit maximization. If this was strictly true the issue for competition law would be relatively straightforward: the task of the law would be to create a structure of penalties where the *likely cost* of unlawful anti-competitive conduct more than outweighed the *likely benefit* to the company of engaging in that conduct. In fact it is not apparent that all companies have profit maximization as their goal all of the time. Even were they to do so, there may be a difference between the goals of the organization as a whole and those of its individual officers. Competition within a company might have the effect of encouraging managers to take risks that are disproportionate to the potential rewards where those risks are not borne directly by that manager: if an unlawful informal agreement between managers in two companies works well, the revenue flow to that manager's division may be greatly improved; if the agreement is discovered the punishment will be spread across the company as a whole. There have been occasions where individual officers have demonstrated a blatant disregard for the strictures of competition law. For example, in *Pioneer* 80/256 (1980) OJ L60/21 a letter written by one, of the officers involved in the maintenance of a restrictive practice read: 'I am well aware of EEC rules regarding parallel exports but quite frankly at times I am more concerned with justice than with the law itself'. One of the issues for competition law is that of whether penalties should be imposed on only the company as a whole, or on individual managers too, where they can be shown to be responsible for the infringement. At the Community level the fines permitted under Regulation 17 may be levied only against the undertaking which is the subject of Community law. In the UK fines may be imposed against the company in breach of the Chapter I and Chapter II prohibitions of the Competition Act 1998, and individual officers may be fined or imprisoned where they have obstructed an investigation or provided misleading information (see Chapter 3).

4.2 The types of penalty

The weapons in the enforcers' arsenal are conduct remedies, structural remedies, and fines and imprisonment. The power to order the modification of corporate conduct (e.g., to determine the price at which a product may be sold), which may go so far as the complete break-up of a company may be the most powerful weapon. There are two significant objections to such modifying orders. The first is that they may often require a continued supervision to ensure compliance, which is burdensome on the relevant enforcer; the second is that they do not always sit well within a framework of free-market economics which competition law is often intended to support. Lastly, third-party remedies—injunctions and damages—also have a role to play. These are considered in the following chapter.

Incarceration is a well-publicized feature of the American system, and is available too in other jurisdictions. In fact imprisonment for antitrust offences is not widely used in America, although some writers have suggested that such a method of enforcement should be potent. It has been pointed out in one study that company officers are, as a group, 'exquisitely sensitive to status deprivation' (Geiss, G., 'Deterring Corporate Crime' in Ermann, M. D., and Lundmann, R. J. (eds), *Corporate and Governmental Deviance*, Oxford, OUP (1978), p. 278). In the late 1950s the 'electrical conspiracy cases' resulted in imprisonment for some company officers, and enforcement officials believed that these convictions had a salutary effect on conduct over the immediately following years; but over time these effects diminished. Although offenders are still regularly sent to prison the threat is not considered to be great, and it is unlikely that these isolated incidents have a significant impact within the majority of companies, although they may encourage the maintenance of compliance programmes. The UK Government intends to introduce imprisonment as a penalty for the operation of 'hard-core' cartels in the Enterprise Bill expected to be introduced in the summer of 2002.

The argument in favour of the efficacy of fines is a persuasive one: companies take part in anti-competitive conduct in order to boost profits; remove those profits and the incentive for illegal conduct vanishes. Elzinga, K., and Breit, W., in *The Antitrust Penalties*, New Haven, Yale UP (1976) argue in favour of the imposition of massive fines, which are more efficient than the other options. Incarceration is an expensive choice for society—longer periods of incarceration are increasingly expensive—but to impose a higher fine is generally no more costly for society than the imposition of a lesser one. Within the Community and the separate European jurisdictions there is now a consensus in favour of the imposition of fines based on turnover. Whether this is the appropriate measure is less certain. While turnover figures have the advantage of being available through the requirements to maintain accounts, and are not readily open to manipulation, they are not always an accurate indicator of an ability to pay. A company fined 5 per cent of turnover in a high-turnover, low-profit-margin business will be harder hit than a company fined 5 per cent of turnover in a low-turnover, high-profit-margin business. However, the solution advanced by Viscount Trenchard, 'to devise a maximum penalty which would have an equal effect in its application to all companies' (Hansard (HL) 30 October 1997, col. 1176), is clearly flawed. A single-figure maximum does *not* have an equal effect on all companies. If the maximum fine were, say, £10m, this would have less deterrent effect, and less impact, on a company with a turnover of £1bn than it would on a company with a turnover of £50m. Further, a set figure allows companies to conduct cost–benefit analyses as to whether to break the law or not. Such strategic behaviour can be redressed only by a variable level of penalty, such that the wrongdoer cannot, before the event, calculate its risk with certainty, or, as is the case in the EC, by the expectation that *at the minimum* the fine will recover all profit reaped by the illegal activity. The UK has adopted in the 1998 Act the same measure as the EC, which is to say that fines may be levied at up to 10 per cent of turnover (see below). Even this measure was described in the debate on the Bill as being 'grossly excessive' (Lord Fraser of Carmyllie, Hansard (HL) 30 October 1997, col. 1152).

4.3 The European Community

4.3.1 Fines

Article 15 of Regulation 17 gives the Commission the power to impose fines where breaches of the law have occurred. Article 15(1) sets a tariff for procedural infringements of the Regulation itself. In these cases the Commission's discretion is severely limited, and the sums of money involved, which run from €100 to €5,000, are unlikely to be such as to cause concern to the larger undertakings that are likely to be subject to Community law. The most important provision of Community law dealing with fines lies in art. 15(2) of Regulation 17, which provides that

The Commission may be decision impose on undertakings or associations of undertakings fines of from 1,000 to 1,000,000 units of account, or a sum in excess thereof but not exceeding

10 per cent of the turnover in the preceding business year of each of the undertakings participating in the infringement where, either intentionally or negligently:

(a) they infringe Article [81(1)] or Article [82] of the Treaty; or

(b) they commit a breach of any obligation imposed pursuant to Article 8(1).

In fixing the amount of the fine, regard shall be had both to the gravity and to the duration of the infringement.

Article 15(4) provides that '[d]ecisions taken pursuant to paragraphs 1 and 2 shall not be of a criminal law nature'. Lastly, by virtue of art. 16, the Commission may impose periodic penalty payments ranging from 50 to 1,000 units of account per day, in the circumstances set out. Primarily these may be imposed in order to compel those in breach 'to put to an end an infringement of Article [81] or [82] of the Treaty'.

The range within which the fines for substantive infringements may fall is a wide one, and it was only at the end of 1997 that the Commission considered the setting of clear guidelines ('Karel Van Miert submits to the Commission clear guidelines on the method for the setting of fines in the context of European "antitrust" legislation', IP/97/1075, 3 December 1997). That the Commission has a wide discretion both as to whether a fine should be imposed at all and as to the level of any such fine, is clear from the wording of art. 15 itself. The use of 'may' and the inclusion of factors to which the Commission should have regard confirm this. This discretion is fettered by the general principles of law developed in the context of art. 230 EC. However, when challenges against the level of fines have been upheld this has generally been on the grounds that the factual findings of the Commission have been incorrect, not that it has acted beyond its powers in imposing the fine at all. In *Miller International Schallplatten GmbH* v *Commission* case 19/77 [1978] 2 CMLR 334, Advocate General Warner argued that

a fine of 10 per cent of turnover may be taken to be appropriate to an intentional infringement of the gravest kind and of considerable duration. At the other end of the scale, a fine of less than 1 per cent is appropriate for a merely negligent infringement, of the most trivial kind and continuing only for a short time, in a case where, nonetheless, the circumstances warrant the imposition of some fine.   (p. 346)

Under the guidelines

a base sum defined with reference to the duration and of the gravity of the infraction will be calculated without reference to turnover. It will then be raised when aggravating circumstances exist or reduced to take into account . . . attenuating circumstances. Corrections could be made to the resulting amount to take account of the individual circumstances of the case.   (ibid.)

The guidelines thus appear to dismiss altogether the calculation of fines by reference to turnover, and the only recognition of this as a determining factor appears where the Commission notes that 'it goes without saying that the final amount calculated according to this method may not in any case exceed 10 per cent of the world-wide turnover of the undertakings'. In assessing the level at which any fine should be imposed the article itself makes reference only to the 'gravity' and the 'duration' of the infringement, and the guidelines make clear that the basic amount will be defined in reference to these.

The determination of the level at which the undertaking would be fined prior to the guidelines had involved the consideration of a number of factors, most of which are reflected in the guidelines. Within the structure as set out in the guidelines the gravity of the infringement will be determined with reference to three criteria: the nature of the infringement; its impact on the market; and the size of the relevant geographical market. The application of these criteria will result in a restriction being placed in one of three categories:

Minor infringements: These might be trade restrictions, usually of a vertical nature [see Chapter 6], but with a limited market impact and affecting only a substantial but relatively limited part of the Community market. Likely fines: ECU 1,000 to 1 million.

Serious infringements: These will more often than not be horizontal or vertical restrictions [see Chapter 6] of the same type as above, but more rigorously applied, with a wider market impact, and with effects in extensive areas of the common market. They might also be abuses of a dominant position . . . Likely fines: ECU 1 million to 20 million.

Very serious infringements: These will generally be horizontal restrictions such as price cartels and market-sharing quotas, or other practices which jeopardise the proper functioning of the single market . . . and clear cut abuses of a dominant position by undertakings holding a virtual monopoly . . . Likely fines: above ECU 20 million.

These figures will be subject to variation, both to allow the requisite individual treatment of the position of each undertaking and to allow the 'duration' to be factored in. The impact of the duration on the level of fine set out above is as follows: short term (generally less than one year)—no impact; medium term (one to five years)—an increase of up to 50 per cent on the amount determined for gravity; long term (five years plus)—an increase of up to 10 per cent per year. Even having published the guidelines the Commission is not under an obligation to spell out precisely how it arrives at the final figure for a penalty imposed on it in an adverse decision. In *Mo Och Domsjo AB* v *Commission* case C–283/98P [2001] 4 CMLR 322 the ECJ held that it was sufficient, having regard to the wording of art. 15(2) of Regulation 17, for the Commission to indicate in its decision 'the factors which enabled it to determine the gravity of the infringement and its duration' (para. 44).

The fact that fines are to be increased in direct proportion to the longevity of the infringement is designed to put further pressure on cartels, an issue which is dealt with in part by the Commission's reducing the penalties on cartel members who 'blow the whistle' (see below).

The fining guidelines also set out aggravating and attenuating circumstances that will affect the basic amount. The non-exhaustive list of aggravating circumstances is as follows:

- repeated infringement of the same type by the undertaking;
- non-cooperation or obstruction during the course of the Commission investigation;
- a leading role in the infringement;

- any retaliatory measures taken against other undertakings designed to reinforce the anti-competitive actions;
- consideration of any profits made by virtue of the unlawful conduct when it is possible to calculate this (see the discussion of this aspect of the calculation of penalties in section 4.4.1.1).

The list of attenuating circumstances is as follows:

- a passive, or 'follow my leader' role taken in a cartel;
- less than full compliance with any restrictive agreement;
- prompt termination of the infringement following the intervention of the Commission;
- reasonable doubt on the part of the undertaking as to the fact that the conduct was in breach of Community law;
- infringement negligently or unintentionally committed;
- cooperation with the Commission in the course of the proceedings.

Undertakings have persistently called for a clarification of the Commission's fining policy, and some pressure has also come from cases in the human rights field, such as *Société Stenuit* v *France* (1992) 14 EHRR 509. In *Musique Diffusion Française SA* v *Commission* cases 100–103/80 [1983] 3 CMLR 221, the Commission argued (at 263) that

since there are so many unquantifiable criteria to be taken into consideration, no mathematical formula of general application is possible. Different approaches may be used in different cases. Even where it is possible to connect the size of the fine to a quantifiable criterion, such as turnover, the decision as to what must be the relationship between the fine and the criteria thus measured is a question of appraisal rather than simple calculation.

The guidelines have moved on from this position, and strike what may be an acceptable compromise between calculation and judgment. The criteria were largely drawn from existing practices, reflecting the approach both of the Commission and of the Court of Justice. It has always been the case that the Commission has been particularly concerned by breaches of art. 81 which are likely to lead to the division of the common market, and any practice threatening economic integration will be strongly condemned. Thus, for example, in *IPTC Belgium* 83/773 (1983) OJ L376/7, the Commission made the point that

It is well known that business practices seeking to prevent parallel imports and to erect artificial trade barriers within the Community, and thus to undermine the unity of the common market, are regularly investigated and condemned by the Community authorities.   (para. 15)

The Commission has been particularly harsh on recidivism. In *Flat glass* 84/388 (1984) OJ L212/13, the Commission emphasized the fact that two of the parties were guilty of previous infringements. The fact that they had negotiated an agreement with the Commission and then observed the letter, but not the spirit, of the undertaking, led to the imposition of a higher fine than would otherwise have been the case. The fines imposed in *LdPE* 89/191 (1989) OJ L74/21 were also influenced by the fact that several of the parties had previously been the subject of Commission action in *Dyestuffs* (*ICI* v *Commission* case 48/69 [1972] CMLR 557) In *Tetra Pak II* 92/163 (1992) OJ L72/1, the Commission imposed a then record fine of ECU 75 million on the undertaking, and in doing so stressed that it would attempt to recover illicit profits where these could be identified. This point was reiterated in the *21st Report on Competition Policy*:

> The financial benefit which companies . . . have derived from their infringements will become an increasingly important consideration. Wherever the Commission can ascertain the level of this ill-gotten gain, even if it cannot do so precisely, the calculation of the fine may have this as its starting point. (point 139)

While the profit level will not, under the guidelines, be the starting-point for the assessment of the fine, the fact that the Commission will attempt at the absolute minimum to recover any profit made remains a guiding principle.

The Commission has reduced the fines imposed in the past where participants in cartels have played a reduced role in relation to the hard-core members. This was the case in *LdPE* (above) where Shell and BP were fined reduced amounts, reflecting the restricted level of their involvement in the cartel meetings. Undertakings may have their fines reduced if they are merely responding to another's illegal activity (*Welded steel mesh* 89/515 (1989) OJ L260/1). Cooperation during the course of the investigation was rewarded in *IPTC Belgium* (above). The 'reasonable doubt' attenuation provision of the guidelines reflects the fact that undertakings have been subjected to lesser penalties in the past where the Commission has not previously penalized the behaviour which is the subject of the fine. For example, in *BDTA* 88/477 (1988) OJ L233/15 the Commission dealt with the actions of a trade association which organized trade exhibitions. It reduced the fine because this was the first exhibition policy case in which one had been imposed. In *Wood pulp* 85/202 (1985) OJ L85/1 the Commission reduced or removed altogether the fines for undertakings that were based in the United States and were operating within American antitrust law (see further Chapter 18).

It is clear that over time the average amount of the fines imposed by the Commission has greatly increased. From 1970 to 1974 the average level was €411,604; from 1990 to 1994 the average level was €4,135,220. This reflects partly the fact that the Commission is taking a greater proportion of its proceedings against larger undertakings and cartels, where both the impact of the infringement and the ability to pay are greater. It also reflects the fact that the Commission has quite deliberately increased the tariff from time to time to strengthen the enforcement of competition policy. This was the case, for example, in *Pioneer* 80/256 (1980) OJ L60/21, where the fines imposed amounted to between 2.4 to 4 per cent of turnover, whereas previously fines had amounted to 2 per cent of turnover at the most. The Commission argued that this was necessary in view of the increasing maturity of the Community regime, and that in deciding to increase levels generally they had not exceeded their discretion. On appeal (*Musique Diffusion Française SA* v

Commission cases 100–103/80 [1983] 3 CMLR 221) the Court agreed with the Commission, holding that 'the proper application of the Community competition rules requires that the Commission may at any time adjust the level of fines to the needs of that policy' (para. 109). It appears that the resolution of cases within the guidelines will, over time, likewise lead to some increase in the overall cost of infringements, although at the time of writing it is too early to be certain about this. However, in January 1998 the Commission broke the record that it had established in *Tetra Pak* by imposing a fine of ECU 102 million on Volkswagen following a finding that the company had, in breach of art. 81(1), prevented Italian dealers in its cars from reselling these to customers from other parts of the Community (*VW* 98/273 (1998) OJ L124/61, on appeal *Volkswagen AG v Commission* case T–62/98 [2000] 5 CMLR 853—as a result of which the fine was reduced to (ECU 90 million). The decision is a further demonstration of the extremely strong stance that the Commission will take against any practice which results in the re-creation of the trade barriers it has sought so hard to dismantle. In September 1998 record fines totalling €273 million were imposed on parties to the Trans-Atlantic Conference Agreement following a finding that they had abused a position of joint-dominance under art. 82 (IP/98/811, 16 September 1998).

On the other hand, where infringements are genuinely committed negligently, fines may be only token. For example, in *1998 Football World Cup* 2000/12 (2000) OJ L5/55 the Commission drew the conclusion that the French ticketing authorities adopted arrangements similar to those taken in earlier competitions, and that the area was so specific that clear guidance could not be drawn from earlier decisions. As a result, having found the relevant undertaking to have abused its dominant position, the Commission imposed a fine that was only €1,000.

4.3.1.1 *Leniency for 'whistle-blowers'*

The Commission is attempting to use its fining policy to put particular pressure on cartels, which it has admitted are hard to detect (see Chapter 3). This pressure stems in part from the Commission Notice on Immunity from fines and reduction of fines in cartel cases, reissued on 13 February 2002 (IP/02/247). The previous version of the Notice was sometimes referred to as the 'whistle-blower's Notice', a terminology the Commission would prefer to avoid. The Notice is aimed at 'secret cartels between two or more competitors aimed at fixing prices, production or sales quotas, sharing markets including bid-rigging or restricting imports or exports' (para. 1). The problem for undertakings engaged in cartels is that the fines increase year-on-year of participation if the cartel is detected, and some members may be looking for a way out. However, the increased fines mean that members might be reluctant to disclose the existence of the cartel to the authorities. The Commission has taken the view that the 'interests of consumers and citizens in ensuring that secret cartels are detected and punished outweigh the interest in fining those undertakings that enable the Commission to detect and prohibit such practices' (para. 4). Accordingly the Commission Notice is aimed at encouraging undertakings involved in cartels to come forward with the evidence the Commission needs to take action.

Total immunity from any fine that would ordinarily be imposed by the Commission is guaranteed where either:

8(a) the undertaking is the first to submit evidence which in the Commission's view may enable it to adopt a decision to carry out an investigation in the sense of article 14(3) of Regulation No 17 in connection with an alleged cartel affecting the Community; or

(b) the undertaking is the first to submit evidence which in the Commission's view may enable it to find an infringement of article 81EC in connection with an alleged cartel affecting the Community.

In respect of para. 8(a) the immunity will apply as long as the Commission did not already have sufficient evidence to launch an investigation, and under para. 8(b) the requirement is that the Commission did not have the evidence, and no other undertaking had been granted immunity from fines under para. 8(a). However, there are also three further conditions to the grant of immunity, set out in para. 11. First the undertaking must cooperate fully throughout the investigation. Second the undertaking must end its own involvement in the cartel at the same time as it provides the necessary information to the Commission, and third the undertaking must not have taken any steps to coerce any other undertaking to join the cartel.

Even in situations where an undertaking does not qualify for a total immunity from a fine penalties may be reduced. This will particularly be the case where the undertaking in question provides information which has a 'significant added value with respect to the evidence already in the Commission's possession' (para. 21). The first undertaking to meet this point will earn a reduction of some 30–50 per cent, the second a reduction of 20–30 per cent, and any subsequent undertaking a reduction of up to 20 per cent.

The criticism of the previous version of the Notice, issued in 1996, was that it was too vague in its application for undertakings to be able to calculate beforehand whether they were likely to benefit from immunity, and the extent to which they might do so. The new Notice goes some way to addressing these concerns, although there may still be situations in which undertakings in a cartel are nervously watching the Commission and unable to determine if it is worth giving evidence in the hope that they will be the first to do so. At least under the terms of the Notice even in these conditions the undertaking will be able to calculate its likely benefit under para. 21, an improvement on the situation that used to exist.

4.3.2 **Other orders**

By virtue of art. 3(1) of Regulation 17, the Commission 'may by decision require the undertakings or associations of undertakings concerned to bring such infringement to an end'. This implies a substantial power, the limits of which have not yet been fully tested. The wording of the Regulation is such that the Commission may make any order that it considers appropriate, subject to the right of challenge that is available under art. 230 EC. This could include, *inter alia*, the admittance of an undertaking into a sales network, the resumption of supplies, the disentangling of a joint venture, and perhaps even the determination of the prices at which a product was to be sold.

4.4 The United Kingdom

4.4.1 The 1998 Act

4.4.1.1 *Fines*

The Competition Act 1988 introduced into domestic law a penalty system that is similar to that of Community law. By virtue of s. 36 of the Act, the Director may impose a penalty where either the Chapter I or the Chapter II prohibitions are infringed. Section 36(8) provides that 'no penalty fixed by the Director under this section may exceed 10 per cent of the turnover of the undertaking (determined in accordance with such provisions as may be specified in an order made by the Secretary of State)'. Turnover is to be calculated in accordance with The Competition Act 1998 (Determination of Turnover for Penalties) Order 2000, SI 2000/309. 'Section 36(8)' turnover is not restricted to the turnover in the relevant product and geographical market.

The turnover threshold may be amended by order of the Secretary of State, but it is unlikely that this figure would ever be revised upwards. Companies may appeal against any fines levied, which become recoverable by the Director as if they were a civil debt (s. 37). Turnover is to be UK turnover, not world-wide or EC turnover. Appeals may be made against decisions of the Director, to the Competition Commission and then to the Court of Appeal (s. 49(1)(b)). Unlike the Court of First Instance, the Competion Commission Appeals Tribunal (CCAT) reviews the decision taken by the DGFT from scratch, in relation both to penalties and to any required conduct changes and is required to consider the case 'on the merits' (Sch. 8, para. 3(1)), and if it is necessary and appropriate to 'make any other decision which the Director could have made (Sch. 8, para. 3(2)(e)). In regard to penalties the CCAT may raise, lower, or revoke altogether any penalty (Sch. 8, para. 3(2)(b)). Also, the CCAT is not bound by any guidance issued by the DGFT in relation to penalties, and as the CCAT recognized in *Napp*, 'the CA98 contains no provision which requires the Tribunal to even have regard to that Guidance' (para. 497). The general approach whereby the CCAT would start from first principles, although in doing so it would clearly have in mind any penalty imposed by the DGFT is, the CCAT commented in *Napp*, consistent with the requirements of the European Convention on Human Rights, art. 6. In the case it was accepted by all parties that the penalties are 'criminal' within the meaning of the Convention, even though they are characterized in English law as a 'civil debt'. An appeal may be made from the CCAT to the Court of Appeal in relation to the level of any penalty imposed (s. 49(1)(b)). The Director is required to publish guidance as to the appropriate penalties (see below).

Given the emphasis in the 1998 Act on conformity with Community law, it is likely that fines will be assessed in a way similar to that employed by the CCAT. It was confirmed by the CCAT in *Napp Pharmaceuticals Holdings Ltd* v *The Director General of Fair Trading* [2002] CompAR 13 that in determining the broad policy relating to fines Community law should be followed (see para. 455). However, in relation to the calculation of the exact fine within the broad parameters set out in the Act, dealt with in the relevant guideline (see below), the CCAT took the view that differences between the approach taken by the DGFT and that by the EC Commission's guideline were 'relevant' for the purposes of s. 60 of the Act. This is to say that the CCAT did not feel obliged to take into account the EC guidelines in making its own decisions. In situations where the condemned conduct has also been subject to the imposition of a penalty under Community law by the Commission, the Director is to have regard to that penalty in assessing the level of the fine under domestic law. 'Small agreements', as defined by secondary legislation (and see s. 39), and 'conduct of minor significance' otherwise falling within the Chapter II prohibition (s. 40) have limited immunity from the imposition of fines. However, this immunity may, in certain circumstances, be withdrawn by the Director.

The relevant thresholds are set out in The Competition Act 1998 (Small Agreements and Conduct of Minor Significance) Regulations 2000, SI 2000/262. These provide that small agreements (s. 39(1)) are those where the combined applicable turnover in the year preceding the infringement did not exceed £20 million (para. 3). The threshold in respect of s. 40(1) is £50 million (para. 4).

The approach that will be taken to the setting of penalties is set out in *Director General of Fair Trading's Guidance as to the Appropriate Amount of a Penalty*, which the OFT had a statutory duty under s. 38(1) of the Act to produce. Reference should also be made to the *Enforcement* guideline. However, there are some who would have preferred that such guidance not be published, on the basis that there is a fear that companies may be able to conduct a cost–benefit analysis as to whether infringement is a viable option, balancing the profit reaped against the likely penalty discounted by the risk of detection. The tone of the guidance is set at the outset, where the Director explains the policy objectives underlying the approach. These are 'to impose penalties on infringing undertakings which reflect the seriousness of the infringement and to ensure that the threat of penalties will deter undertakings from engaging in anti-competitive practices'. Accordingly, the Director intends 'to impose financial penalties which are severe' (para. 2.1).

The broad approach is similar to that adopted by the EC Commission. A five-step approach will be adopted:

1. calculation of the starting-point by applying a percentage determined by the nature of the infringement to the 'relevant turnover' of the undertaking;
2. adjustment for duration;
3. adjustment for other factors;
4. adjustment for further aggravating or mitigating factors;
5. adjustment if the maximum penalty of 10 per cent of the turnover would be exceeded, and to avoid double jeopardy.

These factors are discussed further in the guidelines.

The first penalty imposed by the DGFT under the Act was a fine of £3.21m levied against Napp Pharmaceuticals (*Napp Pharmaceutical Holdings Ltd* CA98/2/2001 [2001] UKCLR 597, on appeal *Napp Pharmaceuticals Holdings Ltd* v *The Director General of Fair Trading* [2002] CompAR 13). The undertaking had been condemned for discriminatory predatory pricing to one customer base, and for excessive pricing to another. One of the points which concerned the CCAT related to an attempt by the DGFT to recover any profits made as a result of Napp's illegal conduct. Such an adjustment is dealt with as part of the third step in the calculation of the penalty, the amount of profit made being 'another factor'. The first concern of the CCAT related to the difficulty of calculating what the gain actually was. In the case in question the parties were unable to agree within a million pounds. Even were a figure produced the CCAT felt that this would most likely underestimate the gain, as it would not be able to take into account the long-term benefit to the under-taking of an enhanced reputation for toughness and competitiveness. The CCAT expressed the view that 'this method of calculation, so it seems to us, is more suited to the process for assessing the damages in civil litigation, rather than the fixing of a deterrent penalty' (para. 508).

The operating of a compliance programme is expressly recognized as a mitigating factor in the *Enforcement* guideline (paras 4.35–4.36), but in order for this to apply the parties must show that the programme is active, visibly supported by senior management, backed up by appropriate procedures and appropriate training, and properly audited and reported.

4.4.1.2 Leniency for 'whistle-blowers'

The OFT approach to 'whistle-blowers' was more influenced by the similar US pro-gramme than by the one operated by the EC Commission. It is now, however, following revisions to the EC scheme (discussed above) similar to that scheme. It was invoked for the first time in the decision *Market Sharing by Arriva plc and First-Group plc* (CA98/9/2002, 30 January 2002), in which both companies benefited from the operation of the scheme as they provided the Director with evidence of cartel activity. Arriva's fine was reduced by 36 per cent, and FirstGroup avoided penalty altogether. FirstGroup did not approach the Director until after the investi-gation had begun, but was the first of the two parties to do so. A letter offering a 100 per cent reduction was issued on 2 November 2000, and was conditional on First-Group providing evidence of the cartel, cooperating with the Director throughout the investigation, and complying with all the conditions set out in the *Guidance on Penalties* (paras 70–71). Under the UK guidelines the Director 'will offer *total immunity* from financial penalties . . . to a member of a cartel who is the first to come forward and who satisfies the requirements set out in para 9.3.2 [or] 9.3.4' (para. 9.1). Paragraph 9.3.2 relates to those who come forward *before* an investigation has commenced. The conditions are that the undertaking in question must:

(a) give full disclosure of relevant information;

(b) cooperate fully throughout the investigation;

(c) not have compelled any other undertaking to join the cartel, have instigated the cartel, or played a leading role; and

(d) cease any involvement in the cartel from the time it comes forward.

Paragraph 9.3.4 relates to those who come forward once an investigation has commenced. In this case immunity may be available where the undertaking is the first to come forward before the Director has given written notice of his intention to make a decision to the effect that the Chapter I prohibition has been breached, and the conditions set out above are also met. The Director will, so far as is possible, attempt to maintain confidentiality as to the identity of any undertaking coming forward under this part of the procedure (para. 9.7). However, given the dynamics involved in the investigation of a cartel, and the fact that there will already be in place links between the undertakings concerned, it is difficult to see how this will work in practice. Copies of draft letters setting out the terms and conditions on which the leniency programme operates are available on the OFT website.

4.4.1.3 *Criminalization*

In its White Paper *A World Class Competition Regime* (Cm. 5233), the Department of Trade and Industry proposed that certain aspects of competition law in the UK be criminalized. In particular it was suggested that criminal penalties should attach to hard-core cartel conduct. Following this suggestion the OFT commissioned a report to investigate the issue. The final report, *Proposed Criminalisation of cartels in the UK*, was published in November 2001 (see [2002] UKCLR 97). In it the authors recommended that a new criminal offence should be created, not linked directly either to art. 81 EC, or to the Chapter I prohibition. Instead the offence should 'incorporate the concept of individuals *dishonestly* entering into agreements with each other in order to implement 'hard core' cartel arrangements' (para. 1.10). The report also recommended that it should be the Serious Fraud Office, rather than the OFT, which would investigate any such case, and that the maximum gaol term on conviction should be not less than five years, to reflect the view of the Government of the seriousness of the offence. If these proposals are accepted, as appears likely, it would mark a sea change in the treatment of anti-competitive conduct in the UK. It would also, inevitably, lead to some very complex and lengthy trials.

4.4.2 **Orders, undertakings, and contempt of court**

One of the most glaring differences between the old domestic regime and the Community competition law was the lack of penalties for past conduct under any of the relevant Acts. None of the older Acts made immediate provision for the imposition of penalties in respect of conduct which was found to be contrary to those Acts. Even in the case of the Resale Prices Act, which was unique in imposing a per se prohibition on conduct falling within its scope, s. 25(1) provided that 'no criminal proceedings lie against any person' in contravention of the Act. The enforcement of the Fair Trading Act 1973 and the Competition Act 1980 depended in the first instance upon the making of an order, or the acceptance of an undertaking by a party, to require modification of conduct which had been found to be in breach of the relevant provisions. This continues to be the case in respect of that part of the Fair Trading Act left in place under the new regime. The subsequent breach of an order or undertaking would bring the offending party into contempt of court. The position in relation to the Restrictive Trade Practices Acts was similar.

This curious situation led to invidious comparisons with the greater powers of the EC Commission, and it was not until *Re Supply of Ready Mixed Concrete (No. 2): Director General of Fair Trading* v *Pioneer Concrete (UK) Ltd* [1995] 1 All ER 135 that it became clear that the system nevertheless had teeth. In that case the Restrictive Practices Court (RPC) had imposed penalties on several members of a concrete cartel that had been maintained notwithstanding a finding that the agreement was in breach of the Restrictive Trade Practices Act 1976 (*Re Supply of Ready Mixed Concrete* [1991] ICR 52). In arriving at a judgment against the parties the court argued that 'it is not to be tolerated that four or five years after a court order is made seeking to stamp out this kind of covert anti-competitive operation, [the companies] are found through their employees to be engaged in the same potentially harmful conduct' (at 70). At the Court of Appeal the companies argued successfully that they should not be held liable at all, given that they had issued instructions to their employees to abandon any unlawful agreements, and should not then be held responsible when these instructions were ignored. The DGFT appealed to the House of Lords which, at the same time as rejecting these arguments, was highly critical of the 'derisory fines' (*per* Lord Templeman at 140) imposed by the RPC. It became clear, therefore, that much higher penalties might be imposed in similar circumstances in the future.

It should be recalled also that the court has wide discretion as to how to punish those in contempt, including the power to order imprisonment, although the prospect of any business manager being sent to prison for a breach of the Fair Trading Act in the future seems unlikely.

5

Third-party rights

5.1 Introduction

Although this chapter is addressed to the rights of third parties rather than to the position of those in breach of the law, or of society as a whole, it should be recognized that there is a relationship between third-party rights and the enforcement of competition law (see the previous chapter). In particular, the effect on the infringing party of paying damages is little different than if a fine were being levied. The effect upon the legal system, however, is more noticeable, and the burden of enforcement will pass from the relevant public authorities to wronged individuals, who may often have greater motivation to bring actions. This is a very obvious and prominent feature of the American antitrust system, where individual enforcement is a vital part of the regime, and is encouraged by the availability of triple damages under s. 4 of the Clayton Act, which provides that

[a]ny person who shall be injured in his business or property by reason of anything forbidden in the antitrust laws may sue therefor ... and shall recover threefold the damages by him sustained, and the cost of suit, including a reasonable attorney's fee. (15 USC s. 15)

The nature of the regimes in the United Kingdom and the European Community is that public regulation is to the fore, and any individual rights are ancillary to this. There is also a very clear difference between the legal culture of the United States, where parties bring actions much more readily, and of Europe, where there is a greater reluctance to involve the courts in commercial matters. This factor is clearly a matter of some exasperation to the EC Commission, which is overworked and would like to see far more actions brought directly by injured parties in the Member States. Alexander Schaub, then Director General of the Competition Directorate, responding to a question from *In Competition* which suggested that businesses find it unattractive to take such steps, answered that 'it should be interesting to use national courts, maybe it is not well enough known. They should play a much bigger role. I don't think it is in [the Commission's] interest to systematically centralise decision-making' ((1996) *In Competition*, 30 September). 'During debates on the passage of the Competition Act 1998 suggestions were made by members on the Conservative benches that the penalties for breaches of the new UK law should be reduced as enforcement would flow from third parties. However, the Government recognized that

ordinary consumers and small companies, who will commonly be the victims of anti-competitive agreements and abuses by small and medium sized enterprises, are less likely and less able to pursue their rights through courts than would a big business.   (Hansard (HL) 17 November 1997, col 436)

And Lord Borrie, former DGFT, made the point that

small businesses have been extremely reluctant to take action themselves because of the expense. With some reason they have thought that the [OFT], set up especially to enforce the law, should take action at public expense. That is the real deterrent.   (ibid.)

It is in part because of these factors that the Government introduced strong publicly imposed penalties in the new law.

For an excellent general discussion of this area see Jones, C. A., *Private Enforcement of Antitrust Law in the EU, UK, and USA*, Oxford, OUP (1999).

5.2 European Community law

5.2.1 Involvement in proceedings

The Commission receives many complaints from third parties about anti-competitive activity, but is significantly overburdened and not able to take effective action in all appropriate cases. In 1999, for example, 388 new cases were registered, of which 149 were based on complaints made by third parties; 582 cases were closed; and 1,013 cases were left outstanding. These figures are not encouraging for third parties seeking redress through an administrative route, although the Commission will focus its activity on the most serious breaches.

In *Automec srl* v *Commission* case T-24/90 [1992] 5 CMLR 431, the applicant relied on art. 232 EC in an attempt to compel the Commission to act in response to a complaint. Article 232 is in the following terms:

Should the European Parliament, the Council or the Commission, in infringement of this Treaty, fail to act, the Member States and the other institutions of the Community may bring an action before the Court of Justice to have the infringement established.

The action shall be admissible only if the institution concerned has first been called upon to act. If, within two months of being so called upon, the institution concerned has not defined its position, the action may be brought within a further period of two months.

Any natural or legal person may, under the conditions laid down in the preceding paragraphs, complain to the Court of Justice that an institution of the Community has failed to address to that person any act other than a recommendation or an opinion.

The Court held that the Commission was entitled to prioritize its workload, that the emphasis in enforcement policy would inevitably shift from time to time in response to the wide range of factors that the Commission was expected to consider, and that the Commission was not obliged necessarily to follow every case presented to it, but was entitled to select which cases it could address its attention to. This case has been often cited by the Commission in its attempts to persuade courts and authorities in the Member States to assume more of the burden of enforcement.

Where the Commission has taken action in response to a complaint, the person who made that complaint will have the necessary *locus standi* to bring an action challenging the act on the basis of art. 230 (see, e.g., *Timex Corp* v *EC Council and Commission* case 264/82 [1985] 3 CMLR 431). The relevant part of this article is as follows:

Any natural or legal person may, under the same conditions, institute proceedings against . . . a decision which, although in the form of a regulation or a decision addressed to another person, is of direct and individual concern to the former.

The link between these two articles was emphasized in *Guerin Automobiles* v *Commission* case C–282/95P [1997] 5 CMLR 447. The Court of Justice held in *Guerin* that the Commission is obliged to take a decision in a reasonable period of time where it has received a complaint. However, the decision taken may be merely a formal statement that the Commission does not intend to pursue the matter. If the decision is not taken following a complaint, the complainant may rely on art. 232 to enforce the obligation, and may use art. 230 to challenge the decision when it is eventually made. While the case appears slightly to strengthen the position of a complainant beyond that established in *Automec*, in that it emphasizes that the Commission must act definitively, the number of procedural hurdles to be overcome, and the time and cost that this can entail, are likely to be beyond the reach of many applicants. Nevertheless, in *UPS Europe SA* v *Commission* case T–127/98 [2000] 4 CMLR 94, the plaintiff was successful in its art. 232 action.

A successful challenge to a rejection of a complaint was also mounted in *Micro Leader Business* v *Commission* case T–198/98 [2000] 4 CMLR 886. Here the applicant had complained to the Commission about various practices engaged in by Microsoft that restricted the ability of Micro Leader Business to obtain Microsoft products in Canada for resale in the EC. The Court held that the evidence put forward by the complainant was sufficient at least to indicate that there might be an abusive practice, and that the Commission should have examined this part of the complaint more carefully. The Commission's rejection of the complaint was therefore annulled, and the Commission was obliged to consider the complaint again, as well as to pay the costs of the complainant's court action. Similarly, in *Union Francaise de l'Express (UFEX)* v *Commission* case T–77/95 [2001] 4 CMLR 35 the CFI held that the Commission had failed adequately to assess the seriousness and duration of the complained of infringements and had not therefore been in a position to determine whether the Community interest would best be served by pursuing the complaint.

In Regulation 2842/98 1998 OJ L354/18, dealing with hearings and procedures (see Chapter 3), some recognition is made of the fact that third parties may become involved. Here it is provided that

if parties other than those referred to [earlier in the Regulation] apply to be heard and show a sufficient interest, the Commission shall inform them in writing of the nature and subject matter of the procedure, and shall set a date by which they may make their views known in writing'.(art. 9(1)).

It is uncertain what criteria have to be met for a third party falling in this section to show 'a sufficient interest'. A complainant does not have the right to be heard during the oral proceedings (*Kish Glass & Co Ltd* v *Commission* case T–65/96 [2000] 5 CMLR 229, paras 32–3).

5.2.2 **Direct effect and** *Garden Cottage Foods*

Given that there is no direct access to the ECJ other than through the 'judicial review' provisions of the Treaty (arts 230, 232, and 288), the individual plaintiff seeking to rely on EC law must do so through the courts of Member States under the principle of direct effect. When the Treaty of Rome originally entered into force in 1958 it was not clear that it was intended to give rise to such actions on the part of individuals. However, in the landmark case of *NV Algemene Transport-en Expeditie Onderneming Van Gend en Loos* v *Nederlandse Belastingadministratie* case 26/62 [1963] 1 CMLR 105, it was established that where articles of the Treaty are clear, precise, and unconditional they are capable of creating rights vested in individuals which can be enforced against Member States ('vertical direct effect').

In *Defrenne* v *Sabena (No. 2)* case 43/75 [1976] 2 CMLR 98, the principle was extended to allow such rights to be enforced against other persons not being part of the state ('horizontal direct effect'). The principle applies equally to regulations, which are, by the wording of art. 249 'binding in [their] entirety and directly applicable in all Member States'. Both art. 81(1) and (2), and art. 82 meet the criteria for direct effect set out in *Van Gend*. The effect of this then is that an undertaking engaging in conduct that falls within the prohibitions may therefore face actions before national courts by those harmed by that action (see, e.g., *Belgische Radio en Televisie (BRT)* v *Société Belge des Auteurs, Compositeurs et Editeurs (SABAM)* case 127/ 73 [1974] 2 CMLR 238). The case of *Francovich* v *Italian Republic* cases C 6 and 9/90 [1993] 2 CMLR 66, in which it was established that a Member State becomes liable for its breaches of Community law to those who can show harm as a result of the breach where an identifiable right has been infringed, and should then compensate accordingly, placed further emphasis on the place of remedies in the Community legal order.

The most important case in the United Kingdom dealing with these issues in relation to competition law is that of *Garden Cottage Foods Ltd* v *Milk Marketing Board* [1983] 2 All ER 770, HL. The plaintiff was a distributor of butter sold in bulk that obtained its supplies from the defendant, and then made a profit by distributing the butter to purchasers elsewhere in the Community. The plaintiff, over the relevant period, made 90 per cent of its purchases from the defendant, and made 95 per cent of its sales to a single Dutch company. In March 1982, the defendant, which was a statutory body and undeniably in possession of a dominant position in the market in England and Wales, announced a new sales policy. The effect of this was that it would in the future sell bulk butter to only four companies, which did not include the plaintiff. The result of this decision was that the plaintiff would in the future be required to pay more for any butter that it obtained. The substance of the case revolved around the issue of whether an injunction would be granted to restrain the defendant from altering its selling practices. At the Court of Appeal an injunction had been granted ([1982] 3 All ER 292, CA) and this decision was reversed by the House of Lords. What was important in this case was not the approach of the Court to the granting of an injunction in competition cases, although that is a matter of note, but the *obiter dictum* of Lord Diplock relating to the duty imposed by art. 82. His Lordship, first referring to the judgment of the ECJ in *BRT* v *SABAM*, suggested that

The rights which the article confers on citizens in the United Kingdom accordingly fall within section 2(1) of the [European Communities Act 1972]. They are without further enactment to be given legal effect in the United Kingdom and enforced accordingly.

A breach of the duty imposed by article [82] not to abuse a dominant position in the Common Market or in a substantial part of it can thus be categorised in English law as a breach of statutory duty that is imposed not only for the purpose of promoting the general economic prosperity of the Common Market but also for the benefit of private individuals in whom loss or damage is caused by a breach of that duty.

If this categorisation be correct, and I can see none other that would be capable of giving rise to a civil cause of action in English private law on the part of a private individual who sustained loss or damage by reason of a breach of a directly applicable provision of the EEC Treaty, the nature of the cause of action cannot, in my view, be affected by the fact that the legislative provision by which the duty is imposed takes the negative form of a prohibition of particular kinds of conduct rather than the positive form of an obligation to do particular acts. (pp. 775–6)

This is now generally accepted as the correct position, although there has been inevitable debate about the characterization of the right of action as being one for breach of statutory duty. In practice this pigeon-holing of the action, which is a consequence of the dualist approach taken by the United Kingdom to international law, is of little significance, and the route taken to obtain a Community-derived remedy is less important than the fact that the remedy is available.

It remains the case that there has been no reported action in the United Kingdom in which a party has successfully sued for damages on the basis of Community competition law. In fact, it was not until the summer of 1997 that there was *any* reported case of damages being obtained before a Community national court on the basis of a breach of either, art. 81 or art. 82. The position altered when British Telecom obtained an order for compensation from the German courts following an allegedly unlawful implementation by Deutsche Telekom and France Telecom of a joint venture before they had complied with conditions set by the EC

Commission. This decision, which was not reported, was immediately appealed by the defendants (see (1997) *In Competition*, 3 June).

There are difficulties in pursuing cases in national courts. One of these is that the courts in the United Kingdom have shown themselves to be generally reluctant to deal with the economic issues that competition law raises (see Chapter 18 for the approach taken by the courts under common law) and have little expertise in this area. Another is that the courts are understandably reluctant to contribute to a multiplicity of actions. In *MTV Europe* v *BMG Records (UK) Ltd* ((1995) 17 July, CA (unreported)) the plaintiff was seeking damages for an alleged breach of arts 81 and 82 and was at the same time pressing a complaint before the EC Commission. The defendant succeeded in persuading the Court of Appeal to confirm the decision of the judge at first instance delaying proceedings at least until the Commission had considered the matter.

National courts are encouraged to apply competition law themselves in the *Notice on Cooperation between National Courts and the Commission* ((1993) OJ C39/6)), in which the Commission makes clear its view that there are strong advantages to claimants in taking this course. In particular the Commission points out that:

(a) it is unable to award damages to injured parties;

(b) national courts can order interim measures;

(c) national and EC-based claims may be combined before national courts; and

(d) the national court may be able to award costs to the successful plaintiff.

The Commission recognizes that it in turn 'has a duty of sincere cooperation *vis-à-vis* judicial authorities of the Member States' (para. 33) and that if national courts require assistance from the Commission they may, to the extent that national law permits, ask the Commission for certain information in order to assist the court (para. 37).

National courts ruling on directly effective Community law may also have recourse to the art. 234 EC procedure. This provides a formal link between any court or tribunal in a Member State and the ECJ:

The Court of Justice shall have jurisdiction to give preliminary rulings concerning:

(a) the interpretation of this Treaty;

(b) the validity and interpretation of acts of the institutions of the Community.

Where such a question is raised before any court or tribunal of a Member State, that court or tribunal may, if it considers that a decision on the question is necessary to enable it to give judgment, request the Court of Justice to give a ruling thereon.

Where any such question is raised in a case pending before a court or tribunal of a Member State against whose decisions there is no judicial remedy under national law, that court or tribunal shall bring the matter before the Court of Justice.

The article, the purpose of which is to restrict the scope for divergence in the application of EC law by national courts and to facilitate the availability of Community law rights, does not serve as an appeal process—questions must be asked in the abstract and the answers provided by the ECJ are unlikely to be such as to determine the outcome of the case on the facts. The jurisdiction of the CFI does not extend to art. 234 references (art. 225(1)), all references being made directly to the ECJ. Domestic courts have shown themselves to be willing to make references in competition cases. Article 10 EC would be applicable were they reluctant to do so; the courts, being emanations of the state to which the duties of art. 10 are addressed, are equally bound to cooperate in the application of Community law.

A problem that is particularly noticeable in domestic law is that established case law makes it difficult to obtain injunctions in relation to competition law matters. The criteria for the granting of injunctions set out in *American Cyanimid Co.* v *Ethicon Ltd* [1975] AC 396, HL, mean, *inter alia*, that injunctions will not be granted where damages are an adequate remedy. This was clearly a problem for the plaintiff in *Garden Cottage Foods*. It should be noted that the view of the EC Commission, expressed in para. 11 of the *Notice on Cooperation* is that injunctions should be readily available.

While some commentators have called for the Commission to promulgate a directive on remedies, introducing what would be a welcome level of harmonization and certainty, this proposal has been resisted by the Competition Directorate.

5.3 United Kingdom law

5.3.1 The Competition Act 1998

Third-party rights have not been a traditional feature of the competition law regime of the United Kingdom, although the original common law developments grew out of a rights-based jurisprudence (the common law developments and rights are considered in Chapter 18). In a Department of Trade and Industry consultation document, 'Tackling Cartels and the Abuse of Market Power' (March 1996), the following passage appeared at para. 6.15:

the government [then Conservative] believes that the part played by private actions will grow over time to form a significant part of the enforcement system. The threat of such actions, with the risk of damages, would add to the deterrent effect of the new system.

Such comments were inspired by long-term criticisms of the difficulties faced by third parties seeking recompense for harm done to them by anti-competitive activity.

This was an important factor in the shaping of the new regime, and attention was drawn to this during the progress of the Bill:

The current regime under the Fair Trading Act needs strengthening. It does little to deter dominant firms from abusing their position. Worse, serious anti-competitive behaviour can continue unchecked while lengthy investigations are conducted. A period of nine years is not unknown. As a result firms can sometimes be driven out of business unfairly before abuses can be investigated and stopped. Consumers and competitors who are harmed by such abuses have no redress or right to compensation . . . the [1998] Act will give businesses and consumers effective rights of redress. (Lord Simon, Hansard (HL) 30 October 1997, col. 1146)

5.3.1.1 *Third-party involvement in public enforcement*

There are some provisions in the Act that allow for specific consideration of third-party interests. Chief of these is s. 35, which provides that the Director may impose interim measures if 'it is necessary for him to act under this section as a matter of urgency for the purpose:—(a) of preventing serious, irreparable damage to a particular person'. Generally the involvement of third parties in the Act's procedures will be limited to that of making representations to the Director complaining about anti-competitive conduct, and the circumstances in which third parties may be involved in the proceedings are restricted.

Section 47 provides that third parties who can show a sufficient interest in certain decisions taken by the Director 'may apply to the Director asking him to withdraw or vary a decision'. Where the Director decides that the person lacks sufficient interest, or that there is no reason to vary or withdraw his decision, the applicant may appeal to the Competition Commission (s. 47(6)). *Locus standi* under these provisions is significantly wider than is the case under art. 230 EC and is intended in part to address the concerns of groups such as the National Consumer Council (NCC) that had argued for the specific appointment of a consumer representative within the OFT, to represent consumer interests during the process of investigation and evaluation of potentially unlawful conduct. The decisions that may be challenged by third parties are those falling within s. 46(3), paras (a)–(f), *viz*:

    (a) as to whether the Chapter I prohibition has been infringed,
    (b) as to whether the Chapter II prohibition has been infringed,
    (c) as to whether to grant an individual exemption,
    (d) in respect of an individual exemption,
        (i)   as to whether to impose any condition or obligation under section 4(3)(a) or 5(1)(c),
        (ii) where such a condition or obligation has been imposed, as to the condition or obligation,
        (iii) as to the period fixed under section 4(3)(b), or
        (iv) as to the date fixed under section 4(5),
    (e) as to—
        (i)   whether to extend the period for which an individual exemption has effect, or
        (ii) the period of any such extension,
    (f) cancelling an exemption . . .

Opposition members of the House suggested that appeals by third parties should be to the CC, not to the Director. The Government's view was that this might be overly cumbersome and restrictive where, for example, a third party merely wanted to bring further matters to the attention of the Director. The decision to allow actions by representative third parties, as well as by individuals who have been directly harmed, was also challenged. However, the arguments in favour of this step are overwhelming. As noted at the beginning of this chapter, individual consumers are unlikely to have sufficient incentives or the resources to bring matters forward. Permitting actions by groups such as the NCC and Consumers Association (CA), will greatly enhance the role of the consumer in the process.

Other provisions are designed to allow third parties to comment at various stages of proceedings. Thus, for example, sch. 5, para. 5, requires the Director either to publish the intention of granting an individual exemption or, where it is more appropriate to do so, to seek information from 'one or more particular persons other than the applicant'.

5.3.1.2 *Private actions in the courts*

In the draft Bill published by the Department of Trade and Industry in August 1997, the provision of third-party rights appeared to be more restricted than some had hoped would be the case. Third-party actions were to be admitted only following non-compliance with a direction issued by the Director. Thus cl. 31(1)(a) provided that where any person had failed, without reasonable excuse, to comply with a direction 'his default is actionable by any person who suffers loss or damage which is attributable to it'. This limited provision was then dropped from the Bill, and the Act makes no explicit provision at all for third-party actions based on its terms. Section 34, as cl. 31 became, now merely provides that where a person fails to comply with a direction 'the Director may apply to the court for an order . . .'. However, in the debate on the Bill, Lord Simon for the government expressed his view that the cumulative effect of these provisions was still such as to allow rights to injured third parties, noting that the Bill included 'provisions to facilitate rights of private action in the courts for damages' (Hansard (HL) 30 October 1997, col. 1148). Later, in response to a direct challenge at the Committee stage, Lord Simon confirmed that 'it is true that third parties have rights to seek damages in the courts as a result of actions held there' (Hansard (HL) 17 November 1997, col 456). Section 58 of the Act makes oblique reference to third-party actions, in providing that the Director's factual findings are, in most situations, binding in respect of proceedings relating to the prohibitions brought by parties 'otherwise than by the Director'. Further explanation of this point was made at the end of the Committee stage, with the government providing important clarification:

third parties have a right of private action. Our clear intention in framing this Bill is that third parties may seek injunctions or damages in the courts if they have been adversely affected by the action of undertakings in breach of the prohibitions. This is an important element of the regime. There is no need to make explicit provision in the Bill to achieve that result. Third party rights of action under the domestic regime are to be the same as those under articles [81 and 82]. (Hansard (HL) 25 November 1997, col. 955)

A limited confirmation of this principle was then inserted in the Act near the end of its passage, and s. 60 (see further Chapter 16) which requires domestic law to be interpreted consistently with EC law, includes a specific reference to 'civil liability of an undertaking for harm caused by its infringement of Community law'.

It is thus recognized in the Office of Fair Trading (OFT) guideline on *Enforcement* that:

Third parties who consider that they have suffered loss as a result of any unlawful agreement or conduct have a claim for damages in the courts. Section 60 provides for the United Kingdom authorities to handle cases in such a way as to ensure consistency with Community law, and expressly refers to decisions of the European Court and the European Commission as to the civil liability of an undertaking for harm caused by its infringement of Community law. (para. 5.1, and see s. 60(6)(b))

5.3.1.3 Private actions taken

As of May 2002 a limited number of private actions had been reported under the Act, and none of these was an unqualified success for the complainant. The first reported case was brought on the basis of an alleged breach of the Chapter II Prohibition (*Claritas (UK) Ltd* v *The Post Office and Postal Preference Service Ltd* [2001] UKCLR 2) was unsuccessful when the Court found that the alleged abuse had not taken place on a 'relevant market for the purposes of s. 18' and dismissed the application. However, the OFT later found that there was a relevant market, and stressed that 'in order to establish an infringement of the Chapter II Prohibition it is not necessary to show an abuse on the market which an undertaking dominates' (*Consignia plc and Postal Preference Service Limited* CA98/4/2001 [2001] UKCLR 846—following *Tetra Pak International SA* v *EC Commission* case C–333/94P [1997] 4 CMLR 662).

In *Synstar Computer Services (UK) Ltd* v *ICL (Sorbus) Ltd and International Computers Ltd* [2001] UKCLR 585 there was an allegation that a software maintenance contract system maintained by the defendant was in breach of both the Chapter I Prohibition and the Chapter II Prohibition. The complainant had also made a complaint to the OFT, and the Court stayed the proceedings pending the outcome of the OFT investigation which it was considered likely would be appealed to the CCAT. All parties in the case recognized that the CCAT was better equipped to deal with the sensitive issues, and in particular market definition, which this case was likely to revolve around. The OFT subsequently made a finding that there had been no breach of the Act, and no appeal was made to the CCAT (*ICL/Synstar* CA98/6/2001 [2001] UKCLR 902).

More substantial arguments were developed in *Hendry and others* v *The World Professional Billiards and Snooker Association Ltd* [2002] UKCLR 5. Here the claimants were snooker players and a company incorporated for the purpose of exploiting the Internet in relation to snooker. They argued that World Professional Billiards and Snooker Association (WPBSA) rules were in breach of both the Act's prohibitions. The Court found that Rule A5 of the WPBSA rules was in breach and was void. Rule A5 provided in part that 'members shall not enter or play in any snooker tournament, event or match without the prior written consent of the Board'. The Court found that this may not have been intended to restrict competition, but that its effect was to do so, by limiting the sources of income to which players could have access. Damages sought by the claimants were not awarded however as the bulk of the claim was dismissed.

5.3.2 **The Fair Trading Act 1973**

Under the Fair Trading Act 1973. s. 93(2) provides that a civil action can be brought in the case of a breach, or anticipated breach, by any party of an order made against that party under ss. 56, 73, 74, or 89 of the Act. The most important of these provisions, s. 56, allows for the making of an order by the appropriate Minister so as to give effect to any recommendations of the Competition Commission (CC) following a monopoly reference. Sections 73 and 74 relate to orders made in relation to mergers, and s. 89 to interim orders made under restricted circumstances. Third-party actions can similarly be brought following the breach or apprehended breach of any undertaking accepted by the Secretary of State or other appropriate Minister. A consequence of this approach is that under the Act it would be possible for a business to pursue an aggressive course of anti-competitive conduct designed to injure a rival, knowing that such conduct would be likely to be condemned following examination by the Director or the CC, and yet not owe any remedy to the injured party. Damages would become available only in situations where conduct was made subject to an order under the Act, and then where a breach nevertheless continued, to the detriment of a third party. In extreme cases companies were driven out of business during the course of CC enquiries, yet they would have no recompense. Given the applicability of the Competition Act 1998 such a position should no longer arise.

5.4 **Conclusion**

While it has been already established that those injured by anti-competitive conduct in the United Kingdom will be able to recover damages on the basis of Community law where the relevant criteria are fulfilled, the extent to which the Competition Act 1998 allows third parties effective redress remains to be tested. It will be an unsatisfactory position if better rights are available on the basis of Community law than on the basis of national law. Neither the EC Commission nor the OFT has the necessary resources to address all matters brought to their attention, and the competition law regime will, in both cases, be better enforced if injured third parties have a significant stake in the process. It is to be hoped that as the principles of competition law become increasingly familiar additional credence is given to individual rights in the system, following, to a limited extent, the vigorous American model.

6

An introduction to the economics of agreements, collusion, and parallel conduct

6.1 Introduction

Multi-firm conduct is often a more difficult phenomenon to analyse and to identify than is single firm or monopoly conduct. It is dealt with in this book ahead of unilateral conduct because that is the order in which the EC Treaty deals with them. At the most general level the point is simply made: if a single firm can damage the market and produce unwelcome welfare effects, then so too can a group of firms which act together *as if* they were a single firm. This is known as the 'cartel', or 'cartelization'. The difficulty inherent in the economic analysis of multilateral conduct has meant that the legal response in the EC and UK is to attack such situations either where observed market conduct is indicative of anti-competitive behaviour, or where physical evidence, such as documents and communications, shows that firms have attempted, even if unsuccessfully, to coordinate conduct. Legislation in this area usually makes reference to 'agreements, decisions, or concerted practices' between firms. In practice the distinction is often not made, and in this chapter the word 'agreement' is taken to apply to all three situations.

6.2 Horizontal restraints

The issue of horizontal agreements, which is to say agreements between firms at the same level of production or distribution, will in most cases be of concern to authorities, as the inevitable tendency of such agreements is to approximate the circumstances of monopolistic competition, and such agreements will be often proscribed. Thus in America one of the long-standing rules of antitrust is that price fixing is to be condemned per se, and is not brought within the 'rule of reason' (*United States v Trans-Missouri Freight Association* 166 US 290 (1897)). Even where the ostensible purpose of such agreements is apparently benign, such as to agree standards or to harmonize technology, the underlying purpose may in fact be anti-competitive. The attainment of monopoly pricing by a cartel is likely to be accompanied by more deleterious effects than in the case of a true monopoly; a group of smaller firms is unlikely to have attained the efficiencies of production that flow from a monopolist's economies of scale. Cartels and collusion are discussed in Bishop, S., and Walker, M., *The Economics of EC Competition Law*, London, Sweet & Maxwell (1999) (hereinafter *The Economics of EC Competition Law*), paras 4.06–4.23.

6.2.1 The problem of oligopoly

In atomistic markets where there are a great number of competitors, agreements between firms operating at the same level of production are unlikely to be of concern to competition authorities (although note that in *Vereniging van Samenwerkende Prijsregelende Organisaties in de Bouwnijverheid (SPO) v Commission* case T–29/92 [1995] ECR–II 289 an investigation into the Dutch building industry involved thousands of undertakings). Much effort would be required to put an agreement in place, and in the absence of a mechanism to punish firms that broke the agreement—which would be illegal in any regime—cheating would be inevitable. The more concentrated the market is, the more likely it is that the firms will be able successfully to agree to dampen or restrict competition. An oligopolistic market is one in which only a few firms compete, or in which a few firms hold the bulk of the market power, albeit with numbers of smaller competitors at the periphery (banking, petrol, etc.). It is in these markets, where business managers may be unable to resist 'a bit of corporate nookie' (Lord Lucas, Hansard (HL) 30 October 1997, col. 1161), that competition concerns arise most readily. A problem for any authority or plaintiff becomes that of distinguishing between conduct which is based on agreements, whether formal or informal, and conduct which is the result of each firm responding rationally to the actions of the others. For example, if petrol prices generally rise by the same margin within a short time, is that because the companies have agreed to raise their prices together, or because once one company does so it makes sense for the others to follow suit? The MMC has consistently held that the petrol market in the UK is competitive, in spite of public concerns to the contrary (see, e.g., Cm. 972, *The Supply of Petrol* (1990)).

It was early suggested by the economist Cournot, in 1838, that, even assuming *independent decisions* made by oligopolists, prices in such markets would be higher than in perfectly competitive markets, and such markets can achieve what is now referred to as a 'Nash–Cournot equilibrium'. Distinguishing between the anticipated higher price of oligopolistic industry and 'artificially' maintained higher prices is one of the central problems facing competition authorities.

6.2.2 Cartels

A cartel may be defined as 'an explicit arrangement designed to eliminate competition' (Kaserman, D. L., and Mayo, J. H., *Government and Business: The economics of antitrust and regulation*, Fort Worth, The Dryden Press (1995), p. 152). Cartels are attractive to participants: if the cartel succeeds, total profits to the participants will be higher than would be the sum of individual profits in what would otherwise be a competitive market. A perfect cartel would be one in which the group as a whole set production where marginal cost for the group equalled marginal revenue, which is to say that the cartel would collectively behave exactly like a single-firm monopoly. In practice such perfection will be unobtainable.

For the EC Commission the danger of cartels is that they

generate situation rents for the most powerful companies since they need not make an effort either to improve the quality of their products or to improve productivity. At the same time, however, cartels artificially keep the least efficient companies in the market, weaken the productive apparatus and thus inflict considerable damage on the economy in general and eventually also on EU jobs.   (IP (98) 1068, 3 December 1998 [1999] 4 CMLR 13)

The example of a cartel that is most often used in economics texts is that of the Organization of Petroleum Exporting Countries (OPEC), which for a time successfully controlled the world market in oil. Even here, in a situation in which the participants, being sovereign nations, were not subject to the rigours of national antitrust laws, the cartel was unable to raise prices to the level that would have been obtained under a monopoly situation. The challenge for antitrust enforcement with respect to cartels is to exacerbate the inherent weaknesses in order either to make membership so unattractive as to force the abandonment of the cartel, or to minimize the effects of the anti-competitive arrangements.

There are two major problems that economists have identified as facing any cartel: these may be characterized as the problems of 'agreement' and 'adherence'. In the mid-1950s emphasis was placed on the difficulties cartel members would have in agreeing on matters of fundamental policy, such as the correct response to make to a new entrant, or the trade-off between short- and long-term profits. One researcher identified a cartel where prices had not changed for 10 years, in spite of rising costs, because the two largest members which were able to block any changes preferred to maintain low prices to keep new entrants out of the market (Fog, B., 'How are Cartel Prices Determined' (1956) 5 *Journal of Industrial Economics* 16). There are several factors that make it difficult for cartels to reach agreement. For example, product differentiation will require cartel members to agree on what may be a very complex price schedule, rather than a single price. This was a problem for OPEC, as oil is not a homogeneous product but is produced at different grades with different sulphur contents. Differences in the costs facing firms in the industry will also make agreement harder: larger firms in the cartel, which are more likely to benefit from economies of scale, may want lower prices than the smaller firms, and it may become difficult to put into place arrangements acceptable to all to limit production.

Once the agreement problem is overcome, the second, more significant, problem relates to adherence. The problem facing cartels is as follows:

If a cartel is successful in restricting its joint output and raising price, it creates an incentive for individual member firms to cheat, expand their outputs, and undermine the cartel. A *single* firm will always profit by cheating on the cartel. But *all* firms have this same incentive, and if all firms expand their output, the cartel breaks down. On this reasoning, cartels are inherently unstable. (Martin, S., *Industrial Economics: Economic Analysis and Public Policy*, MacMillan, 2nd edn (1994), p. 162)

The position may be explained by reference to game theory, on which most cartel/oligopoly models are now based. Game theory, which was developed by John von Neumann and Oskar Morgenstern (*Theory of Games and Economic Behaviour*, Princeton, Princeton UP (1944)), is, at its most elaborate, incredibly complex, but a simple demonstration will show how the problem may be addressed. A branch of game theory deals with the 'Prisoner's Dilemma' which can be related to the behaviour of two competing oligopolists. Consider the following situation: Eileen and Stuart rob an off-licence; they are arrested by Susan, who is convinced of their guilt but does not have the evidence to obtain a conviction unless she can obtain a confession. Susan does have the evidence to obtain convictions on a lesser charge of dangerous driving, and if convicted of this offence both the prisoners will go to prison for one year. If either one of the prisoners confesses and is prepared to testify against the other, that prisoner will receive no gaol term at all and the other will go to prison for 10 years. If both prisoners confess each will go to prison for five years. The prisoners are held separately in the police station and do not have the opportunity to coordinate their conduct. The resulting strategic position therefore looks like this:

		Eileen's strategies	
		Don't confess	Confess
Stuart's strategies	Don't confess	−1, −1	−10, 0
	Confess	0, −10	−5, −5

(For example, if Stuart does not confess, and Eileen does, Stuart faces 10 years in prison, and Eileen none.)

In this position the combined welfare of the parties dictates that neither should confess, and both will go to prison for one year. The incentive for each of the parties to break the fraternal criminal bond and grass on the other is strong, but of course if both do this then each faces a longer prison sentence than if each had remained silent. Only if the two prisoners can exchange information during the process, and are prepared to forgo some short-term benefit in order to improve their collective position, can it be assured that the outcome will be optimal to the two. If two companies are substituted for Eileen and Stuart, and profit figures for the prison sentences, the game becomes applicable to a two-firm cartel situation.

Finding physical, documentary evidence of the existence of cartels is a difficult matter. Baroness O'Caithan drew attention in the Lords to a case resolved by the RPC:

The paint-makers' price fixing cartel, which was ended by an undertaking to the [RPC] in early June [1997] had been going on for years. It was quite obvious that the companies involved knew exactly what they were doing and knew it was illegal. Why else would they have used assumed names to book hotel conference facilities? (Hansard (HL) October 30 1997, col. 1167)

The problem in the UK was compounded under the old regime by the OFT's limited powers of investigation and the lack of deterrent penalties. Given the difficulties of establishing the existence of such cartels, a tactic employed by most authorities is to implement measures designed to destabilize cartels.

Analysis of the instability of cartels is based largely on pioneering work done by George J. Stigler ('A Theory of Oligopoly' (1964) 72 *Journal of Political Economy* 44). Stigler focused on the fact that much of the conduct in a cartel will be furtive, and that a poor flow of information will mean that strategic activity is carried out largely on the basis of conjecture and guesswork. A price-cutting firm is unlikely to announce the fact, and published prices may reflect no change at all. Instead any price cuts are likely to be agreed discreetly with customers. In a cartel situation firms will in any case be facing a reduced demand as price rises with the implementation of the cartel, and it will be difficult for firms to determine if demand reductions are the result of this inevitable process or the cheating of other members. Firms will also be used to a variation in sales, and only if the reduction is below their expectations may they suspect cheating. Stigler's results show that the greater the number of firms in the cartel, the greater is the likelihood of cheating being able to go undetected. On the other hand, if firms are able to pool their information the probability of detection of any cheating rises dramatically. It is then clear that one of the tasks of competition policy is to make such information exchange risky, and in all regimes the availability of hard physical evidence of cartelization is likely to bring swift condemnation.

The prediction that there is an inverse relationship between numbers in cartels and the likely success of cartels is a logical one. In a cartel with 15 members there is a total of 105 paired relationships between members. This rises to 190 relationships in a cartel of 20 members, and 1,225 in a cartel with 50 members (formally the number of paired relationships is given by $N(N-1)/2$). Only if a central control mechanism, normally through a trade association, can be established are larger cartels ever likely to be successful. The activities of trade associations tend to be closely scrutinized by competition authorities. A survey of antitrust actions against cartels taken in the United States found that where only a few firms were involved, and the market conditions were relatively uncomplicated, there were few instances of formally structured collusion. In 606 cases studied the mean number of participants was just under 17, and as the number of participants in each case increased, so too did the complexity of the arrangements that were put in place to facilitate the success of the cartel (Fraas, A. G. and Greer, D. F., 'Market Structure and Price Collusion: An Empirical Analysis' (1977) 26 *Journal of Industrial Economics* 21).

6.2.3 **Price leadership**

It can be difficult to distinguish between cartels in which prices are maintained across a range of producers or suppliers, and other situations in which price leadership is present. Markham distinguished three categories of price leadership, none of which is likely to be condemned by competition authorities without further evidence of actual collusion (Markham, J. W., 'The Nature and Significance of Price Leadership', (1951) 41 *American Economic Review* 891).

Dominant firm leadership occurs where in any market one firm is sufficiently large in relation to other producers to be the only one capable of significantly affecting the market. In such a case the dominant firm is likely to set prices as if it were a monopolist, and the smaller firms will have little to gain from diverging much from this price. Competition law will accept such situations, and does not require firms to price at what would be irrational levels in order to maintain a fiction of vigorous price competition.

Barometric price leadership is more complex, and is a characteristic of markets in which the price leader changes frequently, and in which the response to any change in price tends to be less swift than in the situation where there is a single dominant firm. Whether a price will be followed will depend not on the identity of the company setting the price, but on whether the change, even if set by a small company, reflects a generally perceived need in the market for a price adjustment. This was considered to be the case by the EC Commission in *Zinc producer group* 84/405 (1984) OJ L220/27.

The third situation, which poses the greatest problem for competition law, arises in markets where the product is homogenous, and where there are few producers facing similar costs. Here any one firm would accurately reflect the situation facing each firm, and it is likely that any one firm choosing to adopt a price leadership role would be followed. Conditions similar to these may be found in the United Kingdom in the banking and petrol industries, although the position in the petrol market is changing following the entrance into the market of supermarket chains.

In *Industrial Market Structure and Economic Performance*, Frederic Scherer and David Ross set out some interesting case studies of price leadership (Boston, Houghton Mifflin, 3rd edn (1990), pp. 250–60).

6.3 **Vertical restraints**

In the case of most goods, and some services, there is a chain of production before the product reaches the consumer. Typically this will extend from the gathering of the raw material, and its first processing, to the retailer with whom the customer deals. Thus, for example, in the case of the motor industry the vertical chain begins with steel and plastics manufactures, through the various stages of production of components and the cars themselves, to distributors and individual retailers. A vertical agreement is one between firms at different stages of the chain of production, and it will be immediately apparent that this is an essential and pervasive feature of commercial life. In the absence of vertical agreements the raw material would not arrive at the manufacturer's plant, and the finished car would not end up on a garage forecourt. A vertical agreement is to some extent a substitute for vertical integration. It was a matter of some surprise, therefore, when the EEC Commission, as it then was, attacked an agreement between a manufacturer and a distributor as being anti-competitive in a very early competition decision (*Re Grundig* 64/556/EEC [1964] 1 CMLR 489; on appeal *Establissements Consten SARL and Grundig-Verkaufs-GmbH* v *Commission* cases 56 and 58/64 [1966] CMLR 418; see further discussion of this case in the following chapter). Concerns as to the effects of vertical restraints have also underpinned several MMC and OFT inquiries, including, for example, that into *Foreign Package Holidays*, completed in 1997. The question whether verti- cal restraints are anti-competitive remains a matter of debate, with the Chicago school in the 1980s arguing broadly that any and all vertical restraints should be legal, although the authors of the Commission Green Paper (below) note that a consensus is emerging, with economists being reluctant to generalize in what is a difficult area, and both the UK and EC authorities continue to examine the issue. In 1996 the OFT published its 12th Research Paper 'Vertical Restraints in Competition Policy' (Dobson, P. W., and Waterson, M.; and see also Bond, C., 'Vertical Restraints', (1997) *Fair Trading*, Summer, p. 7), and in early 1997 the EC Commis- sion published its *Green Paper on Vertical Restraints in EC Competition Policy* (COM(96) 721 final; for subsequent developments, see the following chapter). The UK regime's view of vertical restraints is less hostile than that of the EC, and the great majority of such arrangements are excluded from the operation of the Competition Act 1998.

Broadly, the argument made in favour of examining vertical restraints is that while they may encourage inter-brand competition, for example competition between Nissan and Toyota cars, they may restrict intra-brand competition, for example competition between two sellers of Nissan cars.

If vertical restraints or agreements are to be considered a problem, the analysis must take into account situations in which firms at the lower level of the chain, nearer consumers, exercise power over firms higher up the chain. Thus the OFT report recognizes that retailers hold increasing power in setting the contract terms on which they will deal with suppliers, and suggests that competition concerns may be raised where either party in the chain is in possession of market power. The threefold consideration put forward in the report is as follows:

(a) Is there horizontal market power at either the level of manufacturer or the level of retailer?

(b) Is the consumer likely to be significantly affected by the restriction?

(c) Is the result of the restriction to generate efficiency gains?

If the answer to (a) is in the affirmative then consideration of (b) and (c) may allow a determination of whether the restriction is against the public interest. Even if the answer to (b) and (c) would be in the affirmative, the authors conclude that in the absence of horizontal market power there is unlikely to be any benefit from conducting further examination of the practice for anti-competitive effects.

It is a common assumption that vertical restraints are necessarily imposed to benefit the party higher up the chain of production, but this is not always the case. One of the strongest forms of vertical restraint is resale price maintenance (RPM), under which resellers are restricted in their ability to set prices. Usually the manufacturer or supplier specifies a minimum price below which the reseller may not sell the product. It is not easy to create scenarios in which this operates to the benefit of the supplier, and the immediate beneficiary tends to be the retailer. These sorts of restraints therefore may be requested by retailers, and are a particularly effective way to ensure that cheating is minimized in price-fixing cartels. It is perhaps in response to this possibility that, until the Competition Act 1998, the taking of any steps to enforce RPM was the only activity condemned per se in the UK regime. Chicagoan economists have argued that this supposition cannot be correct as there will be too much competition at the retail level to allow the retailers to impose conditions on those supplying to them. This conclusion is probably wrong, and it has been pointed out by Porter that retailers tend to operate in oligopolistic markets because they are dependent in turn on the ability of local customers to travel to them (Porter, M. E., *Interbrand Choice, Strategy, and Bilateral Market Power*, Cambridge Mass, Harvard UP (1976)).

Vertical restraints are discussed in *The Economics of EC Competition Law*, paras 4.24–4.40.

7

Article 81

1. The following shall be prohibited as incompatible with the common market: all agreements between undertakings, decisions by associations of undertakings and concerted practices which may affect trade between Member States and which have as their object or effect the prevention, restriction or distortion of competition within the common market, and in particular those which:

   (a) directly or indirectly fix purchase or selling prices or any other trading conditions;

   (b) limit or control production, markets, technical development, or investment;

   (c) share markets or sources of supply;

   (d) apply dissimilar conditions to equivalent transactions with other trading parties, thereby placing them at a competitive disadvantage;

   (e) make the conclusion of contracts subject to acceptance by the other parties of supplementary obligations which, by their nature or according to commercial usage, have no connection with the subject of such contracts.

2. Any agreements or decisions prohibited pursuant to this Article shall be automatically void.

3. The provisions of paragraph 1 may, however, be declared inapplicable in the case of:

   — any agreement or category of agreements between undertakings;

   — any decision or category of decisions by associations of undertakings;

   — any concerted practice or category of concerted practices;

   which contributes to improving the production or distribution of goods or to promoting technical or economic progress, while allowing consumers a fair share of the resulting benefit, and which does not:

   (a) impose on the undertakings concerned restrictions which are not indispensable to the attainment of these objectives;

   (b) afford such undertakings the possibility of eliminating competition in respect of a substantial part of the products in question.

7.1 Introduction

Article 81 is intended to apply to any conduct, howsoever structured, between two or more undertakings, and is more concerned with the economic impact of a practice than with its legal form. In *La Technique Minière* v *Maschinenbau Ulm GmbH* case 56/65 [1966] 1 CMLR 357, the ECJ held that the condemnation of any restrictive practice will depend 'not so much on its legal nature as on its relations, on the one hand, with "trade between the Member States" and, on the other, with "the play of competition"' (p. 374). Recognizing that the ingenuity of undertakings to devise new ways of structuring or describing arrangements between them knows no bounds, the choice of words is deliberately as wide as possible, and the phrase 'all agreements between undertakings, decisions by associations of undertakings and concerted practices' should be interpreted as extending to any form of multilateral coordinated conduct (see below). Although the article applies to any formally drafted contract, it applies equally to situations where undertakings act in concert with each other by informal means. It is this aspect in particular that makes the application of the article fraught with problems. As we have seen in Chapter 6, in oligopolistic markets it has proven very difficult to distinguish between conduct which is collusive and conduct which is the natural result of the market structure. In this chapter the word 'agreement' is used to apply to all three of these heads unless the discussion is specifically about 'decisions' or 'concerted practices'.

Further problems arise because the prohibition of art. 81(1), which is sufficiently precise as to be directly effective, applies to a great number of contracts entered into by undertakings, and on the face of it would proscribe more beneficial than harmful economic conduct. Many steps have therefore been taken to limit the application of art. 81(1) only to those situations where the conduct identified is harmful, or likely to be harmful: under art. 81(3) agreements may be exempted on an individual case-by-case basis (see below) or en bloc (see Chapter 8) where the somewhat vague criteria are fulfilled, and the ECJ has established that the article does not apply unless the harm caused by the agreement is substantial. The situation thus approximates to, but is not the same as, that in the United States where the 'rule of reason' has been developed to limit the scope of the application of s. 1 of the Sherman Act (see below).

In this chapter the general principles covering art. 81 will be considered; the specific block exemption regulations, which are technical in their draftsmanship and application, will be examined in the next chapter. It is easiest to approach the article by analysing each of its parts, and then by considering its operation as a whole. For the meaning of 'undertaking', see Chapter 2.

7.2 **Article 81(1): the prohibition**

It is immediately apparent that the effect of art. 81 is to make conduct falling within its ambit illegal, and the article may be relied upon by injured competitors. Undertakings in breach are liable to be fined by the Commission, and many of the largest fines handed out have been to those engaged in illicit cartels (see Chapter 4). As noted in the introduction to this chapter, the article is drafted so as to apply to any form of multilateral anti-competitive conduct, and 'has been interpreted so broadly and formalistically that any restriction on the freedom to act has been deemed to fall under the prohibition, irrespective of its impact on competition' (Amato, G., in *Robert Schuman Centre Annual on European Competition Law 1996*, p. 126). The Commission does not always distinguish between the various forms that a breach of the article may take, and indeed in some cases has expressly refused to do so. In *Cartonboard* 94/601 (1994) OJ L74/21, for example, the Commission said that it did not consider it 'necessary, particularly in the case of a complex infringement of long duration, for the Commission to characterise it as exclusively an agreement or concerted practice. Indeed, it may not even be feasible or realistic to make any such distinction' (para. 128). However, the approach taken to evidence of the breach, particularly by the courts, and perhaps to the penalty, may depend on the form that the proscribed conduct takes.

7.2.1 Agreement between undertakings

That any contract between two undertakings may be held to fall within art. 81 is clear, and many distribution, franchise, and service agreements have been examined, modified, and at times condemned. However, 'agreement' does not require that a formal contract be in place, or indeed that any more than one party behaves in a certain manner. The primary requirement of this part of art. 81(1) is that at least two parties must be involved. The article cannot in any circumstance be applied to entirely unilateral conduct.

In *Polypropylene* 86/398 (1986) OJ L230/1, for example, the Commission found that the producers of polypropylene had been party 'to a whole complex of schemes, arrangements and measures decided in the framework of a system of regular meetings and continuous contact' (para. 80). Although the parties contended that no agreement was in place, the Commission held that it was not necessary for it to establish the presence of an agreement 'intended as legally binding upon the parties'. In the Commission's view an agreement exists wherever there is the necessary consensus between the parties 'determining the lines of their mutual action or abstention from action in the market', and it was certainly not necessary for the agreement to be made in writing. This point was emphasized in *National Panasonic* 82/853 (1982) OJ L354/28, where National Panasonic UK somehow managed to operate a dealership system throughout the UK without the benefit of written agreements. The company did not dispute that an agreement existed, and in fact had provided the Commission with evidence of the terms and conditions that it expected dealers to comply with if they were to be admitted into the network.

It has been stressed already that art. 81 cannot apply to unilateral conduct, which may be addressed only if art. 82 is applicable, but there are situations in which it appears as if only one party may be acting. In *Johnson & Johnson* 80/1283 (1980) OJ L377/16, the Commission investigated a situation in which the undertaking and its subsidiaries, including Ortho UK, acted to prevent the export from the UK to Germany of pregnancy-testing kits. In January 1977 Ortho had changed the contracts of sale that applied between it and its dealers so as ostensibly to permit the export of the testing kits within the EC. However, on investigation the Commission found that the company had acted unilaterally in making threats to dealers to withhold supplies, or to delay supplies, if the dealers in fact made exports even within the Community. While it is possible that this conduct could have been attacked under art. 82, the Commission chose to proceed under art. 81 and found that although the action was apparently unilateral the dealers all knew what the position was and that in effect the contracts of sale 'were still, therefore, subject to prohibitions of exports, which prohibitions formed an integral part of agreements within the meaning of art. [81(1)]' (para. 28).

7.2.2 Decisions by associations of undertakings

It is standard practice in many industries for those in the industry to belong to an association that acts on behalf of its member companies. Such actions might include industry-wide promotional compaigns, public education, market research, standards setting, and perhaps even charitable functions on behalf of workers in the industry. These associations may also act as a front for collusive activity: a unilateral statement from the association as to, for example, the desirability of price stability, might be followed by action by all its members, each of them denying that they have in any way colluded with the others.

A classic example of such a situation arose in *Roofing felt* 86/399 (1986) OJ L232/15, where the action taken related primarily to the Cooperative Association of Belgian Asphalters (Belasco) which represented seven members in the industry. The members had collaborated in drawing up an agreement, initially valid for five years but thereafter renewable, which provided for, *inter alia*: bans on bribes to induce customers to choose a particular supplier; joint advertising; and the studying of ways of standardizing and rationalizing the production and distribution of roofing felt. While all of these are laudable aims, and by themselves would have been unlikely to attract the attention of the EC Commission, further objectives set out in the agreement included: the adoption of a price list and minimum prices for all roofing felt supplied in Belgium; the allocation of quotas between members; and penalties for breaches of decisions made under the agreement, which taken together would fall within the prohibition set out in art. 81(1). Although the Commission was able to establish the presence of agreements between the individual members of Belasco, and some outside parties, it pointed too to the role played by Belasco, which it found 'was involved in a number of ways in the operation of the agreement'. In particular, it was Belasco which had managed the quota system, unilaterally employing an accountant for the purpose and administering the compliance mechanism.

Where an association of undertakings is found to exist the steps that it takes do not have to be binding on its members to fall within art. 81(1). If this were to be a requirement avoidance would be all too easy. In *Fire insurance* 85/75 (1985) OJ L35/20 (on appeal *Verband der Sachversicherer eV v EC Commission* case 45/85 [1988] 4 CMLR 264) for example, an association of undertakings was found to exist, but argued in its defence that the 'recommendation' it had made was expressly described as 'non-binding'. However, the Commission was not persuaded to this view and made its position clear:

In spite of the fact, therefore, that the title of the recommendation describes it as being 'non-binding', the recommendation was in the nature of a 'decision' by an association of undertakings within the meaning of Article [81]. It is sufficient for this purpose that the recommendation was brought to the notice of members as a statement of the association's policy.   (para. 23 of the Decision)

Here the association's objective was to represent, promote, and protect the business interests of insurers providing industrial fire insurance in Germany. Following a long period during which insurance premiums in the sector had fallen, although there had been no apparent reduction in the risks being insured or their costs, a recommendation, described as 'non-binding', laid down a collective flat rate and an across-the-board rise in premiums. By its decision taken in 1984 the Commission rejected an application for negative clearance and the association appealed. The Court, taking into account the nature of the recommendation, noted that shortly after it was made the members of the association altered their contracts of reinsurance so as to comply with the recommendation. The statutes of the association gave it the power to coordinate the activities of its members, particularly in relation to competition, and decisions or recommendations taken by a special committee set up under it were deemed to be 'definitive'. In view of these facts the Court held that the recommendation 'regardless of what its precise legal status may be, constituted the faithful reflection of the applicant's resolve to coordinate the conduct of its members . . . it must therefore be concluded that it amounts to a decision of an association of undertakings' (para. 32).

This case was followed by the EC Commission in *Fenex* 96/438 (1996) OJ L181/ 28, in which action was taken against an association of undertakings in the freight market in The Netherlands. The association had, for nearly 100 years, issued 'recommendations' to its members relating to various scales of charges. In its defence the association argued that the recommendations were non-binding and were therefore not 'decisions' within the meaning of art. 81. The Commission noted that: the system had been in existence for a long time; the recommendation was drawn up and updated annually by a specialist body within the association; the recommendation would then be adopted by the board of directors of the association; and it would be published accompanied by a circular drafted in strong terms, such as, for example, 'in view of the result arrived at members are *urgently recommended* to pass on the above mentioned tariff increase [5 per cent] in full' (at para. 38, emphasis added). In the light of these facts the Commission held that 'the recommendation must be interpreted as being the faithful reflection of the association's resolve to coordinate the conduct of its members on the relevant market' (para. 41).

Consistently the Court has expressed concern that the rules governing trade associations should not be more than is necessary to achieve the *legitimate* object-ives of that association. The fact that this was not the case was important in *Gottrup-Klim Grovvareforeninger* v *Dansk Landbrugs Grovvarelskab* case C–250/92 [1996] 4 CMLR 191. Here an association existed that had as its task, facilitating cooperative purchasing of supplies, and the Court held that 'in order to escape the prohibition laid down in Article [81(1)] of the Treaty, the restrictions imposed on members by the statutes [of the association] must be limited to what is necessary [to ensure the legitimate aims of the association]'. There will even be situations in which the rules of a trade association may be such as to make the creation of the association, or membership of it, a breach of art. 81(1) without the need for the Commission to consider the actual operation of the association in practice. This appears to have been the case in *National Sulphuric Acid Association* 80/917 (1980) OJ L260/24, where the Commission indicated that the terms of the association in question were automatically such as to breach art. 81(1) (paras 29–36).

7.2.3 Concerted practices

Concerted practice is perhaps the most nebulous of the three categories and covers a wide range of conduct, ranging from a situation in which an agreement appears to exist but is difficult to establish evidentially, to the very difficult situations in which the conduct that is observable in the market diverges from that which would be expected so as to suggest that firms are in some degree colluding. In an American antitrust case it was pointed out that 'the picture of conspiracy as a meeting by twilight of a trio of sinister persons with pointed hats close together belongs to a darker age' (*William Goldman Theatres Inc.* v *Loew's Inc* 150 F2d 738, 743n. 15 (3rd Cir 1945)) and the modern-day enforcers of competition policy are confronted with companies using a full range of practices by which to coordinate their behaviour, whether by way of conventions held in luxury hotels, unrecorded telephone calls and emails, or apparently innocent market announcements in the press.

The first significant case in which the ECJ dealt with concerted practices was *ICI* v *Commission, 'Dyestuffs'* case 48/69 [1972] CMLR 557, in which it upheld a Com-mission decision where the undertakings were condemned on the basis of evidence of collusion in the setting of prices. The definition of concerted practice applied in that case was approved and expanded on in the next important case, *Suiker Unie* (*Coöperatieve Vereniging 'Suiker Unie' UA* v *Commission* cases 40–48/73, 50/73, 54–56/73, 111/73, 113–114/73 [1976] 1 CMLR 295), when the Court held that

The concept of a 'concerted practice' refers to a form of coordination between undertakings which, without having been taken to the stage where an agreement properly so-called has been concluded, knowingly substitutes for the risks of competition cooperation in practice between them which leads to conditions of competition which do not correspond to the normal conditions of the market, having regard to the nature of the products, the importance and number of the undertakings as well as the size and nature of the said market. Such cooperation in practice amounts to a concerted practice *inter alia* when it enables the persons concerned to consolidate established positions to the detriment of effective freedom of movement of the products in the Common Market and of the freedom of consumers to choose their suppliers. (paras 26–7 of the judgment)

The difficulties of establishing the existence of such a situation are compounded in particular where the market is an oligopolistic one, in which case a degree of similarity of conduct is to be expected: if it is appropriate for one producer to raise its prices it is quite probably appropriate for all to do so. In such a situation it is not the fact that prices have risen at the same time, by possibly the same level, that will induce condemnation under art. 81(1). The task of the Commission is to show that this has been achieved by other than the operation of normal market forces—it is the method, and not the result, that is being condemned. This is made clear by the Court in the *Dyestuffs* case:

while it is permissible for each manufacturer to change his prices freely and to take into account for this purpose the behaviour, present and foreseeable, of his competitors, it is, on the other hand, contrary to the competition rules of the Treaty for a manufacturer to cooperate with his competitors, in whatever manner, to determine a coordinated course of action relating to an increase in prices. (para. 118)

It is exceptionally difficult to distinguish between situations in which an undertaking acts *intelligently* in response to another's conduct (which is quite lawful), and acts *with knowledge* of another's conduct (which may be in breach of art. 81(1)). In *Cimenteries CBR SA v Commission* joined cases T 25–26/95, etc. [2000] 5 CMLR 204 (in summary only) the CFI explained that

The concept of concerted practice implies the existence of reciprocal contacts. That condition is met where one competitor discloses its future intentions or conduct on the market to another when the latter requests it or, at the very least, accepts it. Thus, failure by an applicant to object to or express reservations where a competitor reveals its position regarding the relevant market will deny the former the defence of being a purely passive recipient of information unilaterally passed on without any request on the part of the applicant. (para. 1849)

A similar stance was taken in *Tate & Lyle plc, British Sugar plc and Napier Brown plc v Commission* joined cases T–202/98, etc. [2001] 5 CMLR 22 where the Court held that an undertaking would be implicated in the existence of a concerted practice where it attended a meeting whose purpose was limited 'to the mere receipt of information concerning the future conduct of their market competitors' (para. 58). This would apply even where that information could be obtained through legitimate channels by the undertakings.

In *Zinc producer group* 84/405 (1984) OJ L220/27, the Commission investigated coordination in the market for zinc under an agreement that extended from 1964 to 1977. When the agreement ended in 1977 the market structure meant that there was no one firm that could break ranks and set its own prices independently of the rest of the market. In such a situation, known as 'barometric price leadership' (see Chapter 6), undertakings do not have true economic independence but, in law, are not acting in a concerted fashion where all companies set the same prices. The Commission was careful to isolate this position from that which existed between

1964 to 1977, and did not condemn the undertakings in relation to subsequent conduct, notwithstanding the similarity in behaviour (paras 75–6).

There are, in essence, two ways in which the Commission may attempt to establish the existence of collusive conduct. The first, and most satisfactory, is to collect the physical evidence that supports such a conclusion. Records of meetings, copies of letters, statements by company personnel, and evidence presented by customers may all provide the necessary evidence. Although such evidence may often lead to the conclusion that an agreement is in place it may fall short of the required formality but still be indicative of collusion. An alternative, and more difficult, route is for the Commission to base a case on the analysis of the market in question, arguing that there is a divergence between the conduct that would be predicted under competitive conditions and the conduct observed, and that the only explanation for such a divergence is that the relevant undertakings are colluding. This was the way in which the Commission proceeded in its decision in relation to *Wood pulp* 85/202 (1985) OJ L85/1 (on appeal *Re Wood Pulp Cartel: A Ahlström Oy* v *Commission* cases C 89, 104, 114, 116, 117, and 125–129/85 [1993] 4 CMLR 407; note that at [1988] 4 CMLR 901 the issue of territorial jurisdiction was dealt with—see Chapter 18.

In *Wood Pulp* the Commission took action against 43 undertakings producing bleached sulphate pulp, used in the manufacture of fine quality paper, based in both the Community and other producing states, including Canada and the United States. World-wide about 800 companies produced bleached wood pulp, with over 50 firms selling into the Community. There were a large number of customers based in the Community, and one firm alone supplied about 290 different paper manufacturers. Producers announced prices in advance for the following quarter-year. Such announcements were highly visible and were reported in the specialist trade press, and were likely to be followed quickly by similar announcements from competitors. Over a number of years prices in the Community rose steadily, irrespective of the fact that over some of this period the stocks of pulp held by producers were increasing, and that production costs varied. Prices were also constant irrespective of the source of the product, when it might have been expected that imports from Canada and the United States would be more expensive than those from Scandanavia. The core of the Commission's argument was that

The fact that the addressees of this Decision have coordinated their market conduct contrary to Article [81(1)] of the EEC Treaty is proved by:

— their parallel conduct in the years 1975 to 1981 which, in the light of the conditions obtaining on the market in question and following a proper economic analysis, cannot be explained as independently chosen parallel conduct in a narrow oligopolistic situation . . .

Given the particular competitive conditions obtaining on the pulp market, such uniform market behaviour can be explained only by a concerted practice on the part of the addresses of this Decision.   (paras 82–3)

The factors that the Commission considered to be determinative of the issue included the following:

- the presence on the market of 50 producers and several hundred customers;
- the fact that some of these producers were large enough to pursue an independent competitive policy;
- the wide range of products offered the potential for the introduction of price competition;
- the deliberate creation of a transparent market by the system of early announcements of prices;
- the fact that prices rose evenly and uniformly, with none of the divergences that would be expected were the firms moving independently towards a new equilibrium price;
- the uniform approach to prices could not be explained by the presence of a single market leader, as no company held this position;
- the absence of any explanation of the rapid spread of price information across products, companies, and countries;
- coincidence was ruled out; and
- prices bore little relationship to fluctuations in costs.

Following the imposition of fines, and the negotiation of an undertaking with which the Commission would be satisfied, several of the companies appealed to the ECJ. The Court's rejection of the Commission's main arguments was robust. The question whether the mere system of price announcements denounced by the Commission could itself constitute an infringement of art. 81(1) was rejected by the Court. The stance taken by the Court was that each individual price announcement was made by a producer to a consumer or consumers, and not to other producers. This being so, no one announcement would 'lessen each undertaking's uncertainty as to the future attitude of its competitors' (para. 64 of the judgment). There was, the Court suggested, no guarantee that any one price announcement would be followed by that undertaking's competitors. In fact the announcement could result in a competitor taking the opportunity to announce a lower, more competitive price. The fact that 'the Commission [had] no documents which directly establish the existence of concertation between the producers concerned' meant that the Court took a rigorous approach to the conclusion reached by the Commission. The key paragraphs in the judgment are as follows:

In determining the probative value of those different factors, it must be noted that *parallel conduct cannot be regarded as furnishing proof of concertation unless concertation constitutes the only plausible explanation for such conduct*. It is necessary to bear in mind that, although Article [81] EEC prohibits any form of collusion which distorts competition, it does not deprive economic operators of the right to adapt themselves intelligently to the existing and anticipated conduct of their competitors . . .

Accordingly it is necessary in this case to ascertain whether the parallel conduct alleged by the Commission cannot, taking account of the nature of the products, the size and the number of the undertakings and the volume of the market in question, be explained otherwise than by concertation.   (paras 71–2, emphasis added)

Unusually in this case the Court commissioned its own expert report into the characteristics of the market in question. The experts' conclusions differed from those of the Commission; in particular the experts pointed out that the system of price announcements had been requested by customers, rather than being imposed by producers. This, the experts said, was the result of the cyclical nature of the market, and the fact that producers of paper wanted to know as soon as possible what the biggest constituent cost of their end product was going to be. The fact that the response to price announcements was almost simultaneous was explained by the applicants as being the result not of concertation, but of the highly transparent nature of a market in which both producers and customers were sophisticated and well-informed. This analysis too was supported by the Court's experts. In a second report requested by the Court the experts concluded that the parallelism in prices could also be explained by the natural structure of the market. Following these analyses the response of the ECJ was to accept that 'in this case, concertation is not the only plausible explanation for the parallel conduct' (para. 126).

In annulling this decision the Court has made it difficult for the Commission to proceed against collusive practices. Although it is likely that in the majority of cases the Commission will be able to find physical evidence of collusion, there are likely to be some situations where the Commission is unable to do so. In such cases it is still going to have to fall back on economic analysis. The level of economic debate and evidence brought in the *Woodpulp* case takes it beyond the expertise of lawyers and into the realms of pure industrial economists. Given the differences of approaches to this subject it is likely that in many cases alleged wrongdoers will be able to commission a reputable economist to produce an argument that runs counter to that brought forward by the Commission. Only if the Commission is able to anticipate each and every possible argument will it be able to build a case that will, if *Woodpulp* is followed, satisfy the ECJ.

The more recent action in the *Ferry operators—currency surcharge* decision (97/84 (1997) OJ L26/23) hints at the range of approaches that the Commission may now take. Here various operators of ferry services between the UK and continental Europe imposed surcharges on customers who had paid in sterling following the 17 per cent fall in the value of the pound in September 1992. The additional charges, which were designed to protect the operators from the full impact of the devaluation of the currency, were levied at the same amount, and their imposition took effect at the same time and was announced in identical terms. The Commission both indicated that this was not a plausible result in light of the fact that the operators faced very different cost structures dependent upon their size and management systems, and also relied on evidence and admissions of collusion collected in the course of a Regulation 17 investigation.

Concerted practices may be distinguished from naked cartels (or 'hard-core' cartels), where there is an explicit agreement between undertakings. In practice, however, the link is blurred as evidence of the agreement may be difficult to obtain. At the end of 1998 the Commission created a new unit expressly to fight cartels

(IP (98) 1068, 3 December 1998, [1999] 4 CMLR 13). One of the best examples of cartel decisions is *Pre Insulated Pipe Cartel* 1999/60 (1999) OJ L24/1, an infringement that began with a national cartel in Denmark in 1990, and by 1994 had been extended to cover the entire Community. The list of restrictions of competition set out in para. 147 of the Decision is an impressive one, and, even allowing for some reductions in the level of fines imposed in accordance with its notice on the non-imposition of fines in cartel cases (see Chapter 4), the total fines amounted to €92,920,000. A very good description of the operation of this cartel, and the steps taken to counteract it, written by the head of the Cartels unit of the Competition Directorate, may be found in *Competition Policy Newsletter* (1999) February, p. 27.

One of the most high-profile cartel cases of recent years attracted the attention of competition authorities around the world when the existence of the cartel was exposed to the FBI. In the EC the investigation, during which competition authorities cooperated, culminated in the EC Commission decision *Amino Acids Cartel—Archer Daniels Midland Co and others* 2001/418 2001 OJ L152/24. Here a number of leading companies in the production of amino acids, led by the US company Archer Daniels Midland, put in place elaborate cartel arrangements to market share and fix prices. The story of the uncovering of the cartel is told in Eichenwald, K., *The Informant*, New York, Broadway Books (2000), which is highly recommended.

7.2.4 Peripheral involvement in restrictive conduct

The fact that an undertaking has only a peripheral role in any breach of art. 81, and is not a driving force in the illegal conduct, is not a defence to any action brought under the article. However, if fines are imposed on the offending undertakings these may be less for those undertakings that have played a less significant role in the activity. Thus, for example, in the *Polypropylene* decision (86/398 (1986) OJ L230/1) the Commission drew a distinction between the four largest producers which between them 'formed the nucleus of the arrangements and constituted an unofficial directorate' and other members that had played a less prominent role. However, the fact that Shell 'did not attend the plenary sessions', or that Hercules 'did not communicate its own detailed sales figures to other producers' was in neither case considered to be a mitigating factor in assessing the existence of a breach by those undertakings.

The strictness of this approach was even more evident in *LdPE* 89/191 (1989) OJ L74/21, which again related to a cartel operating in the plastics market. The decision related to 17 undertakings, but three, BP, Shell, and Monsanto, required 'special examination'. None of these undertakings took a central role in the cartel, and the Commission acknowledged that, at worst, their participation could be considered 'only a partial one'. As the Commission recognized, 'mere knowledge of the existence of a cartel does not constitute involvement in the infringement'. Neither would it constitute an infringement to have knowledge of a cartel's existence and to base one's own conduct on the basis of that knowledge. This was the argument made by BP and Shell, which both argued that documents obtained by the Commission that showed they were aware of impending price rises and planned their own rises in the light of that knowledge were simply the result of their making use of 'legitimate market intelligence' or other published sources (para. 32). The three companies were all allocated quotas by the cartel, but argued that this was unconnected with them and simply the result of the cartel optimistically setting quotas for all the producers in the industry. It is clear from the terms of the decision that the Commission found these arguments persuasive, but the Commission had established that the undertakings had attended at least some of the meetings of the cartel. 'In the absence of any evidence of attendance at meetings or other contacts the Commission might well have given these three undertakings the benefit of the doubt' (para. 33), but even the minimal contact that could be shown was considered to be sufficient to establish the applicability of art. 81(1) to those undertakings. The fines that the undertakings were required to pay, however, were far less than those meted out to the other participants: BP, for example, was fined ECU 750,000, compared to Bayer AG's fine of ECU 2,500,000.

7.2.5 'Object or effect'

It should be apparent from the wording of the article that an agreement may be condemned if it has *either* the object *or* the effect of preventing, restricting, or distorting competition. It would be an unusual position were undertakings to be allowed to conspire, ineffectually, to breach the law and be condemned only were they successful. In *La Technique Minière* v *Maschinenbau Ulm GmbH* case 56/65 [1966] 1 CMLR 357, the Court examined a distribution agreement between a German producer of industrial earth-levellers and a French distributor. Following a disagreement between the parties La Technique Minière had asked the Cour d'Appel in Paris to declare the contract void on the grounds that it breached art. 81(1). Maschinenbau Ulm argued that the agreement did not partition the market and did not therefore fall within the prohibition. As this case arose under art. 234 EC the Court was not being asked to resolve the issue, but in its answers to the Cour d'Appel the Court indicated that

these [criteria] are not cumulative but alternative conditions, indicated by the conjunction 'or', suggest[ing] first the need to consider the very object of the agreement, in the light of the economic context in which it is to be applied. . . . Where, however, an analysis of the said clauses does not reveal a sufficient degree of harmfulness with regard to competition, examination should then be made of the effects of the agreement.   (p. 375)

That the Commission is willing to bring actions against cartels even where they are not entirely successful is demonstrated by, *inter alia, Polypropylene* 86/398 (1986) OJ L230/1. During the course of investigations into the market for bulk thermoplastic polypropylene throughout the Community, the Commission uncovered substantial documentary evidence of 'an institutionalised system of meetings between representatives of the producers at both senior and technical managerial levels' (para. 1). At these meetings, 'the producers developed a system of annual volume control to share out the available market between themselves according to agreed percentage or tonnage targets, and regularly set target prices' (para. 1). The appendices attached to the decision, listing meeting dates and venues, show the extent to which the Commission may be able to obtain irrefutable evidence of attempts to coordinate activity. Such conduct is a classic example of cartelization, where producers seek collectively to limit supplies, raise prices, and monitor observance of the agreement to alleviate the risk of its collapsing through strategic cheating on the part of the cartel members. As the Commission put it:

By planning common action on price initiatives with target prices for each grade and national currency effective from an agreed date, the producers aimed to eliminate the risks which would be involved in any unilateral attempt to increase prices. The various quota systems and other mechanisms designed to accommodate the divergent interests of the established producers and newcomers all had as their ultimate objective the creation of artificial conditions of 'stability' favourable to price rises: (para. 89)

In fact the agreement was not as successful as the participants had hoped. The price level achieved in the market generally lagged some way behind the targets set at the meetings, and the price initiatives often ran out of steam, occasionally resulting in a sharp drop in prices. Over the period in question the industry was characterized by substantial over-capacity, and in such circumstances the temptation on the part of the cartel members to cheat would have been hard to resist. Faced with the evidence garnered by the Commission some of the producers in fact appeared to rely on their own cheating as a defence, pointing to sometimes substantial discrepancies between the delivery targets they had been set and the actual deliveries they had made. In one particular year, 1980, the targets for tonnage deliveries had to be revised continually. Some of the alleged participants pointed also to the fact that market shares had changed substantially over the relevant period, a fact that they said was evidence of 'unrestricted' competition. The Commission rebutted most of these arguments. It argued that while there had been price instability this was usually arrested by a revision of the targets and agreements, and that further falls which would have benefited consumers were thus prevented. That market shares had changed had been envisaged under the targets which had taken into account the ambitions of some of the newer entrants into the market. However, as the Commission also made clear, art. 81(1) would have been applicable notwithstanding failures in the cartelization of the market:

The fact that in practice the cartelisation of the market was incomplete and did not entirely exclude the operation of competitive forces does not preclude application of article [81]. Given the large number of producers, their divergent commercial interests and the absence of any enforceable measures of constraint in the event of non-compliance by a producer with agreed arrangements, no cartel could control totally the activities of their participants. (para. 92)

The 15 identified participants in the cartel were fined a total of ECU 5,785,000.

A similar position was reached in *Ferry operators—currency surcharge* 97/84 (1997) OJ L26/23 (discussed above) where the fact that the operators found it extremely difficult actually to impose the charge that they had agreed to levy did not serve to exonerate them from the fact that they had, in breach of art. 81, colluded to impose the charge.

7.2.6 **Unilateral conduct**

For the prohibition of art. 81(1) to be invoked there must be multilateral conduct. Unilateral conduct will be condemned under EC competition law only where it falls within art. 82. However, there are situations in which it may appear at first sight that art. 81 has been applied to unilateral conduct. Such a situation arose in *AEG-Telefunken* v *Commission* case 107/82 [1984] 3 CMLR 325, in which the undertaking contested a Commission decision (82/267 (1982) OJ L117/15) on the grounds that there had been no other undertakings involved in the condemned conduct. AEG had maintained a selective distribution system and refused to supply certain distributors which met the criteria laid down by AEG but which had a reputation for price cutting—AEG itself described its strategy as a 'high price policy'. It appeared from the wording of the decision that AEG was indeed the only offending party, and the decision was addressed only to it. However, when the undertaking appealed, the conclusion reached by the ECJ was that the refusals to supply, which had been endemic, were an integral part of the operation of the distribution system, and involved all the members of that system, who stood to benefit from the refusals. In effect, the ECJ found that the nexus of interest between AEG and its distributors was such that it was implicit in the agreements between AEG and each of the distributors that AEG would refuse to supply price-cutters. There have been other cases since where the Commission has pursued a similar line, notably *Sandoz* 87/409 (1987) OJ L222/28 and *Vichy* 91/153 (1991) OJ L75/57 (see also Lidgard, H. H., 'Unilateral Refusal to Supply: an Agreement in Disguise?' [1997] *ECLR* 352).

7.3 **The prevention, restriction, or distortion of competition: the application of article 81(1)**

An agreement between two or more undertakings will not be caught within art. 81(1) where it does not prevent, restrict, or distort competition. Such a position may be confirmed by the grant of negative clearance following an application to the Commission (see Chapter 3). As noted earlier, there are strong advantages accruing to those undertakings whose agreements do not fall within art. 81(1), and although an exemption granted under art. 81(3) (see below) allows the undertaking to continue to operate the agreement, such an exemption may require that certain conditions be met and allow the Commission to exercise a degree of supervision over the operation of the agreement. A negative clearance will clear the undertakings from any further involvement with the Commission unless there is a material change in the circumstances, or the negative clearance was granted on the basis of misinformation.

There is a substantial and vibrant debate about the way in which the Commission has applied this part of art. 81(1). It is clear that not all clauses within agreements prevent, restrict, or distort competition, and that there are situations in which agreements, even at the horizontal level, are incapable of having such an effect, or the only distortion of competition may be a beneficial one (see in particular the *Agreements Guidelines on the Applicability of Article 81 to Horizontal Cooperation*, 2000, at para. 3). The debate is similar to that surrounding the application of the rule of reason in American antitrust law which is referred to at the end of this chapter. In one of the leading cases in this respect, *Gottrup-Klim v Dansk Landbrugs Grovvareselskab* case C-250/92 [1994] ECR I–5641, the ECJ held that the extent to which clauses in contracts were compatible with EC competition law could not be assessed 'in the abstract', but depended on both their content, and the 'economic conditions prevailing on the markets concerned'. In this case the ECJ ruled that it was not necessarily anti-competitive for a cooperative association to include a rule which prohibited members from also joining other cooperatives. The Court found that membership of competing co-operatives could impinge upon the proper operation of the cooperative, and its contractual arrangements. Accordingly, the term in question could potentially 'have beneficial effects on competition' (paras 31 to 34).

In the *Guidelines on Vertical Restraints*, the Commission sets out the factors that are important in determining whether a vertical agreement falls within art. 81(1) (see para. 121, and the subsequent discussion in paras 123–33). These are:

(a) market position of the supplier;

(b) market position of competitors;

(c) market position of the buyer;

(d) entry barriers;

(e) maturity of the market;

(f) level of trade;

(g) nature of the product; or

(h) other factors.

In *European Night Services* v *Commission* joined cases T–374/94, etc. [1998] ECR II–3141 the matter was expressed this way:

in assessing an agreement under [art. 81] account should be taken of the actual conditions in which it functions, in particular the economic context in which the undertakings operate, the products or services covered by the agreement and the actual structure of the market concerned unless it is an agreement containing obvious restrictions of competition such as price-fixing, market-sharing or the control of outlets. In the latter case, such restrictions may be weighed against their claimed pro-competitive effects only in the context of [art. 81(3)] of the Treaty, with a view to granting an exemption . . . It must be stressed that the examination of conditions of competition is based not only on existing competition between undertakings already present on the relevant market but also on potential competition, in order to ascertain whether, in the light of the structure of the market and the economic and legal context within which it functions, there are real concrete possibilities for the undertakings concerned to compete among themselves or for a new competitor to penetrate the relevant market and compete with the undertakings already established in it. (paras 136–7, references omitted)

Much earlier than this the Court in *Remia* v *Commission* case 42/84 [1985] ECR 2545 had held that a clause in an agreement relating to the transfer of a business, under which the seller agreed not to compete with the new owner of the business would not fall within art. 81. The EC Commission had found that such a clause did fall within the prohibition, and had offered only a limited concession in its application of art. 81(3) (*Nutricia/Zuid—Hollandse Conservenfabriek* 83/670 (1983) OJ L376/22). The Court held on appeal that against the background in which the agreement operated 'non-competition clauses . . . have the merit of ensuring that the transfer has the effect intended. By virtue of that very fact they contribute to the promotion of competition' (para. 19). *Remia* was cited with approval by the Commission in *Glaxo Wellcome* 2001/791 (2001) OJ L302/1, relating to a system designed to restrict the flow of parallel imports of cheap pharmaceutical products from Spain into the more expensive EC Member States. In response to an application for negative clearance, the Commission held *inter alia* that

The Court of Justice (and Court of First Instance) have always qualified agreements containing export bans, dual-pricing systems or other limitations of parallel trade as restricting competition 'by object'. That is to say, prohibited by art. 81(1) without there being any need for an assessment of their actual effects. In principal they are not eligible for exemption pursuant to art. 81(3).

This reference to certain restrictions as being restrictive of competition 'by object' (see also *Volkswagen AG* v *Commission* case T–62/98 [2000] 5 CMLR 853, paras 89 and 178) brings the approach under art. 81(1) close to the US approach to the 'rule of reason' although the EC Commission has stated that such a rule has no place to play in the art. 81 system (see section 7.7).

The principles developed in these cases may also be seen at play in *Visa International* 2001/782 (2001) OJ L293/94 in which the Commission made a decision of negative clearance in respect of the agreement between some 20,000 financial institutions responsible for the operation of the Visa network system. The Commission held that the rules relating to the operation of the agreement were not restrictive of competition. In particular a rule under which a member of the Visa network could not acquire the right to join without issuing cards exploiting the network was not restrictive of competition as it ensured a large card base, thereby making the system as a whole more attractive to merchants (paras 18 and 65).

Perhaps the clearest discussion of the state of the law relating to this difficult issue is that given by Advocate General Lenz, in *Union Royale Belge des Societes de Football Association ASBL* v *Jean-Marc Bosman* case C-415/93 [1995] ECR I–4921 at paras 262–9).

Where undertakings operating in different markets, and which are not current competitors, enter into an agreement relating to a third market this *may* fall outside the remit of art. 81(1). This was the case, for example, in *Elopak/Metal Box—Odin* 90/410 (1990) OJ L209/15, where Elopak and Metal Box collaborated in a joint venture to produce a new form of packaging carton for foodstuffs. The Commission held that the joint venture agreement fell outside the terms of art. 81 as the parties were not competitors, and the joint venture company, Odin, would effectively operate as an independent entity. This decision, along with *Konsortium ECR 900* 90/446 (1990) OJ L228/31, is an example of the Commission applying some of the principles of a 1983 policy statement on a 'realistic' approach to competition.

A similar approach was taken in the late 1990s case of *Cegetel* (1999) OJ L218/14 in which the Commission found that a joint venture relating to the provision of a fixed voice telephony service in France, the founding companies of which were large operators in France, Germany, and the USA, did not fall within art. 81(1). The Commission held that as the parent companies were each unable to enter this market by themselves the existence of the joint venture did not restrict either actual or potential competition.

Generally, however, the Commission will take a broad view of the potential danger of restrictive conduct, and is more likely to find that such situations are encompassed within art. 81(1) but may benefit from an exemption (see, e.g., *KSB/Goulds/Lowara/ITT* 91/38 (1991) OJ L19/25).

7.3.1 Vertical agreements

Article 81(1)(a)–(e) set out some of the classes of restriction to which the article is intended to apply. This list is not intended to be exhaustive, however. The article applies to both inter-brand and intra-brand competition. Inter-brand competition is that *between different brands*, for example, competition between Ford and Nissan motor cars. Intra-brand competition is that *between goods of the same brand*, for example, competition between different retailers of Nissan motor cars. Typically this means that EC competition law is applicable to vertical restraints (see generally Chapter 6), which are often considered to have a pro-competitive effect, the aim being to improve methods of distribution and to make it easier to bring products to the market. This conclusion, which seems to flow obviously from the wording of the prohibition, is one of the most contentious reached in the application of EC competition law and came as a surprise to many when the position was first established. It was driven largely by the fact that one of the underlying imperatives of EC competition law is to facilitate the integration of the national markets. Where vertical restraints obstruct such an integration, by, for example, allocating particular national or regional markets and territories to particular distributors, they are likely to be condemned. The key decision was that in *Etablissements Consten SARL and Grundig-Verkaufs-GmbH* v *Commission* cases 56, 58/64 [1996] 1 CMLR 418, which remains the most important case to be considered under art. 81, and one that demonstrates the application of most aspects of that article. It is therefore discussed here in some detail.

7.3.1.1 *Consten and Grundig*

Grundig-Verkaufs-GmbH was a German manufacturer of consumer electronic goods (radios, tape recorders, television sets, and dictating machines). In April 1957 it entered into an exclusive distribution contract with the French firm Etablissements Consten. Under the terms of this contract Consten was to be Grundig's sole representative in France, the Saar, and Corsica. Consten was required, *inter alia*, to purchase a certain minimum percentage of Grundig's exports into France, to adequately promote Grundig's products, and to provide an adequate after-sales service and maintain supplies of spare parts. Along with these obligations Consten undertook not to sell competing products, and not to make any deliveries, direct or indirect, of its supplies to territories outside its contract area. Similar terms were to be found in the contracts Grundig maintained with its distributors in other European territories, and with the main German wholesalers. Grundig itself was enjoined from supplying, other than through Consten's the relevant goods into Consten's allocated territory. In order to reinforce Consten's exclusive rights it was assigned in France the trademark GINT (Grundig International), which was carried on all Grundig products. The effect of this was that Consten would be able to bring an action, based on the infringement of its intellectual property rights, against any importer of Grundig's goods into France. Under the terms of the assignment if Consten ceased being Grundig's sole distributor in the relevant territory it was to return the GINT trademark to Grundig. The firm UNEF obtained Grundig products from German distributors in spite of the fact that they were not meant to supply such customers, and sold them into France at prices below those charged by Consten. Consten brought two actions against UNEF in the French courts, one based on the French law of unfair competition, the other for infringement of the GINT trademark. In 1962 the case was adjourned following an application made by UNEF to the Commission which sought a declaration to the effect that the agreement between Consten and Grundig was in breach of art. 81(1). Grundig notified its agreements with both Consten and its other exclusive distributors to the Commission on 29 January 1963, and sought a decision to the effect that art. 81(1) did not apply to such an agreement, or that if it did the agreement should be exempt by virtue of the application of art. 81(3). By a decision of 23 September 1964 (*Re Grundig's Agreement* 64/566/EEC; the official text is not published in English, but see [1964] CMLR 489) the Commission held that the contracts in question, and the assignment of the trademark, constituted an infringement of the provisions of art. 81. Both Consten and Grundig brought actions to have the decision annulled. When the cases came before the ECJ the Italian and German governments were admitted as intervening parties, both of them in support of the two firms.

After rehearsing the facts Advocate General Karl Roemer noted that the case had 'taken on unusual proportions because of the economic and legal importance of the problems dealt with and the number of parties involved'. Various technical points made by the applicants were dismissed by the Advocate General, who then dealt in more detail with the more significant arguments about the applicability of art. 81(1) to vertical restraints. Consten had argued that it was incumbent on the Commission to provide a theoretical justification for the position it had taken. Advocate General Roemer roundly dismissed this suggestion, pointing instead to the limited body of case law already decided by the ECJ in the area of restrictive agreements. Following on from the first such case considered by the Court (*Bosch v De Geus* case 13/61 [1962] 1 CMLR 1), he noted that the Court had held that it was not possible in that case to come to a general conclusion about the application of art. 81(1) to a particular class of agreements, and that the task instead was to decide in each particular case whether the article was applicable. It was of no doubt, the Advocate General said, that 'contracts involving exclusive supply and purchase undertakings can have the effect of limiting competition, especially when they are accompanied by an absolute territorial protection'. Grundig had suggested that the absolute territorial protection afforded under the contract was irrelevant, for even without it the distributor would be the only 'offeror' of the product in question. Clearly this 'argument could not be supported, for it was precisely the presence of other 'offerors', in particular UNEF, that had led to Consten bringing action before the French courts to enforce its territorial claims.

There were, however, points that concerned the Advocate General. In particular he was concerned that the approach of the Commission was apparently to consider only the 'object' of the agreement and not its concrete 'effect'. 'Article [81(1)]' the Advocate General said, 'requires really the comparison of two market situations: that which arises after the conclusion of an agreement and that which would arise in the absence of the agreement'. Such a concrete examination, if undertaken, might lead to the conclusion that an agreement in a particular case 'only has effects which are likely to *promote* competition'. In particular this might be the case, it was suggested, where it would not be possible for a manufacturer to gain a purchase on the market unless it were to do so by way of appointing an exclusive distributor. Thus, the Advocate General opined, 'such an examination might have led to a finding that in the Grundig–Consten case the *suppression* of the sole sales agency would have involved a noticeable reduction in the offer of Grundig products on the French market'. A second argument was made by the German government which the Advocate General felt 'deserves complete approval'. This was that a consideration of the competition between various distributors of Grundig products missed the point, and that any consideration of the market should have as its starting point an analysis of the competition between *similar competing* products. This is the distinction between intra-brand and inter-brand competition that is still a matter of debate in the Community (see below). The Advocate General was of the opinion that the Commission was simply 'wrong in taking *exclusive* account of that internal competition ... and in neglecting completely in its consideration competition with similar products'. Competition, it was suggested, should be judged in this case at the level of the wholesaler, where the dealers were technically competent to distinguish between the different brands of equipment, and to pass on the relevant details to the retailers. In fact, the market share held by Grundig in France in tape recorders and dictating machines was only about 17 per cent. There must therefore have been vigorous competition from other brands of similar, although not identical, products. In the market for televisions and radios it appeared that the competition, particularly from foreign imports, was intense, and there was evidence that the prices charged for Grundig products had been reduced in response to this on several occasions. Taking these factors into account the Advocate General felt that 'the conclusions reached by the Commission in examining the criterion of "interference with competition" should be considered as insufficiently based and consequently should be disregarded'.

The Commission, in considering the requirement that the practice 'may affect trade' (see below), had found it sufficient to demonstrate that 'following an agreement restricting competition the trade between Member States develops *in other* ways than it would have done without the agreement'. It was the Commission's contention that this requirement was merely a 'criterion of competence', but the Advocate General was 'convinced that the very text of 'article [81(1)] prevents justification of that opinion'. His view was that in some of the Treaty's official languages the requirement was that there be an *unfavourable* influence on trade and that it was insufficient merely to demonstrate an influence. In the Advocate General's view it was the suppression of such exclusive arrangements that could have a harmful effect on trade and obstruct the integration of the market, as such steps could in fact reduce the flow of goods between the Member States. These various criticism, he felt, were sufficient to annul the decision. Further arguments merely reinforced this view. Prominent amongst these was the fact that the Commission had found simply that the agreement was in breach of the article. The Advocate General, however, felt that this position led to 'intolerable' legal uncertainty, and that, particularly at such an early stage in the development of the law relating to restrictive agreements, undertakings should be told precisely what *clauses* of the agreement were in breach. This would both lend greater clarity and precision to the Commission's decisions, and also give the undertakings concerned the chance to amend their agreements to bring them into line with Community law without requiring them to lose all the legal benefits flowing from those agreements.

The Advocate General considered also the refusal of the Commission to grant an exemption to the contested agreement under art. 81(3). The Commission had accepted that it might be possible to contend that the agreements contributed to improving production and distribution, but not that consumers received any share in the resulting benefit. This, the Commission had held, would be impossible as long as the agreement conferred absolute territorial protection on Consten. Noting that the German Law against Restraint on Competition, one of the strictest regimes in the Community, took a lenient approach to exclusive distribution agreements, the Advocate General felt that the Commission should do likewise in the application of art. 81(3), because 'as a general rule competition between *similar* products of different producers constitutes a sufficient regulator of the market'. In its application to the Court the Commission had argued that because art. 81(1) provided the *rule*, and art. 81(3) only the *exception*, it fell to the undertakings in particular cases to justify the application of the exemption. This would allow the Commission to adopt a role that was, in the view of the Advocate General, unacceptably passive. Thus it was argued that the role of the Commission was to 'raise questions on its own initiative and make conscientious enquiries together with the undertakings concerned'. Whether the individual criteria for the grant of an exemption had been fulfilled was also a matter of some debate. Although accepting that the agreement could lead to the requisite improvement in production and distribution, the Commission had suggested that the requirement that Consten undertake promotion of the products on behalf of Grundig was a restraint that was unnecessary. The Commission had not, the Advocate General felt, adequately argued this point, and had failed to show that the bearing of this cost by Consten had not resulted in any benefit to the market. For an exemption to be granted consumers are expected to reap some of the benefits of the restrictive agreement along with the undertakings themselves. The Commission had argued that that was not the case here. As the Advocate General noted, this requirement is 'a particularly delicate and difficult criterion to grasp', and found the submission of the German government particularly helpful on this point. This had suggested that it should be sufficient to show that there was lively competition between manufacturers of different products, as 'that guarantees at the same time that the consumers have a fair share in the profit, because [they] should only pay the price which develops on the market under the influence of effective competition'. Pointing to the likelihood that such exclusive dealing arrangements would promote competition the Advocate General suggested that consumers might then be sharing the rewards and, as important to his conclusion, that the Commission had failed to consider this aspect. In conclusion Herr Roemer, supporting the arguments of the applicants and the two interested Member States, argued that the contested decision should be annulled *in toto* and referred back to the Commission for reconsideration.

As is usual in Community case law the judgment is somewhat shorter than the Advocate General's submission (13 pages and 46 pages respectively). On the question of whether art. 81(1) could be applied to vertical restraints, which was a matter that the Italian government had strongly contested, the Court held that

Neither the wording of article [81] nor that of article [82] gives ground for holding that the two articles are limited in effect according to the positions of the contracting parties in the economic process. Article [81] refers in a general way to all agreements which distort competition within the Common Market and does not establish any distinction between those agreements as to whether or not they were made between operators competing at the same stage or between non-competing operators placed at different stages. In principle no distinction should be made where the Treaty does not make any distinction.

The Court was equally dismissive of the arguments made by the Advocate General, the German government, and the parties to the effect that the conferment of absolute territorial protection in a case where there existed competition at the level of the producers need not necessarily be condemned. The Court pointed to the basic objectives of the Treaty: 'The Treaty, whose preamble and text aim at suppressing the barriers between Member States and which in several provisions gives evidence of a stern attitude with regard to their reappearance, could not allow undertakings to restore such barriers'.

The Court further agreed with the Commission that the primary purpose of the requirement that trade between Member States be affected was to allow for jurisdictional competence to be determined. The Commission was not therefore required to show that trade would have been greater had the agreement not been in place. The Court, in holding that 'the fact that an agreement favours an increase, even a large one, in the volume of trade' brings the agreement within art. 81, could not have made the position clearer, nor more roundly rejected the argument of the Advocate General.

On the questions of the benefits of inter-brand over intra-brand competition, particularly advanced by the German government, the ECJ found that it was quite acceptable for the Commission's analysis to proceed solely with reference to the competition in the market for Grundig's products, and held that

Although competition between producers is generally more noticeable than that between distributors of the same make, it does not thereby follow that an agreement tending to restrict the latter kind of competition should escape the prohibition of article [81(1)] merely because it might increase the former.

Lastly, the Court was satisfied that the Commission had properly considered the points relating to the award of an art. 81(3) exemption. The Commission's decision was annulled by the Court only in so far as it related to the entire agreement concluded between the parties, the Court holding that those parts of the agreement which did not breach the art. 81(1) prohibition could not be condemned by the Commission.

While *Consten and Grundig* saw the Commission and Court taking a relatively inflexible approach to the nature of competition in so far as it applied to exclusive distribution agreements, a more flexible approach may be seen in *Metro-SB-Grossmärkte GmbH & Co. Kg v Commission* case 26/76 [1978] 2 CMLR 1. In this case a selective distribution system operated by SABA, a German manufacturer of radios, television sets, and tape recorders, was approved by the Commission (*SABA* 76/159 (1976) OJ L28/19). This followed a complaint by a cash-and-carry wholesaler which, by reducing the level of service that it offered to consumers, was able to charge lower prices than would usually be charged by SABA's distributors. Metro had argued to the Commission that it was denied access to the distribution system established by SABA, and that this distribution system was in breach of art. 81(1) and therefore unlawfully maintained. Referring to the flexibility afforded by the concept of 'workable competition', the ECJ held that the nature of the competition could vary depending on the products and services in question, and the structure of the market. The Commission had found selective distribution systems to be unobjectionable as long as the resellers were chosen on the basis of objective criteria which had a genuine relationship to the product in question and as long as such criteria were not applied in a discriminatory manner. The argument was raised by Metro that such systems could lead to higher prices for consumers, and that the application of art. 81(1) required that price competition be maintained effectively. The Court's response was that

It is true that in such systems of distribution price competition is not generally emphasised either as an exclusive or indeed as a principal factor. . . . However, although price competition is so important that it can never be eliminated, it does not constitute the only effective form of competition or that to which absolute priority must in all circumstances be accorded. The powers conferred upon the Commission under article [81(3)] show that the requirements for the maintenance of workable competition may be reconciled with the safeguarding of objectives of a different nature and that to this end certain restrictions on competition are permissible. . . . For specialist wholesalers and retailers the desire to maintain a certain price level, which corresponds to the desire to preserve, in the interests of consumers, the possibility of the continued existence of this channel of distribution in conjunction with new methods of distribution based on a different type of competition policy, forms one of the objectives which may be pursued without necessarily falling under the prohibition contained in article [81(1)]. (para. 21)

Thus, although recognizing the primacy of price competition, which in the Court's words 'is so important that it can never be eliminated', the Court and the Commission both recognized that there could be situations in which some restriction on price competition would be acceptable if that restriction fostered other types of competition. Here the nature of the product was such that a number of large and medium-scale producers offered products that consumers would regard as being generally interchangeable. In such a circumstance any restrictions on prices maintained by one producer would be constrained by the existence on the market of acceptable substitutes, and could be justified if the effect of the constraint was to make available to the consumer a level of supply, service, and after-sales commitment that would not be available in the absence of the restraint.

7.3.1.2 *Agency agreements*

In May 2000 the Commission published its *Guidelines on Vertical Restraints*, which deal, at paras 12–20, with agency agreements, and which replace the *Notice on Exclusive Dealing Contracts with Commercial Agents of 1962*. Agency agreements, according to the *Guidelines*,

cover the situation in which a legal or physical person (the agent) is vested with the power to negotiate and/or conclude contracts on behalf of another person (the principal), either in the agent's own name or in the name of the principal, for the:

— purchase of goods or services by the principal, or
— sale of goods or services supplied by the principal.

Genuine agency agreements do not fall within art. 81(1). Non-genuine agency agreements are likely, subject to the market share provisos, to fall within block exemption 2790/99, discussed in Chapter 8. The determination of whether an agency agreement is genuine or not goes to the question of the allocation of risk. If the agent does not bear the risks for the contracts negotiated, or bears only a minimal risk, then it is a 'genuine' agency agreement. In these cases the agent is, in effect, not exercising any independent economic activity, and is subsumed within the principal undertaking.

7.3.1.3 *Vertical restraints—the Commission Green Paper and responses*

The decision in *Consten and Grundig* continues to loom large over the application of EC competition law. In January 1997 the Commission published its *Green Paper on Vertical Restraints in Competition Policy* (COM(96) 721 final, 22 January 1997). This invited comments on four options, against a background of criticism in which it was widely argued that the current Community rules were too restrictive, were not conducive to legal certainty, and failed adequately to consider the economic impact of any particular arrangement. Noting the 'ambiguous' nature of the impact on competition such restraints have, the Commission set out the broad problem in the opening paragraphs:

(1) The single market represents an opportunity for EU firms to enter new markets that may have been previously closed to them because of government barriers. This penetration of new markets takes time and investment and is risky. The process is often facilitated by agreements between producers who want to break into a new market and local distributors. Efficient distribution with appropriate pre- and after-sales support is part of the competitive process that brings benefits to consumers.

(2) However, arrangements between producers and distributors can also be used to continue the partitioning of the market and exclude new entrants who would intensify competition and lead to downward pressure on prices. Agreements between producers and distributors (vertical restraints) can therefore be used pro-competitively to promote market integration and efficient distribution or anti-competitively to block integration and competition. The price differences between Member States that are still found provide the incentive for companies to enter new markets as well as to erect barriers against new competition.

(3) Because of their strong links to market integration that can be either positive or nega-tive, vertical restraints have been of particular importance to the Union's competition policy. Whilst this policy has been successful in over 30 years of application a review is now necessary.

The four options suggested by the Commission were:

(a) maintain current system;

(b) increase the scope of the block exemptions;

(c) make the block exemptions more focused; and

(d) reduce the scope of art. 81(1).

In inviting comments the Commission stressed that 'absolute territorial protec-tion . . . which may affect trade between Member States will not only continue to fall *per se* within Article [81(1)] but [is] unlikely to be exempted' (para. 39).

The Commission's response to the consultation process became clear in September

1998 when it issued both a Communication (or White Paper) and two proposals for regulations to give effect to its proposals (COM(1998) 546 final). The communication made it clear that the aim of the Community should be to develop 'a more economics based approach' in which 'vertical agreements should be analysed in their market context'. In order to address the shortcomings identified under the current regime the Commission considered that 'a profound change of policy is necessary' which was to take the form of 'one, very wide Block-Exemption regulation covering all vertical restraints concerning intermediate and final goods and services, except for a limited number of hardcore restraints'. This process became reality from 1 June 2000 when Regulation 2790/99 on the application of art. 81(3) of the Treaty to categories of vertical agreements and concerted practices (1999) OJ L 336/21, entered into force. This regulation is discussed in detail in Chapter 8.

There is a plethora of cases dealing with territorial restrictions in distribution agreements, and work carried out on behalf of the government during the passage of the Competition Act 1998 demonstrated that single-market considerations played the leading role in many of the cases dealing with vertical restraints. More recent decisions include *Novalliance/Systemform* 97/123 (1997) OJ L47/11, in which the infringing company quickly amended the terms of its distribution agreements following their notification to the Commission; *ADALAT* 96/478 (1996) OJ L201/1, dealing with export bans imposed in relation to a range of medicinal products by Bayer AG; and *BASF Lacke + Farben AG and Accinauto SA* 95/477 (1995) OJ L272/17, dealing with the market for car paints, upheld on appeal, *BASF Coating AG* v *Commission* case T–175/95 [2000] 4 CMLR 33. The ECU 102m fine imposed on Volkswagen in January 1998 (*VW* 98/273 (1998) OJ L124/61)—on appeal (*Volkswagen AG* v *Commission* case T–62/98 [2000] 5 CMLR 853) the fine was reduced by the Court to €90 m—is in itself proof of the Commission's abhorrence of distribution agreements which are operated so as to prevent parallel imports. In that case Italian distributors of the manufacturer's cars were effectively prevented from reselling them to Austrian and German consumers.

At the same time as it issued its Communication the Commission brought forward two enabling amendments to Regulations 17/62 and 19/65. Regulation 1216/99 (1999) OJ L148/5 allows exemptions to be granted retrospectively from the date of notification in order to reduce the number of initial notifications. Regulation 1215/99 (1999) OJ L148/1 gives the Commission the authority to issue a block exemption wider in scope than that previously permitted.

In May 2000, to coincide with the entry into force of Regulation 2790/99 on 1 June 2000, the Commission published its *Guidelines on Vertical Restraints*. At paras 119–36 these set out general rules for the assessment of vertical restraints. The starting point is the recognition of the fact that 'for most vertical restraints competition concerns can only arise if there is insufficient inter-brand competition', and that in unconcentrated markets, defined as those where the Herfindahl Hirshman Index (HHI) is less than 1,000 (the use of the HHI formula is discussed below in relation to horizontal agreements), it will be assumed that non-hard-core vertical restraints will not have appreciable effects. On the other hand, vertical restraints which have the effect of reducing inter-brand competition will be analysed with greater concern. Some analysis of specific categories of vertical restraint is provided in paras 137–229 of the *Guidelines*. The practices dealt with there are: single branding, exclusive distribution, exclusive customer allocation, selective distribution, franchising, exclusive supply, tying, and recommended and maximum resale prices. In each case, the *Guidelines* should be read through carefully.

7.3.2 **Horizontal agreements**

The position taken in relation to damaging cartels, and to concerted practices, has already been considered above. These are the two obvious situations in which horizontal agreements—those between undertakings operating at the same level in the market—may be condemned. It should be noted that there is some debate as to whether a 'concerted practice' may be classed as an agreement, but the *effect* is the same as that for a more formal agreement.

Guidelines on the Applicability of Article 81 EC to Horizontal Cooperation Agreements, published in January 2001. These *Guidelines* replace a number of earlier guidelines and notices, including, importantly, the 1968 *Notice on Agreements, Decisions and Concerted Practices in the Field of Cooperation between Enterprises* ((1968) OJ C75/3).

The difficulty in dealing with benign horizontal cooperation is that there is always a risk that parties will coordinate in an anti-competitive fashion, and that such coordination can have serious consequences both for economic welfare, and for the integration of the single market. Thus it is recognized in the introduction to the *Guidelines* that:

1. In most instances, horizontal cooperation amounts to cooperation between competitors . . .

3. Companies need to respond to increasing competitive pressure and a changing market place driven by globalisation, the speed of technological progress and the generally more dynamic nature of markets. Cooperation can be a means to share risk, save costs, pool know-how and launch innovation faster. In particular for small- and medium-sized enterprises cooperation is an important means to adapt to the changing market place.

7.3.2.1 *Potentially benign horizontal agreements*

The analysis of horizontal agreements is not straightforward. Although the temptation may be to condemn all such agreements the range of material about which undertakings at a horizontal level agree is vast, and includes not only prices and market sharing, but also practices which are wholly pro-competitive, or whose pro-competitive effects may outweigh the anti-competitive effects. We have already seen above that in the case of *European Night Services* v *Commission* joined cases T–374/94, etc. [1998] ECR II–3141 the Court drew a distinction between different types of horizontal agreements. The first task, the Court said, was to carefully assess the competitive conditions in which such agreements operated. It might be the case that a horizontal agreement would not even fall within art. 81(1) if it had no deleterious effect on competition. However, where certain restrictions are present, set out in the case as being price fixing, market sharing, or the control of outlets (para. 136), it must be presumed automatically that art. 81(1) applies. It would then become necessary to analyse carefully the competitive conditions in order to see if the requirements for the application of art. 81(3) were met.

The issues relating to less harmful horizontal agreements are explored in the relevant EC Commission. However,

> 2. Horizontal cooperation may lead to competition problems. This is for example, the case if the parties to a cooperation agree to fix prices or output, to share markets, or if the cooperation enables the parties to maintain, gain or increase market power and thereby causes negative market effects with respect to prices, output, innovation or the variety and quality of products.

The *Guidelines*, which go some way to clarifying the position in relation to horizontal cooperation and should be read carefully, focus on cooperation between competitors, which includes both 'actual' and 'potential' competitors. They have a further limitation in that they are concerned only with cooperation which may generate efficiency gains, by which the EC Commission means 'agreements on R&D, production, purchasing, commercialisation, standardisation, and environmental agreements' (para. 10). Research and development agreements, and production agreements, which include specialization agreements, are considered in the following chapter, because they are subject to block exemptions.

The *Guidelines* deal first with the situations in which such agreements may fall within art. 81(1). Some agreements are unlikely to fall within art. 81(1), particularly where there will be no coordination of competitive conduct. This will be the case where the parties are not competitors, or where (as was the case in *Elopak/Metal Box—Odin* 90/410 (1990) OJ L209/15, discussed above) the parties could not independently carry out the activity covered by the cooperation. In these cases, notwithstanding that there is an element of cooperation, it will be in an entirely new activity. This new activity would not exist without that level of cooperation, and therefore pre-existing competition is not being undermined.

Agreements will almost always fall within art. 81(1), and will almost always be prohibited, where they 'have the object to restrict competition by means of price fixing, output limitation or sharing of markets or customers' (para. 25). Agreements that do not fall within these categories have to be analysed more fully to determine whether they fall under art. 81(1).

The central consideration will be 'the position of the parties in the markets affected by the cooperation' (para. 27), because it is the undertakings' market power which is likely to be determinative of whether harmful effects flow from the agreement. The base line of the Commission is that such agreements cannot be tolerated where they have the effect of 'eliminating' competition (see art. 81(3)).

One of the indices used by the Commission is the Herfindahl-Hirshman Index, or HHI, which is a tool employed by the US authorities in merger control. It provides a useful first indicator of market concentration. Formally the HHI is the sum of the squared market shares of the companies on the relevant market, or $\Sigma s1^2 \ldots sn^2$

(where sn is the market share of firm n). Thus, in a market with four firms, each of which has a 25 per cent market share, the HHI would be $25^2 + 25^2 + 25^2 + 25^2 = 2,500$. In a total monopoly market the HHI would be 10,000 (100^2), and in a market of 100 firms, each with only 1 per cent market share, it would be 100. Where the HHI is less than 1,000, the concentration will be characterized as low, between 1,000 and 1,800 it will be moderate, and over 1,800 high. As the *Guidelines* make clear, a post-cooperation HHI may in some cases 'be decisive for the assessment of the possible market effects of a cooperation'. It refers to the following example:

A market consisting of four firms with shares of 30%, 25%, 25% and 20%, has a HHI of 2,550 (900 + 625 + 625 + 400) pre-cooperation. If the first two market leaders would cooperate, the HHI would change to 4,050 (3,025 + 625 + 400) post-cooperation.   (footnote 22, para. 29)

As well as conducting such analysis it must be demonstrated that the requirements of art. 81(3) are met (which are discussed below). For a detailed consideration of the approach to be taken in relation to each of the categories of agreement referred to in the *Guidelines* reference should be made to the relevant section in the *Guidelines*.

7.3.2.2 *Information agreements*

The *Guidelines* do not deal with information-sharing agreements. There has not been a great deal of case law in relation to these. In its 1968 *Notice on Cooperation Agreements* the Commission indicated that certain information agreements would not be caught by art. 81. These agreements were:

(1) Agreements having as their sole object:
— an exchange of opinion or experience,
— joint market research,
— the joint carrying out of comparative studies of enterprises or industries,
— the joint preparation of statistics and calculation models.

Agreements whose sole purpose is the joint procurement of information which the various enterprises need to determine their future market behaviour freely and independently, or the use by each of the enterprises of a joint advisory body, do not have as their object or result the restriction of competition. But if the scope of action of the enterprises is limited or if the market behaviour is coordinated either expressly or through concerted practices, there may be a restraint of competition. This is in particular the case where concrete recommendations are made or where conclusions are given in such a form that they induce at least some of the participating enterprises to behave in an identical manner on the market.

Although this notice has been replaced by the horizontal guidelines, it remains the most substantial source of comment relating to information agreements. It implies that agreements relating to the exchange of information between actual or potential competitors are therefore capable of being in breach of art. 81. A distinction should in this respect be made between three classes of information agreements:

(a) information exchanges concerning price;

(b) information exchanges which do not relate to price, but do contain information that may underpin other anti-competitive activity, such as, for example, information that allows firms in an industry to pinpoint exactly who is making what sales to whom; and

(c) information which is neither about price nor about other anti-competitive activity.

In the case of the first two categories the Commission is likely to take the approach that the agreement invites condemnation, having the object, if not in fact the effect, of being anti-competitive. In the third category the Commission will examine the situation more carefully, the presumption being that there is no anti-competitive object, but that there may nevertheless be an anti-competitive effect in practice. The Commission will be highly swayed by the extent to which the information is individualized. In its *7th Annual Report on Competition Policy* it explained its position at some length. In short the position is that the 'provision of collated statistical material is not in itself objectionable' but that 'the organised exchange of individual data from individual firms . . . will normally be regarded by the Commission as practices . . . which are therefore prohibited' as having the object or effect of preventing, restricting, or distorting competition. The leading cases in this respect are *UK Tractors Information Agreement* 92/157 [1992] OJ L68/19 and *Fatty Acids* 87/1 (1987) OJ L3/17.

In the latter case an agreement was entered into by the four major producers in the EC of various chemicals. Under the agreement the parties, having first established their respective average market shares over the previous three years, set out to exchange information regarding their total sales in Europe for each quarter, with the intention of allowing each party to monitor the behaviour of each other, and to adjust its own conduct accordingly. As the Commission noted the information exchanged was 'of a kind normally regarded as business secrets' (para. 1). At para. 45 of the decision the Commission held that an agreement

based on an exchange of confidential information on the one hand about traditional market positions and on the other hand providing a means of monitoring their future performance, has inherent restrictive effects upon competition. . . through the exchange of information they artificially increased transparency between them by obtaining knowledge of each other's activities which they would not have had in the absence of the agreement. The Commission considers that this will inevitably have led them to temper their competitive behaviour towards each other.

7.3.2.3 *Standards-setting agreements*

Agreements relating to standards setting are dealt with in Part 6 of the *Guidelines*. Standardization agreements are defined as those which 'have as their primary objective the definition of technical or quality requirements with which current or future products, production processes or methods may comply' (para. 159). In high-tech industries, such as computing, where equipment needs to be able to interface with other equipment standards setting is increasingly important. Standards may be set by either public or private bodies. In the case of public bodies it is unlikely that competition law will involve itself, and the only requirement in the EC is that any such standards do not distort competition, and are not used to raise barriers to trade.

In relation to private standards setting the general principles set out in the *Guidelines* follow previous decisions taken by the Commission. Where standards are 'open' they are unlikely to fall within art. 81(1). An open standard is one which is open to all, and is not discriminatory or exclusionary. For example, in *TUV/Cenelec* (*28th Annual Report on Competition Policy* 1998, p. 159) the Commission negotiated a settlement whereby a standard developed by Cenelec was 'opened' up to all qualified certifiers, a procedure which the Commission hoped would 'serve as a model for application procedures in related fields'. Standards may, however, be used to restrict competition by setting criteria which are unattainable by some parties. The question then becomes one of whether art. 81(3) may be applied. If that is to be the case the standard must serve a valid end, and meet the general criteria for exemption discussed below.

The leading decision dealing with the application of art. 81(3) to a standards-setting agreement is that of *X/Open Group* 87/69 (1987) OJ L35/36. In this case a number of significant undertakings in the computing industry, such as Bull, Ericsson, and ICL notified the Commission of an agreement to standardize various matters relating to the use of the computer operating system UNIX. The objective was to increase the number of applications that could be written to work with UNIX. The group intended to limit its membership, with a requirement that applicants be 'major manufacturers in the European information technology industry, with their own established expertise concerning UNIX'. The revenue of any applicant to the group would be expected to be about US$500m from information technology activity. The Commission found that the agreement would fall within art. 81(1), but that it would be exempt under art. 81(3). A crucial factor was that the standards created by the group would be well publicized and relevant technical information would be made widely available. The Commission further found that

the advantages involved in the creation of an open industry standard (in particular the intended creation of a wider availability of software and greater flexibility offered to users to change between hardware and software from different sources) easily outweigh the distortions of competition entailed in the rules governing membership which are indispensable to the attainment of the objectives of the Group Agreement.   (para. 42).

7.3.3 Mergers and joint ventures

The application of art. 81 to mergers and joint ventures is considered in Chapter 16.

7.4 **Article 81(2): void agreements**

Where art. 81(1) has been found to apply to any agreement an important consequence is that the agreement, or relevant parts of it, is void. Because of the nature of the prohibition there need not be any formal decision to the effect that art. 81(1) applies for this to be the case. This position is made clear in *Beguelin Import Co.* v *GL Import Export SA* (case 22/71 [1972] CMLR 81) where the Court held that 'since the nullity imposed by Article [81(2)] is absolute in character, an agreement which is void because of that provision has no effect between the contracting parties and cannot be pleaded against third parties' (para. 29). Thus any national court dealing with the issue may find that a contract or parts of that contract are void where one of the parties to an action can demonstrate that art. 81(1) applies to the situation.

The effect of art. 81(2) runs either from the date at which art. 81(1) became effective, or the date of the conclusion of the agreement, whichever is the later. National courts may not, however, apply art. 81(2) to 'old' agreements which existed at 13 March 1962 or the date of accession of the relevant Member State (*Brasserie de Haecht SA* v *Wilkin (No. 2)* case 48/72 [1973] CMLR 287). As long as these agreements have been notified to the Commission in accordance with Regulation 17/62 only the Commission has the power to strike these down. However, once the Commission has indicated to the parties that it is unlikely to grant an exemption to the parties under art. 81(3) this 'provisional validity' comes to an end, and national courts may then apply art. 81(2) themselves. It appears that the Commission notification to this effect need not take the form of a formal decision, but that any clear communication to that effect by an appropriate official will achieve the same effect (*SA Lancôme* v *Etos BV* case 99/79 [1981] 2 CMLR 164).

Article 81(2) does not necessarily apply to an agreement in its entirety. Where the offending clauses can be separated from the agreement without stripping the essence of the agreement, this will be permitted. Whether this is possible is to be determined in the light of all the relevant circumstances objectively and not necessarily by reference to the views of the parties themselves. Thus in *La Technique Minière* v *Maschinenbau Ulm GmbH* case 56/65 [1966] 1 CMLR 357, the Court held (at 376) that

The automatic nullity in question applies only to those elements of the agreement which are subject to the prohibition or to the agreement as a whole if those elements do not appear severable from the agreement itself. Consequently, all other contractual provisions which are not affected by the prohibition, since they do not involve the application of the Treaty, fall outside the Community law.

The Court has also held that where the matter falls to be decided before a national court the test of severability is to be that which would normally be applied in equivalent national law (*Société de Vente de Ciments et Bétons de L'Est SA* v *Kerpen and Kerpen GmbH* case 319/82 [1985] 1 CMLR 511). There is therefore the potential for a different result to be arrived at depending on the country in which an action is brought, although it is unlikely that this will be a matter of great difficulty in practice.

As has been discussed in Chapter 5, competition law is not used as a sword as often as it could be. One of the most common ways for EC competition law to be introduced before the national courts is for a party contesting a contractual obligation to raise what has become known as the 'Euro-defence'. In such a case the defendant pleads that there is no obligation because the clause or contract in question is in breach of art. 81(1) (see, e.g., *Chemidus Wavin Ltd* v *Société pour la Transformation et l'Exploitation des Resines Industrielles SA* [1978] 3 CMLR 514). English courts have tended to be wary of these 'defences', recognizing the potential of such a defence to serve as an effective delaying tactic: if an art. 234 reference is made in such a case the matter may take up to 18 months to be resolved. Nevertheless if the argument is made it will have to be addressed properly at trial. Such 'defences' may also be raised on the basis of art. 82 although this is less likely. Again the courts may be sceptical of the claims made (see, e.g., *Hoover plc* v *George Hulme (Stockport) Ltd* [1982] FSR 565).

It is for national courts to rule on the validity of contracts falling within art. 81(1) in actions relying on the direct effect of EC law. There has been uncertainty as to the approach that would be adopted by courts in the UK. The issue has been discussed recently in two cases, *Gibbs Mew* v *Gemmell* (unreported (1998) CA) and *Passmore* v *Morland plc* (unreported (1998) High Court). Both cases arose out of challenges to leases between pub tenants and breweries. In *Gibbs Mew* the Court found that the primary purpose of art. 81 was to protect third-party competitors rather than the parties to the agreement itself. Adopting a rule of some severity for the parties, the Court held that a contract falling within art. 81(1) would, for the purposes of English law, be an illegal one. Accordingly there would be no right to damages for either party arising out of the performance of obligations purported to be set out in the contract.

The issue was referred to the ECJ by way of an art. 234 reference from the Court of Appeal in the cases of *Crehan* v *Courage Ltd and others* [1999] UKCLR 110 and 407. The questions that have been asked are important ones, and the answers may have a significant impact on the way in which art. 81 is applied in contractual disputes throughout the Community. The questions, in full, are as follows:

1. Is art. 81 EC to be interpreted as meaning that a party to a prohibited tied house agreement may rely upon that article to seek relief from the courts from the other contracting party?

2. If the answer to Q1 is yes, is the party claiming relief entitled to recover damages alleged to arise as a result of his adherence to the clause in the agreement which is prohibited under art. 81?

3. Should a rule of national law which provides that Courts should not allow a person to plead and/or rely upon his own illegal actions as a necessary step to recovery of damages be allowed as consistent with Community law?

4. If the answer to Q3 is that in some circumstances such a rule may be inconsistent with Community law what circumstances should the national court take into consideration?

Late in 2001 the ECJ provided the answer to these questions (*Courage Ltd* v *Crehan* case C–453/99 [2002] UKCLR 171) and held in particular that, while it was for the national court to determine the appropriate procedures by which the rights given under art. 81 should be invoked, national courts should take into account 'the economic and legal context in which the parties find themselves and . . . the respective bargaining power and conduct of the two parties to the contract' (para. 32). The Court stressed that in cases where a small agreement was concluded within a network of similar agreements 'the party contracting with the person controlling the network cannot bear significant responsibility for the breach of art. 81, particularly where in practice the terms of the contract were imposed on him by the party controlling the network' (para. 34).

In *Passmore* the court accepted that a contract falling within art. 81(1) would be a nullity but adopted a sophisticated approach in recognizing that careful analysis would be needed to determine whether a contract was indeed caught by art. 81, and that the situation could change over time, depending on, for example, the market shares of the parties. Such an approach may raise a great number of problems, and its wisdom has been doubted.

7.5 Trade between Member States

Article 81 will apply only where the practice under consideration 'may affect trade between Member States'. This is a jurisdictional test that applies also in respect of art. 82. The purpose of the provision

is to define, in the context of the law governing competition, the boundary between the areas respectively covered by Community law and the law of the Member States. Thus Community law covers any agreement or any practice which is capable of constituting a threat to freedom of trade between Member States in a manner which might harm the attainment of the objectives of a single market between the Member States, in particular by partitioning the national markets or by affecting the structure of competition within the Common Market. On the other hand conduct the effects of which are confined to the territory of a single Member State is governed by the national legal order. (*Hugin Kassaregister AB and Hugin Cash Registers Ltd* v *Commission* case 22/78 [1979] 3 CMLR 345, at 373)

In practice it will not be difficult to show that most transactions of any real size are capable of affecting trade between Member States, and the ECJ's definitive statement of the meaning of the requirement in *Société Technique Minière* v *Maschinenbau Ulm* case 56/65 [1966] ECR 235 does not provide a very satisfactory clarification: 'it must be possible to foresee with a sufficient degree of probability on the basis of a set of objective factors of law or of fact that the agreement in question may have an influence, direct or indirect, actual or potential, on the pattern of trade between the Member States' (at 249; the problems with translation of cases become apparent if the alternative report, [1966] CMLR 357, at 375, is referred to, as the wording is substantially different, although the sense is not altered).

An extreme reading of this report ('possible to foresee an indirect potential influence on the pattern of trade') would again permit the application of EC law to almost any situation. However, in the 2001 notice on agreements of minor importance ([2001]) OJ C368/13) the Commission recognizes that 'agreements between small and medium-sized undertakings . . . are rarely capable of appreciably affecting trade between member states' (para. 3). For these purposes small and medium-sized undertakings are defined as those with fewer than 250 employees and having an annual turnover not greater than €40m, or an annual balance sheet total not greater than €27m. And in *The Dutch Acceptance Giro System* 1999/687 1999 OJ L271/28 the Commission found that an agreement between undertakings in The Netherlands relating to inter-bank commission payments, with only a negligible involvement by banks from other Member States, would not affect trade between Member States.

7.6 Limits on the application of article 81

From the above it becomes apparent that the prohibition of art. 81(1) is broad and indiscriminate. It applies to multilateral anti-competitive conduct irrespective of the form that the conduct takes; it applies to a wide range of practices; and the jurisdictional test of an effect on Community trade is not a demanding one. At the same time as the prohibition has been widely drawn the limits on the application of the prohibition have become more clearly defined. Most obviously the article is ameliorated in the application of art. 81(3). The ECJ has also developed *de minimis* criteria which are not themselves set out in the article.

7.6.1 Individual article 81(3) exemptions

7.6.1.1 *Procedure*

Article 81(3) provides the major mechanism by which the reach of the prohibition set out in art. 81(1) is curbed. Where the criteria set out in the article are met the Commission has the sole power at present to declare that conduct falling within art. 81(1) is nevertheless to be permitted. The exemption takes the form of a formal decision by the Commission declaring art. 81(1) to be 'inapplicable' to the agreement or arrangements described in the decision. This is similar to, but not the same as, the application of the 'rule of reason' in American antitrust law. In that case the rule's application means that conduct is deemed not to fall within the relevant provisions of the Sherman Act. The award of an exemption under art. 81(3) does not exclude the conduct in question from the ambit of art. 81(1). The position is rather that otherwise illegal conduct will be exempted under certain restricted conditions. These are that the practice in question contributes to improving the production or distribution of goods or to promoting technical or economic progress, while allowing consumers a fair share of the resulting benefit, and which does not:

(a) impose on the undertakings concerned restrictions which are not indispensable to the attainment of these objectives;

(b) afford such undertakings the possibility of eliminating competition in respect of a substantial part of the products in question.

Any such exemption is legally binding and therefore serves as a defence in any action before a national court based on a claim to the effect that the practice identified in the decision is unlawful. The exemptions provided for exist in two main forms: individual exemptions are granted on a case-by-case basis; block exemptions, taking the form of regulations, encompass classes of agreements. In this chapter the focus will be on individual exemptions; block exemptions are considered separately in the following chapter.

Article 9(1) of Regulation 17 provides that: 'Subject to review of its decision by the Court of Justice, the Commission shall have sole power to declare article [81(1)] inapplicable pursuant to Article [81(3)] of the Treaty.'

Exemptions may be granted only following the notification of the agreement provided for in Regulation 17, art. 4:

1. Agreements, decisions and concerted practices of the kind described in Article [81(1)] of the Treaty . . . in respect of which the parties seek application of Article [81(3)] must be notified to the Commission. Until they have been notified, no decision in application of Article [81(3)] may be taken.

Save in tightly defined circumstances exemptions may not be backdated so as to be applied prior to the notification of the agreement (Regulation 17, art. 6(1)). This is not the case where agreements have been notified within the appropriate time limits, or where the criteria set out in art. 4(2) apply. In 1999 art. 4(2) was amended by Regulation 1216/1999 in order to enable vertical agreements to benefit from an exemption under art. 81(3) from the inception of the agreement. This will be the case even where notification occurs later, and it is the Commission's hope that this will reduce the number of notifications. As noted in the *Guidelines on Vertical Restraints*, 'if a dispute arises, an undertaking can still notify, in which case the Commission can exempt the vertical agreement with retroactive effect from the date of entry into force of the agreement if all four conditions of art. 81(3) are fulfilled' (para. 63). The Commission also makes it clear in the *Guidelines* that 'unless there is litigation in national courts or complaints, notifications of vertical agreements will not be given priority in the Commission's enforcement policy' (para. 65). The Commission requires that notifications be made in accordance with rules laid down in Commission Regulation 3385/94 ('On the form, content and other details of applications and notifications provided for in Council Regulation No. 17' (1994) OJ L377/28). Form A/B, set out as an Annex to the Regulation, is to be used for this purpose, and 17 copies along with copies of relevant documents must be sent to the Commission in Brussels.

The other important provision of Regulation 17 relating to exemptions is found in art. 8, which provides that

1. A decision in application of Article [81(3)] of the Treaty shall be issued for a specified period and conditions and obligations may be attached thereto.

2. A decision may on application be renewed if the requirements of Article [81(3)] of the Treaty continue to be satisfied.

3. The Commission may revoke or amend its decision or prohibit specified acts by the parties:

    (a) where there has been a change in any of the facts which were basic to the making of the decision;

    (b) where the parties commit a breach of any obligation attached to the decision;

    (c) where the decision is based on incorrect information or was induced by deceit;

    (d) where the parties abuse the exemption from the provisions of Article [81(1)] of the Treaty granted to them by the decision.

In cases to which subparagraphs (b), (c) or (d) apply, the decision may be revoked with retroactive effect.

As para. 1 says, such exemptions are to be time limited. It was held in *European Night Services* v *Commission* joined cases T–374/94, etc. [1998] ECR II–3141, that 'the duration of any exemption must be sufficient to enable the beneficiaries to achieve the benefits justifying such exemption' (para. 230). In this case the CFI held that, having regard to the size of the investment necessary to achieve the aims of the agreement, the Commission's eight-year exemption was probably too short.

National courts are not at present able to grant exemptions under art. 81(3), although see below. Where they are considering the application of art. 81 the court should, according to the 'Notice on cooperation between national courts and the Commission in applying Articles [81] and [82] of the EEC Treaty' ((1993) OJ C39/6), 'check whether [the agreement, decision, or concerted practice] is or will be the subject of an exemption by the Commission under Article [81(3)]' (para. 24). There are three situations that may arise. First, there may exist a formal Commission decision, which must be followed, or a comfort letter, which 'the Commission considers that national courts may take account of . . . as factual elements' (see Chapter 3). Secondly, an agreement might fall within a block exemption regulation, which must also be followed by the national court. The position is more complex in the third category of cases where an individual exemption has not been awarded and a block exemption does not apply. Here the national court should

first examine whether the procedural conditions necessary for securing exemption are fulfilled, notably whether the agreement, decision or concerted practice has been duly notified in accordance with Article 4(1) of Regulation No. 17. Where no such notification has been made, and subject to Article 4(2) of Regulation No. 17, exemption under Article [81(3)] is ruled out, so that the national court may decide, pursuant to Article [81(2)] that the agreement, decision or concerted practice is void.   (para. 28)

Where the agreement has been notified the national court is asked to anticipate the Commission's likely decision. The Notice refers the national court to 'the relevant criteria developed by the case law of the Court of Justice and the Court of First Instance and by previous regulations and decisions of the Commission'. This may therefore be a complex matter, and in practice the national court is more likely to stay proceedings to await the result of the Commission's deliberation (as, for example, was the case in *MTV Europe v BMG Records (UK) Ltd* (1995) 17 July, CA, unreported).

In its *Modernisation White Paper* the EC Commission sets out a reform programme for the application of art. 81. This

involves the abolition of the notification and exemption system and its replacement by a Council Regulation which would render the exemption rule of [art. 81(3)] directly applicable, without prior decision by the Commission. Article [81] as a whole would be applied by the Commission, national competition authorities and national courts. (para. 12)

The modernization process is expected to be completed sometime in 2002.

7.6.1.2 *The application of the substantive criteria*

The Commission possesses a wide margin of discretion in deciding whether to grant an exemption in individual cases, although this discretion is subject to judicial control (see Regulation 17, art. 9(1) and, e.g., *Metro-SB-Grossmärkte GmbH & Co. KG v Commission* case 26/76 [1978] 2 CMLR 1, para. 45). The review by the Court will be limited to determining whether the procedural rules have been complied with, including the provision of adequate reasoning, whether the facts have been accurately stated, and whether there has been any manifest error or misuse of powers. The Court is not expected therefore to review all the economic aspects of the particular decision (see, e.g., *BAT Ltd and RJ Reynolds Industries Inc v Commission* cases 142 and 156/84 [1988] 4 CMLR 24, para. 62).

The article calls for a balance to be drawn between the restriction and the positive impact that this has. No clear criteria have been established by which it is possible to determine what the outcome will be in any particular instance, although the great majority of exemptions will fall to be granted under one of the block regulations and agreements will, where possible, be tailored so as to comply with these.

The Commission may take into account wider social considerations as well as matters that relate strictly to competition policy. In September 1998, for example, an art. 81(3) comfort letter was issued to members of the European Council for Automotive Research and Development (EUCAR) relating to an agreement between major manufacturers to collaborate in research aimed, *inter alia*, at reducing car emissions. In doing so, the Commission noted that 'research must be at the pre-competitive stage' (Press Release IP/98/832, 25 September 1998). Environmental concerns also led to the Commission granting an art. 81(3) exemption in respect of an agreement between manufacturers and importers of washing machines to reduce sales of the least efficient machines (*CECED Agreement* 2000/475 [2000] OJ L187/47). In *Metro* the Commission took into consideration the fact that several Member States had enacted legislation that differentiated between resale and wholesale outlets with the aim of providing a limited protection to retailers from competition from wholesalers, in order to increase the range of outlets. The Court's view was that it was acceptable for the Commission to apply a similar policy when deciding whether to grant an exemption under art. 81(3) to the selective distribution system maintained by SABA (at para. 29 of the judgment). This is of concern to some commentators who would prefer that the scope of the review be limited strictly to competitive matters. However, the fact that the Court has held repeatedly that Community competition policy is to be reviewed in the light of the other objectives of the Treaty would suggest that such a wider application is appropriate—another objective of the Treaty should not be obstructed by a rigid interpretation of art. 81(3) (see also *Remia BV* v *Commission* case 42/84 [1987] 1 CMLR 1, at para. 42).

Although the article provides that consumers must benefit from the restriction in order for the exemption to be granted, there is some scepticism within consumer organizations as to the rigour with which this analysis is conducted. Often it will simply be assumed that if the process of competition itself benefits from the application of the agreement then the benefit will flow naturally to the consumer. For example, in the *Metro* case the Court first considered the fact that the agreement assured 'a more regular distribution' of the goods in question to the benefit of both producer and retailer (para. 43). Then the Court held that

In the circumstances of the present case regular supplies represent a sufficient advantage to consumers for them to be considered to constitute a fair share of the benefit resulting from the improvement brought about by the restriction on competition permitted by the Commission ... the grant of exemption may ... in the present case be considered as sufficiently justified by the advantage which consumers obtain from an improvement in supplies. (para. 48)

This is not always the case, however. In condemning the operation of an association of building contractors in The Netherlands market the Commission, supported by the CFI, found that although the contractors undeniably benefited from the operation of the rules determined by the association this benefit was not passed on to the customer. As the Court put it, 'the claimed limitation of transaction costs operates almost exclusively to the benefit of the contractors'. Even accepting that some of the benefits the contractors claimed did exist, because, for example, the customer would have to consider fewer bids, 'that benefit is limited by comparison with the disadvantages which he must bear and the benefits obtained from that system by contractors' (*Vereniging van Samenwerkende Prijsregelende Organisaties in de Bouwnijverheid (SPO)* v *Commission* case T–29/92 [1995] ECR–II 289, para. 295).

The meaning of 'consumer' is not necessarily limited to the end-user of a product purchasing it through a retail outlet. The industrial user of a product, or a manufacturer purchasing a component to be used in its production process may also be a consumer for the purposes of art. 81(3). For example, in *Kabel-metal-Luchaire* 75/494 (1975) OJ L222/34, an agreement between two industrial companies was exempted when 'electrical-equipment and motor-vehicle manufacturers and their customers, obtain[ed] a fair share of the benefits ... for as a result of this agreement

they have at their disposal in the common market goods tailored to their needs'
(para. 11).

Some concern has been expressed that in giving pre-eminence to the role of price
competition the Commission has not permitted the consumer to benefit from
other types of competition in some cases. For example, in *VBBB/VBVB* 82/123
(1982) OJ L54/36 (on appeal *Vereniging ter Bevordering van het Vlaamse Boekwezen
(VBVB) and Vereeniging ter Bevordering van de Belangen des Boekhandels (VBBB) v
Commission* cases 43/82 and 63/82 [1985] 1 CMLR 27) the Commission considered
an agreement operated by the main Dutch and Belgian book publishers and sellers
under which resale price maintenance was applied. This position had its counterpart in the Net Book Agreement operated in the United Kingdom. Under the terms
of the agreement booksellers would be prevented from increasing their individual
market share by competing with other booksellers on price. In seeking an exemption for this agreement the parties claimed that it produced benefits that were
shared by the consumers. In particular it was claimed that the agreement increased
both the range of books published and the number of outlets in which they could
be purchased.

Similar arguments were made before the ECJ following the Commission's finding
that the agreement was in breach of art. 81(1) and that no exemption would
be granted. The applicants also relied, unsuccessfully, on art. 10 of the European
Convention on Human Rights which guarantees the right to freedom of expression. As was the case in *Metro*, the applicants claimed that while the effect of the
agreement was to restrict price competition, here by resellers in relation to each
individual book, it left unimpaired competition between the various publishers.
The applicants felt that by taking the view that price competition was the essential
ingredient in competition the Commission had ignored the particular characteristics of the book market. The Commission did not share the applicants' view
that for the consumer the consideration put on the price of a book was secondary
to that relating to the diversity of stocks. The Court, noting the Commission's
argument that 'the resale price maintenance system totally eliminates price
competition at retail level' (para. 43 of the judgment), rejected the applicants'
arguments. Accepting that there might be situations in which art. 81(1) would not
be breached by a restriction on price competition that was more than balanced by
other factors, the Court nevertheless held that in this case the agreement's effects
were too marked to be removed from the scope of the prohibition by the granting
of an art. 81(3) exemption.

On the other hand, in *REIMS II* 1999/687 (1999) OJ L275/17 the EC Commission
exempted an agreement between 16 European postal operators which fixed the
fees for the costs of delivering cross-border mail (so-called terminal dues). At
para. 65 the Commission noted that 'it has to be acknowledged that the REIMS II
Agreement is a price-fixing agreement with unusual characteristics'. Some sort of
arrangement was clearly necessary in order for the postal system to work, and in
the absence of a general agreement there would need to be a system of bilateral
agreements, with the costs entailed by this. Further, the agreement would clearly

produce the substantial advantage of an increase in the quality of cross-border mail services (paras 69–76).

The fact that an undertaking has the benefit of an exemption will not necessarily serve as a defence to an action brought on the basis of art. 82. The exemption relates specifically to the application of art. 81(1) and not to EC competition law in general. This point was clarified by the CFI in *Tetra Pak Rausing SA v Commission* case T–51/89 [1991] 4 CMLR 334, where the Court rejected Tetra Pak's argument to the effect that the principle of legal certainty would be undermined if an art. 81(3) decision could not be relied on in all circumstances. A similar view was taken by the Commission in *Cewal* 93/82 (1993) OJ L34/20 (at para. 20) where it held that the fact that the parties benefited from one of the block exemptions did not prevent the application of art. 82.

7.6.2 The Commission's exclusive power

The fact that the Commission alone has the competence to award an individual exemption is often seen as a hindrance to the effective application of art. 81. The argument that these powers should also be given to either the relevant national authorities or to national courts is driven by the inability of the Commission to deal with the number of cases brought before it. In 1999, for example, 388 new cases were registered by the Commission, of which 162 were notifications by the parties to various practices. The Commission closed only 68 cases by formal decision, while a further 514 were dealt with less formally, whether by comfort letters, or by simple administrative closure of the file (1999 *Annual Report*, p. 57). The argument against such a devolution of application, which is consistent with the principle of subsidiarity, is that it might carry with it the serious risk of inconsistencies in approach, and in the worst case to flagrant abuses of the process. These arguments are not convincing, and it is unlikely that the harm to competition policy from occasionally inconsistent national decisions would be any greater than that arising from the logjam of cases in front of the EC Commission, or the great number of informal steps taken to resolve this problem. In 1995 Karel Van Miert, the Commissioner in charge of competition policy, accepted that

After almost forty years of enforcement of competition law by the European institutions such a risk no longer exists. Much progress has been made in recent years towards an achievement of the seamless web of enforcement of competition law in Europe. . . . This is a natural consequence of the integration process, which creates pressure for a level playing field throughout the Community and also affects application of Community law by national authorities.

The *Modernisation White Paper* has been referred to above. The Commission is advocating the adoption of a 'directly applicable system', which it explains thus:

Within the framework of the prohibition system provided for in the Treaty, there exists another option for reform, which would be to adopt a directly applicable exception system allowing for *ex post* supervision of restrictive practices. The switch to such a system can be achieved by a Council Regulation, based on art. 83 of the Treaty, which would stipulate that all national authorities or courts before which the applicability of art. 81(1) of the Treaty was invoked would also consider the applicability of art. 81(3). Article 81 would then become *a unitary norm comprising a rule establishing the principle of prohibition, unless certain conditions are met.* The whole of art. 81 would then become a directly applicable provision which individuals could invoke in court or before any authority empowered to deal with such matters. This interpretation would have the effect of making restrictive practices which are prohibited by art. 81(1), but which meet the tests of art. 81(1), lawful as from the time they were concluded, without the need for any prior decision. Similarly, restrictive practices that restricted competition would be unlawful once the conditions of art. 81(3) are no longer fulfilled. This new framework would mean that restrictive practices would no longer have to be notified in order to be validated. The arrangements for implementing art. 81 as a whole would then be identical for art. 81(1) and art. 82.

7.6.3 Block exemption regulations

Because many thousands of agreements would need to be individually notified to the Commission in order to seek the benefit of the art. 81(3) exemption, various block exemptions now relate to a range of agreements. Some of these are considered in more detail in the following chapter.

7.6.4 *De minimis* rules and the notice on agreements of minor importance

On its face art. 81(1) prohibits all anti-competitive agreements where trade is affected, irrespective of the size of the parties in question or the impact that the agreement will have. Were this in fact the case the article would paralyse business activity, and steps have been taken to remove from its scope the great majority of situations where agreements are in place. The initial approach of the Commission and the Court was to remove from the application of the article those agreements where the market share of the parties concerned was only minimal. For example, in the case of *Franz Völk v Ets Vervaecke SPRL* case 5/69 [1969] CMLR 273, an agreement was not condemned under art. 81(1) even where it contained clauses that, in other contexts, would have been clearly in breach. The agreement was an exclusive distribution agreement providing absolute territorial protection, between a German producer of washing machines and a Belgian-based distributor. The manufacturer's market share was, at 0.6 per cent, considered to be insignificant, and the agreement related to only 600 units. In these circumstances the Court held that 'an agreement escapes the prohibition of Article [81] when it only affects the market insignificantly, account being taken of the weak position held by the parties on the market in the products in question' (para. 3). It should be noted, however, that art. 81 will still apply at market shares greatly below those necessary to establish the presence of a dominant position under art. 82.

These *de minimis* decisions have been 'codified' in a Commission notice on agreements of minor importance, which has been regularly overhauled since the first notice was introduced. While such notices cannot have the force of law, and do not bind the Commission, they are considered to be of the status of at least 'soft law' by those seeking guidance from them, and are likely to reflect accurately current Commission policies. In the most recent version of the notice the Commission makes it clear that where undertakings rely on the notice in good faith and assume that an agreement is covered by the notice the Commission will not impose fines on them if it subsequently finds them to be in breach. In cases where the notice does apply 'the Commission will not institute proceedings either upon application or its own initiative' (para. 4).

The most recent version of the *de minimis* notice was published in 2001 ((2001) OJ C368/13) and is the most detailed version of the notice published to date and, according to the accompanying press release (IP/02/13, 7 January 2002), 'reflects an economic approach'. Thresholds provided for in the earlier versions of the notices have been raised. Under the 2001 notice the relevant thresholds for the application of art. 81(1) are different depending on whether agreements are made between competing or non-competing undertakings. In the case of competitors, or potential competitors, the threshold is 10 per cent of any of the relevant markets affected by the agreement(s) (para. 7(a)). Where the undertakings are not competitors or potential competitors the threshold is 15 per cent (para. 7(b)). In situations in which it is not readily easy to determine whether the relevant undertakings are competitors or not the lower threshold is to be the applicable one.

For the first time the notice sets out a threshold to apply to situations in which there exists a network of small agreements which have a cumulative effect, although in this respect the formula is a little more complex. Both the thresholds set out in para. 7 are reduced to 5 per cent in respect of individual agreements, and a cumulative foreclosure effect is considered to be unlikely to exist if less than 30 per cent of the relevant market is affected by a network of parallel agreements. This is to say that, for example, where there is a network of parallel agreements which covers 20 per cent of the market, and a new one is entered into between parties which have less than 5 per cent of the overall market, both the individual agreement and the network of similar agreements will be found not to be appreciable.

Certain 'hard-core' restrictions are considered sufficiently onerous as to invite condemnation even where they are entered into by parties whose market shares would be such as to fall within the application of the notice. In relation to competitors these are agreements which have as their object of the fixing of prices when selling the products to third parties, the limitation of output or sales, and the allocation of markets or customers (these are the same exceptions as found in block exemption 2790/99—see Chapter 8). In the case of agreements between non-competitors the following restrictions are prohibited: those which restrict the ability of a buyer to determine its minimum sale price, the maintenance of absolute territorial protection, various restrictions relating to the operation of selective distribution systems, and restrictions on the ability of a supplier of components to a manufacturer that would limit the ability of the supplier to make those components available as spare parts (these are the same exceptions as found in block exemption 2658/2000—see Chapter 8).

The fact that an agreement or conduct falls above the thresholds set out in the notice does not mean that such agreements necessarily appreciably restrict competition. It is noted in para. 2 of the notice that such agreements 'may still have only a negligible effect on competition and may therefore not be prohibited by Article 81(1)'. However, such agreements would not benefit from the shortcut to safety provided by the *de minimis* notice.

7.7 **Article 81 and the rule of reason**

Similarities between the approach of arts 81 and 82 EC and that of the Sherman Act, ss. 1 and 2, have encouraged speculation as to the place of doctrines developed in the American context in Community law. There has been much discussion of the place of the 'rule of reason' in EC law. Section 1 of the Sherman Act is, in part, in the following terms:

Every contract, combination in the form of trust or otherwise, or conspiracy, in restraint of trade or commerce among the several States, or with foreign nations, is declared to be illegal. Every person who shall make any contract or engage in any combination or conspiracy hereby declared to be illegal shall be deemed guilty of a felony.

As was noted in Chapter 1, on its face this provision would condemn a wide range of competitive activity, much of it beneficial. American courts responded to this legislative straitjacket by developing an approach, itself based on the common law, in which the question is asked whether the restraint under attack 'is one that promotes competition or one that suppresses competition' (*National Society of Professional Engineers* v *United States* (1978) 435 US 679 at 691). The test was first introduced in *Standard Oil Co. of New Jersey* v *United States* (1911) 221 US 1, and was given some shape in 1918. Thus the

true test of legality is whether the restraint imposed is such as merely regulates and perhaps thereby promotes competition or whether it is such as may suppress or even destroy competition. To determine that question the court must ordinarily consider the facts peculiar to the business to which the restraint is applied; its condition before and after the restraint was imposed; the nature of the restraint and its effect, actual or probable. The history of the restraint, the evil believed to exist, the reason for adopting the particular remedy, the purpose or end sought to be attained, are all relevant facts.   (*per* Brandeis J in *Chicago Board of Trade* v *United States* (1918) 246 US 231 at 238)

Under the rule of reason a plaintiff must generally show first that the practice in question is likely to damage competition. If this can be demonstrated it is then for the defendant to establish that there are clear benefits that flow from the restraint, and that the restraint is necessary in order for those benefits to be achieved. *Inter alia* vertical restraints fall to be considered under the rule of reason and it is unlikely that a vertical restraint will be condemned except in situations where inter-brand competition is very weak (see, e.g., *Tunis Bros Co.* v *Ford Motor Co.* (1991) 952 F.2d 715).

While many have been unable to resist the temptation of comparing the operation of the rule of reason with the process whereby matters are considered under art. 81, the argument is a complex one and of doubtful value. The availability of the art. 81(3) exemption has meant that major problems have not been created for undertakings when their arrangements are brought within the scope of art. 81(1), albeit a negative clearance is to be preferred to an exemption. The analysis undertaken for the purposes of art. 81(3) is akin to, but not the same as, that carried out in applying the rule of reason. Generally arguments based on an application of the rule of reason in relation to art. 81 are designed to remove from the scope of the article altogether many of the agreements which now fall to be considered under art. 81(3), and would thus deprive the Commission of much of its current flexibility. However, one undeniable benefit of such an approach would be to reduce the costs to undertakings of compliance with the regulatory structure as presently operated.

In its *Modernisation White Paper* the Commission accepts that it is, in effect, advocating an approach similar to that taken under the rule of reason, and notes, in relation to arguments about the rule of reason, that

the Commission has already adopted this approach to a limited extent and has carried out an assessment of the pro- and anti-competitive aspects of some restrictive practices under art. [81(1)] . . . However, the structure of [art. 81] is such as to prevent greater use being made of this approach.   (para. 57)

Later the Commission expressly rejects the casting aside of art. 81(3), which is what advocates of the rule of reason are implicitly asking for, and in some cases explicitly suggesting. The Commission's view is that it would be 'paradoxical' to do so, 'when that provision in fact contains all the elements of a "rule of reason"' (ibid.).

8

Block exemption regulations under article 81

8.1 Introduction

The authority for the making of block exemptions stems from art. 83 EC, which provides that the secondary legislation necessary to give effect to the principles set out in arts 81 and 82 'shall be laid down by the Council, acting by a qualified majority on a proposal from the Commission'. Such legislation may be designed, *inter alia,*

(b) to lay down detailed rules for the application of Article [81(3)], taking into account the need to ensure effective supervision on the one hand, and to simplify administration to the greatest possible extent on the other.

Block exemption regulations are made on the basis of the experience gained by the EC Commission in the individual application of art. 81(3), and are designed to ease the administrative burden for both the Commission and the relevant undertaking that is seeking the benefit of an exemption. Where the terms of any practice that falls within art. 81(1) are entirely within the permissive terms of any of the block exemptions then individual notification of that practice is not necessary and art. 81(1) is automatically disapplied. Two Council Regulations establish the general framework within which block exemptions may be made. These are Regulation 19/65 ((1965) JO 533) and Regulation 2821/71 ((1971) JO L285/46). Regulation 19/65 gave the Commission the authority to issue regulations relating to bilateral exclusive dealing arrangements, and Regulation 2821/75 an equivalent power applicable to categories of agreements relating to intellectual property. Regulation 19/65 was amended in 1999 by Regulation 1215/99 (1999) OJ L148/1, which was part of the follow-up to the *Green Paper on Vertical Restraints* discussed in the previous chapter. Recital (9) of 1215/99 made clear the thrust of the changes that were to be effected, stating that 'the Commission should be empowered to replace the existing legislation with legislation which is simpler, more flexible and better targeted, and which may cover all types of vertical agreements'.

The amendment also made specific reference to various categories of intellectual property, and their assignment or use.

Importantly, in relation to the balance of power between the Member States and the Commission a new para. 7(2) was added to Regulation 19/65, which gives the

Member States the power to withdraw the benefit of a block regulation in cases where an agreement falling within its terms has 'certain effects which are incompatible with the conditions laid down in art. 81(3) . . . in the territory of a Member State, or in part thereof, which has all the characteristics of a distinct market'. The block exemptions considered in this chapter are those that were enacted under these instruments. Further authorization has been given in specific areas such as transport and insurance.

The following summarizes the position of the main block exemptions as of May 2002:

- Regulation 2790/99 on the application of art. 81(3) of the Treaty to categories of vertical agreements and concerted practices (1999) OJ L336/21;
- Regulation 2658/2000 on the application of art. 81(3) of the Treaty to categories of specialization agreements (2000) OJ L304/3;
- Regulation 2659/2000 on the application of art. 81(3) of the Treaty to categories of research and development agreements (2000) OJ L304/7;
- Regulation 1475/95 on the application of art. [81(3)] of the Treaty to certain categories of motor vehicle distribution and servicing agreements (1995) OJ L145/25;
- Regulation 240/96 on the application of art. [81(3)] of the Treaty to certain categories of technology transfer agreements (1996) OJ L31/2.

There has been considerable change to the block exemption landscape since late 1999. Regulation 2790/99 has replaced two earlier blocks dealing with exclusive distribution and exclusive purchasing (Regulations 1983/83 and 1984/83, both published in corrected versions at (1983) OJ L281/24). It has also replaced Regulation 4087/88 relating to franchising agreements ((1988) OJ L359/46). Although there are situations in which the terms of these block exemption regulations could be relevant, for example in relation to a private action brought in contract law alleging the illegality of an agreement, only the terms of the new regulation are dealt with here. Those seeking detailed analysis of the regulations it replaces are referred instead to Green, N., and Robertson, A., *Commercial Agreements and Competition Law—Practice and Procedure in the UK and EC*, Kluwer 2nd edn (1997). The detailed terms of Regulation 2790/99 are considered below.

In addition to this fundamental change, the Commission published late in 2000 new block exemptions dealing with specialization and research and development agreements. It also published its *Guidelines on the Applicability of Article 81 to Horizontal Cooperation Agreements*, which should be read alongside these two block exemptions. Two older block exemption regulations, relating to motor vehicle distribution and technology transfer, continue to be in force.

8.2 **Vertical agreements**

8.2.1 **Regulation 2790/99**

It has already been seen in the previous chapter that the approach taken in *Etablissements Consten SARL and Grundig-Verkaufs-GmbH* v *Commission* cases 56, 58/64 [1966] CMLR 418 confirmed, to the surprise of some, that art. 81 could be applicable to vertical agreements, including those designed to facilitate the marketing and distribution of goods. While the majority of such agreements, if notified, would be likely to benefit from an individual exemption this is a procedure that neither the Commission nor the undertakings themselves would wish for. Following the application of Community competition law, when Regulation 17 entered into force, a very large number of such agreements were notified to the Commission, which gave it the expertise to determine which clauses were likely to feature in such agreements, and which it was likely to find in breach of the Treaty. Regulation 67/67 initially covered both exclusive distribution and exclusive purchasing agreements, but this was broken down in 1983 into two block exemptions. The Regulation enacted in 1999 is therefore a move back to a more general approach, but without the straitjacket imposed by the earlier regulations. Regulation 2790/99 should be read alongside the Commission Notice, *Guidelines on Vertical Restraints*, published in May 2000.

Recital (3) of the Regulation identifies a range of vertical agreements which can normally be regarded as satisfying the conditions laid down in art. 81(3) for the granting of an exemption. This category

includes vertical agreements for the purchase or sale of goods or services where these agreements are concluded between non-competing undertakings, between certain competitors or by certain associations of retailers of goods; it also includes vertical agreements containing ancillary provisions on the assignment or use of intellectual property rights.

This includes not only standard distribution agreements, but also franchising agreements, and the *Guidelines*, at paras 42–44 deal with the assignment of know-how that is central to franchise agreements.

The preamble to the Regulation iterates the arguments made in favour of such agreements in the case law and previous decisions. The preamble is an integral part of the Regulation and on several occasions the ECJ interpreted provisions of Regulation 67/67 in the light of its preamble, as, for example, in *De Norre* v *NV Brouwerij Concordia* case 47/76 [1977] 1 CMLR 378. It is recognized therefore that:

(6) Vertical agreements of the category defined in this Regulation can improve economic efficiency within a chain of production or distribution by facilitating better coordination between the participating undertakings; in particular they can lead to a reduction in the transaction and distribution costs of the parties and to an optimisation of their sales and investment levels.

(7) The likelihood that such efficiency-enhancing effects will outweigh any anti-

competitive effects due to restrictions contained in vertical agreements depends on the degree of market power of the undertakings concerned.

It is this focus on market power which marks the most significant difference between the operation of this Regulation, and its predecessors. Where the earlier regulations set out detailed lists of acceptable, 'white' clauses, and unacceptable, 'black' clauses, the new Regulation provides that, with some limited exceptions, all vertical restraints are acceptable unless they are coupled to significant market power. Recognizing that there may still be some situations in which the effect of agreements may be harmful, and in particular those in which there are parallel networks of vertical agreements which have a foreclosure effect, there is mention in recital (13), and later in the Regulation, of the power of the Commission to withdraw the benefit of the exemption (see also art. 6).

Article 1 of the Regulation defines basic terms relevant to its application, and the core provision is that of art. 2, which provides that:

Article 81(1) shall not apply to agreements or concerted practices entered into between two or more undertakings each of which operates, for the purposes of the agreement, at a different level of the production or distribution chain, and relating to the conditions under which the parties may purchase, sell or resell certain goods or services ('vertical restraints').

The exemption applies also to agreements between associations of undertakings and their members as long as all members are retailers of goods, and if no individual member has a turnover in excess of €50m. This does not affect the possible application of art. 81(1) to horizontal agreements between members of the association (art. 2(2)). The three main elements of this definition are set out in para. 24 of the *Guidelines*. The agreement must be between two or more undertakings, and agreements with final consumers not operating as an undertaking do not therefore count. It does not matter if each undertaking operates at various levels of the market, as long as the specific agreement is between elements operating at a different level, and the purpose of the Regulation is to 'cover purchase and distribution agreements'. Rent and lease agreements are not covered.

Article 2(3) includes provisions relating to the assignment of intellectual property rights where the assignment is a legitimate part of a vertical agreement otherwise covered by the exemption. Five conditions are set out for this to be valid, the main purpose being to 'ensure that the [Regulation] applies to vertical agreements where the use, sale or resale of goods or services can be performed more effectively because IPRs are assigned to or transferred for use by the buyer' (*Guidelines*, para. 31).

The limiting principle is set out in art. 3, para. 1, which provides that

the exemption provided for in art. 2 shall apply on condition that the market share held by the supplier does not exceed 30% of the relevant market on which it sells the contract goods or services.

A similar market share of 30 per cent applies in relation to buyers where the vertical agreement relates to exclusive supply obligations (art. 3(2)). Agreements as a whole will not be covered by the exemption in situations in which, either by themselves or in combination with other factors, they have one of a number of objectives (art. 4). These include:

(a) setting fixed or minimum sale prices (maximum prices may be set in some circumstances);

(b) setting territorial restrictions except in certain defined, limited circumstances;

(c) restricting cross-supplies in a selective distribution system;

(d) restrictions accepted by a buyer of components which prevent the supplier of those components from selling them as spare parts to end-users or repairers not approved of by the buyer.

The approach to territorial restrictions follows that long established by the Commission, in that the protection of exclusively assigned territories must permit passive sales, although active sales may be prevented. The *Guidelines* provide definitions of 'active' and 'passive' sales, that for the first time deal also with the issue of marketing over the Internet. The definitions, in full, are as follows:

'Active' sales mean: (1) actively approaching individual customers inside another distributor's exclusive territory or exclusive customer group by, for instance, direct mail or visits, or (2) actively approaching a specific customer group or customers in a specific territory allocated exclusively to another distributor through advertisement in media or other promotions specifically targeted at that customer group or targeted at customers in that territory, or (3) establishing a warehouse or distribution outlet in another distributor's exclusive territory.

'Passive' sales mean responding to unsolicited requests from individual customers, including delivery of goods or services to such customers. General advertising or promotion in media or on the Internet that reaches customers in other distributors' exclusive territories or customer groups but which is a reasonable way to reach customers outside those territories or customer groups, for instance, to reach customers in non-exclusive territories or in one's own territory, are passive sales. (para. 50)

The question of Internet sales is an important one, and it is generally recognized that the development of e-commerce threatens to change radically concepts of 'exclusivity' and assigned territories. At para. 51 of the *Guidelines* the Commission deals with the issue at some length, taking as the starting point the basic principle that

[e]very distributor must be free to use the Internet to advertise or sell products. A restriction on the use of the Internet by distributors could only be compatible with the [Regulation] to the extent that promotion on the Internet or sales over the Internet would lead to active selling into other distributors' exclusive territories or customer groups.

The Commission considers the situation where a customer contacts a distributor through the distributor's web site, and places an order, to be one of passive selling. Further, the language used on the web site will be irrelevant. Outright bans on selling on the Internet will be permitted only where there is an objective justification. The position here is likely to have been influenced by the experience gained in America, where the issue of Internet selling has already led to some difficulties. It was reported in 1998, for example, that Tupperware had prohibited its more than

7,000 'sales consultants' from selling Tupperware through the consultants' own web sites. Tupperware had argued that the product needed live demonstrations in order to be most effectively sold.

Article 5 provides that certain obligations within an agreement will not be covered by the block exemption, although to the extent to which these can be separated out from the agreement as a whole, the latter will still benefit. There are few of these, and the first two relate to various non-completion obligations, while the third relates to any provision under which members of a selective distribution system are prevented from selling competing brands.

The right of Member States to withdraw the benefit of the block exemption in accordance with the conditions laid down in Regulation 19/65 is confirmed in art. 7.

Article 9 relates to the issue of the calculation and assessment of market share. Although the Regulation resolves many of the problems that flowed from the overly formalistic approach adopted under the earlier block exemptions, it does not provide a solution to every problem that will always be simple. To some extent it has replaced formalistic legal analysis with sophisticated economic analysis, and although for a great many small- and medium-sized undertakings this will not present any problem, there will be a class of firms for which there may be genuine doubt whether they are operating at the 30 per cent threshold. Paragraph 1 of art. 9 refers to the by now standard definition of goods or services 'sold by the supplier, which are regarded as interchangeable or substitutable by the buyer, by reason of the products' characteristics, their prices and their intended use'. The effect of this is to require the analytical framework of the Commission Notice on Market Definition (discussed in Chapter 11) to be applied. Market shares are to be calculated on the previous year's data where these are available, and they may, for a two-year period, exceed 30 per cent as long as they do not rise above 35 per cent. If they are initially below 30 per cent, but then rise to above 35 per cent, the period of grace shall be limited to one year.

8.2.2 Motor vehicle distribution and servicing agreements— Regulation 1475/95

Regulation 1475/95 replaced an earlier version (Regulation 123/85 (1985) OJ L15/16), and the earlier version still applies to agreements concluded before 30 September 1995. Following the earlier Regulation's entry into force, all the European car distributors structured their arrangements so as to comply with the terms of the Regulation, and the Commission was able to abandon many investigations that it had under way in this sector. The peculiarities of the motor vehicle market are noted in the preamble to the Regulation. This position is established in recital 4, where the Commission explains that

motor vehicles are consumer durables which at both regular and irregular intervals require expert maintenance and repair, not always in the same place. Motor vehicle manufacturers cooperate with the selected dealers and repairers in order to provide specialised servicing for the product. On grounds of capacity and efficiency alone, such a form of cooperation cannot be extended to an unlimited number of dealers and repairers.

Article 1 of the Regulation provides that it may apply to agreements to which only two undertakings are party, where one is awarded a specific territory, which need not be exclusive to that party, and the motor vehicles are supplied for resale. The Regulation does not cover motor cycles, or three-wheel cars. The supplier may be restrained from itself supplying final customers, or providing servicing (art. 2). Many of the acceptable terms are designed to protect investment made by the supplier in the dealership. It is common, for example, for the manufacturer/ supplier to arrange for training for mechanics that is specific to the particular range of cars, or to provide specialist equipment required for their servicing. Article 3(4) allows restrictions, for example, that prevent any third party using a common workshop to benefit unduly from the investment of the supplier. Other permissible restrictions relate to standard safety criteria: the dealer may be prevented from using spare parts supplied by other manufacturers unless these match the suppliers' parts in quality and function (art. 3(5)). In the white list of art. 4 provisions relating to standards are to the fore. The supplier may also require that the dealer endeavours to sell minimum quantities (art. 4(1)(3)), and to maintain set stock levels (art. 4(1)(4)). Article 5 sets out further requirements that *must* appear if the Regulation is to be applied. The first requirement is that such agreements must include an obligation on the dealer to honour guarantees and provide free of charge to the end customer any servicing or repair work that falls under the warranty. One of the main changes made from the earlier Regulation is that agreements must now include a provision under which the dealer will be permitted to sell other makes of vehicles where 'the dealer shows that there are objective reasons for doing so' (art. 5(2)(1)). The inclusion of this requirement was designed to open up the market, reducing the force of the tie on the dealers and appears in this regard to have been less than wholly successful.

The blacklist contains 12 restrictions that will remove the agreement from the scope of the Regulation. These are designed to maintain competition as far as possible within a market in which vertical ties are a prominent and necessary feature. An agreement cannot, for example, be exempted if there are restrictions on the ability of the dealer to determine the price of the contract goods (art. 6(1)(6)), or if there are restrictions on the spare parts that may be used subject to quality requirements (art. 6(1)(10)).

The Regulation is due to expire on 30 September 2002, and in February 2002 the Commission published its proposals for a new, greatly changed, version of the regulation.

The draft regulation is based more closely on Regulation 2790/99 (see above). The effect of this is that the regulation will not be prescriptive, and allows manufacturers greater choice as to the way in which they arrange to sell cars. In particular 'providing an agreement corresponds to the basic conditions for the application of the regulation, everything is permitted with the exception of a defined blacklist of "hardcore" restrictions' (IP/02/196, 5 February 2002). A feature of the new regime that is stressed is that retailers will have the ability to 'actively' sell outside their assigned territory, and may not be penalized in any way for doing so. It is hoped by the Commission that this will put pressure on what it terms the 'extraordinarily high price differentials that exist between member states' (ibid.).

8.2.3 Technology transfer agreements—Regulation 240/96

Regulation 240/96 replaced both Regulation 2349/84 on patent licensing ((1984) OJ L219/15) and Regulation 556/89 on know-how licensing ((1989) OJ L61/1) and applies to agreements entered into from 1 April 1996. It is a matter of common commercial practice for the holder of intellectual property not itself to directly exploit the knowledge, technology, or processes governed by that property, but to license to someone else the right to do so in return for a royalty or commission on the profits accruing to the licensee.

The Commission early took the view that patent licences would fall within art. 81(1) unless the licence merely confirms the existence of the property right in the patent. The most important case in this respect is that of *LC Nungesser KG and Kurt Eisele v Commission* case 258/78 [1983] 1 CMLR 278 ('the *maize seed* case'). This dealt with the commercial exploitation of a modified type of maize seed, where the right owner granted an exclusive licence. The approach taken by the Court was that such an exclusive licence might be necessary to persuade the licensee to take the risk of commercially exploiting someone else's invention. Where this was the case, the Court held, such an assignment might not fall within art. 81(1) at all. Although the intellectual property dealt with in this case was the 'plant breeder's right', the Court indicated that the same approach could be applied to other types of intellectual property, including, presumably, patents and know-how. In following this judgment the Commission has consistently stressed that restrictions imposed to allow a product to be brought to the market cannot continue indefinitely. While a restriction might be acceptable for the first few years of a product's exploitation, this will not remain the case once it becomes clear that the initial risk hurdle has been overcome. This approach was followed in the earlier two specific block exemption Regulations, and has carried through to the replacement Regulation.

The Regulation is applicable to pure patent, pure know-how, and mixed patent and know-how licensing agreements to which only two undertakings are party. Patent agreements will qualify for exemption where patents have been granted under either national law, or the Community systems. Patents are deemed, in art. 8, to include: patent applications; utility models; applications for registration of utility models; topographies of semiconductor products; *certificats d'utilité* and *certificats d'addition* under French law; protection certificates for medicinal products; and plant breeder's certificates. Know-how licensing requires that the know-how takes the form of 'a body of technical information that is secret, substantial and identified' (art. 10(1)). All these terms are further defined in the Regulation.

The terms identified as acceptable in art. 1 include those which are necessary to the granting of exclusivity in favour of the licensee in a defined territory. A significant difference between this Regulation and the rules that may be generally expected to appear is that in this case the licensee may be prohibited not only from pursuing an active sales policy outside of the assigned territory, but also from responding to unsolicited orders that have their origin outside that territory (art. 1(1)(6)). This recognizes that it is in the nature of intellectual property to confer absolute territorial protection, but is tempered by the fact that the restriction may not be granted for 'a period exceeding five years from the date when the licensed product is first put on the market' (art. 1(2)). This five-year protection is therefore seen to be all that is necessary to allow the rewards for taking the initial risk to be recouped. Other restrictions that may be accepted include those protecting the right itself, including obligations on the licensee not to divulge the know-how (art. 2(1)(1)), or to sublicense (art. 2(1)(2)), or to continue to use the knowledge after the termination of the agreement if that knowledge is still protected under intellectual property laws (art. 2(1)(3)). The licensee may be required to pass on to the licensor any improvements to the process that are developed by the licensee (art. 2(1)(4)), and to observe minimum quality standards which are technically justifiable and applied equally to any other licensees (art. 2(1)(5)). Further permissible obligations include clauses relating to royalty payments and those necessary to protect the integrity of the product and the value of the brand name or trademark.

Any restriction imposed in relation to the setting of prices (art. 3(1)) or quantities that may be produced save in strictly defined circumstances (art. 3(5)) shall take the agreement outside the scope of the block exemption, as shall restrictions on parallel importing that are not objectively justifiable or related to the intellectual property rights in specific territories (art. 3(3)). By virtue of art. 5 the Regulation does not apply to situations in which undertakings collectively pool patents or know-how, or to situations in which licences are granted between competing undertakings which hold interests in a joint venture.

The Regulation shall apply until 31 March 2006.

In 2000 the Commission published an *Evaluation Report on the Transfer of Technology Block Exemption Regulation No 240/96*, which was critical of a number of aspects of the operation of the Regulation. It was criticized as being too formalistic, too complex, and too narrow in its scope. Agreements relating to technology transfer which were not unduly harmful were not covered by the Regulation as it stands at present. The Commission took the view that it might have to devise new rules for licensing agreements, and that these would be most likely to take the same form as the newer block exemption regulations, probably being 'a wide, umbrella-type block exemption regulation in combination with a set of Guidelines' (para. 178). The process of reform in this area will not however be a quick one, and given that the existing Regulation does not expire until 2006 this will not be a priority for the Commission, although the commission recognizes that parts of the Regulation may not be entirely consistent with the changes being instituted in the modernization programme.

8.3 **The horizontal block exemptions**

Not all cooperation between undertakings that are competitors, or potential competitors, is necessarily bad, and two special cases are dealt with by way of block exemption regulations. In their broad approach, both these regulations resemble Regulation 2790/99.

8.3.1 **Research and development**

There is a general commitment on the part of the EC to the fostering of research and development (R&D) which is emphasized in the Treaty itself. Article 163, introduced by the Single European Act, is, in part, in the following terms:

1. The Community shall have the objective of strengthening the scientific and technological bases of Community industry and encouraging it to become more competitive at international level, while promoting all the research activities deemed necessary by virtue of other chapters of this Treaty.

2. For this purpose the Community shall, throughout the Community, encourage undertakings, including small- and medium-sized undertakings, research centres and universities in their research and technological development activities of high quality; it shall support their efforts to cooperate with one another, aiming, notably, at enabling undertakings to exploit the internal market potential to the full, in particular through the opening up of national public contracts, the definition of common standards and the removal of legal and fiscal obligations to that cooperation.

Generally, R&D agreements are among the small class of horizontal agreements that are actively encouraged by the competition authorities, and the Commission has made it clear that in many cases it does not consider that R&D agreements are in any way restrictive of competition, and are not therefore caught by art. 81(1). In its *14th Annual Report on Competition Policy* (1984) the EC Commission recognized the importance of R&D to the development of the EC economy:

Competition . . . relies increasingly on innovation . . . The introduction of new processes and products on the market stimulates competition within the common market, and helps to strengthen the ability of European industry to compete internationally. . . . R&D plays an essential role. In fact R&D promotes and maintains dynamic competition, characterised by initiation and imitation and in doing so assures economic growth.

. . . in many cases the synergy arising out of a cooperation is necessary because it enables the partners to share the financial risks involved and in particular to bring together a wider range of intellectual and mental resources and experience, thus promoting the transfer of technology. In the absence of such cooperation, the innovation may not take place at all, or otherwise not as successfully or efficiently. Also the present situation in the Community demands more rapid and effective transformation of new ideas into marketable products and processes, which may be facilitated by joint efforts by several undertakings.

The Commission has always shown a favourable attitude towards R&D cooperation provided that competition is maintained by the existence of different independent poles of research.

While statements such as these continue to demonstrate a flexible attitude to R&D agreements, evidence of which can also be found in previous Commission decisions, it is a general requirement that such agreements should not contain restrictions which go beyond those necessary to undertake the project successfully and to exploit its fruits. Particular attention will be paid to terms which limit the conduct of the participants after the conclusion of the project. Further, the Commission is more likely to be cautious in the granting of individual exemptions in markets which are highly concentrated. These factors have informed the block exemption, in which R&D is defined as

the acquisition of know-how relating to products or processes and the carrying out of theoretical analysis, systematic study or experimentation, including experimental production, technical testing or products or processes, the establishment of the necessary facilities and the obtaining of intellectual property rights for the results.   (art. 2(4))

The Regulation exempts from the application of art. 81(1) agreements under which undertakings pursue

(a) joint research and development of products or processes and joint exploitation of the results of that research and development;

(b) joint exploitation of the results of research and development of products or processes jointly carried out pursuant to a prior agreement between the same parties; or

(c) joint research and development of products or processes excluding joint exploitation of the results.   (art. 1(1))

Ancillary restrictions which are not directly about R&D but the presence of which is a necessary component of the agreement will also be covered by the operation of the block. Article 3 sets out four conditions for the granting of an exemption. These are, in brief, that:

(a) all parties must have access to the results;

(b) where the agreement is only in relation to pure R&D the parties must be free to exploit it in any way they wish;

(c) where the agreement includes provisions for joint exploitation this can only be permitted where the results are protected by intellectual property, and are 'decisive for the manufacture';

(d) where the agreement makes provision for manufacture by way of specialisation, the undertakings engaged in such manufacture must fulfil orders from all the parties, unless the agreement also provides for joint distribution.

Article 4 provides the market share test that is similar to that of Regulation 2790/99, and which is 'consistent with an economics based approach which assesses the impact of agreements on the relevant market' (recital (7)). Where the parties are not competing at the time of the agreement the exemption will last for the duration of the R&D. When the agreement provides for the joint exploitation of results the exemption will last for seven year from the date at which the contract products are first put on the market (art. 4(1)). At the end of this period the exemption will continue to apply for as long as the market share of the parties does not exceed 25 per cent (art. 4(3)). This balances the fact that it is likely to be the case that R&D agreements may lead to the development of a market in which the parties are the only players, and will have a 100 per cent market share, against the fact that without the joint R&D such a market might not exist at all. It is thus possible to have a seven-year exemption in respect of a very high market share where the parties do not start off as competitors. Where two or more of the parties are competing in the market for products which can be improved or replaced by the contract products, the exemption shall last for the same period as set out in art. 4(1), but only for as long as the parties do not have a combined market share of more than 25 per cent of the relevant market (art. 4(2)).

Article 5 of the Regulation removes from its scope entire agreements that have one of 10 objectives. These include: (a) the elimination of independent poles of research; (b) agreements which purport to prevent challenges to the validity of intellectual property rights; (c) limiting output or sales; (d) price fixing; (e)–(j) a number of territorial restrictions, having their origins in various practices.

Provisions in art. 6 relating to the calculation of market shares are similar to those set out in Regulation 2790/99.

Art. 7 sets out the power of the Commission to withdraw the benefit of the block exemption from individual agreements in a range of circumstances. In addition to the market share tests of art. 6, these provisions allow the Commission to act where the agreement's existence impairs substantially the scope for third parties to carry out R&D in the relevant field because of limited research capacity available elsewhere (art. 6(a)). The remainder of these provisions are largely concerned with situations in which, for a number of possible reasons, effective competition in relation to the products in question is impaired. The Regulation will apply until 31 December 2010 (art. 9).

8.3.2 Specialization agreements

In the *Guidelines on the Applicability of Article 81 to Horizontal Cooperation Agreements* published at the same time as the horizontal block exemption regulations, specialization agreements are dealt with as part of the wider set of 'production agreements'. This recognizes the fact that there are a number of forms in which production agreements can manifest themselves, and that specialization agreements, in which 'the parties agree unilaterally or reciprocally to cease production of a product and to purchase it from the other party' (*Guidelines*, para. 79), are merely one such form. The benefits of specialization agreements are referred to in recital (8) of the Regulation, which recognizes that:

Agreements on specialisation in production generally contribute to improving the production or distribution of goods, because the undertakings concerned can concentrate on the manufacture of certain products and thus operate more efficiently and supply the products more cheaply. Agreements on specialisation in the provision of services can also be said to generally give rise to similar improvements. It is likely that, given effective competition, consumers will receive a fair share of the resulting benefit.

The agreements covered by the block exemption are set out in art. 1, and include: (a) unilateral specialization agreements, (b) reciprocal specialization agreements; and (c) joint production agreements. Related purchasing and marketing agreements are also covered (art. 3). The market share limit set out in art. 4 is a combined market share of 20 per cent, a level lower than that set out in the R&D block exemption, reflecting the fact that the restrictions on competition in the case of specialization agreements can be more severe than that in R&D. Where the market shares are initially less than 20 per cent they may rise to a maximum of 25 per cent for two consecutive years, or may exceed 25 per cent for one year, without the benefit of the exemption being lost (art. 6(2) and (3)).

Article 5 sets out the categories of agreements which cannot benefit from the block exemption, which are those that: (a) fix prices; (b) limit output or sales; and (c) allocate markets or customers. However, to the extent that it is necessary to set prices or produce agreed amounts in the context of a production joint venture, this will be permitted as part of the integration of functions within the joint venture.

The benefit of the block exemption may be withdrawn in accordance with art. 7 where the Commission finds that it has effects which are incompatible with the conditions set out in art. 81(3). In particular this may be the case where: (a) the agreement is not yielding the expected results; or (b) there is no effective competition in respect of the products which are the subject of the agreement in the common market, or a substantial part of it. The Regulation shall apply until 31 December 2010.

In situations in which the market shares set out in the Regulation are exceeded it is almost certain that the requirements of art. 81(1) will be met, and an individual analysis under art. 81(3) will be necessary. The Commission is still inclined to take a favourable view of such agreements (see, e.g., *Bayer/Gist-Brocades* 76/172 (1976) OJ L30/13, and *Jaz-Peter* 78/194 (1978) OJ L61/17).

9

The control of anti-competitive agreements under United Kingdom law

9.1 Introduction

The Competition Act 1998 rewrote virtually all the relevant domestic law relating to the control of multilateral anti-competitive conduct. The single exception arises where arrangements between companies that are considered to be part of a complex monopoly are dealt with under the relevant provisions of the Fair Trading Act 1973 (this situation is dealt with in Chapter 12). Under the old domestic regime three Acts related to the control of multilateral conduct: the Resale Prices Act 1976; the Restrictive Trade Practices Act 1976; and the Restrictive Trade Practices Act 1977. These are not dealt with here, and readers seeking more detail in relation to the Restrictive Trade Practices Acts should refer to one of the older practitioner texts, such as Livingstone, D., *Competition Law and Practice*, FT Law & Tax (1995).

9.2 Agreements under the Competition Act 1998

9.2.1 The Chapter I prohibition

Section 2 of the Competition Act 1998 puts into place a prohibition on anti-competitive agreements that is similar to that of art. 81 EC. Section 2 is set out here in full:

2.—(1) Subject to section 3, agreements between undertakings, decisions by associations of undertakings or concerted practices which—

    (a)   may affect trade within the United Kingdom, and

    (b)   have as their object or effect the prevention, restriction or distortion of competition within the United Kingdom,

are prohibited unless they are exempt in accordance with the provisions of this Part.

(2) Subsection (1) applies, in particular, to agreements, decisions or practices which—

    (a)   directly or indirectly fix purchase or selling prices or any other trading conditions;

    (b)   limit or control production, markets, technical development or investment;

    (c)   share markets or sources of supply;

(d)   apply dissimilar conditions to equivalent transactions with other trading parties, thereby placing them at a competitive disadvantage;

(e)   make the conclusion of contracts subject to acceptance by the other parties of supplementary obligations which, by their nature or according to commercial usage, have no connection with the subject of such contracts.

(3) Subsection (1) applies only if the agreement, decision or practice is, or is intended to be, implemented in the United Kingdom.

(4) Any agreement or decision which is prohibited by subsection (1) is void.

(5) A provision of this Part, which is expressed to apply to, or in relation to, an agreement is to be read as applying equally to, or in relation to, a decision by an association of undertakings or a concerted practice (but with any necessary modifications).

(6) Subsection (5) does not apply where the context otherwise requires.

(7) In this section 'the United Kingdom' means, in relation to an agreement which operates or is intended to operate only in a part of the United Kingdom, that part.

(8) The prohibition imposed by subsection (1) is referred to in this Act as 'the Chapter I prohibition'.

Because of the overriding nature of s. 60, requiring this provision to be interpreted consistently with EC law, it should be applied in much the same way as art. 81 EC. However, the extent to which single market issues have been determinant in some of the EC case law may lead to divergence and to some difficulty. In the *Guidelines relating to the Chapter I Prohibition* (referred to throughout this chapter as 'the Chapter I guidelines') the Office of Fair Trading (OFT) indicates that:

The obligation to ensure consistency applies only to the extent that this is possible, having regard to any relevant differences between the provisions concerned. This means that there will be certain areas where the Community principles will not be relevant. For example, the Community single market objectives designed to establish a European common market would not be relevant to the domestic prohibition system. (para. 2.2)

It is not for nothing that s. 60 (the operation of which is discussed in further detail in Chapter 16) has been nick-named 'the Klondike clause'. It is inevitable that in this area there will be much debate as to whether particular principles of law and practice are 'single market' issues. For example, is the case of *Consten and Grundig* (discussed in detail in Chapter 8) determined by the desire to integrate the French and German markets, or by the desire to have competition law applied equally to intra- and inter-brand competition? If the answer is yes to the latter, is this in turn only because intra-brand competition must be regulated because of the effect that restrictions may have on the single market? This means, for example, that as is the case under art. 81, where an offending clause can be deleted from an agreement the agreement as a whole may not be void. Attempts in the Lords to introduce refinements to cover specific categories of agreements, or exemptions, were rejected by the government. Specific classes of agreements will be dealt with by way of exemptions and rules made under the Act (schs. 1–4). Vertical restraints have been largely excluded from the prohibition on the basis of rules made under s. 50, although it is intended to change this. Were this to be done on the face of the Act itself it would be difficult to respond to any new developments at the Community level.

9.2.2 **Exemptions**

Exemptions to the general prohibition in s. 2 may come in one of three ways. Section 3 of the 1998 Act sets out generalized exclusions which include: mergers and concentrations, which continue to be dealt with under the relevant provisions of the Fair Trading Act 1973 (sch. 1) (see Chapter 15); agreements which are examined under other Acts, which may include activities that are supervised directly by one or other of the industry regulators (sch. 2); and professional rules (sch. 4). The Secretary of State has been given the power to modify these excluded classes, by either adding to the list or removing from the list those items already on it. Further, the prohibition will apply only where an agreement has an appreciable effect on trade and competition, although the government rejected calls for an explicit test embodied in the Act (Hansard (HL) 13 November 1997, col. 259). The most important exclusions are those set out in The Competition Act 1998 (Land and Vertical Agreements Exclusion) Order 2000, SI 2000/309, which is discussed below. The grant of an exemption from the scope of the Chapter I prohibition is not intended to confer immunity from the application of the Chapter II prohibition. Thus, in relation to an individual exemption, the Director will be expected to consider the extent to which the conduct might fall within Chapter II. Where an agreement falls within a block exemption that individual assessment is lost, and the rule is that a block exemption relates *only* to conduct falling within Chapter I, and will not therefore cover conduct that falls also under Chapter II.

9.2.2.1 *Individual exemptions*

The procedure for the award of individual exemptions is set out in ss. 4–5. The position here is similar to that operating under art. 81(3) EC, which is to say that an individual exemption may be granted by the Director only where an agreement has been notified under s. 14 of the Act (s. 4(1)(a)). Notification carries the same benefits as it does under Community law, which is to say that it confers immunity from penalties for such time as no decision in respect of that agreement is taken (s. 14(4)), and allows the notifying undertaking to benefit from legal certainty once a decision has been taken. When any agreement is notified the Director will decide whether the prohibition has been infringed; or if not, whether this is because the agreement does not fall within the prohibition, or because it satisfies the criteria for the award of an individual exemption. The criteria for the making of both individual and block exemptions are set out in s. 9, which provides that exemptions may be available in the case of any agreement which

(a) contributes to—
    (i) improving production or distribution, or
    (ii) promoting technical or economic progress,
while allowing consumers a fair share of the resulting benefit; but
(b) does not—

(i) impose on the undertakings concerned restrictions which are not indispensable to the attainment of those objectives; or

(ii) afford the undertakings concerned the possibility of eliminating competition in respect of a substantial part of the products in question.

It should be immediately apparent that this is virtually a word-perfect rendering of art. 81(3) into domestic law, which, coupled with the principle of interpretation set out in s. 60, will mean that the case law and Commission decisions taken under this part of Community law are likely to be determinative of the position adopted under domestic law. While these provisions have been generally welcomed, the Consumers' Association (CA) expressed its concern that the EC Commission has been inconsistent in its treatment of consumer interests, and advocated greater clarity for the status accorded to consumer interests. In its response to the DTI consultation exercise the CA therefore argued that

In order to ensure that consumer interests are fully integrated into the application of the Chapter 1 exemption, two things are needed. First, the source and likely scale of the potential benefits from an agreement need to be identified together with the time frame over which such benefits are likely to accrue. Second, there needs to be an assessment of the extent to which the benefits identified are likely to accrue to consumers in practice. In other words, we think a consumer cost–benefit calculation should form part of any decision to exempt agreements under the Chapter I exemption. (*A Prohibition approach to anti-competitive agreements and abuse of dominant position: Consumers' Association response to the DTI draft Bill*, September 1997, p. 7)

In practice it is likely that the approach to the benefit arising to consumers will be much the same as it is under Community law, which is to say that where it can be clearly shown that the notified practice does contribute towards improving production or distribution, or promoting technical or economic progress, consumer interests will be presumed to benefit unless the agreement is clearly restrictive.

Individual exemptions may be granted 'subject to such conditions or obligations as the Director considers it appropriate to impose' (s. 4(3)(a)), and the decision must specify a time when the exemption will expire (s. 4(4)), although any exemption may be renewed (s. 4(6)). Exemptions may be withdrawn where the Director 'has reasonable grounds for believing that there has been a material change of circumstance since he granted an individual exemption' (s. 5(1)), or where the exemption has been granted on the basis of false or misleading information (s. 5(2)), or where the company benefiting from the exemption has failed to comply with any obligation attaching to the grant of the exemption (s. 5(4)). If a condition attaching to the exemption is breached then no further action is necessary by the Director to remove the benefit of an exemption, as the exemption will be automatically terminated (s. 5(3)). In any case in which the Director takes steps to cancel an exemption the cancellation may be backdated, which is likely to have the effect of increasing the penalty faced by the company, and may expose it to an increased risk of civil action. Because the prohibition renders void contracts which fall within it, the backdated removal of an exemption could have serious consequences for companies, and it is unlikely that any will be so culpable as to place themselves in this position.

Notifications are to be made on Form N. One aim of the OFT, having learnt from the experience of the EC Commission, is to reduce the number of speculative notifications. Accordingly, unlike the position in the Community, a fee will be charged for undertakings wishing to avail themselves of the exemption process. The fee for the exemption of an agreement under s. 14 is £13,000 (Competition Act 1998 (Director's Rules) Order 2000, SI 2000/293, para. 6, and Annex 2).

Only a small number of agreements have been notified to the OFT for consideration for either a negative clearance or exemption. Following consultation leading to some adaptation of the agreement a decision of negative clearance was made in respect of the standard conditions for licensing the commercial exhibition of films (*Film Distributors' Association Ltd* CA98/10/2002, 1 February 2002). Exemptions were granted to *Link Interchange Network Limited* CA98/7/2001 [2002] UKCLR 59, and in respect of the *Memorandum of Understanding on the Supply of Fuel Oils in an Emergency* CA98/8/2001 [2002] UKCLR 74.

9.2.2.2 *Block exemptions*

Block exemptions may be made to cover categories of agreements which fall within the terms of s. 9. Any such exemption must be proposed and published by the Director (ss. 6 and 8), and may be made by the Secretary of State as an Order in Parliament. Express provision is made for the incorporation of opposition procedures similar to those found in some of the block exemptions examined in Chapter 8 (s. 7). Although it is likely that block exemptions will be largely similar to those enacted at Community level, this may not necessarily be the case and the position taken in relation to vertical agreements is very different (see below). The parallel exemptions provided for in s. 10 (see below) may render such an approach largely unnecessary, and there are clear differences of approach between the DTI and the EC Commission in the matter of vertical restrictions, where the domestic regime is likely to take a more lenient stance although there are plans to change this position. As of May 2002 only one block exemption had been created—the Competition Act 1998 (Public Transport Ticketing Schemes. Block Exemption) Order 2001, SI 2001/319.

9.2.2.3 *Parallel exemptions*

In s. 10 it is provided that '[a]n agreement is exempt from the Chapter I prohibition if it is exempt from the Community prohibition', i.e., from art. 81(1). This section therefore makes concrete the notion of the one-stop shop with regard to agreements. In any situation where an agreement operating in the UK has been notified to the EC Commission and granted an exemption individually under art. 81(3) or falls within a block exemption, that agreement will not be caught by the operation of domestic law. The provision in fact goes further than this, for it applies not only to agreements which are already exempt from art. 81(1), but also to those which would be, by virtue of the operation of a block exemption, where the agreement in question is not actually subject to Community law because it has no impact on trade between the Member States (s. 10(2)). One effect of this section then is to import wholesale into the United Kingdom domestic arena, which falls outside the ambit of Community law, all Community block exemptions, without the need for them to be incorporated under ss. 6–8 of the 1998 Act.

The Director is granted the power to cancel the benefit of the parallel exemption (s. 10(5)). While it is unlikely that this power will be used to any great extent, if at all, circumstances could arise in which the Community interest would be served by the granting of an exemption, but where the brunt of any anti-competitive impacts were felt within the UK, leading to the revocation of the exemption on the basis of domestic law.

There is a lacuna in this part of the Act relating to comfort letters granted by the Commission. As has been noted earlier (see Chapter 3), the Commission resolves a great many cases by way of comfort letters rather than by the award of an individual exemption under art. 81(3). The benefit of the parallel exemption does not extend to those companies in possession of a comfort letter, and it will remain necessary for them to notify the agreement to the Director under s. 14 in the expectation, given the obligation of s. 60, that an exemption will be granted from the Chapter I prohibition. Given that the Government repeatedly emphasized the desire both to ensure consistency with Community law and to minimize the compliance costs to industry of the new regime, it would have been better had the parallel exemption extended to comfort letters, perhaps by way of an opposition procedure whereby the holder of a comfort letter would notify the Director of that fact but would be exempted from the Chapter I prohibition until such time as the Director made a decision to the contrary, any such decision being required to be taken in a strict time limit. In draft guidance, 'EC "comfort" letters', the OFT noted the lack of specific provision in the Act, but its comments are encouraging:

> the Director General considers that a comfort letter preceded by a notice in the Official Journal under art. 19(3), Reg. 17/62, is sufficiently authoritative to constitute a 'statement' of the Commission to which the Director General and courts are obliged to have regard. Although he may revoke such a 'parallel exemption' in certain specified circumstances, as a general rule, the Director General will not depart from the Commission's assessment of an agreement. (para. 2)

This guidance was not formally published, but the approach taken in the Chapter I guidelines (paras 7.11–7.12) is consistent with this.

9.2.2.4 *De minimis thresholds and appreciability*

During the passage of the Act the Government indicated that, subject to later consultation, classes of agreements would be exempt from the imposition of financial penalties, but not from any other adverse consequences of breach in accordance with s. 39 ('small agreements') where the turnover of the parties in question was between £20m and £50m (Hansard (HL) 17 November 1997, col. 434). The relevant thresholds are set out in the Competition Act 1998 (Small Agreements and Conduct of Minor Significance) Regulations 2000, SI 2000/262. These provide that small agreements (s. 39(1)) are those where the combined applicable turnover in the year preceding the infringement did not exceed 20 million (para. 3). The threshold in respect of s. 40(1) is £50 million (para. 4).

In following EC law, an appreciability test will be applied in relation to agreements falling under the Act. In the Chapter I guidelines the threshold for appreciability is set at a combined market share of 25 per cent, although there may be some circumstances in which this is not the case (para. 2.19). Agreements which fix market prices or which share markets, or impose minimum resale prices, or are part of a network of similar agreements which have a cumulative effect, may have an appreciable effect even where the parties' market shares are below the 25 per cent threshold.

9.2.3 Horizontal and vertical agreements

At the time of writing the prohibitions have not been in effect for sufficient time to generate a body of case law, and it is only possible to discuss in the most general terms the situations in which specific agreements may be condemned. Reference should be made at present to the various guidelines dealing with agreements, and of course to EC precedent, bearing in mind always the 'single market' caveat. The guidelines deal with both horizontal and vertical restraints, and make reference where necessary to Community cases. However, they predate the final publication of both the *Guidelines on Vertical Restraints* by the EC Commission, and the *Draft Guidelines on Horizontal Cooperation*. One of the benefits of adopting guidelines, however, is that they may be updated as necessary, and do not have the rigidities of a formalized case or legislative system.

9.2.3.1 *Horizontal agreements*

Section 2(2) of the Competition Act 1998 itself includes the list of examples of anti-competitive agreements which mirrors that of art. 81. As with art. 81 this 'is a non-exhaustive, illustrative, list and does not set a limit on the investigation and enforcement activities of the Director General' (Chapter I guidelines, para. 3.3). The guidelines themselves deal expressly with price fixing, which is likely to infringe the prohibition in all cases, as is market sharing, agreements to limit or control production or investment, and collusive tendering.

The first cartel to be penalized by the Director under the new regime demonstrated sharply the improvements that the Competition Act 1998 has made to the system of competition enforcement in the UK. While anti-competitive conduct in the bus industry had bedevilled the operation of the Competition Act 1980, in *Market Sharing by Arriva plc and FirstGroup plc* CA98/9/2002, 30 January 2002, the Director was able to deal decisively with this market. In the case in question the Director concluded that the two undertakings had breached the Chapter II prohibition by entering into a market-share agreement in respect of bus routes within Leeds. The OFT investigation followed the receipt of an anonymous complaint which alleged that Arriva Yorkshire had entered into an agreement with First Leeds to swap bus routes. The market affected was small, and the initial complaint referred only to two local routes. On-site investigations were carried out in October 2000, and both companies benefited from the operation of the leniency scheme in relation to the operation of cartels (see Chapter 4). One of the board members of Arriva Yorkshire, Mr Peter Harvey, had arranged a meeting in a private room at a Yorkshire hotel where the participants were senior staff of both Arriva and First-Group. These meetings were not declared by the FirstGroup participants on a form linked to training in compliance procedures with the Competition Act, which asked the participants to note all contacts with competing companies. The Director found that the object of the agreement reached between the undertakings was 'clearly to share markets geographically by mutual withdrawal from the relevant bus routes' (para. 42). Penalties were imposed, although FirstGroup's was reduced to nil following the application of the leniency scheme.

Information-sharing, advertising, and standardization agreements are all capable of infringing the prohibition, but need to be examined more carefully. Again the principles are those established by the EC, although in relation to advertising, for example, there is a paucity of relevant precedent.

9.2.3.2 *Vertical agreements*

Early on in its preparation for the 1998 Act, the DTI indicated that it was intended to remove most vertical agreements from the scope of the Chapter I prohibition. Research carried out on behalf of the DTI indicated that in the majority of formal decisions and cases decided in relation to vertical agreements under EC law, single-market considerations were to the fore. Such considerations would clearly be largely irrelevant in the UK, and Lord Simon, in the House of Lords, suggested that

There remains a case therefore for special treatment of vertical agreements under the Bill to avoid the burden of unnecessary notification and to ease the so-called 'straitjacket' which existing European block exemptions impose.   (Hansard (HL) 9 February 1998, col. 901)

In February 2000 the Government introduced the statutory instrument, made under the power conferred by s. 50 of the Act, which was to give effect to this broad intention. The Competition Act 1998 (Land and Vertical Agreements Exclusion) Order 2000, SI 2000/310, defines a vertical agreement in the following terms:

'Vertical agreement' means an agreement between undertakings, each of which operates, for the purposes of the agreement, at a different level of the production or distribution chain, and relating to the conditions under which the parties may purchase, sell or resell certain goods or services and includes provisions contained in such agreements which relate to the assignment to the buyer or use by the buyer of intellectual property rights, provided that those provisions do not constitute the primary object of the agreement and are directly related to the use, sale or resale of goods or services by the buyer or its customers.

This definition therefore includes exclusive distribution agreements, exclusive purchasing agreements, selective distribution agreements, and franchise agreements.

Paragraph 3 of the Order provides that 'the Chapter I prohibition shall not apply to an agreement to the extent that it is a vertical agreement'. This very broad exclusion, which contains no explicit market power test, and is therefore somewhat different to the approach taken in Regulation 2790/99 (discussed in Chapter 8), is limited only by the effect of para. 4, which excludes from this exemption situations in which the agreement, whether by itself or in combination with other factors, restricts 'the buyer's ability to determine its sale price, without prejudice to the possibility of the supplier imposing a maximum sale price or recommending a sale price, provided that these do not amount to a fixed or minimum sale price'.

Alongside the publication of the Competition Act 1998 (Land and Vertical Agreements Exclusion) Order 2000 the OFT published its *Guidelines on Vertical Agreements and Restraints* which should be read together with the Exclusion Order, and which relates also to vertical agreements which do not fall within the terms of the Exclusion Order (and which are considered more generally in the guideline *Assessment of Individual Agreements and Conduct*—in particular this deals with price fixing which is relevant in relation to the withdrawal of the exclusion). In the latter case the starting point for the analysis is that market power is relevant, and that the appreciability provisions, discussed above, are such that where the market share of the parties does not exceed 25 per cent the Chapter I prohibition will not apply, unless there are harmful network effects. Even below this threshold, however, agreements which have as their object or effect the setting of minimum prices may be considered to be capable of having an appreciable effect on competition.

In order to fall within the terms of the Exclusion Order the guidelines focus on the two elements that must be met. The economic relationship between the undertakings involved must be genuinely vertical, although it could be a vertical relationship within the chain of production, for example. More than one undertaking may be a party to the agreement, but if this is the case, each of them must be at a different level. Thus, an agreement between a manufacturer and five retailers would not be within the exemption, as the five retailers would be operating at the same level. On the other hand, an agreement between a manufacturer, a wholesaler, and a retailer would be exempt. It should also be noted that this assessment is to be made in the light of the purposes of the agreement under consideration, so an agreement between a wholesaler and a retailer which related to retailing would be exempt, even if the wholesaler was also engaged in retailing.

The second element to be considered is the terms of the agreement itself. As the guidelines make clear, 'conditions which relate to matters other than the conditions of purchase, sale and resale are not covered by the exclusion' (para. 2.8). Ancillary restrictions relating to intellectual property will be covered, but these must not be the primary purpose of the agreement, and must relate directly to the goods or services which are the main subject-matter of the agreement. It is not necessary for all elements of an agreement to fall within the exclusion. The exclusion will apply to those elements of a vertical agreement which are within its terms, and any other elements of the agreement will fall to be considered separately.

The benefit of the exclusion can, as indicated above, be withdrawn. In the guidelines it is suggested that 'it is likely that the Director General will exercise these powers only rarely' (para. 5.2). Nevertheless, complaints relating to excluded agreements will be considered carefully, and there may be some situations in which the withdrawal of the benefit will be justified. Where this is the case the Director General

must consult the parties to that agreement. Such a direction must specify the date from which it is to take effect; it may not take effect from a date earlier than the date on which it was given. If the Director General gives such a direction he will publish it on the public register that he maintains. (para. 5.3)

Even where the benefit of the exclusion is withdrawn this does not mean that the agreement is automatically caught within the Chapter I prohibition, but rather that the Director is given the power to make an individual assessment of the agreement.

In *Dixons Stores Group Limited/Compaq Computer Limited/Packard Bell NEC Limited* CA98/3/2001 [2001] UKCLR 670 the Director sent a clear signal that vertical agreements were not considered to be a significant problem. Here an agreement was entered into between Dixons Stores Group Retail Ltd ('DSG') and Compaq Computer Ltd under which DSG was to be Compaq's exclusive distributor in the UK. A similar agreement was entered into between DSG and Packard Bell Limited. The John Lewis Partnership complained that the subsequent withdrawal of supplies from them was in breach of both the Act's prohibitions. The Director found that there was no dominant position within the meaning of the Chapter II prohibition, and in respect of the Chapter I prohibition held that the agreements were vertical agreements within the meaning of the Exclusion Order, and that although the power existed to withdraw the benefit of this, 'in practice it is likely that the Director will exercise these powers only rarely' (para. 110).

As has been discussed elsewhere the relationship of Community law to national law, in which the former is supreme, means that an exemption granted under the Competition Act 1998 is relevant only in the context of the national standard, and does not mean that an agreement or practice which would otherwise be caught by art. 81(1) is exempted from that provision as well. It is therefore possible that some vertical agreements which will fall within the Exclusion Order may, by virtue of the market shares of the parties, still not fall within Regulation 2790/99, and may be condemned under art. 81(1). Unfortunately this means that there is still the possibility for actions in the national courts to be based on this provision, even where there would be no domestic right.

The Exclusion Order also removes land agreements (which create, alter, transfer, or terminate an interest in land, or an agreement to enter into such an agreement) from the scope of the Chapter I prohibition. This is a more technical provision than that relating to vertical agreements, and reflects in part the fact that there has been no Community law relevant to this area, largely because such agreements would be likely to fall within the *de minimis* provisions, or lack an impact on trade. It was foreseen, however, that there would be concerns about the application of the prohibition at the national level.

Where vertical agreements lie outside the exclusions, and within s. 2 of the Act, the guideline *Assessment of individual agreements and conduct* should be referred to. At paras 6.6–6.33 this deals in particular with the following categories of vertical restraints: resale price maintenance, selective distribution, exclusive distribution, exclusive purchasing or dealing, tie-in sales and bundling, full-line forcing, quantity forcing, and fidelity discounts. This guideline recognizes that these restrictions 'are common business practices and are not prohibited unless they lead to a significant reduction in competition' (para. 6.6). In order to determine whether such restraints are to be condemned therefore it will be necessary to establish whether they have the effect of leading to market foreclosure, or of raising rivals' costs (para. 6.30). However, this is not to say that full analysis of each agreement will be considered. Rather the approach taken will be that of determining whether the restraint is the least restrictive way to achieve any benefit alleged for the agreement.

The Government intends to repeal this provision bringing the assessment of vertical agreements back within the mainstream of the Act (see the White Paper *Productivity and Enterprise*). Regulation 2790/99 would apply by way of the provisions for parallel exemptions.

9.2.4 Exclusions

Alongside the individual, block, and parallel exemptions are a number of exclusions set out in schs. 1–4 to the Competition Act 1998 which remove categories of individual agreements from the Chapter I prohibition. The list of such agreements can be altered by the Secretary of State.

One of the more controversial areas, which is under review by the OFT, relates to the exemption granted for professional rules (sch. 4, para. 1; see also the Competition Act 1998 (Application for Designation of Professional Rules) Regulations 1999, SI 1999/2546, and the guideline *Trade Associations, Professions and Self-Regulating Bodies*). In March 2001 the OFT published two significant documents relating to competition in the professions. The first of these was a report prepared by the economic consultancy LECG, and the second (OFT328, [2001] UKCLR 352) was the response of the DGFT to the issues raised in the LECG report. Broadly the conclusion was that restrictions within the professional sectors operated to the detriment of the public, and were not outweighed by the advantages arising from any such restrictions. Thus in its response to the LECG report the DGFT recognized that

The professions are entrusted with the delivery of services of considerable public importance. They work within a framework of law, but within that framework their governing bodies have important degrees of freedom to control rights to enter and practise the relevant professions. The exercise of these powers can have a significant impact on the economy, on the interests of consumers, and on society generally, especially where the professions concerned have exclusive rights to supply certain services. Restrictions on supply in the case of professional services, just as with other goods and services, will tend to drive up costs and prices, limit access and choice and cause customers to receive poorer value for money than they would under properly competitive conditions. Such restrictions will tend also to inhibit innovation in the supply of services, again to the ultimate detriment of the public.

The accompanying OFT press release (PN 10/01, 7 March 2001 [2001] UKCLR 530) indicated that the OFT was particularly concerned about the operation of various rules in relation to the legal and accountancy professions. Amongst other concerns raised was that relating to the division of the Bar into junior barristers and QCs, which the OFT pointed out 'has no parallel in other markets'. The OFT found it 'hard to see what benefits it brings to consumers and the public'. The Director recommended that the right to exclusion from the Chapter I prohibition for professional rules should be removed. Two days later the DTI announced that it intended to accept this recommendation (P/2001/141, 9 March 2001 [2001] UKCLR 707), stating that 'the professions should be fully subject to competition law'. In the White Paper *Productivity and Enterprise*, the Government confirmed that it intends to carry this reform through. In *Conte* v *Rossi* case C–221/99 [2002] 4 CMLR 8, a reference from an Italian court, the ECJ held that art. 81 did not preclude national rules 'which provides that the members of a profession may set at their discretion the fees for certain services they provide' (para. 28). However, the examination of the issue in this case was somewhat cursory due to the nature of the questions asked in the reference.

Schedule 1 to the Act removes from the Chapter I and II prohibitions, agreements or conduct which would result in a merger. Merger situations continue to be dealt with under the Fair Trading Act 1973 (see Chapter 15).

9.2.5 Consideration of agreements by the Director

The powers of the Director to conduct investigations where it is suspected that the prohibitions of the Act are being breached, and the penalties available in those situations, are dealt with in Chapter 3. Procedural aspects of the Act relating exclusively to the Chapter I prohibition include provisions relating to the seeking of guidance from the Director and the legal effects of decisions taken by the Director to the effect that the prohibition is not being infringed.

Under s. 12 of the Act, any party to an agreement may ask the Director to examine the agreement in order to determine whether or not it is in breach of the Chapter I prohibition. The procedure to be adopted in any such case is set out in full in sch. 5. Under s. 13, parties to agreements may similarly apply for guidance from the Director as to 'whether or not in his view, the agreement is likely to infringe the Chapter I prohibition'. In this case the Director may indicate whether the agreement would be likely to be granted an exemption if it were properly notified in accordance with s. 14. Although no penalties will accrue to agreements notified under s. 13 it is likely that this section will be of use primarily to companies that are contemplating a new agreement, and that wish to ascertain whether they can proceed in the certainty that they will not be in breach of the prohibition. Where the guidance given is to the effect that:

(a) the agreement is unlikely to infringe the Chapter I prohibition, regardless of whether or not it is exempt;

(b) the agreement is likely to be exempt under—
   (i)   a block exemption,
   (ii) a parallel exemption, or
   (iii) a s. 11 exemption; or
(c) he would be likely to grant the agreement an individual exemption if asked to do so (s. 15(1))

then no further action is to be taken by the Director in relation to that agreement until such time as there is a material change in the circumstances (s. 15(2)(a)), or if the guidance has been given on the basis of false or misleading information (s. 15(2)(b)), or if the agreement is formally notified under s. 14 (s. 15(2)(c)), or if a complaint is subsequently made about that agreement (s. 15(2)(d)). These circumstances are wider than the equivalent provisions in s. 16 relating to the situation in which a formal decision has been taken regarding an individual exemption, and it is in this particular that the benefit of the formal decision over this less formal guidance is most pronounced. It is further provided that no penalty shall be levied in respect of any agreement where such guidance has been given, although this immunity may be removed in the circumstances specified in s. 15(4). Although the words are not used, the effect of s. 13 is to import the concept of the 'comfort letter' into domestic law. The section operates so as to confer the benefit of legal certainty without the necessity of the agreement being put through the formal notification procedure, and suitably limits the circumstances in which the benefit of the guidance/comfort letter may be removed. In this respect the procedure is more rigorous and transparent than that adopted at the Community level, where the practice relating to comfort letters has arisen through custom and guidance and is not formally prescribed by way of secondary legislation.

10

An introduction to the economics of monopoly abuse

10.1 Introduction

The arguments advanced in Chapter I support the need for some intervention in the competitive structure, but do not necessarily justify action against individual monopolists. The Harvard/Chicago debate is not a purely theoretical one, and nowhere is this more significant than in relation to the policy prescriptions relating to the control of monopoly conduct. If the extreme Chicago approach is correct there would be little need to apply competition law to the conduct of privately maintained monopolies. Article 82 EC (see Chapter 11) could, along with parallel provisions in domestic law, be abandoned, leaving competition regulators to focus on the twin problems of distortions to the competitive structure resulting from state conduct and the maintenance of cartels. State aids and state-maintained, or created, barriers to entry have indeed received increasing attention from the EC Commission, and much time has been taken up in the UK with deregulation initiatives in the utilities sectors (see the discussion of natural monopolies, below). If, on the other hand, the Harvard school adherents are correct the anti-competitive conduct of a single firm in possession of a significant degree of market power may still raise genuine concerns that cannot be resolved by the operation of the market place in the absence of regulatory intervention. This is the assumption underpinning art. 82 and its domestic equivalents. The economics of monopoly control is considered in Bishop, S., and Walker, M., *The Economics of EC Competition Law*, London, Sweet & Maxwell (1999), ch. 5.

10.2 Individual monopolies

To the economist a monopoly is, quite simply, a market in which the industry is in the hands of one producer. Competition law, however, extends to situations which are monopolistic—which is to say a market in which there are a number of sellers, into which new firms may enter, but in which each firm has a degree of control over price by virtue of selling products that are not identical to those of its competitors. Generally, potentially anti-competitive actions undertaken by a single firm will be subject to legal proceedings only where that firm has a significant degree of market power. It is a source of some confusion that legislation and case law make reference to 'monopoly' to describe such market power, disregarding the stricter economic definition. Market shares are usually used as a proxy by which to establish, prima facie, the appropriate market power at which intervention may be triggered. In the UK the market share adopted under the Fair Trading Act 1973 was the relatively low level of 25 per cent; in the EC shares of around 50 per cent generally require the undertaking to demonstrate that it is *not* in a dominant position (see further Chapter 11); and in the USA a share of at least 50 per cent, and likely around 70 per cent, will establish the degree of monopoly power required under the Sherman Act (see, for a survey of the relevant authorities, *Domed Stadium Hotel, Inc.* v *Holiday Inns, Inc* 732 F.2d 480 at 489–90).

The attractions to company directors of attaining monopoly have never been better expressed than in *The Godfather*.

Like any good businessman he came to understand the benefits of undercutting his rivals in price, barring them from distribution outlets by persuading store owners to stock less of their brands. Like any good businessman he aimed at holding a monopoly by forcing his rivals to abandon the field or by merging with his own company. . . . Like many businessmen of genius he learned that free competition was wasteful, monopoly efficient. (Puzo, M., *The Godfather* (1969), ch. 14)

Expressed this way the strategy may not be far removed from that adhered to in many boardrooms, although clearly Don Vito Corleone was prepared to resort to anti-competitive practices that would be better addressed by way of the criminal law than by way of competition law. The problems to be addressed by competition law are that, first, monopolies may not always be efficient and, secondly, the pursuit of predatory or exclusionary tactics may have harmful welfare effects as well as, less abstractly, damaging individual target firms, along with their investors and managers.

The allegations faced by monopolists most frequently are that:

(a) the monopoly price is higher than the price would be in a competitive market, which is the area that is usually of most concern to consumer advocates;

(b) output is lower and therefore potential demand that could be efficiently met is going unanswered, a corollary of which is that the income that would have been spent on the monopolist's product is being spent elsewhere, distorting other prices in the economy;

(c) predatory behaviour may directly damage the interests of other legitimate competitors and indirectly harm consumers; and

(d) the monopolist, in order to protect a profitable position, may erect barriers that prevent new entrants coming into the market to correct the behaviour referred to in (a) and (b).

Ancillary concerns are that monopolists, contrary to the Godfather's view, may be *less efficient* than firms in a more competitive market and may stifle innovation. Following Leibenstein this type of inefficiency is sometimes called 'X-inefficiency', and relates primarily to an inefficient use of existing resources. X-inefficiency arises if the same inputs might result in more outputs (Leibenstein, H., 'Allocative Efficiency v. X-Efficiency', (1966) 59 *American Economic Review* 392). Competition law is not well placed to deal directly with X-efficiency concerns, which would require a strongly interventionist approach, or with the problem of reduced monopoly output. Instead the focus of the law is on facilitating the emergence of stronger competition to the monopolist by tackling predation, exclusion, and barriers to entry. *Ceteris paribus* stronger competition should reduce the other identifiable harms. Depending on the emphasis given to individual rights and consumer welfare in the relevant regime, other issues such as high pricing or refusal to deal may be addressed where they are readily identifiable.

10.2.1 **Higher prices/lower output**

The formal proof by which higher pricing and lower output arises in monopoly markets is a standard feature of industrial economics and is not unduly technical. The aim of all firms is assumed to be profit maximization, and although this may not be the case in all situations, it is a reasonable working assumption. The consequence of this is that, when considering what quantity of any product to market, firms will set the level where the marginal cost (MC) of production is equal to the marginal revenue (MR) the firm makes from that unit of production: if the MC is £5 and the MR is £10 a profit-maxizing firm would produce the extra unit as it would make a £5 profit on the sale; if the MC is £10 and the MR is £5 the firm would not produce it as it would make a £5 loss.

Whereas in perfect competition the firm has no control whatsoever over the price at which the item is sold, and takes the price set by the market, a monopolist *makes* the price. Adam Smith famously suggested that 'the price of monopoly is upon every occasion the highest which can be got'. It is the essence of monopoly that the monopolist has the power to set the price of his product, which is effected by altering the amount that is supplied. As with perfect competition, marginal cost will be set equal to marginal revenue, but the outcome is very different, as Figure 10.1 shows. In the case of perfect competition price = MC, with the outcome being PC, QC. In the case of monopoly MR = MC, with the outcome being PM, QM. The monopoly price, PM, is higher than the competitive price, PC, and the quantity produced, QM, is less than would be produced in a perfectly competitive market, QC.

10.2.2 **Monopoly profits**

Measuring the variables discussed above, and assessing the extent of the loss of wealth caused by any one monopoly, is exceptionally difficult. In the UK in particular, but not exclusively, assessments have been made in some cases of the profits

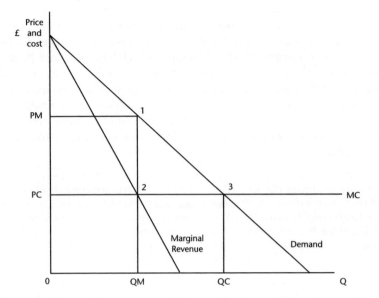

Figure 10.1 Demand and supply curves

Notes: 1. The assumption of constant marginal cost is a simplifying one, and is unlikely to be matched in the real world. However, to relax this assumption does not change the analysis.

2. The rectangle PM, PC, 2, 1, represents a transfer of wealth from consumer to the monopolist. The triangle 1, 2, 3, shows 'dead-weight welfare loss', potential demand that could be supplied efficiently but, under single-price monopoly, is not (see Chapter 1).

made by individual monopolists to determine whether these are 'excessive' and indicative of abuse. A report prepared for the OFT's research paper series offers an interesting, although at times very technical, approach (Graham, M., and Steele, A., *The Assessment of Profitability by Competition Authorities*, London, OFT (1997)). A problem with assessing profits, recognized by the authors, is that 'high levels of profit are associated with both competition failure and successful competitive advantage ... the competition authorities must ... distinguish high profits due to successful advantage from those due to failures of competition' (para. 1.2). Even where very high profits are identified these may simply be the result of very efficient production and innovation, and not be evidence of market abuse. Similarly, the fact that a monopoly makes low profits does not necessarily mean that it is not abusing its position. It might rather be very inefficient, and be surviving only because it is engaged in perpetrating abuses.

10.2.3 Predatory and exclusionary conduct

Predation may be broadly defined as conduct intended primarily to harm competitors, which is likely to result in a short-term loss in order to allow a long-term gain. It is most generally associated with pricing policies, and predatory pricing is considered in some detail in Chapter 13. As Myers emphasizes, there are other categories of anti-competitive conduct involving low prices that are not, strictly, predatory and that may be better described as 'exclusionary' (Myers, G., *Predatory Behaviour in UK Competition Policy*, London, OFT (1994)). Whether predation or exclusionary conduct can be successful is a matter of sharp disagreement, and while economic modelling may be of assistance it is suggested that the issue cannot be resolved simply by reference to abstract analysis. Decisions as to whether to enter any given market are made by entrepreneurs who will to some extent be swayed by their individual assessment of risks. Thus one commentator has evocatively recognized that

A house with a high wall surrounding its property, iron bars on the windows and a moat will be hard to enter without the permission of the owner. It has 'structural' barriers to entry. A second house with a small 'No Trespassing' sign and a two-foot high white picket fence has low structural barriers to entry. It has been pointed out, however, that if the second house has, in addition to the sign and the fence, a lawn strewn with the lifeless corpses of failed entrants, the next entrant may be effectively deterred. (Rapp, R. T., 'Predatory Pricing Analysis: A Practical Synthesis', NERA. Working Paper No. 2, 1990, pp. 6–7)

It is clear from the case law that the competition authorities recognize reputation effects as playing a significant role in strengthening or maintaining a company's strong position (such an acknowledgement was made by the OFT in its decision *Predation by Aberdeen Journals Ltd* CA98/5/2001 [2001] UKCLR 856, (para. 56)), although less well recognized is the impact that competition law actions may have in enforcing reputation effects. For example, the EC Commission has supported a claim of dominance against the largest producer of soda ash in the Community by referring to 'the perception of Solvay by other Community producers as the dominant producer and their reluctance to compete aggressively for Solvay's traditional customers' (*Soda Ash—Solvay* 91/299 (1991) OJ L152/21, para. 45).

10.2.4 Barriers to entry

'The concept of barriers to entry is', as Bork notes, 'crucial to the antitrust debate' (Bork, R. H., *The Antitrust Paradox*, New York, The Free Press (1993), p. 310). The question to be considered is whether economic theory suggests that a monopolist is able to so harm the market structure as to remove or reduce the threat of competition from other companies. It will be immediately apparent that the answer to this question lies at the heart of the Chicago/Harvard debate. A recognition of the role of barriers to entry supports the Structure–Conduct–Performance model advanced by the Harvard School, and discussed in Chapter 1.

Michael Porter, associated with the Harvard Business School, approaches competition issues from the perspective of a company that wishes to strengthen or protect its position, and is not therefore primarily concerned with competition law. The problem for an incumbent is that 'new entrants to an industry bring new capacity, the desire to gain market share, and often substantial resources. Prices can be bid down or incumbents' costs inflated as a result, reducing profitability'. The threat of entry, he argues, depends 'on the barriers to entry that are present, coupled with the reaction from existing competitors that the entrant can expect' (Porter, M. E., *Competitive Strategy*, New York, The Free Press (1980), p. 7). Porter lists five major barriers to entry: economies of scale; product differentiation; capital requirements; switching costs (i.e., the costs to a buyer of switching to a new supplier); and access to distribution channels. By exploiting and reinforcing these barriers it is suggested that incumbents can increase their power to act independently of competition. Whether competition law can be invoked to reduce these barriers will depend on the circumstances of the particular case: notably the law has tackled product differentiation (e.g., *Contraceptive Sheaths* (Cmnd. 8689, 1982 and Cm. 2529, 1994)) and access to distribution channels (e.g., *Films* (Cm. 2673, 1994)). The presence of economies of scale, which is a form of efficiency, or the requirement that entrants must meet the capital costs of entrance are not matters that should, or can, be addressed by competition law.

The real question to be resolved in any case 'is whether there exist *artificial* entry barriers that are *not forms of superior efficiency*' (*Bork, The Antitrust Paradox*, above, p. 311, emphasis added). Many economists and antitrust commentators would not, in fact, accept that any of the 'barriers' on Porter's list should fall to be resolved by the application of competition law. It is also here that the theoretical debate is at its most intense, and it is not likely to be resolved in the foreseeable future. In practice the competition lawyer may not need to pursue this debate, as many of the cases may be resolved on the basis of observable conduct. Where, for instance, firms have entered and become established in an industry that in itself will negate the need for debate about barriers in most legal proceedings. This may also be the case where there is clear evidence of failed attempts at entry over time.

The issues of vertical integration and vertical restraints which may be associated with both monopolistic and competitive structures are considered in Chapter 6.

10.2.5 Natural monopolies

In one situation a monopoly *is* the efficient market solution. Whether this is the case is determined by the scope of economies of scale: if these are very large in relation to market demand, formally, such that there is no price at which two firms could cover their costs, costs of production are at their lowest level when only one firm is in the market. This will be the case where marginal costs are still falling when the final consumer's demand is satisfied, and will arise in particular where fixed costs are by far the greater component of production, with variable costs being of relatively minor importance. Traditionally such industries have been found to exist where a large and expensive infrastructure is an integral part of that industry (i.e., the utilities, rail transport, and telecommunications). Another type of natural monopoly may also exist under situations of 'network returns'. These arise in industries which are heavily reliant on standards and on product compatibility. A good example is the computing industry. If two operating systems for desktop computers exist, one of which is a superior product (it may even be cheaper) and one of which is already on most computers, it is likely that the requirement that one computer be able to communicate with another will mean that the more popular package will remain dominant, irrespective of other features. The role of such network economies played an important role in the debate about Microsoft's practices and its place in the market.

Developing successful strategies to control these industries has been difficult, and for many years the tendency in 'mixed' economies was to take them into public ownership and therefore direct state control. In the late 1970s and throughout the 1980s the United Kingdom led the way in replacing state ownership with private shareholder ownership, regulating conduct by way of licensing systems that restrict both price rises and the return on capital that can be retained by the company. In some cases this has been achieved by separating the various elements of the infrastructure of what were once highly vertically integrated industries. Typically the approach now is to create strict licence conditions for the elements of the infrastructure that remain natural monopolies, and to encourage competition among the remaining elements, whether downstream or upstream.

10.3 Social concerns

Senator Kefauver, author of the United States' Celler–Kefauver Act 1950, argued in support of the Act that 'the history of what has taken place in other nations where . . . economic control [is] in the hands of a very few people is too clear to pass over', thus suggesting that competition law may be employed in the pursuit of socio-political goals. The fact that monopolies redistribute income, generally from the poor to the wealthy (see, e.g., Powell, I., 'The Effect of Reductions in Concentration on Income Distribution', (1987) 69 *Review of Economics and Statistics* 75), may also be used in some quarters to support interventionist arguments. There is no reason why tools of competition law cannot be used in support of wider social objectives, such as income redistribution, but the efficiency of any such move must be doubted. It is unlikely that the application of a sophisticated, and therefore costly, competition law can be more effective in this area than the imposition of, say, a windfall tax on monopoly profits. Fears as to the concentration of power in the hands of the few are also probably better addressed other than by way of competition laws. A well-developed competition law that follows clear economic criteria should, in any event, play its part in raising welfare generally by supporting the competitive process.

10.4 **Conclusion**

The approach taken to monopolies under competition law is determined in part by the recognition accorded to individual rights in the competitive process. When the Chicago economists posit efficiency tests as the only acceptable standard by which to frame legislation, they do so without regard to an individual businessman whose efforts have been stifled by the predatory conduct of a more powerful incumbent and without due recognition of 'reputation' effects. The fact that sooner or later the incumbent will be challenged successfully will be of little concern to the bankrupt entrepreneur who has made the first effort, but the position of the failed business is not, in the overall economy, significant. The recent changes in the United Kingdom law and the recognition of direct effect (see Chapter 2) have placed an increasing emphasis on individual rights and remedies, and in both regimes enforcement is largely complaint driven. This forces the courts, and therefore economists as expert witnesses, to consider the (anti-)competitive impact of short-run activity that might be expected to have little long-run impact. Whereas in the 1960s and 1970s such analysis might have been considered to be of questionable value, more recent developments in economic modelling have shown that harmful welfare effects may, in fact, flow from such conduct, although the debate is by no means settled.

11

Article 82

Any abuse by one or more undertakings of a dominant position within the common market or in a substantial part of it shall be prohibited as incompatible with the common market in so far as it may affect trade between Member States.

Such abuse may, in particular, consist in:

   (a) directly or indirectly imposing unfair purchase or selling prices or other unfair trading conditions;

   (b) limiting production, markets or technical development to the prejudice of consumers;

   (c) applying dissimilar conditions to equivalent transactions with other trading parties, thereby placing them at a competitive disadvantage;

   (d) making the conclusion of contracts subject to acceptance by the other parties of supplementary obligations which, by their nature or according to commercial usage, have no connection with the subject of such contracts.

11.1 Introduction

Article 82 forms the basis of actions far less often than does art. 81—not only does it necessarily apply to fewer undertakings but those to which it does apply, being among the larger organizations, are more likely to be aware of their obligations under competition law. As the guidelines on fines note (see Chapter 4), 'large undertakings usually have legal and economic knowledge and infra-structures which enable them more easily to recognise that their conduct consti-tutes an infringement and be aware of the consequences stemming from it under competition law'.

Because art. 82 condemns only the 'abuse' of a dominant position the mere holding of such a position, or tactics employed by undertakings to attain a dominant position when they are not yet dominant, is not outlawed. In America, in contrast, s. 2 of the Sherman Act, which condemns 'monopolisation', is designed to control the practices whereby firms *gain* market power (although only where the firm already has a sizeable market share), and in *United States v Grinnel Corp.* 384 US 563 (1966) the court sought to attack the 'wilful' acquisition of monopoly power as opposed to the attainment of monopoly through better commercial practices. In *Europemballage Corp. and Continental Can Co. Inc.* v *Commission* case 6/72 [1973]

CMLR 199, the ECJ made clear the position that the *creation* of a dominant position could not be condemned under art. 82—only its subsequent abuse could be controlled (see para. 26 of the judgment).

The result of the application of art. 82 is that a differential standard of conduct applies to undertakings in a dominant position than to others in the market place. This can be a source of some distress to the managers of an undertaking who may not be able to respond to competitive situations as they would wish, and as perhaps they might have been lawfully able to do when the undertaking was still climbing towards its dominant position. The ECJ has explained the situation thus:

A finding that an undertaking has a dominant position is not in itself a recrimination but simply means that, irrespective of the reasons for which it has such a dominant position, the undertaking concerned has a special responsibility not to allow its conduct to impair genuine undistorted competition on the Common Market.   (*Nederlandsche Banden-Industrie Michelin N.V. v Commission* case 322/81 [1985] 1 CMLR 282, para. 57)

As an undertaking in a dominant position in a relevant market has greater capacity to distort the market through its actions, it may be reasonable to maintain such a differential standard and to impose this 'special responsibility'. A similar sentiment is clear in *Hoffmann-La Roche & Co. AG v Commission* case 85/76 [1979] 3 CMLR 211, where the ECJ held that

The concept of abuse is an objective concept relating to the behaviour of an undertaking in a dominant position which is such as to influence the structure of a market where, as a result of the very presence of the undertaking in question, the degree of competition is weakened . . .   (para. 91)

Once it has been determined that an undertaking is in breach of art. 82, whether that determination is made by the EC Commission or by a national court in the context of an action based on the principle of direct effect (see Chapter 2), there is no opportunity for an exemption to be sought from the application of the prohibition. As Advocate General Lenz stressed in *Ahmed Saeed*, this was a deliberate decision taken by the writers of the Treaty and is implicit in the adoption of the term 'abuse': 'abuses cannot be approved, or at any rate not in a community which recognises the rule of law as its highest principle' (*Ahmed Saeed Flugreisen and Silver Line Reisebüro GmbH v Zentrale zur Bekämpfung Unlauteren Wettbewerbs eV* case 66/86 [1990] 4 CMLR 102 at 116). Negative clearance under art. 2 of Regulation 17 may be granted in respect of both arts 81 *and* 82 (see Chapter 3), but undertakings are understandably reluctant to notify the Commission of practices that might potentially fall within the art. 82 prohibition, with only the hope that they will not, and the procedure is hardly ever used. This is not to say, however, that there is no scope for flexibility in the application of the article—the concept of 'abuse' is a flexible' one and will usually be determined only after careful analysis of each situation. Another significant difference between art. 82 and art. 81 is that whereas the latter condemns 'anti-competitive' conduct, the prohibition of art. 82 may be extended to situations in which an undertaking exploits its position of dominance purely for its own benefit without reference to the effect that this behaviour may have on competitors. Indeed in some situations exploitative conduct, such as charging 'excessive' prices, may serve as a spur to more effective competition by, for instance, sending a signal to potential entrants as to the high level of profits that may be earned in the market, yet may be condemned as an abuse.

The questions to be asked in relation to the application of art. 82 are:

(a) Is there an undertaking holding a dominant position?

(b) Does this dominant position extend to a substantial part of the common market? 40%?

(c) Is the dominant position being abused?

(d) Is the nature of this abuse such as to affect trade between Member States?

These questions will now be dealt with in turn.

11.2 The meaning of 'dominant position' (f.T.A 25%)

The ECJ has held that:

The dominant position referred to in [art. 82] relates to a position of economic strength enjoyed by an undertaking which enables it to prevent effective competition being maintained on the relevant market by giving it the power to behave to an appreciable extent independently of its competitors, customers and ultimately of its consumers.   (*United Brands Co.* v *Commission* case 27/76 [1978] 1 CMLR 429, para. 65)

Dominance does not require that there be *no* competition. In *Hoffmann-La Roche & Co. AG* v *Commission* case 85/76 [1979] 3 CMLR 211, the court held that a finding of dominance 'does not preclude some competition . . . but enables the undertaking which profits by it, if not to determine, at least to have an appreciable influence on the conditions under which that competition will develop, and in any case to act largely in disregard of it' (para. 39).

This attempt to define a standard by reference to genuine economic analysis, but which creates legal problems and leads, inevitably, to extensive litigation, may be contrasted with the legally neat, but economically unsatisfactory, 25 per cent market share test of the Fair Trading Act. There is no fixed formula by which the dominance referred to in art. 82 may be established. Rather by analysis of each case the following matters must be resolved:

(a) the relevant product market within which dominance is alleged;

(b) the relevant geographical market over which the alleged dominance extends;

(c) the relevant time period; and

(d) the relative strength of the alleged dominant undertaking.

The last matter may itself call for an examination of several aspects, most important but not exclusive of which is the market share of the relevant product held by the undertaking. Some care must be taken in defining the 'relevant market', which has a different meaning from the word 'market' in general commerce. The 'relevant market' may not be limited to the undertaking's definition of its sales area or the traditional definition applied by the industry to its sector.

11.2.1 **The relevant product market**

Generally it is in the interests of a defendant undertaking to describe the product market as broadly as possible, and for the Commission to define it narrowly. The more narrowly the market is defined the greater the market share of any one undertaking will be. Thus the manufacturer of the Nissan Micra motor car will have a 100 per cent share of the market, which is to say a total monopoly, if the product market is defined as being 'new Nissan Micras'. If the market is extended to that of small saloon cars the market share will drop to a level that probably remains significant but falls well short of monopoly and if the relevant market is extended to include all motor cars, including perhaps secondhand vehicles, and certain forms of public transport which to some extent compete with new cars, the market share will be insignificant.

The most important factor in defining the relevant product market is that of substitutability (or 'cross-elasticity'). Thus, in *Hoffmann-La Roche*, the ECJ stated that '[t]he concept of the relevant market presupposes that there is a sufficient degree of interchangeability between all the products forming part of the same market'. Substitutability can be analysed from the perspective of both the consumer of the product ('demand substitutability') and the suppliers or potential suppliers of the product ('supply substitutability'). In its notice on market definition (see below) the Commission points to the formal test of 'demand substitution arising from small, permanent changes in relative prices', that is to say, to what extent would customers switch to readily available substitutes in response to a hypothetical, small (5–10 per cent) change in price of the product whose market is being assessed? In the United States this is referred to as the 'SSNIP' test, where SSNIP stands for a 'small but significant non-transitory increase in price'. Supply substitution requires that suppliers of other products are able to switch production in the short term in response to small but permanent changes in price. Necessarily, as these postulated changes in price are small and as an effect of the switch in supply is likely to result in smaller market shares for all suppliers, the cost of switching production must be small and the risk not substantial.

One of the most important European cases arose in relation to the market for bananas. In 1975 the Commission adopted a decision relating to certain conduct carried out by United Brands Continental, a subsidiary of an American firm accounting for 35 per cent of world banana exports. After finding that United Brands had engaged in a range of abusive conduct the Commission fined the company, and United Brands brought an action before the ECJ seeking an annulment of the Commission decision (*United Brands Co. v Commission* case 27/76 [1978] 1 CMLR 429). In particular the undertaking challenged the definition of the relevant product market adopted by the Commission, which had held that the market in question was that specifically for bananas, as against a more general market for soft fruit or for all fruit. The ECJ defined the problem as being one of whether bananas were 'reasonably interchangeable by consumers with other kinds of fresh fruit' (para. 12). United Brands argued that bananas 'compete with other fresh fruit in the same shops, on the same shelves, at prices which can be compared, satisfying the same needs: consumption as a dessert or between meals' (para. 13), and was able to point to statistics prepared by the United Nations agency, the Food and Agricultural Organization, that showed that consumers switched from buying bananas to buying other types of fruit in the summer months when the alternatives became readily available. The Commission, on the other hand, argued that it was right to treat bananas as being part of a discrete market, and pointed in particular to the fact that 'the banana is a very important part of the diet of certain sections of the community' (para. 19), namely, the very young, the elderly, and the sick, and that the banana possessed unique characteristics: 'appearance, taste, softness, seedlessness [and] easy handling' (para. 31). Further, at that time, bananas were unusual in being available all the year round, and the same statistics relied on by United Brands showed that the demand and price for bananas were generally unresponsive to the supplies of other fruits, with the single exception of grapes and peaches in Germany. In conclusion the Court held that 'a very large number of consumers having a constant need for bananas are not noticeably or even appreciably enticed away' by other fruit and that 'consequently the banana market is a market which is sufficiently distinct from the other fresh fruit market' (para. 35).

It may often be possible to establish that, because of a set of preferences peculiar to that group, particular groups of consumers are insensitive to the price of a given product. However, care should be taken before concluding from this that a separate market exists over which dominance is more easily established. The question is not one of how much the monopolist could in theory charge that group for the product, but one of whether the remaining consumers' behaviour will act as a limit on pricing decisions. Unless a monopolist seller of bananas can isolate the sick and elderly, and force them to pay more, the price can be raised only across the entire supply. This might increase the revenue from that one group, but it is likely to be more than offset by a fall in revenue from other consumers who are able to switch to different products. Market analysis should, if results are to be meaningful, focus on the group of consumers who can switch consumption at the margin, and not on the group who cannot—this is the essence of the SSNIP test.

Similar analysis to that of *United Brands* was conducted in *Nederlandsche Banden-Industrie Michelin N.V.* v *Commission* case 322/81 [1985] 1 CMLR 282. Here the Commission had condemned Michelin, the well-known tyre manufacturer, for, *inter alia*, its policies relating to dealer discounts and bonuses. In challenging the decision Michelin argued that the Commission had incorrectly defined the relevant market and, in so doing, had inflated the market share of Michelin. Had the market been defined correctly, Michelin asserted, the market share would have fallen to 37 per cent, a level which would not support a conclusion of dominance. The market for tyres is a complex one: tyres are supplied both with the original vehicle purchase and as replacements; they are available in different sizes, qualities, and treads, depending in part upon the vehicle to which they are to be attached; old tyres may be given new treads ('retreads') and these compete with new replacement tyres. In taking its decision the Commission defined the relevant market as that for new replacement tyres for lorries, buses, and similar vehicles. For this market Michelin's sales amounted to between 57 per cent and 65 per cent over the period in which the Commission was interested. The Court appeared to be unimpressed with arguments made by Michelin to the effect that the relevant market should include also car and van tyres. While Michelin contended that these should be taken into account as they occupy similar positions on the market, and that suppliers might therefore be able to switch from manufacturing car and van tyres to manufacturing heavy vehicle tyres, the Court made the point that 'there is no interchangeability between car and van tyres on the one hand and heavy-vehicle tyres on the other' (para. 39). Responding to the supply-side substitutability argument, the Court noted that to switch production between tyres for heavy vehicles and those for cars and vans was no easy matter and would require the investment of considerable time and money by manufacturers. Neither did the Court accept that retreads competed directly with new replacement tyres, even though there might be an element of substitution—Michelin had itself conceded that a retread would not always be as safe or reliable as a new tyre.

It is interesting to note that in 1980 the courts in the United States found, basing their view in part on the existence of a $30 price differential, that separate markets existed in the case of radial and non-radial tyres in the case of *Donald B. Rice Tire Co. v Michelin Tire Corp.* 483 F. Supp. 750 (D. Md. 1980).

While the Commission has usually been successful in defending its market definitions it lost the notable case of *Europemballage Corp. and Continental Can Co. Inc. v Commission* case 6/72 [1973] CMLR 199. Here the Court held that the Commission had failed adequately to justify its reasoning in defining the three relevant markets as being those 'for light containers for canned meat products', 'light containers for canned seafood', and 'metal closures for the food packing industry'. The Commission did not give adequate reasons in the contested decision as to why these three areas constituted separate markets or why they stood apart from the wider market for can containers 'for fruit and vegetables, condensed milk, olive oil, fruit juices and chemico-technical products'. It also failed to consider the possibility of food packagers producing their own containers, and the Court was generally dismissive both of the quality of the reasoning in the decision and of the use of inconsistent facts to support arguments.

Demand- and supply-side substitutability may be the most important factor in the determination of the relevant product market, but the Commission and Court have made reference to other factors. In some instances, such as in *AKZO Chemie BV v EC Commission* case C–62/86 [1993] 5 CMLR 215 (the discussion of predation in this case is considered in further detail in Chapter 13), the Court has accepted the Commission's view that the action of the allegedly dominant undertaking is itself evidence of the bounds of the product market. It is surely correct that if an undertaking apparently engages in an abusive practice, which would be commercially beneficial only if a dominant position was held, the presumption that it has correctly defined the relevant market, and does indeed have a dominant position, should be raised.

The failure to come to court with a carefully considered market analysis may have fatal consequences for the progress of the case. In *Sockel GmbH* v *The Body Shop International plc* [2000] UKCLR 262, an action was dismissed largely because the claimant had failed to adequately define the market. In this case the claimant had alleged an abuse of a dominant position on the part of Body Shop, and had depended on the fact that the franchise system itself set out the bounds of the relevant market, without any consideration of competition from other brands and other outlets.

11.2.1.1 *Spare parts and ancillary products*

The issue of spare parts and ancillary products was first dealt with by the EC authorities in some detail in the case of *Hugin* (*Hugin Kassaregister AB and Hugin Cash Registers Ltd* v *Commission* case 22/78 [1979] 3 CMLR 345). The Commission had taken a decision that the non-dominant supplier of cash machines held a dominant position in the market for spare parts for those machines (78/68, (1978) OJ L22/23). The Court agreed with the Commission that, based on arguments relating to substitutability, the spare parts were not interchangeable with spare parts for other machines, and neither was it reasonable to suggest that a consumer purchase a new cash register from a different supplier as an alternative to fitting a spare part in an existing machine. The case has been followed since (see, e.g., *Volvo AB* v *Erik Veng (UK) Ltd* case 238/87 [1989] 4 CMLR 122) but it has raised concerns. It may be argued that a consumer choosing an initial purchase (in *Hugin* a cash register, and in *Volvo*, a motor car) must consider, as part of that decision, aspects such as the costs of maintenance and after-sales servicing, of which the availability of spare parts is just one element. In neither of the above cases did the undertaking hold a dominant position in the primary market, and as the consumer is able to make a choice at this stage it is very much to the disadvantage of the undertaking if it has thrust upon it unexpected and unwelcome responsibilities in the secondary market, for which it may not have budgeted, following a finding of dominance in that market. This argument is persuasive as long as the assumption of symmetry of knowledge between consumer and undertaking remains valid, but falls down where the consumer has neither the information nor ready access to it, on which to base such calculations at the point of original purchase.

A similar argument may be made in relation to ancillary products (or 'consumables'/'lock-ins') such as toner cartridges for printers, or semi-manufactured products to work with industrial machinery, and again it might be expected that the consumer, even more so than with spare parts, is in a position to factor in the ancillary items at the time of making the initial purchase. Two major cases, *Hilti* (*Hilti AG v Commission* case T–30/89 [1992] 4 CMLR 16) and *Tetra Pak II* (*Tetra Pak International SA v Commission* case T–83/91 [1992] 4 CMLR 76), dominate the case law. In *Hilti* the Court held that a distinction could be made between three separate markets: a nail-gun used in the construction trade; the cartridge strip in which the nails were placed; and the nails themselves. As with *Hugin*, *Hilti* did not hold a dominant position in the market for fixing systems for use in the construction industry, but did hold such a position in relation to the two ancillary markets. In *Tetra Pak II* the Commission argued that the market for filling machines to package liquid foods into cartons was a different market from that for the cartons themselves into which the foods were placed (92/163 (1992) OJ L72/1). Tetra Pak had argued that it was a supplier of integrated systems, and could not be said to have a dominant position in the market for cartons for its machines as no such separate market existed. On the facts the Court held that there were inconsistencies in the arguments made by Tetra Pak, including the fact that it supplied cartons to users of other manufacturers' machines, and that it would not need to impose restrictive contract terms on its customers for its own cartons if no other manufacturers' cartons could be used. This would be an example of supply-side substitutability where manufacturers making cartons for their own machines could also, with minimal adjustment to production lines, produce cartons for other machines.

In its *25th Report on Competition Policy* (COM (96) 126 final) the Commission accepted that this is a difficult area in which complaints can be resolved only on a case-by-case basis, with the Commission taking into account 'all important factors such as the price and life-time of the primary product, transparency of prices of secondary products, prices of secondary products as a proportion of the primary product value, information costs and other issues' (point 86). Such an approach was taken in *Pelikan/Kyocera* (point 87) where the Commission dealt with a complaint relating to activity in the market for toner cartridges for printers. The Commission was persuaded that Kyocera was not dominant in a secondary market for cartridges to be used with its printers, as consumers 'were well informed about the price charged for consumables and appeared to take this into account in their decision to buy a printer'.

Four factors were set out as being important when making the assessment whether a secondary market existed independently of the primary market:

(1) Would the consumer be in a position to make an informed choice at the point of initial purchase about the life cycle of the product, and the associated costs of any consumables? For example, in the case of a printer and toner cartridges would the consumer be able to 'punish' a company that appeared to abuse its power in the aftermarket by making a different choice in the primary market?

(2) Would the consumer actually make that choice?

(3) Would a sufficient number of consumers respond to apparent abuses in the aftermarket by adjusting their choices in the primary market?

(4) Would the response time of consumers be quick enough to protect those locked in to the aftermarket?

There has been much criticism of the approach taken by the EC Commission in this area, and of the *Hugin* decision in particular, but some support for such a course may be adduced from the American case of *Eastman Kodak Co.* v *Image Technical Services Inc.* 504 U.S. 451 (1992), where a broadly similar stance was taken in relation to 'locked-in' customers for spare parts where the cost of switching would be high. This has been followed in similar cases in the United States.

11.2.2 **The relevant geographical market**

Having considered what the relevant product market is the Commission must then show the geographical boundaries of that market. In a form of words used frequently in decisions 'this examination enables the Commission to identify the actual and potential competitors of the undertaking in question and other constraints which may exist on the exercise of its supposed market power'. This is an important consideration, because while an undertaking may be dominant in a very small area—the classic example of which is the bus company that is dominant with respect to a single route—art. 82 requires that a dominant position extend to a 'substantial part' of the Community (see below). The close link between these two considerations has been made clear by the ECJ, which has held that for art. 82 to apply 'presupposes the clear delimitation of the substantial part of the [EC] in which it may be able to engage in abuses which hinder effective competition and this is an area where the objective conditions of competition applying to the product in question must be the same for all traders' (*United Brands Co.* v *Commission* case 27/76 [1978] 1 CMLR 429, para. 44). An examination of the geographical market should also take into account the fact that it may be the case that an undertaking may appear to be dominant in one territory, but actually face competition or the threat of competition from outside of that territory that acts as a restraint on its conduct.

In the *United Brands* case, the Commission considered that the geographical market constituted Germany, Denmark, Ireland, and the Benelux countries, but excluded the other three Member States (the UK, Italy, and France) on the grounds that the legacy of history was such that there existed special circumstances relating to the import of bananas in those countries. The undertaking was happy that these countries be excluded, but argued further that the Commission should have held that each Member State constituted a separate market as the conditions of competition were different in each state, with different customs systems and different patterns of consumption. In the three excluded states the Court noted that United Brands would not be in a position to compete on equal terms with other bananas sold in those states, but that while the six other states displayed different characteristics the market in each of them was free, and the conditions of competition were the same for all undertakings trading in them, with the result that 'these six states form[ed] an area which [was] sufficiently homogenous to be considered in its entirety' (at para. 53). It is the conditions of competition, and not the result of that competition, that are important in determining the boundaries of the geographical market. Thus the fact that there are price differences between various areas is not in itself evidence of different markets (see, e.g., *Soda Ash—Solvay* 91/299 (1991) OJ L152/21).

In some instances the identification of the relevant area will be a relatively straightforward matter. There may, for instance, be specific evidence pointing to a clear boundary to the market. Thus in a series of cases relating to television guides and television listings the relevant areas were, in each case, those in which the television programmes themselves were intended primarily to be received (see, e.g., *RTE* v *Commission* case T–69/89 [1991] 4 CMLR 586 (Ireland) and *BBC* v *Commission* case T–70/89 [1991] 4 CMLR 669 (UK)). The action of a state monopoly, or of state regulation, may also define the market strictly, as, for instance, was the situation in *British Leyland plc* v *Commission* case 226/84 [1987] 1 CMLR 185, which related to the system of a national approval certificate for motor cars. The position may be more complicated where there is an apparently national market, as might be the case for any national newspaper, but where there is nevertheless some inter-state trade. If *The Times* is sold on news stands in the major cities in Europe in small numbers, is the relevant geographical market that of the UK or a wider market extending into Europe?

There has been some criticism of the approach taken by the Commission and the ECJ in defining the geographical market in *Michelin*. Although it was recognized that the main tyre companies competed at the global level, the Commission had argued that the actions of each subsidiary were tailored to the specific conditions of each national market and had treated The Netherlands as a separate market from the rest of the Community. The Court agreed that it was 'at that level that the objective conditions of competition [were] alike for traders', and although it accepted that 'in practice dealers established in The Netherlands obtain their supplies only from suppliers operating in The Netherlands' (*Nederlandsche Banden-Industrie Michelin N.V.* v *Commission* case 322/81 [1985] 1 CMLR 282, para. 26), it may be argued that the possibility of consumers going outside The Netherlands for their tyres should have been discussed more fully. It is likely that the competitive conditions in The Netherlands were, at the least, moderately affected by the availability of supplies from elsewhere in the Community.

As a rule of thumb the size of the market is in inverse proportion to the product's transportation costs relative to the value of the product: a product with a high value and a low transportation cost will have a large geographical market; and a product with a low value and a high transportation cost will have a small geographical market. That transport costs may be highly influential in determining the boundaries to the market may be seen in *Napier Brown–British Sugar* 88/518 (1988) OJ L284/41. In finding that British Sugar had abused a dominant position in its market the Commission considered that the UK constituted a geographical market separate from that of the rest of the Community. *Inter alia* the Commission was swayed by the fact that imports into the UK over the period immediately preceding its action had amounted to only 5–10 per cent of consumption, and noted that this was in part the result of 'the natural barrier of the English Channel, which gives rise to additional transport costs' (at para. 44(i)) (a similar conclusion had been reached by the MMC in two reports into mergers in the domestic sugar industry which the Commission in part relied upon). Sugar represents a classic example of a product which has high transport costs in relation to value: it is both bulky and relatively cheap.

In situations where transport costs do not constitute a significant barrier to trade, the relevant geographical market may often be that of the entire Community (see, e.g., *ECS/AKZO* 85/609 (1985) OJ L374/1, para. 66). Thus in *Tetra Pak I (BTG Licence)*, which concerned the market for packaging machines and consumables for liquid foods, of which milk was the most important, the Commission held that 'even if there exist the differing demand conditions between Member States, the [EC] is the relevant geographical market . . . transport costs for both machines and cartons are not significant. In fact carton packaging machinery supplied to dairies in the [EC] comes from producers all over the world' (88/501 (1988) OJ L272/27, para. 41).

11.2.3 **The relevant time period**

Time is a factor that must be considered in order to establish the relevant period:

(a) over which the dominance is alleged; and

(b) over which the alleged abuse may have been perpetrated.

However, it is extremely rare for the analysis of the temporal market to be a significant feature of a decision or case. The most notable example arises out of the 1973/74 oil crisis, with the Commission taking a decision holding that one consequence of the crisis was to create a series of temporarily defined separate markets in favour of each supplier as customers were unable to switch to alternative suppliers, supplies being rationed by suppliers and made available only to their traditional customers (*ABG Oil companies operating in the Netherlands* 77/327 (1977) OJ L117/1). While the Commission lost the case on appeal on different grounds, the Court left intact the temporal arguments (*BP* v *Commission* case 77/77 [1978] 3 CMLR 174). Generally the Commission's determination of the temporal constraints over which the relevant market is defined is not likely to be successfully challenged, but there may well be arguments as to the duration of the alleged abuse as this is a factor in assessing the level of any fines imposed (see Chapter 4).

11.2.4 **The Commission Notice on market definition**

In 1997 the Commission published a Notice on the definition of the relevant market for the purpose of Community competition law ((1997) OJ C372/5). Such notices are not binding—although as they often do little more than 'codify' the previous case law the grounds for challenging them may be limited—and are 'without prejudice to the interpretation which may be given by the [CFI and ECJ]'. They are unlikely to be disregarded by the Commission, however, being in effect a statement of current policy, and are highly persuasive on other authorities or courts dealing with matters of EC competition law. The notice applies equally to analysis conducted for the purposes of applying arts 81 and 82 and Regulation 4064/89 (see Chapter 15), as well as the European Economic Area Agreement and the ECSC Treaty. The reason for issuing the notice is made apparent in the introduction:

> The definition of the relevant market in both its product and geographic dimensions often has a decisive influence on the assessment of a competition case. By rendering public the procedures the Commission follows when considering market definition and by indicating the criteria and evidence on which it relies to reach a decision, the Commission expects to increase the transparency of its policy and decision making in the area of competition policy.

The Notice firmly places the SSNIP test at the heart of market definition. In its decision relating to the *1998 Football World Cup* 2000/12 (2000) OJ L5/55 the Commission was explicit in its application of the Notice's SSNIP test to define the relevant market (paras. 66–74), although in *Virgin/British Airways* 2000/74 (2000) OJ L30/1 the Commission indicated that it was not required to perform the SSNIP test, and that the methodology set out in the Notice was merely an illustration of the way in which markets operated.

The Commission recognizes that, because the purpose for which competition law is being applied may be different under each legislative head, the methodology outlined above 'might lead to different results depending on the nature of the competition issue being examined', but that certain basic principles apply in all cases. These economic constants are the factors that serve as competitive restraints on the undertaking whose conduct or concentrative transaction is being analysed: demand substitution and supply substitution.

Supply-side substitution, which is a factor in market definition, is to be distinguished from potential competition, which is not. The Notice makes clear the fact that the Commission does not consider it appropriate to consider potential competition (see, e.g., *Europemballage Corp. and Continental Can Co. Inc. v Commission* case 6/72 [1973] CMLR 199) at the stage of market definition. This is not to say that this factor is disregarded by the Commission, but that 'the conditions under which potential competition will actually represent an effective competitive constraint depend on the analysis of specific factors and circumstances related to the conditions of entry' and that, if required, such analysis will be carried out only *after* the relevant market has been defined. The key distinction between supply-side substitution and potential competition lies in the time period over which each may take place, with potential competition arising only over a longer time-frame.

The Notice sheds useful light on the practicalities of market analysis and the extent to which the Commission may be able to avoid the sort of analysis undertaken in, for example, the *United Brands* case. It is apparent that in the right circumstances cases will be fairly quickly dealt with where the issue is simply one of 'whether product A and product B belong or do not belong to the same product market', and where the determination that they do will at once eliminate any competition concerns. Where more detailed analysis is called for the Commission may contact main customers, main companies, relevant professional associations, the undertakings directly involved, and where appropriate companies involved in upstream markets, which are defined as those closer to the original source of production or raw input. Not all such contacts will be by way of formal decisions taken under the appropriate secondary legislation, and the Commission may often simply discuss matters with company officers on the telephone, or arrange informal visits to allow it to gain a clearer understanding of the operation of the relevant market. Factors that may serve as evidence to define product markets include: an analysis of the product characteristics; evidence of substitution in the recent past; various econometric and statistical approaches; views of customers and competitors; consumer preferences as perhaps identified by consumer surveys commissioned within the industry in the past; barriers and costs of switching consumption; and the possible existence of different groups of consumers and price discrimination.

A broadly similar approach is taken to the geographic market, the objective being, as indicated above, 'to identify which companies selling the products in the relevant market are actually competing with the parties and constraining their behaviour, with the focus placed on prices'. The evidence that the Notice suggests may be used to define the geographic market includes: past evidence of diversion of orders to other areas; basic demand characteristics, including factors such as national preferences; views of customers and competitors; current geographic patterns of purchases; trade flows; and barriers and costs of switching sources.

The Notice does not deal with the issue of the temporal definition of the market.

11.2.5 The relative strength of the alleged dominant undertaking

Having established the relevant market—product, geographical area, and time period—the next requirement for art. 82 to apply is that dominance in that market be established. Dominance may be attributed to an undertaking by virtue of a variety of factors of which the most important is market share. However, market share may not be the sole determinant of dominance, and situations may arise in which an undertaking commands a large market share yet is not dominant. This might be the case, for example, where there is the serious threat of *potential* competition (see above). Likewise there may be situations where an undertaking has a seemingly innocuous market share yet is still dominant because of the relatively weak positions of its main competitors.

11.2.5.1 *Market share*

The classic statement as to the role of market share in determining dominance is to be found in the case of *Hoffmann-La Roche*. The ECJ held that

although the importance of the market shares may vary from one market to another the view may legitimately be taken that very large shares are in themselves, and save in exceptional circumstances, evidence of the existence of a dominant position. An undertaking which has a very large market share and holds it for some time, by means of the volume of production and the scale of the supply which it stands for—without those having much smaller market shares being able to meet rapidly the demand from those who would like to break away from the undertaking which has the largest market share—is by virtue of that share in a position of strength which makes it an unavoidable trading partner and which already because of this secures for it, at the very least during relatively long periods, that freedom of action which is the special feature of a dominant position.   (*Hoffmann-La Roche & Co. Ag* v *Commission* case 85/76 [1979] 3 CMLR 211, para. 41)

In that case the appellant undertaking manufactured various vitamins, each of which was treated as a separate product market, and the analysis of the ECJ is revealing as to the role market shares play and the extent to which a particular share may, by itself, be relied upon in establishing the existence of a dominant position. Where a range of shares is given it is cover a three-year period, in which membership of the Community grew from six to nine Member States, and both share by value and share by quantity:

- *Vitamin A*: The market share stood at 47 per cent, and dominance was established, in part by reference to other criteria (paras 50–2).
- *Vitamin B_2*: 75–87 per cent 'so large that they are in themselves evidence of a dominant position' (para. 56).
- *Vitamin B_3*: 19–51 per cent 'Market shares of this size either in value or in quantity . . . do not in themselves constitute a factor sufficient to establish a dominant position . . . insufficient evidence of the existence of a dominant position held by Roche for the period in question' (paras 57–8).
- *Vitamin B_6*: 84–90 per cent 'market shares are . . . so large that they prove the existence of a dominant position' (paras 59–60).
- *Vitamin C*: 63–66 per cent 'evidence of the existence of a dominant position' but further evidence used to support the conclusion (paras 61–3).
- *Vitamin E*: 50–64 per cent 'significant', but further evidence used to support the finding of dominance (paras 64–6).
- *Vitamin H*: 93–100 per cent 'with the result that it in fact has a monopoly' (para. 67).

In *AKZO* the Court, having first cited *Hoffmann-La Roche* to make the point that very large market shares may by themselves be conclusive evidence of dominance, held that a share of 50 per cent would satisfy this test (*AKZO Chemie BV* v *Commission* case C–62/86 [1993] 5 CMLR 215).

The Commission appears on occasion to be more conservative than the Court in its use of market share. In *BBI/Boosey & Hawkes: interim measures* 87/500 (1987) OJ L286/36, Boosey & Hawkes, the leading manufacturer of musical instruments for brass bands, was found to have 'a market share of some 80 per cent to 90 per cent' but the Commission, noting that 'a high market share does however not on its own create a presumption of dominance', pointed also to other evidence. It was significant that the undertaking's own documents claimed that their instruments were 'the automatic first choice of all the top brass bands', and that no other competitor had been able to make a significant impact on the market, in spite of Yamaha making strenuous efforts to do so (para. 18). However, there are clear instances where a finding of dominance is made by exclusive reference to market share. In *Decca* (*Decca Navigator System* 89/113 (1989) OJ L43/27) the undertaking had a legal monopoly in relation to the relevant market for the period during which it held patents in respect of the relevant technology, and thereafter held a market share such as to constitute a de facto monopoly. The Commission did not point to any other evidence to establish its finding of dominance.

Generally the approach appears to be that a market share of 70 per cent and above will almost certainly constitute a dominant position; a share of 50–70 per cent will raise a presumption of dominance; a share of 40–50 per cent may support a conclusion of dominance; and a share of below 40 per cent is highly unlikely to permit the finding of dominance unless other evidence is overwhelming, although the Commission in its *10th Report on Competition Policy* suggested that an undertaking could still be found to enjoy a dominant position with a market share as low as 20 per cent. In *Virgin/British Airways* 2000/74 (2000) OJ L30/1 the Commission found dominance to exist at a point when BA's market share of the total airline sales in the UK in 1998 amounted to 39.7 per cent (para. 41). This is the lowest figure at which a finding of dominance has been sustained, and even here there were other factors strongly indicative of dominance, including the relatively low market shares of other parties.

11.2.5.2 *Competitors' positions*

The relative size of the competitors' market shares were determining evidence as to the existence of a dominant position in relation to the vitamins C and E market in *Hoffmann-La Roche* (above) and supporting evidence in relation to the vitamin A market. In the market for vitamin C the Court, for instance, pointed to the fact that 'the gap between Roche's shares (64.8 per cent) and those of its next largest competitors (14.8 per cent and 6.3 per cent) was such as to confirm the conclusion' of dominance (para. 63) and a similar position was found to exist in relation to vitamin E. The comments made in relation to vitamin A, where the market shares were 47 per cent to Roche, and 27 per cent, 18 per cent, 7 per cent, and 1 per cent to the other producers, are more telling:

Since the relevant market thus has the particular features of a narrow oligopolistic market in which the degree of competition by its very nature has already been weakened, Roche's share, which is equal to the aggregate of the shares of its two next largest competitors, proves that it is entirely free to decide what attitude to adopt when confronted by competition. (para. 51)

In *Sabena* (*London European v Sabena* 88/589 (1988) OJ L317/47) the Commission found that the market share held by Sabena of the relevant market of computerized airline reservation systems in Belgium was between 40 per cent and 50 per cent. As such a share would not, by itself, support a claim of dominance, the Commission noted that 'the ratio of market shares held by the undertaking concerned to those held by its competitors is also a reliable indicator' (para. 24). In this case the five competing systems were each used by no more than 20 agencies, as compared to the 118 agencies using the Sabena system.

11.2.5.3 *Barriers to entry*

As noted in Chapter 10, the role played by barriers to entry in industrial economics and antitrust analysis is of vital importance. The establishment of the market share of the allegedly dominant undertaking cannot by itself determine the competitive restraints under which the undertaking operates. It is possible, albeit unlikely, that an undertaking could have a 100 per cent market share and yet not be able to reap significant profits if it is constantly aware of the danger of potential competition, which might be triggered by higher prices signalling to entrepreneurs that profits can be made in the market. Barriers to entry are not, however, easily analysed and often require a more dynamic long-term view of market structure than does a straightforward static analysis of current market shares. The situation is further complicated by disagreements between industrial economists as to the meaning of the term 'barrier to entry' and as to those factors that may legitimately be considered to be barriers. It is in the definition of this term that one of the most dramatic differences lies between the Harvard and Chicago schools. In the various decisions taken under art. 82 the Commission has pointed to the existence of identifiable barriers to entry, but has rarely made convincing or detailed arguments and has not developed an entirely satisfactory framework. For example, in *Tetra Pak I* (88/501 (1988) OJ L272/27), as well as relying on the undertaking's 91.8 per cent market share in the relevant market—'machines capable of filling cartons by an aseptic process with UHT-treated liquids'—the Commission considered that the 'barriers to entry to produce aseptic packaging machines are particularly high, which severely limits the entry of new competitors' (para. 44.3). This may be true, but it is not adequately supported by detailed analysis found within the decision itself.

In the absence of a sophisticated analysis the Commission has turned instead to a range of evidence which it considers to be indicative of dominance, and has not always made clear whether these secondary factors are considered also to be evidence of barriers to entry or of dominance per se.

11.2.5.4 *The resources, size, and commercial superiority of the undertaking*

In *British Plasterboard* (*BPB Industries plc* 89/22 (1989) OJ L10/50), once the Commission found that the undertaking's share of the plasterboard market in Great Britain was between 98 per cent and 96 per cent for the relevant period it may seem unnecessary to have referred to other factors to support the argument that the company enjoyed a dominant position. Nevertheless the Commission pointed also to the 'substantial economies in producing on a large scale in integrated industrial complexes' (para. 116) enjoyed by BPB. Further, the extensive product range carried by BPB and the fact that architects were on occasion specific in requiring the use of

BPB's products were further points used as evidence of dominance. The failings of a static, snapshot analysis are perhaps demonstrated by this decision. While on these facts it appears the BPB's position would be unassailable, an MMC report in 1990 (*Plasterboard*, Cm. 1224) found that BPB's market share had fallen, in the space of only two years, from 96 per cent to 65 per cent, following the entry of new competition into the market.

Undertaking which have succeeded in developing an efficient and strong distribution system may find that the existence of such a system is one factor that supports a finding of dominance. Thus, for instance, in *Eurofix-Bauco/Hilti* 88/138 (1988) OJ L65/19 one of the factors that the Commission considered to be relevant was Hilti's 'strong and well-organised distribution system—in the EEC it has subsidiaries and independent dealers integrated into its selling network' (para. 69).

In *Soda Ash* (*Soda Ash—Solvay* 91/299 (1991) OJ L152/21) the company's dominant position was established not just by its near-total monopoly in three of the Member States, but also by reference to, *inter alia*, its manufacturing strength with plant in six of the Member States; its upstream integration as the largest producer of salt (a raw material in the manufacture of soda ash) in the Community; and Solvay's 'excellent market coverage as the exclusive or near-exclusive supplier to almost all the major customers in the Community'.

The Commission may turn not only to product ranges, but also to the services offered by the allegedly dominant company, both where these are the primary activity and where they are ancillary to the supply of the primary product. Thus, for example, in a decision taken in respect of shipping services between Zaire and Angola and various North Sea ports (*Cewal* 93/82 (1993) OJ L34/20), the assertion of dominance was supported by reference to the 'network of routes, the capacities of [Cewal's] fleet and the frequency of the services it can provide' (para. 59). The level of technical support that could be provided by Michelin's large number of representatives (*BF BV/NV NBI Michelin* 81/969 (1981) OJ L353/33), which was greater than that of rival manufacturers, was also considered to be indicative of dominance.

11.2.5.5 *Technical superiority and the possession of know-how and intellectual property*

Technical superiority was considered to be a relevant factor by the ECJ in *Hoffmann-La Roche & Co. AG v Commission* case 85/76 [1979] 3 CMLR 211, which held that: 'Roche's technical lead over its competitors due to the fact that it is the proprietor of several patents relating to vitamin A, even after the expiration of these patents, is a further indication that it occupies a dominant position' (para. 51). Similar considerations were raised in *Eurofix-Bauco/Hilti* 88/138 (1988) OJ L65/19, where Hilti's DX 450 nail gun, which was central to the issue of market power, was commended for its 'novel technically advantageous features' which were subject to patent protection. The Commission also drew attention to Hilti's 'extremely strong research and development position' which it considered to be a factor in establishing dominance. In *Tetra Pak I* 88/501 (1988) OJ L272/27 this factor was also an issue, with the Commission pointing to Tetra Pak's first-mover advantage: 'it was the first to develop the technology and has vast experience . . . its technology and machines are partially protected by patents' (para. 44.2).

The possession of copyright in published material may also lead to a conclusion of dominance if the relevant market is drawn tightly. The Commission dealt with complaints relating to the practices of the IBA, BBC, and RTE television networks, in relation to the programme listings. The undertakings' policy was to reserve to themselves the right to publish advance details of schedules, and they relied in part on their copyright in these listings to obstruct advance publication by magazines that were attempting to compete with the authorized publications. In a short decision, which was subsequently challenged, the Commission held that 'the factual monopoly held by the broadcasting organisations in relation to their . . . listings is strengthened into a legal monopoly' by virtue of the application of copyright laws, and that the companies therefore held a dominant position. (*Magill TV Guide/ITP/ BBC and RTE* 89/205 (1989) OJ L78/43).

11.2.5.6 *Super-dominance*

Recent developments in the law of dominance suggest that a refinement to the 'special responsibility' provided for in the *Michelin* case is being created in the case of undertakings which are 'super-dominant'. This follows from the comments of the Advocate General in the case of *Compagnie Maritime Belge SA* v *Commission* joined cases C 395 and 396/96P [2000] 4 CMLR 1076, and may be deduced also from an analysis of the response to abusive conduct in earlier cases. The key statement of Advocate General Fennelly is found in paragraph 137 of his submission to the Court:

To my mind, art. 82 cannot be interpreted as permitting monopolists or quasi-monopolists to exploit the very significant market power which their superdominance confers so as to preclude the emergence either of a new or additional competitor. Where an undertaking . . . enjoys a position of such overwhelming dominance verging on monopoly, comparable to that which existed in the present case . . . it would not be consonant with the particularly onerous special obligation affecting such a dominant undertaking not to impair further the structure of the feeble existing competition.

The 'particularly onerous special obligation' referred to here may be witnessed at play in some of the 'essential facility' cases discussed in Chapter 13, where the undertakings in question enjoyed total monopoly in some areas of the market, and as a result were able to exclude from other parts of the market potential competition. It had already been recognized by the ECJ in the case of *Tetra Pak* v *Commission (No. 2)* case C–333/94P [1997] 4 CMLR 662 that the scope of the special responsibility provided for in *Michelin* must be considered in the light of the particular facts of each case. The comments of the Advocate General in *Compagnie Maritime Belge* seem to do little more than provide a convenient label to a situation in which the analysis of the particular facts shows that the existing competition to the monopolist is 'feeble' rather than merely 'weakened'.

11.2.5.7 *Joint dominance*

The law relating to joint dominance (also known as 'collective dominance' and 'oligopolistic dominance') is dealt with here in relation to art. 82, and in Chapter 15 in relation to merger control, although it should be recognized that the two threads are inextricably connected. The economics of what is a difficult area are dealt with in Chapter 14.

The leading case relating to joint dominance is that of *Compagnie Maritime Belge SA* v *Commission* joined cases C 395 and 396/96P [2000] 4 CMLR 1076. The case arose by way of an appeal from *Cewal* 93/82 (1993) OJ L34/20 where the Commission had condemned members of a liner conference for attempting, collectively, to eliminate an independent competitor. One of the issues that fell to be dealt with was, following a chain of cases applying the concept in relation to merger control, the extent to which, and the factors conditioning this, a number of undertakings could *collectively* occupy a dominant position. It will be recalled that art. 82 makes reference to a dominant position held by 'one or more' undertakings. The Court held that it was well established that art. 82 could apply to situations in which a dominant position was held by more than one undertaking:

the expression 'one or more undertakings' in art. [82] of the Treaty implies that a dominant position may be held by two or more economic entities legally independent of each other, provided that from an economic point of view they present themselves or act together on a particular market as a collective entity.   (para. 36)

To establish that such a position exists it is necessary, according to the Court, to examine the economic links or factors which give rise to a connection between undertakings. It is not sufficient that the undertakings in question are linked by an agreement or other practice which would fall within art. 81(1) in order to find that a position of joint dominance exists, but such an agreement can result in a position of joint dominance, depending on the way in which the agreement would be implemented. In the present case the way in which the liner conference agreement between the parties operated was such as to place them in the position of presenting 'themselves on that market as a collective entity *vis-à-vis* their competitors, their trading partners and consumers' (para. 44).

Joint dominance was also discussed in the context of art. 82 in *Irish Sugar* 97/624 (1997) OJ L258/1, on appeal *Irish Sugar plc* v *Commission* case T–228/97 [1999] 5 CMLR 1300, paras 38–68. Here it was accepted by all that for joint dominance to exist 'there must be close links between the two entities, and that those links must be such as to be capable of leading to the adoption of the same conduct and policy on the market in question' (para. 45). Here the joint dominance related to a vertical arrangement between a dominant producer of sugar, and the sole bulk distributor of sugar in the same Member State.

11.3 The meaning of 'substantial part'

For art. 82 to apply, the dominant position identified must be found to exist in 'the common market or in a substantial part of it'. Clearly if dominance extends throughout the EC this jurisdictional hurdle is overcome. The meaning of 'substantial part' is, however, open to interpretation, and is likely to be an inconstant factor: an area that would have counted as substantial in a Community of six may no longer be substantial in a Community that has more than doubled to 15 members, meaning that previous case law may not be a fail-safe guide to future determinations. It has been traditionally argued that a market extending to any single Member State will meet the threshold, but this may no longer be the case. While there are obvious political difficulties in either the Commission or a court in a Member State holding that the relevant state is not 'substantial', the increasing strength of the single market might allow the authorities to argue successfully that, particularly with regard to the smaller states, a state-wide market will not automatically be so classed. However, in *Irish Sugar* 97/624 (1997) OJ L258/1 the Republic of Ireland was found to be a substantial part of the Common Market although it accounted for only 1.2 per cent of the market for the sale of sugar in the EC. The concept also must be related to the specific market for the product in question, and not merely to an examination of the size of the absolute geographical area identified in defining the market boundary, although that is undeniably important.'

11.3.1 Examples

While a single Member State may not now automatically be substantial there is no doubt that areas of Member States can be, and that the Community can support several substantial markets in the same product, as long as in each the conditions of competition are different (see the discussion of *United Brands*, above).

The case of *Suiker Unie* (*Cooperatieve Vereniging 'Suiker Unie' UA* v *Commission* cases 40–48/73, 50/73, 54–56/73, 111/73, 113–114/73 [1976] 1 CMLR 295) remains one of the most important in determining the meaning of 'substantial'. The case itself is exceptionally complicated, with the applicants challenging a Commission decision which imposed fines and cease and desist orders on 16 undertakings (*European Sugar Industry* 73/109 (1973) OJ L140/17), on many different grounds. One of the applicants (Raffinerie Tirlemontoise) was alleged by the Commission to occupy a dominant position on the sugar market in Belgium and Luxembourg, which the Commission had held to be a substantial part of the Common Market, and claimed before the ECJ that this position was inconsistent with the small level of production of sugar in Belgium relative to the rest of the Community, and with the small number of consumers in the two Member States (it will be recalled that at the time the contested decision was taken the Community's membership was that of the original six Member States). The view taken by the Court was that in determining whether a specific area amounts to a 'substantial part of the common market' it would be necessary to take into account 'the pattern and volume of the production and consumption of the said product as well as the habits and economic opportunities of vendors and purchasers' (para. 371). Also relevant would be the fact that the organization of the sugar market by the Community had tended to reinforce national boundaries. In the year 1971/72 sugar production in the Community as a whole stood at 8,100,000 tonnes, and Belgian production at 770,000 tonnes (9.6 per cent of the total). Consumption in Belgium stood at 350,000 tonnes, compared to 6,500,000 tonnes in the Community (5.4 per cent) of the total. The Court held that these market shares, taken together with the other relevant factors, were such as to mean that the Belgo-Luxembourg market did constitute a substantial part of the Community.

In relation to another applicant, Sudzucker-Verkauf, the question was whether the 'southern part of Germany' constituted a substantial part of the common market. The population of the area in which the undertaking held its position was 22 million at the time the decision was taken, the undertaking's production was about 800,000 tonnes, and the Court held that this market 'is found to be sufficiently large, so far as sugar is concerned, to be considered . . . as a substantial part' of the Community (para. 448).

11.3.2 Infrastructure and facilities

It was noted above that a straightforward comparison of the relative size of the geographical area of the market with that of the Community as a whole will not always be sufficient to establish the meaning of 'substantial part', and in a chain of decisions very small geographical areas have been held to be 'substantial'. These include airports (Brussels Airport) and ports (Holyhead, Rødby, and Roscoff), all of which may be small in themselves but which may be the essential point of access to a market that is itself substantial (see further Chapter 13).

11.4 The concept of abuse

The list of abusive practices set out in art. 82 'merely gives examples, i.e., not an exhaustive list of the kinds of abusive exploitation of a dominant position prohibited by the Treaty' (*Europemballage Corp. and Continental Can Co. Inc. v Commission* case 6/72 [1973] CMLR 199, para. 26), and accordingly the Commission and Court have condemned practices not set out in the list. In *Continental Can*, for example, this included the acquisition of shares in a competing undertaking, which had the effect of increasing the power of an *already* dominant position (see the discussion of mergers in Chapter 15). The 'special responsibility' that dominant firms have not to impair or distort competition (*Nederlandsche Banden-Industries Michelin N.V. v Commission* case 322/81 [1985] 1 CMLR 282, at 327) suggests that standards of permissible conduct in the EC will be higher than, for example, in the

United States. The meaning of abuse might therefore be such as to go beyond the requirement not to act so as to impair the efficient operation of the market place. In *Hoffmann-La Roche & Co. AG* v *Commission* case 85/76 [1979] 3 CMLR 211, the ECJ held that

the concept of abuse is an objective concept relating to the behaviour of an undertaking in a dominant position which is such as to influence the structure of a market where, as a result of the very presence of the undertaking in question, the degree of competition is weakened and which, through recourse to methods different from those which condition normal competition . . . has the effect of hindering the maintenance of the degree of competition still existing in the market.   (para. 91)

The reference to 'normal competition' in this context is questionable. In fact many practices that have been condemned under art. 82 are not abnormal, but their use by undertakings which are already in a position of some strength has an impact that draws the attention of the EC Commission.

11.4.1 Examples of abusive conduct

Abuses arising out of predatory, discriminatory, and excessive prices, and refusals to supply, are considered in some detail in Chapter 13. The remaining examples given here are not a comprehensive listing, but will give some indication of the range of practices that have been condemned and the sort of evidence that is likely to attract the interest of the EC Commission.

11.4.1.1 *Exclusive purchasing and tie-in sales*
There exists a range of purchasing requirements that are sometimes used in order to extend a dominant undertaking's influence or to increase its profits. The most common of these practices are exclusive purchasing requirements, by virtue of which a purchaser agrees not to buy the same product from any other source, and tie-in sales, whereby the purchaser will be supplied with one product only if another is also purchased. In its extreme position, where tie-in sales extend across the complete range of the dominant supplier, such a practice may be termed full-line forcing.

Exclusive purchasing requirements were first dealt with in detail in *Vitamins* 76/ 642 (1976) OJ L223/27 (on appeal, *Hoffmann-La Roche & Co. AG* v *Commission* case 85/76 [1979] 3 CMLR 211). Hoffmann's strategy in relation to its bulk sales of synthetic vitamins was to conclude exclusive agreements with customers wherever possible. These 'fidelity agreements' were referred to in a circular issued by the Roche parent company in 1970, which was obtained and quoted by the Commission:

According to the experience of various Roche companies, fidelity contracts provide a very efficient protection against competition, especially as far as BASF are concerned. In our today's Management Information we have therefore made a special provision for such contracts. (para. 12)

In essence the structure of the supply contracts was such that Hoffmann would provide the major part of each customer's requirements at the most favourable price in the relevant market, and at regular intervals, which were usually annual, customers would be given a rebate of between 1 per cent and 20 per cent on their purchases if they had indeed obtained most of their requirements from Hoffmann. Hoffmann's ability to obtain information about, and to react to, its competitors' practices was enhanced by an 'English clause' in the contracts, which provided that Hoffmann would meet any price offered to a customer by any reputable supplier, or that if it failed to do so it would not remove the benefit of the rebates if the customer bought from the competing supplier. Generally these contracts were concluded for a period of five years, and would thus guarantee to Hoffmann a stable outlet which would potentially exclude other competitors from developing strength in the market.

The Commission found this conduct to be abusive as 'by its nature it hampers the freedom of choice and equality of treatment of purchasers and restricts competition between bulk vitamin manufacturers' (para. 22) and also took the view that the fidelity rebates fell expressly within art. 82(c), 'applying dissimilar conditions to equivalent transactions', because they were not related to objective cost factors.

When the case came before the ECJ it held that

> An undertaking which is in a dominant position on a market and ties purchasers—even if it does so at their request—by an obligation or promise on their part to obtain all or most of their requirements exclusively from the said undertaking abuses its dominant position.   (para. 89)

The Court further held that in the absence of exceptional circumstances the granting of rebates designed to support exclusive purchase obligations would be caught by art. 82(c).

In *ICI* (*Soda Ash ICI* 91/300 (1991) OJ L152/40) the Commission found that ICI's strategy in the relevant market was to ensure that its main competitors in the UK, Brenntag and General Chemical, 'at least remained in the United Kingdom market as a presence ... which met the need of most large customers for a secondary supplier while in fact presenting no real competitive threat' (para. 58). ICI offered its customers a 'top-slice rebate' under which substantial financial incentives were offered to customers purchasing more than their expected regular 'core' supplies from ICI. By tying its customers in this way ICI was able, in effect, to regulate the remainder of the market, and to control both the quantity and the price at which its competitor was able to sell.

Tying and full-line forcing fall within art. 82(d) ('making the conclusion of contracts subject to acceptance by the other parties of supplementary obligations which, by their nature or according to commercial usage, have no connection with the subject of such contracts') unless there are objective reasons to justify the tie. In the *Michelin* decision the primary issue was that of discounts granted to retailers that were considered to be hard for retailers to calculate and that had the effect of encouraging them to switch orders from Michelin's competitors (*BF BV NV NBI Michelin* 81/969 (1981) OJ L353/33). One of the concerns of the Commission was that, for the year 1977, the bonus system operated in such a way as to link the purchases of light tyres to heavy tyres. This is to say that a customer who would ordinarily purchase its heavy tyres from Michelin and its light tyres from another supplier would be encouraged to purchase all its tyres from Michelin in order to earn the bonus. Some do not consider such a practice to have an anti-competitive effect, but it would appear that the parties themselves believe that it is possible to extend monopoly power from one market to another. If Michelin were the only manufacturer of heavy tyres and informed customers that they would not be supplied with such tyres unless also purchasing Michelin's light tyres, the customers would have little option but to refuse to deal with other suppliers.

The position in *Hilti* was more obvious than in *Michelin*. In this case (*Eurofix-Bauco Hilti* 88/138 (1988) OJ L65/19) the company, which held a dominant position in relation to the market for fastening systems for use in the professional building industry (nail-guns), tied the sales of the two accessories, nails and cartridges, used by them. While there is a clear connection between the three products they may be legitimately viewed as separate markets. Many manufacturers are able to make the cartridges, most of which are in the form of a strip containing usually 10 brass cartridges, that are used to propel the nails, and are also able to make the nails themselves. In several cases Hilti either took, or threatened, legal action, based on its patents, to prevent the manufacture and marketing of cartridges that would be compatible with its nail guns. The Commission found that Hilti had maintained a policy of only supplying the cartridge strips for use in its guns when the purchaser also took the necessary number of nails, although Hilti had denied this when first asked by the Commission. When carrying out its investigation the Commission came across a letter from Hilti GB to Hilti AG referring to a particular customer who 'has now been advised that an embargo has been placed on cartridge-only sales (only a verbal restriction has been passed to the customer with nothing in writing)'. Other evidence obtained included an internal memo to the sales force relating to another customer who 'wanted a large quantity of Hilti cartridges. These would appear to be required in connection with Profix nails and should in no circumstances be supplied to the customer' (para. 31). In yet other cases the company instituted a policy of reducing discounts given on orders of cartridges if nails were not purchased at the same time. The attempt to restrict competition in the market for the two consumables of which Hilti's behaviour was suggestive was found to constitute an abuse. As regards Hilti's customers, the policies pursued left 'the consumer with no choice over the source of his nails and as such abusively exploit him' (para. 75). As a result of these practices Hilti was fined ECU 6m and ordered to bring the practices to an end.

Similar considerations were to the fore in *Tetra Pak II* (92/163 (1992) OJ L72/1). Tetra Pak's standard supply contracts contained two clauses which had the following effects: (i) the obligation that only Tetra Pak cartons would be used on Tetra Pak machines; and (ii) the obligation to obtain supplies exclusively from Tetra Pak. As the Commission noted, these two clauses would 'make the system airtight: not only is it not possible for the purchaser of a machine to use packaging other than that bearing the Tetra Pak mark, but moreover he may not obtain supplies of packaging from any source other than Tetra Pak' (para. 116). Tetra Pak's defence was that it was not possible to drive a wedge between the two markets (machines and packaging) and that it was the supplier of a totally integrated system, of which many elements were integral components. *Inter alia* the company suggested that: the high technology machines demand exact packaging that could be supplied only by Tetra Pak; it could offer full servicing only if all components in the process were purchased from it; and only the use of its cartons prevented health problems. As might be expected (particularly in the light of the company's past record) the practice was roundly condemned. Not only did the two clauses highlighted constitute abuses in their own right, they also raised the possibility of further abuse and placed competitors 'who cannot therefore, unlike Tetra Pak itself, subsidise possible losses on a given product through profits made on another product, in an extremely uncomfortable position' (para. 117). The approach of the ECJ and the Commission to this case was criticized by Lord Fraser of Carmyllie in the Lords debate on the Competition Act 1998. He expressed concern at a line of jurisprudence that seems to suggest that dominance in one market creates duties in another (Hansard (HL) 13 November 1997, col. 307).

Monopolies established by law (i.e., by state action) are, unless art. 86(2) applies, subject to the same art. 82 obligations as are privately run enterprises and on many occasions have been treated accordingly. In *Telemarketing (Centre Belge d'Etudes de Marché-Télémarketing SA v Compagnie Luxembourgeiose de Télédiffusion SA* case 311/84 [1986] 2 CMLR 558—an art. 234 reference from the national court) the Luxembourg TV Broadcaster (CLT) operated under a licence issued by the Luxembourg government, and required the plaintiff telemarketing company to have calls placed in response to advertisements screened on the channel routed through an associated company, IPB. CLT argued that this was a matter of pragmatism, as IPB had good notice of changes to schedules and therefore would better be able to anticipate and respond to customers than the complainant's own company. Further, the television channel took the view that customers believed that they were dealing with it, and that it therefore had an obligation to ensure an appropriate level of service. However, for the first year in which it placed advertisements with the broadcaster the complainant had not been required to use IPB and had been able to advertise its own telephone response number. The national court asked the ECJ whether this extension of power over the television broadcasts into an ancillary market, telephone response numbers for advertising, was an abuse of art. 82, and in response the Court held that the action was in breach both of art. 82(a) and of art. 82(d). In insisting that any advertiser buying telephone time did not use its own agency, but instead use that allied to the company, the company had imposed conditions on all other companies that it did not impose on itself. Further, the tie imposed supplementary obligations with no connection with the true subject-matter of the contract.

11.4.1.2 *Abusive discounts and rebates*

The use of discounts and rebates in order to facilitate tie-in sales and exclusive purchasing has been considered above. There are other cases in which discounts have been used abusively.

When it began to face emerging competition from France and Spain, British Gypsum, a subsidiary of British Plasterboard Industries, sought ways in which to 'reward the loyalty of merchants who remained exclusively' with them (*BPB Industries plc* 89/22 (1989) OJ L10/50, para. 58). Subsequently a scheme was put in place whereby payments were to be made to selected merchants in the form of contributions to promotional and advertising expenses, and this was later extended to provide added bonuses to those entering exclusive contracts. All these rebates were condemned, and the issue was revisited in 1992 when British Gypsum was encouraged to modify other rebate schemes introduced following the earlier decision. As amended, the rebate schemes, which then related to objectively identifiable savings and could be made available to all customers satisfying the appropriate criteria, were accepted by the Commission (*22nd Report on Competition Policy 1992*, p. 422).

It is now well established that rebate or discount schemes will be acceptable only where they are non-discriminatory and therefore do not fall within art. 82(c). Further illustrations may be found in *Brussels National Airport* 95/364 (1995) OJ L216/8 and in *Irish Sugar* 97/624 (1997) OJ L258/1 (on appeal *Irish Sugar plc v Commission* case T–228/97 [1999] 5 CMLR 1300). In the former case British Midland complained that the system of discounts, established by Royal Decree in 1989, was such that only Sabena, its main competitor, could benefit from them. The Commission requested the Belgian authorities to end the system, having found that only the existence of economies of scale could justify such a system, and that that was not the case here. In *Irish Sugar* the company was fined ECU 8.8 m after being found to have abused its dominant position on the Irish sugar market. The company had responded to the threat of imports from France by, *inter alia*, offering various rebate schemes. These extended both to industrial customers making exports of the refined product, and to smaller domestic customers. The rebates were condemned as being ad hoc and without any consistent relationship to objectively identifiable criteria. The effect of the abuse was to maintain prices for sugar in Ireland, and particularly in Northern Ireland, that were significantly higher than in other Member States.

The core allegation made against British Airways, substantiated by the Commission in *Virgin/British Airways* 2000/74 (2000) OJ L30/1 related to the use by BA of the use of commission schemes, in effect discounts, to boost sales of its flights through travel agents at the expense of those of its rivals. The marginal effect of the commission scheme is clearly explained by the Commission in paras 29–30 of the decision. In effect, to combat the offer by BA of a standard commission rate of 7 per cent coupled to a 'performance reward' of 0.5 per cent, at the margin a competing airline would have to offer a commission rate of 17.4 per cent. The Commission accepted that BA would have to offer a marginal rate as high as this to *increase* sales of its own tickets, but noted that 'it is at an advantage over the new entrant who must offer this high rate of commission on all its sales'. Such a scheme was both discriminatory, in that the discounts offered bore no relation to objectively justifiable factors, and exclusionary, at a time when, according to the Commission, BA should have been facing competition in a newly deregulated market.

11.4.1.3 *The abusive use of intellectual property*

The general position in competition law is that property rights cannot be asserted in such a way as to lead to an anti-competitive outcome (see, e.g., *Flughafen Frankfurt/Main AG* 98/190 (1998) OJ L72/31, para. 89). In relation to intellectual property rights this principle becomes strained, and the relationship between intellectual property and competition law is a difficult one. We have already seen in chapter 1 that the term 'monopoly' originally referred to a grant from the Crown that was similar to a modern intellectual property right. The modern theory of intellectual property rests on the presumption that the grant of the exclusive right is a reward that is necessary to encourage innovation, and that a monopoly profit is the proper way to achieve this.

The holding of intellectual property does not necessarily confer a dominant position (*Sirena v Eda* case 40/70 [1971] ECR 69, para. 16) as it may be the case that the relevant market encompasses products, services, or processes other than the one for which the right is held. There are, however, a number of cases in which it has been found that an intellectual property right acts as a barrier to entry, consolidating the strength of a dominant position (see the discussion of this factor earlier in this chapter). In *Tetra Pak I* 88/501 (1988) OJ L272/27 the EC Commission condemned the acquisition of a licence to intellectual property in an area where the undertaking in question was already dominant.

The leading case, although one that is peculiar on its facts, relating to the abusive use of intellectual property is that of *Magill* (*RTE and Independent Television Productions v Commission* cases C 241 and 242/91P [1995] 4 CMLR 418). Here the Commission found that broadcasters in Ireland had abused their dominant position by exploiting the copyright they held in television programme listings to prevent the publication of those listings by third parties. The broadcasters published their own television guides and were able to prevent competition in what was viewed as a separate market from that of the television broadcasting itself. The Court noted that:

The appellants—who were, by force of circumstances, the only sources of the basic information on program scheduling which is the indispensable raw material for compiling a weekly television guide—gave viewers wishing to obtain information on the choice of programs for the week ahead no choice but to buy the weekly guides for each station and draw from each of them the information they needed to make comparisons.

The appellants' refusal to provide basic information by relying on national copyright provisions thus prevented the appearance of a new product, a comprehensive weekly guide to television programs, which the appellants did not offer and for which there was a potential consumer demand. Such refusal constitutes an abuse under heading (b) of the second paragraph of art. 82 of the Treaty.

The conclusion of the Court was that the Commission was in a position to remedy an abuse by ordering the compulsory licence of the intellectual property held by the appellants:

In the present case, after finding that the refusal to provide undertakings such as Magill with the basic information contained in television program listings was an abuse of a dominant position, the Commission was entitled under [Regulation 17], in order to ensure that its decision was effective, to require the appellants to provide that information. As the Court of First Instance rightly found, the imposition of that obligation—with the possibility of making authorisation of publication dependent on certain conditions, including payment of royalties—was the only way of bringing infringement to an end.

While this judgment has been criticized for undermining the very essence of the intellectual property right it is not doubted that it remains good law, although perhaps somewhat limited on its facts (although note that in *IMS Health Inc* v *Commission* case T–184/01R [2002] 4 CMLR 1 the CFI overturned a decision imposing interim measures which required the compulsory licensing of intellectual property). The principle is clear that in the exercise of all types of intellectual property rights, competition law considerations must be carefully considered.

11.5 Trade between Member States

The condemning of an abuse 'in so far as it may affect trade between Member States' is the jurisdictional test of Community involvement, and the same principles apply as for art. 81 (see Chapter 7).

11.6 The relationship between article 82 and article 81

Jurisdiction under arts 82 and 81 is not mutually exclusive, and there will be situations where both apply, as for example a case in which a dominant undertaking obliges its customers or smaller competitors to enter into restrictive agreements. This was acknowledged by the ECJ in *Hoffmann-La Roche* (*Hoffmann-La Roche & Co. AG* v *Commission* case 85/76 [1979] 3 CMLR 211) where one issue considered under art. 82 related to a contract entered into between Hoffmann and Merck. Under the terms of this contract Merck agreed to purchase exclusively from Hoffmann a considerable quantity of vitamin B_6 for a period of five years. The Court found that the purpose of the contract was to eliminate the risk to Hoffmann of a planned increase in production, and that this constituted an abuse. The Court noted that 'the question might be asked whether the conduct in question does not fall within Article [81] of the Treaty and possibly within its paragraph (3)' (para. 116). It will be recalled that art. 81(3) allows for an exemption to be granted to an agreement that falls to be condemned under art. 81(1) where certain criteria are satisfied. Might the potential application of art. 81(3) therefore act as a defence to an action brought under art. 82? The answer is no. The Court went on to hold that art. 82 'is expressly aimed in fact at situations which clearly originate in contractual relations so that in such cases the Commission is entitled . . . to proceed on the basis of Article [81] or Article [82]' (para. 116). The CFI, however, has suggested that this may not be the case where an exemption has been granted on an individual basis. The presumption would be that the Commission would have considered whether art. 82 was in fact relevant, and would not have granted the exemption if that were the case; and in *Tetra Pak* the Advocate General went so far as to say that a practice 'which satisfies the conditions for exemption laid down in Article [81(3)] cannot at the same time be regarded as constituting an abuse' (*Tetra Pak Rausing SA* v *Commission* case T–51/89 [1991] 4 CMLR 334 at 350). In such a case the Commission would be expected to demonstrate either that facts had been withheld from it at the time the exemption was granted, or that there had been a material change in the circumstances in order to succeed with a new claim. Some of the block exemptions (see Chapter 8) expressly state that exemptions granted under their authority do not serve as a defence under art. 82 (e.g., Council Regulation 4056/86 on Maritime Transport (1986) OJ L378/4); and even where no such express provision is made, the general presumption must be that as block exemptions do not require the specific assessment that is needed in the case of art. 81(3) individual exemptions, they cannot serve as a defence to an art. 82 action.

12

Single-firm conduct in the United Kingdom

12.1 Introduction

The changes made to domestic competition law by the Competition Act 1998 had a more drastic impact on that part of the law dealing with multilateral anti-competitive conduct than they had on the control of single-firm conduct. The Fair Trading Act (FTA) 1973 has been left largely intact, albeit with restrictions on its application. The Competition Act 1998 itself, apart from making amendments to the existing structure, introduced in Chapter II (ss. 17–24) the prohibition on abuse of a dominant position (s. 18) that brings the domestic regime largely in line with that of the European Community.

12.2 The Competition Act 1998

The 'Chapter II' prohibition is in the following terms:

18.—(1) Subject to section 19, any conduct on the part of one or more undertakings which amounts to the abuse of a dominant position in a market is prohibited if it may affect trade within the United Kingdom.

(2) Conduct may, in particular, constitute such an abuse if it consists in—

(a) directly or indirectly imposing unfair purchase or selling prices or other unfair trading conditions;

(b) limiting production, markets or technical development to the prejudice of consumers;

(c) applying dissimilar conditions to equivalent transactions with other trading parties, thereby placing them at a competitive disadvantage;

(d) making the conclusion of contracts subject to acceptance by the other parties of supplementary obligations which, by their, nature or according to commercial usage, have no connection with the subject of the contracts.

(3) In this section—

'dominant position' means a dominant position within the United Kingdom; and
'the United Kingdom' means the United Kingdom or any part of it.

(4) The prohibition imposed by subsection (1) is referred to in this Act as 'the Chapter II prohibition'.

The similarity with art. 82 EC should be immediately evident, and as the Act is to be interpreted and applied so as to achieve results consistent with those that would be achieved under Community law (see the discussion of s. 60 in Chapter 16 below) guidance as to its application should be sought in the commentary on art. 82. Only as the prohibition is enforced will it become possible to clarify its terms further. The prohibition does not apply to merger situations, which remain subject to the provisions of the FTA 1973 nor to those identified in sch. 3 (s. 19). Where conduct is of minor significance (s. 40) fines under s. 36(2) may not be imposed, but other decisions may be taken by the Director, and private actions may be brought. The appropriate level is set at a turnover of £50m by the Competition Act 1998 (Small Agreements and Conduct of Minor Significance) Regulations 2000, SI 2000/262 (para. 4).

Provisions similar to those found in Chapter I of the 1998 Act allow parties to notify practices in which they are involved to the Director for guidance (s. 21) or for a formal decision (s. 22). The experience in Community law has been that parties have not notified unilateral actions to the Commission, preferring to hope that the conduct will not be detected. Two main reasons may be advanced for this: first, legal certainty is not generally as important an issue in relation to unilateral conduct as it is in relation to agreements; and, secondly, the lack of involvement of other parties may reduce the scope for detection. The legal effect of guidance issued is to protect the company from the application of the Chapter II prohibition unless there has been a material change in the circumstances (s. 23(2)(a)), the guidance has been issued on the basis of false or misleading information (s. 23(2)(b)), or there has been a complaint made by a third party (s. 23(2)(c)). It is this third provision that will be of most concern to the company operating under the benefit of guidance, and that may in fact deter it from seeking guidance. Companies are likely to be concerned that the more publicity given to a practice that might be considered to be abusive, the more likely it is that a third party will complain to the Director. The company remains free from the threat of penalties, however, even where a complaint is made for conduct engaged in until such time as the Director gives notice that the immunity conferred under the guidance is being removed (s. 23(3)–(4)). The only situation in which penalties may be imposed with retroactive effect is where the guidance was given on the basis of false or misleading information (s. 23(5)). Decisions confer greater legal certainty as they will not be affected by any third-party complaint and may be revoked only in the first two situations outlined in relation to guidance (s. 24).

As of May 2002 two adverse decisions had been taken by the OFT in relation to the Chapter II prohibition. The first of these related to a range of exclusionary and exploitative pricing practices (*Napp Pharmaceutical Holdings Ltd and Subsidiaries* CA98/2/2001 [2001] UKCLR 597, on appeal *Napp Pharmaceutical Holdings Ltd and Subsidiaries v The Director General of Fair Trading* [2002] CompAR 13). The second related to a very specific instance of predatory pricing (*Predation by Aberdeen*

Journals Ltd CA98/5/2001 [2001] UKCLR 856). This latter decision was remitted to the OFT for further consideration on the grounds that the decision had failed to adequately define the relevant product market (*Aberdeen Journals Ltd v The Director General of Fair Trading* [2002] CompAR 167).

12.2.1 **The assessment of dominance and abuse**

12.2.1.1 *Dominance*

Broadly the approach taken to the measurement and control of dominance in the UK will be the same as for that in the EC. The key difference is the territorial scope in the application of the Act. The relevant OFT guidelines, which should be read through carefully, are *The Chapter II Prohibition, Assessment of Individual Agreements and Conduct* (some of the matters raised in this are dealt with in the following chapter), *Assessment of Market Power*, and *Market Definition*. The two basic tests to be applied in relation to the Chapter II prohibition are those of whether an undertaking is dominant, and if so, whether it is abusing the dominant position that it holds.

In order to answer the first question it will be necessary to define the relevant market. The relevant guideline 'in general . . . follows the same approach as the European Commission's Notice on market definition' (para. 1.3) which was discussed in the previous chapter. The guidelines make reference to the value of previous precedent, whether drawn from the 'old' UK regime, or from the EC (para. 5.15). It is recognized that earlier definitions 'can provide a useful shortcut', but that, given that market conditions change over time, the market definition from older cases may not always be appropriate. There are three factors in this respect that are particularly important. The first is that innovation may mean that older definitions are now irrelevant. In the context of the relationship between national and Community law the second factor is the more important. This is that 'a previous product market definition may relate to a particular area, such as another part of the European Union, where substitution is more or less likely. A product definition may therefore be different in different locations'. However, the basic methodology of the EC Commission will be followed, even if it produces a different result because the factual elements are different. The third factor to be considered in this respect is that the definition of the relevant market may actually depend upon the competition problem that is being investigated (see paras 5.16–5.20). A relevant geographic market does not have to extend to the UK as a whole, but could be regional, or local. In *Predation by Aberdeen Journals Ltd* CA98/5/2001 [2001] UKCLR 856 the relevant geographic market was Aberdeen.

Once the market has been defined it is necessary to establish whether the undertaking whose conduct is being examined is dominant in this market. Again the factors are the same as under art. 82. The guidelines refer to the standard definition of dominant position set out by the ECJ in *United Brands Co.* v *Commission* case 27/76 [1978] 1 CMLR 429, discussed in the previous chapter. The guidelines indicate that it is 'unlikely that an undertaking will be individually dominant if its market share is below 40 per cent, although dominance could be established below that if other relevant factors (such as the weak position of competitors in that market) provided strong evidence of dominance' (para. 2.11).

The broad framework for assessing market power is set out in Part 3 of the *Assessment of Market Power* guidelines, the thrust of which in essence is to consider the restraints that would prevent an alleged dominant undertaking from raising its prices. These include existing competitors, potential competitors, and buyer power. In this context the discussion of entry barriers (paras 5.1–5.29) should be examined carefully, as they are likely to play a significant role in the analysis. As the guidelines recognize, 'assessing the effects of entry barriers and the advantages they give to incumbents is complex' (para. 5.25). Overseas competition will be considered in this assessment as it too can 'provide an effective constraint on the ability of domestic undertakings to raise prices' (para. 5.28). This has been a significant factor in a number of recent merger reports in which mergers have been allowed to proceed on the grounds that anti-competitive effects would be mitigated by the growth in international competition (see, e.g., *Universal Foods Corpn and Pointing Holdings Ltd* (Cm. 4544, December 1999)).

Some evidence of dominance may also be adduced from the performance of the undertaking in question, although such analysis must proceed carefully in order to distinguish an 'excessive' rate of profit (para. 6.3) from profit generated by efficient performance.

12.2.1.2 *Joint dominance*

The approach taken to joint dominance should be the same as that taken under art. 82, and to an extent the same as the analysis of this under Regulation 4064/89 (see Chapter 15). However, the difficulties encountered with this approach are one of the major reasons justifying the retention of the Fair Trading Act provisions discussed below.

12.2.1.3 *Abusive conduct*

The list of abuses given in s. 18 of the Competition Act 1998 is the same as that for art. 82. Perhaps unusually the abuse that is first dealt with in *The Chapter II Prohibition* guideline is excessive pricing, which has rarely been dealt with at Community level, although concerns about excessive prices have underpinned a number of MMC/CC reports under the Fair Trading Act (see below) and was raised in the *Napp* decision (CA98/2/2001, [2001] UKCLR 597). Price discrimination, which has been prominently discussed in the context of the Community regime, is somewhat sidelined, with the Director General anticipating that 'he would consider price discrimination to be an abuse only if there were evidence that prices were excessive . . . or that it was used to exclude competitors' (para. 4.16). The treatment accorded to these, and other specific instances of abuse, is considered further in the following chapter.

12.3 The Fair Trading Act 1973

The institutional structure under which the Act operates has been examined in Chapter 2.

12.3.1 Monopoly references

One of the general duties of the Director General of Fair Trading ('the Director') is to: 'keep under review the carrying on of commercial activities in the United Kingdom . . . with a view to his becoming aware of, and ascertaining the circumstances relating to, practices which may adversely affect the economic interests of consumers in the United Kingdom' (s. 2(1)(a)). In furtherance of this task the Director shall take such steps as are practicable to facilitate 'his becoming aware of, and ascertaining the circumstances relating to, monopoly situations or uncompetitive practices' (s. 2(2)).

Section 6 of the 1973 Act defines a 'monopoly situation in relation to supply of goods'. The words of s. 7, which relates to the supply of services, mirror those of s. 6, which is set out here in full:

> 6.—(1) For the purposes of this Act a monopoly situation shall be taken to exist in relation to the supply of goods of any description in the following cases, that is to say, if—
>
> (a) at least one-quarter of all the goods of that description which are supplied in the United Kingdom are supplied by one and the same person, or are supplied to one and the same person, or
>
> (b) at least one-quarter of all the goods of that description which are supplied in the United Kingdom are supplied by members of one and the same group of interconnected bodies corporate, or are supplied to members of one and the same group of interconnected bodies corporate, or
>
> (c) at least one-quarter of all the goods of that description which are supplied in the United Kingdom are supplied by members of one and the same group consisting of two or more such persons as are mentioned in subsection (2) of this section, or are supplied to members of one and the same group consisting of two or more such persons, or
>
> (d) one or more agreements are in operation, the result or collective result of which is that goods of that description are not supplied in the United Kingdom at all.
>
> (2) The two or more persons referred to in subsection (1) (c) of this section, in relation to goods of any description, are any two or more persons, not being a group of interconnected bodies corporate, who whether voluntarily or not, and whether by agreement or not, so conduct their respective affairs as in any way to prevent, restrict or distort competition in connection with the production or supply of goods of that description, whether or not they themselves are affected by the competition and whether the competition is between persons interested as producers or suppliers or between persons interested as customers of producers or suppliers.

It should be recognized that both ss. 6 and 7 leave the person making the reference with an element of discretion, particularly in the terms in which the market is defined. The reference to 'goods of that description' is intended to be a flexible one, and does not require the application of any strict economic criteria. One point of contention between those under investigation and the regulators often stems from the market definition, with the 'monopolist' arguing that the market has been drawn too narrowly. The element of discretion is reinforced by s. 10(7), which allows those making the references to use the criteria they 'think most suitable in the circumstances' in determining which goods may be treated as being of a 'separate description'.

Reports of both the Office of Fair Trading (OFT) and the Competition Commission (CC) will generally define the relevant market early on. It has been determined, for example, that bus transport constitutes a separate market from that of other forms of transport (e.g., *The supply of bus services in the north-east of England* (Cm. 2933, 1995)), and that the market for pay-TV is to be separated from that for television broadcasting in general (*BSkyB's Position in the Wholesale Pay TV Market* (OFT, 1996)). In the latter case BSkyB had argued in favour of the wider market definition, as those under review tend to do, noting that it competed with terrestrial television for viewers. While the OFT accepted that this form of television placed *some* constraint on BSkyB, it was not the case that competition from the BBC and independent terrestrial broadcasters forced BSkyB to set its prices at competitive levels. Even within the pay-TV market narrower markets could be defined in, for example, premium sports and movie channels (paras 2.3–2.7, and 10.1–10.4).

Notwithstanding the wording of s. 6(1)(a) and (b), a monopoly situation may be taken to exist in only a part of the United Kingdom, if it appears to the person making the reference appropriate to do so (s. 9(1)).

The role that political considerations play in the process is demonstrated by s. 12 of the 1973 Act, which sets out the powers of the Secretary of State in relation to the function of the Director. In particular the Secretary of State may indicate priorities regarding both specific matters (s. 12(1)(a)) and classes of goods (s. 12(1)(b)).

Following any investigation undertaken by the Director (see Chapter 3) the Director may then make a reference to the Commission 'where it appears to the Director that a monopoly situation exists or may exist' (s. 50(1)). A reference may also be made by the Secretary of State, or by any other Minister (s. 51). In the alternative the Director may accept an undertaking from a company in lieu of a reference. This follows the introduction of s. 56A to the FTA 1973 by the Deregulation and Contracting Out Act 1994, and given the costs to the company of being involved in a reference there is a strong incentive on the part of the company to accept such an undertaking. However, there are strategic difficulties with this, and the evidence to date suggests that this provision is unlikely to have a significant impact in avoiding investigations. Three factors are prominent. The first is that in any investigation involving more than one party, all would have to agree to the undertaking; and as the impact on each company may be different, such agreement is difficult to achieve and strategic behaviour is to the fore. Well-informed press coverage suggests that this was the case with the inquiring into *Foreign Package Holidays* (Cm. 3813, 1997), and that one company at least would have agreed to the undertakings suggested by the Director prior to the making of the formal reference. Secondly, some companies may see the formal CC enquiry as an opportunity to 'clear the air' and provide a more final resolution of the issue than could be achieved by way of making an undertaking. Thirdly, a company may prefer to take its chances with the somewhat erratic CC, and may think it has more chance of influencing this body, which is composed in part by members with experience of industry, than it has with the Director and the OFT.

Two types of monopoly references may be made. The simpler is a 'monopoly reference limited to the facts' (s. 48). In dealing with such a reference the Commission is required only 'to investigate and report on the questions whether a monopoly situation exists in relation to the matters set out in the reference' (s. 49). While such references are not common there are several cases in which the CC has been called upon to consider a situation but not its relationship to the public interest. This was the case, for example, in its second report into *Contraceptive sheaths* (Cmnd. 8689, 1982), where it was asked to determine whether excessive profits were being earned in the market. Although the inference is that the public interest would be damaged by the making of excessive profits, this is not a conclusion that the CC was being asked to draw. In a reference limited to the facts the factors that the Commission must determine are:

(a) by virtue of which provision of sections 6 to 8 of this Act that monopoly situation is to be taken to exist;

(b) in favour of what person or persons that monopoly situation exists;

(c) whether any steps (by way of uncompetitive practices or otherwise) are being taken by that person or those persons for the purpose of exploiting or maintaining the monopoly situation and, if so, by what uncompetitive practices or in what other way; and

(d) whether any action or omission on the part of that person or those persons is attributable to the existence of the monopoly situation and, if so, what action or omission and in what way it is so attributable.

Under a wider remit the Commission can be asked to consider references not limited to the facts (s. 49). As this is an important section, consideration of which is a vital part of domestic competition law, it is set out in full:

49.—(1) A monopoly reference may be so framed as to require the Commission to investigate and report on the question whether a monopoly situation exists in relation to the matters set out in the reference in accordance with section 47 of this Act and, if so, to investigate and report—

(a) on the questions mentioned in paragraphs (a) to (d) of section 48 of this Act; and

(b) on the question whether any facts found by the Commission in pursuance of their investigations under the preceding provisions of this subsection operate, or may be expected to operate, against the public interest.

(2) A monopoly reference may be so framed as to require the Commission to investigate and report on the questions whether a monopoly situation exists in relation to the matters set out in the reference in accordance with section 47 of this Act and, if so,—

(a) by virtue of which provisions of sections 6 to 8 of this Act that monopoly situation is to be taken to exist;

(b)   in favour of what person or persons that monopoly situation exists; and

(c)   whether any action or omission on the part of that person or those persons in respect of matters specified in the reference for the purposes of this paragraph operates, or may be expected to operate, against the public interest.

(3) For the purposes of subsection (2)(c) of this section any matter may be specified in a monopoly reference if it relates to any of the following, that is to say—

(a)   prices charged, or proposed to be charged, for goods or services of the description specified in the reference;

(b)   any recommendation or suggestion made as to such prices;

(c)   any refusal to supply goods or services of the description specified in the reference;

(d)   any preference given to any person (whether by way of discrimination in respect of prices or in respect of priority of supply or otherwise) in relation to the supply of goods or services of that description;

and any matter not falling within any of the preceding paragraphs may be specified for those purposes in a monopoly reference if, in the opinion of the person or persons making the reference, it is of a kind such that (if a monopoly situation is found to exist) that matter might reasonably be regarded as a step taken for the purpose of exploiting or maintaining that situation or as being attributable to the existence of that situation.

Whenever the Director intends to make a reference, a copy of that reference must be submitted to the Secretary of State. There is then a 14-day period in which the Minister may direct the Commission not to proceed with the reference (s. 50(6)). Once made any monopoly reference may be varied by the person who made that reference (s. 52(1)), although not in such a way as to turn the reference into one that that person would not have been able to make originally (s. 52(3)). Neither may a monopoly reference not limited to the facts be varied so as become a reference limited to the facts (s. 51(2)). Appropriate publicity shall be given to references.

The duties of the CC with respect to the report requested by the reference are set out in s. 54. Amongst other things the Commission is required to set out 'definite conclusions on the questions comprised in the reference' (s. 54(2)). The responsibilities of the Commission when reporting on a reference not limited to the facts are set out at s. 54(3):

(3) Where, on a monopoly reference not limited to the facts, the Commission find that a monopoly situation exists and that facts found by the Commission in pursuance of their investigations . . . operate, or may be expected to operate, against the public interest, the report shall specify those facts, and the conclusions to be included in the report, in so far as they relate to the operation of those facts, shall specify the particular effects, adverse to the public interest, which in their opinion those facts have or may be expected to have; and the Commission—

(a)   shall, as part of their investigations, consider what action (if any) should be taken for the purpose of remedying or preventing those adverse effects, and

(b)   may, if they think fit, include in their report recommendations as to such action.

The 'action' referred to in s. 54(3)(a) is that which may be taken either by those in whose favour the monopoly exists, or by the relevant Minister(s) (s. 54(4)(a), (b)). There is no time limit set in the Act within which Commission reports must be completed following the making of the reference, but s. 55 provides that a time period must be specified in the reference itself. This may subsequently be extended (s. 55(2)).

In addition to its s. 54 duties the Commission is required to 'take into consideration any representations made to [it] by persons appearing to [it] to have a substantial interest in the subject-matter of the reference, or by bodies appearing to [it] to represent substantial numbers of persons who have such an interest' (s. 81(1)(a)). Subject to these constraints on its role the Commission has the discretion to 'determine [its] own procedure for carrying out any investigation on a reference under [the Act]' (s. 81(2)), although it must have regard to such general directions as may be issued from time to time by the Secretary of State (s. 81(3)). The process of investigation is considered in some detail below.

Reports are addressed to the relevant Minister, and it is for the Minister to 'lay a copy of the report before each House of Parliament, and . . . arrange for the report to be published in such a manner as appears to the Minister or Ministers to be appropriate' (s. 83(1)). A copy of every report shall also be sent to the Director (s. 86). There are several provisions made to ensure that matters which are confidential, or the disclosure of which would be contrary to the public interest, are not disclosed. Following a report the Minister may make an order by way of statutory instrument exercising one of the powers conferred by sch. 8 to the Act (s. 56(2)). The power of the Minister to make orders, and the circumstances in which they may be made, are discussed in greater detail below.

The application of the public interest test lies at the heart of the 1973 Act's provisions relating to monopoly conduct. The test, such as it is, is contained in s. 84, which therefore assumes fundamental importance in the context of s. 49 references. Section 84 provides as follows:

84.—(1) In determining for any purposes to which this section applies whether any particular matter operates, or may be expected to operate, against the public interest, the Commission shall take into account all matters which appear to them in the particular circumstances to be relevant and, among other things, shall have regard to the desirability—

(a) of maintaining and promoting effective competition between persons supplying goods and services in the United Kingdom;

(b) of promoting the interests of consumers, purchasers and other users of goods and services in the United Kingdom in respect of the prices charged for them and in respect of their quality and the variety of goods and services supplied;

(c) of promoting, through competition, the reduction of costs and the development and use of new techniques and new products, and of facilitating the entry of new competitors into existing markets;

(d) of maintaining and promoting the balanced distribution of industry and employment in the United Kingdom; and

(e) of maintaining and promoting competitive activity in markets outside the United

Kingdom on the part of producers of goods, and of suppliers of goods and services, in the United Kingdom.

It is clear from the wording of s. 84(1) that the list of matters that may be relevant is not intended to be exhaustive, and it is in the discussion of the nature of the public interest that much of the investigative time is taken up. In its study of the then domestic regime the House of Commons Select Committee on Trade and Industry (Fifth Report, *UK Policy on Monopolies* (1995) HC–249) was critical of the application of the public interest test. The Consumers' Association had presented evidence to the Committee in which it argued that the definition of 'public interest' provided in the 1973 Act was 'unacceptably loose', and the Committee agreed, noting at point 20 of the Report that:

The DGFT defined the public interest as 'consumer well-being' but admitted that 'I do not think anybody could possibly pretend that they could sit down and do some sums and have an answer they can defend against all comers at the end of the day'. The Chairman of the CC said that it was impossible to define the public interest in a general context, and the Minister simply referred to the criteria set out in the Act. These criteria, however, are extremely broad and lack an indication of priorities. (HC 249, vol. I, p. xiii)

The main problem that has been created by this flexible test is that of inconsistency in the inquiries that have been held by the CC and in the reports published. The CC has argued that the terms of the Act require that it operate flexibly and must examine each case on its merits. As a result, the CC argues, it is unable to issue general policy guidance of the type that is published by the American antitrust authorities, and that is mirrored in some of the notices published by the EC Commission.

In its 2001 White Paper, *Productivity and Enterprise* (Cm 5233, July 2001), the Government announced its intention to replace the public interest test in the Fair Trading Act with a competition test.

Every report is directed to the Minister, and the DGFT shall be sent a copy of every report (s. 86) save where the reference was made by a Minister in a circumstance where the DGFT could not have made the reference (s. 86(2)). The Director then may choose to give advice to the relevant Minister regarding any matter arising out of the report, which the Minister is obliged to take into account. Where the Minister decides that action is required following the receipt of the report, it is the duty of the DGFT 'to comply with any request of the [Minister] to consult with . . . the relevant parties with a view to obtaining from them undertakings to take action' (s. 88(1)). The Director shall notify the Minister of any such undertakings and these shall be published in an appropriate manner (s. 88(2), (2A)). Once an undertaking has been given, the Director has an ongoing duty to monitor compliance with that undertaking and the extent to which the undertaking remains appropriate given changing economic circumstances (s. 88(3)).

Where the Minister considers that an order in Parliament is more appropriate to the remedying of any situation than would be the making of an undertaking by the relevant parties, he may make use of his powers under s. 56. The operation of this power is limited by ss. 90 and 91, which should be read in conjunction with sch. 8.

By virtue of s. 89 the Minister may make an interim order after receipt of the report if the Minister intends to make a 'principal order' the effect of which might be obstructed by continuing anti-competitive activities. In making an order the Minister must lay a draft of the order before Parliament, and can act only when the approval of Parliament has been obtained (s. 91(1)). The Minister shall also, in an appropriate manner, publish his intention to make the order and shall accept representations made relating to that order before the order is made (s. 91(2)). Once an order is made any subsequent breach does not give rise to criminal sanctions. However, third parties may bring civil proceedings in respect of a breach and the Crown may seek an injunction or 'any other appropriate relief' (s. 93).

12.3.2 The problem of joint dominance/complex monopoly

One of the undoubted strengths of the domestic competition regime has been its ability to conduct industry-wide reviews and to put in place appropriate remedies to deal with conduct or structure pervasive through the industry which operates, or may be expected to operate, against the public interest, even where such conduct might not be regarded as anti-competitive in an abuse-based regime.

The basis for these actions is found in s. 6(1)(c) and s. 6(2) of the FTA 1973, which are set out above (the equivalent provision with respect to services lies in s. 7(2)). These provisions allow the CC to find that a monopoly situation exists, even in situations where no one company has a 25 per cent share of the relevant market, on the basis that companies 'so conduct their respective affairs'. Section 6(2) should be read in conjunction with the definition of 'group' given in s. 137(2). This provides that:

'group' (where the reference is to a group of persons fulfilling specified conditions, other than the condition of being interconnected bodies corporate) means any two or more persons fulfilling those conditions, whether apart from fulfilling them they would be regarded as constituting a group or not.

It is thus clear that a company may be part of a group for the purposes of this part of the Act without in any way being part of a standard 'corporate structure'. The sole requirement to find that a company is part of a group is that the relevant criteria are being fulfilled, and in this case 'relevant criteria' is to be defined with reference to a pattern of behaviour, which may not even amount to collusion or 'conscious parallelism'. The CC has indicated that the word 'conduct' will be taken to mean that the provision applies only to situations in which the company has an alternative course of action (see, for example, *Credit Card Services*, Cm 718, 1989), although this is not entirely consistent with the immediately preceding words of s. 6(2) 'whether voluntarily or not'. Conduct on which the CC has based a finding of complex monopoly includes, *inter alia*, the practice by the petrol companies of recommending pump prices (*Petrol*, Cm 972, 1990), the similarity in information given to consumers (*Contact lens solutions*, Cm 2242, 1993), and the adoption of standard terms and conditions (*Credit Card Services*). Given the criticisms of these sections it must be stressed again that the finding that a complex monopoly exists does not determine that there is a practice operating against the public interest: it is merely a jurisdictional threshold, the satisfaction of which is necessary in order for further examination of the market to proceed.

The difficulty that industry faces in relation to these provisions is that an individual company may not be aware that it is a complex, or behavioural, monopolist and therefore subject to the strictures of the 1973 Act. It would be an unusual situation were a scale monopolist to be unaware of its position, unless the market definition adopted by the Director in making the reference were a surprising one that narrowed the market substantially. Lawyers do not always appreciate the degree of uncertainty that these provisions give rise to, but as has been demonstrated elsewhere in this book certainty cannot be easily reconciled with the effective application of competition law. This point, made in response to debate about the place of these provisions, has been encapsulated by Rodger:

> The provisions are designed to provide for investigation and suitable prospective remedies for a situation of 'market failure' irrespective of whether there has been collusion or other 'reproachable behaviour'. Firms operating in such a market have to appreciate that the law is aimed at enhancing, through the public interest, the common good, and to balance this, the law is not enforced by sanctions for past behaviour, as law in the area of economic policy and regulation is difficult to formulate with such precision. (Rodger, B. J., 'Decentralisation, the public interest and the "pursuit of certainty"' [1995] *ECLR* 395)

However, the jurisdictional test that has to be fulfilled before this public interest examination can be undertaken is a wide one, and it can lead to the consideration of situations that would rarely fall to be dealt with in any other competition law regime. In particular, markets may be examined which are clearly not oligopolistic. In an unpublished conference paper delivered in 1992 the former DGFT, Sir Bryan Carsberg, noted that of the 38 cases investigated between 1970 and 1992 that were not concerned with scale monopolists, some 42 per cent involved markets where the combined share of the top four firms was less than 25 per cent (see Brent R., 'The certain pursuit of oligopoly: a reply' [1996] 3 *ECLR* 163).

12.3.3 The conduct of the CC investigation

Investigations under the FTA 1973 require an examination of the *market* that has been defined in the reference, the place of particular companies in that market, and the examination of particular practices that raise public interest concerns.

The CC first acquaints itself with the market, often by way of site visits and informal contacts with those involved in the industry. At the same time it develops a factual questionnaire that firms are first asked to comment on in draft, and that is then sent to the more significant parties for completion.

As part of its fact finding the CC is also likely to conduct surveys of smaller participants in the industry, major customers, consumer groups, and industry representatives.

Following the submission of the responses to the questionnaires the CC may in some cases hold a clarification hearing, to resolve matters about which the CC is still uncertain. In all of its hearings the CC prefers to discuss matters with the appropriate company officials rather than with lawyers, as it is the officials who best know their industry. Hearings are generally informal and are not structured in a similar way to tribunals or courts, although each is confidential to the person giving evidence and the CC. The broad view of those who have been put through such hearings is that the process is effective and well balanced.

Following the factual hearing, if one is held, the CC will send the parties a 'public interest letter'. This will state first whether a monopoly situation has been found to exist on the basis of the facts available to the CC. If there is no monopoly situation the CC does not have the jurisdiction even to consider the public interest matters, and will normally expedite proceedings at this stage. If a monopoly situation does exist the CC will raise any concerns that it may have regarding public interest issues, and its initial views as to the possible remedies where it has identified harms. The response to the public interest letter will be another time of heavy involvement on the part of the companies likely to be affected by it, particularly where suggested remedies may have a significant impact. The public interest letter will be responded to in great detail, with arguments advanced by the company supported by economic, accounting, and legal analysis. Following the responses to the letter further 'public interest' hearings with the main parties will be held to discuss the issues arising, and in some cases yet a third hearing, to discuss remedies, will take place.

The CC will then produce a draft report, and details relevant to each of the parties only will be sent to that party for comment. As the Secretary of State, by virtue of s. 83 of the FTA 1973 has the power to exclude certain confidential matters from the published report, companies will be concerned to ensure that these provisions are applied to any material which they do not wish to be published. Such exclusions will be most evident in the annexes setting out financial data and in presentations of market shares, client bases, and other such commercially sensitive matters where publication might give an advantage to competitors. The company will also be given the chance to correct factual inaccuracies but will not, at this stage, be able to challenge further the CC's conclusions. The involvement of the CC will come to an end when the report is made to the Secretary of State, whose role in the process is set out above.

Criticisms of this process focus not only on the vagueness of the 'public interest' criteria that the CC is supposed to apply, but also upon the cost of the procedure to those companies under investigation. Many reports result in a conclusion that the public interest is not being harmed, even where some anti-competitive activity is identified, although the impact of others may be considerable. Price capping in particular can produce a gain to consumers that is considerable in relation to the overall burden.

12.3.4 **Anti-competitive conduct considered under the 1973 Act**

Since 1950 there have been approximately 400 reports made by the MMC/CC, 75 of which were made on the basis of the pre- 1973 legislation. Many of these were made in response to merger investigations, and others to the demands of specific sectoral regulation. Under the FTA 1973 provisions relating to monopoly investigations and the public interest criteria the MMC/CC has made reports into a number of industries. Among its first 25 reports under the post-1973 regime the CC considered, for example, batteries (HC 1, 1974–75), contraceptive sheaths (HC 135, 1974–75—a market that the CC has considered on a number of occasions), building bricks (HC 474, 1975–76), legal services (six reports covering barristers', solicitors', and advocates' services and advertising), frozen foodstuffs (HC 674, 1975–76), cat and dog foods (HC 447, 1976–77), wholesale newspapers and periodicals (Cmnd 7214, 1978), petrol (Cmnd 7433, 1979), and ice cream (Cmnd 7632, 1979). More recent examples include new motor cars (Cm 4660, 2000), supermarkets (Cm 4842, 2000), and milk in Scotland (Cm 5002, 2000).

It is neither practicable nor useful to provide a summary of all the reports undertaken by the CC and the conclusions reached in a book of this nature. What follows is an introduction to some of the approaches that have been adopted by the CC in the past, which might continue to influence its approach in future investigations. Specific matters that are dealt with in more detail in the next chapter include pricing policies, refusal to supply, and the essential facilities doctrine. These are not therefore considered below.

12.3.4.1 *Vertical restraints*

We have already seen that there is an intense debate about the attitude that should be taken towards vertical restraints in competition law, both amongst industrial economists and amongst regulators. Because the FTA 1973 is not addressed exclusively to single-firm anti-competitive conduct but may also examine whether the very structure of a market is competitive, the MMC/CC has considered the extent to which a vertically integrated industry operates against the public interest on a number of occasions. In 1997 the MMC published its report into the retail travel industry (*Foreign Package Holidays* Cm. 3813, 1997), in which it was called upon to consider, *inter alia*, the links between tour operators and the high street retail outlet chains, the larger ones of which are owned by the tour operators whose packages they sell. The MMC did not demand divestiture, which had been the greatest fear of the integrated companies, but did insist that the links between the retail and operational arms were made more transparent to allow the consumer to know of the tie at the time of booking the holiday.

Vertical links may arise contractually where, for example, there are very long-term supply contracts between a producer and a distributor, as well as through direct ownership. In *Cinema Advertising Services* (Cm 1080, 1990) a reference was made following a complaint by Pearl & Dean Ltd to the effect that it had suffered as a result of various unfair practices engaged in by Rank Screen Advertising (RSA). The

OFT had expressed its concerns about the link between RSA and the rest of the Rank Organisation, which had a strong involvement in film distribution. The fear was that this would inhibit independent exhibitors, who were dependent to an extent on Rank's films, from taking the services offered by Pearl & Dean. Further, RSA had exclusive access to the Odeon cinema chain, also part of the Rank Organisation, accounting for 17 per cent of the market. It also had contracts with the Cannon chain, accounting for around 30 per cent of the market, that ran for 14 years. The offering of substantial discounts, which were alleged to be predatory in that they were so significant as to be uneconomic for RSA, to advertisers if they did not place advertisements on screens under contract to Pearl & Dean reinforced the exclusion. The MMC concluded that there was no evidence that the Odeon chain benefited from being part of the Rank Organisation—the various companies within the group operating at arm's length; that the influence that Rank exercised over film distribution was felt not to be sufficiently significant to deter independent screens from taking the service offered by Pearl & Dean; and that the long-term contracts with Cannon were won as 'a result of competition and [RSA] has no reason to expect criticism for this achievement', the length of the contracts arising at the request of Cannon (paras 9.36–9.42). In this case, therefore, the MMC found that 'neither the practice of negotiating long-term contracts nor RSA's relationship with Odeon are facts which operate, or may be expected to operate, against the public interest' (para. 9.45).

The issue of 'freezer exclusivity' (the supply of freezer cabinets to retailers of impulse-ice cream on condition that only the supplier's ice cream be stocked in the cabinets) was considered by the MMC in *Ice Cream* (Cm 2524, 1994). Similar practices were considered almost contemporaneously by the Irish competition authorities and by the EC Commission—see *Van den Bergh Foods Ltd* 98/531 (1998) OJ L246/1. In a market with perhaps as many as 1,000 suppliers, the MMC found that a scale monopoly existed in favour of Birds Eye Wall's Ltd (BEW), and a complex monopoly in favour of BEW, Nestlé UK Ltd, and Mars UK Ltd. The first two had an acknowledged policy of operating freezer exclusivity, and Mars' insistence upon full-range stocking in return for the provision of a freezer achieved something very similar, as the full range of Mars ice cream would leave little space in the freezer for other brands. The MMC recognized that this practice was part of an effective distribution system, necessary because 'demand is not only seasonal, but also subject to extreme short-term fluctuations as the weather changes' (para. 1.3), but addressed the concern that the system might also operate so as to raise barriers to entry. This could be the case in particular where a retailer, most likely a small newsagent, had room for only one freezer and would therefore be faced with a choice of either buying and maintaining its own freezer or being tied to one product range, foreclosing the outlet to other suppliers. In this case the MMC considered the argument of some suppliers and the Consumers' Association that the restrictions on consumers operated against the public interest. In particular the MMC was

not convinced that the uniform adoption of retailers' own cabinets would itself significantly improve choice for consumers: the range of products stocked is likely to be limited by space constraints, and retailers may still prefer mainly to stock one manufacturer's products, given, for example, ease of supply and invoicing arrangements. (para. 9.54)

This conclusion has been widely criticized, and in their OFT research paper Dobson and Waterson point out that if the checklist they advocate were applied to this situation it would strongly suggest that the market is operating against the public interest (see Chapter 6).

If nothing else makes it clear that dealing with oligopolistic markets can present serious problems for competition law the fact that a further reference was made to the MMC in relation to the ice cream market at the end of 1999 would demonstrate the difficulties. In its report published in January 2000 (*The Supply of Impulse Ice Cream*, Cm. 4510, 2000) the CC looked again at 'ice cream purchased for immediate consumption', and in particular the terms on which freezer exclusivity and distribution channels operated. This time the CC recommended that BEW be prevented from entering into any agreement for capacity in relation to any freezer used for storage and/or the display of wrapped impulse ice cream in any outlet in Great Britain, unless 50 per cent of the display space, and the full storage space, could be used for products from other manufacturers. The treatment of the distribution channel as an 'essential facility' follows the approach suggested by the ECJ in *Oscar Bronner GmbH* v *Mediaprint Zeitungs GmbH* case C–7/97 [1999] 4 CMLR 112, which is dealt with in the following chapter. Undertakings were accepted from BEW in April 2000 (DTI Press Release, 7 April 2000, P/2000/260).

12.3.4.2 *Full-line forcing, tie-in sales, and line discounts*

Full-line forcing requires a customer to accept all or part of a supplier's range and denies them the ability to purchase selectively; tie-in sales tie the supply of one product to another. Both were considered by the MMC in its 1981 general report into *Full-line Forcing and Tie-in Sales* (HC 212, 1981). These practices raise concerns where the effect is to allow a producer to extend market power from a market in which it is dominant to one in which it is not. The MMC's general view was that such practices are neither 'consistently harmful, beneficial or neutral but [depend] on the circumstances' (*Tambrands Ltd*, Cm. 3168, 1996, para. 2.35).

The MMC examined the practice of tying sales of toner to the supply of photocopiers on two occasions. Following the first report (HC 47, 1976–77) Rank Xerox Ltd, which had around 90 per cent of the market, gave a number of undertakings to the Secretary of State in 1978. In 1983 the company was released from many of these following altered market conditions, and in 1988 the company sought release from the remainder of the undertakings. The undertaking is quoted here both to illustrate the case and to illustrate the general nature of the form in which companies may be bound following action taken by the OFT and CC:

Toner
1. We will give to all customers, before entering into agreements with them, the option of purchasing toner separately, either from ourselves or from another supplier.
2. We will show on our Rental and Service Agreements our current retail prices for toner

and specify in such Agreements the terms on which customers may change to separate purchase of toner.

3. We will show the amount of the charge for toner on the rental invoices of all customers who do not elect to purchase toner separately.

4. We will inform the [DGFT] of any proposed changes to those terms of our Rental and Service Agreements that relate to the purchase of toner.

In seeking a release from this undertaking the company argued that toner tie-in was a widespread industry practice, and that the company was unfairly restricted by the undertaking. In its review of the situation the OFT identified a number of practices that it felt merited further review by the MMC. The MMC did not entirely accept arguments made by some suppliers that tying of toner to the supply of copiers was justified on technical grounds, but did recognize that manufacturers had 'a legitimate interest in seeking to ensure that suitable toner is used in their machines' (Cm 1693, 1991, para. 9.118). The MMC was swayed by the level of competition in the market, and by the fact that where toner was tied to the copier the package as a whole had to be competitive. Customers who responded to an MMC survey did not, on the whole, object to the practice. The MMC's view was that the public interest would not be jeopardized were Rank Xerox to be released from its earlier undertaking. In 1997 the OFT, while recognizing that matters had improved somewhat, announced that it remained unhappy with several industry practices ('Photocopier Industry Cleans up its Selling Practices', OFT Press Release 9/97, 20 March 1997).

When it considered the range-stocking requirements imposed by Bryant & May, a large manufacturer of matches and disposable cigarette lighters, the MMC found that 'the existence of such provisions in agreements in each case restricts and distorts competition, as customers are likely to buy less matches and disposable lighters from Bryant & May's competitors than they would do otherwise' (*Matches and disposable lighters*, Cm. 1854, 1992, para. 7.50).

In 1996 the MMC published its report made under the now defunct Competition Act 1980 into the practice of Tambrands Ltd, which has a market share of around 60 per cent in the UK and owns the 'must-stock' Tampax mark (Cm 3168, 1996), following a complaint made by the supermarket chain Somerfield Stores Ltd. The company's practice was to offer discounts to a selective group of retailers in return for the acceptance of a condition requiring the retailer to stock the full range of Tampax. Tambrands rejected the 'emotive' description of this practice as 'full-line forcing'. The OFT had been concerned that the requirement to stock across the range could reduce shelf space available to competitors in the affected outlets and thereby raise barriers to entry. Before the MMC Tambrands acknowledged that 'it was seeking to get the broadest possible distribution of its product range . . . and that the range-stocking requirement could be expected to benefit new products' (para. 2.29). The MMC concluded that Tambrands' conduct was not anti-competitive within the meaning of s. 2(1) of the Competition Act 1980, and did not therefore continue to determine whether it lay within the public interest. In *Fine Fragrances* (Cm 2380, 1993) the MMC found that the imposition of range-stocking criteria and minimum purchasing requirements did not operate against the public interest. Although a number of deleterious effects were postulated, the evidence supporting their existence was not strong.

Both minimum-stock requirements and exclusivity were factors present in the distribution system operated by Coca-Cola & Schweppes Beverages Ltd which was considered by the MMC in *Carbonated Drinks* (Cm 1625, 1991). In this case the MMC condemned the operation of the requirements by the scale monopolist as a feature that contributed significantly to the already high barriers to entry. In particular, the fact that distributors had to cease selling competing products in order to quality for certain types of favourable terms distorted the market, and the MMC felt that this would lead to a reduction in consumer choice and therefore to a rise in prices for the product generally.

12.3.4.3 *Anti-competitive use of property rights*

There is a general presumption that an owner of property, whether it is real property or intellectual property, who merely uses that property in a way that falls within that owner's legal right, is not engaging in an anti-competitive practice. However, this is not always the case and, as the OFT has made clear:

it has been established that where the effect is to restrict, distort or prevent competition, the manner in which property rights are exercised may amount to an anti-competitive practice as defined in the Competition Act 1980.   (*The Southern Vectis Omnibus Company Limited: refusal to allow access to Newport Bus Station, Isle of Wight*, 1988, para. 7.4)

Although that case dealt with real property, a bus terminal, the argument is more likely to be raised in relation to intellectual property. The MMC had expressed concerns about the potential of the exploitative use of intellectual property rights in *Ford Motor Company Ltd* (Cmnd 9437, 1985). Here the MMC found that Ford's practice of refusing to grant licences to any person to manufacture or sell spare parts for its cars, and enforcing this through its copyright in those parts, was against the public interest. Effectively the practice gave Ford a complete monopoly over the market. The MMC concluded that it did not have the power to order the granting of a licence to manufacture or sell a copyrighted item, and recommended changes in the law to allow it to do so (for a well-argued sceptical view of the MMC's approach see Liesner, J. and Glynn, D., 'Does Anti-trust Make Economic Sense?' [1987] *ECLR* 344–69). The changes advocated by the MMC were introduced in the Copyright, Designs and Patents Act 1988, s. 144, which provides, in part, that

(1) Where the matters specified in a report of the Monopolies and Mergers Commission as being those which in the Commission's opinion operate, may be expected to operate or have operated against the public interest include—

    (a)   conditions in licences granted by the owner of copyright in a work restricting the use of the work by the licensee or the right of the copyright owner to grant other licences, or

    (b)   a refusal of a copyright owner to grant licences on reasonable terms, the powers conferred by Part I of Schedule 8 to the Fair Trading Act 1973 (powers exercisable for purpose of remedying or preventing adverse effects specified in report of

Commission) include power to cancel or modify those conditions and, instead or in addition, to provide that licences in respect of the copyright shall be available as of right.

A similar situation arose in *BBC/ITP* (Cmnd 9614, 1985), where the practice concerned the refusal of the BBC to grant licences to use its copyrighted programme listings to third parties. Here the MMC found that the practice did not operate against the public interest, although the matter was later redressed, following the application of Community law.

12.3.4.4 *Advertising issues*

Because the test set out in the FTA 1973 is so wide, a wide range of practices may be envisaged as falling within it. An issue that is hard to categorize, but which is related to full-line forcing because it is also about extending monopoly power, arose in the MMC's investigation into the practice of television broadcast companies of using their channels and programmes to promote their own products (*Television Broad-casting Services*, Cm 2035, 1992). The reference followed the Sadler inquiry, initiated by the Secretary of State for Trade and Industry (*Enquiry into Standards of Cross Media Promotion*, Cm 1436, 1991). In the course of this inquiry the BBC's cross-promotion in particular was criticized. When the reference was made, the MMC found that the value of the free airtime given by the BBC to its commercial arm, BBC Enterprises, amounted to as much as £20m in 1990/91. The bulk of this related to promotions of magazines that were linked to BBC TV programmes. At the time BBC Enterprises had a market share in consumer magazines of between 7 and 10 per cent, but in specialist areas market shares were far higher, rising to 90 per cent in relation to food and cookery magazines. The MMC found this practice to be against the public interest, and recommended that 'broadcasting of moving trails . . . should be prohibited, but that still trails by announcement over the end credits of a programme or over a single slide should be allowed' (para. 7.186). Further conditions, such as the length of time that could be used and the requirement to indicate the availability of competing products, were also attached to these.

Restrictions on advertising which limit competition within professions and limit the amount of information available to the public, were condemned in a series of 1976 reports into accountants, solicitors in England and Wales, solicitors in Scotland, stockbrokers, veterinary surgeons, barristers, and advocates. In these reports the MMC took a sceptical stance to claims that restrictions on advertising were necessary to ensure the reputation of the industry. Later, in *Osteopaths* (Cm 583, 1989), the MMC recommended that advertising restrictions should be lifted, provided that any advertising should conform to the British Code of Advertising Practice, not bring the profession into disrepute, and not exploit the lack of knowledge of the consumer. A good discussion of issues relating to advertising may be found in 'Advertising restrictions in professional services' in Amato, G, and Laudati, L. L., *The Anticompetitive Impact of Regulation* (2001, Edward Elgar).

12.3.5 **The continued application of the 1973 Act**

Many commentators considered that a straightforward application of art. 82 EC to the United Kingdom would lose the benefit of the complex monopoly provisions of the FTA 1973. One option facing the Government was to add to any domestic incorporation of art. 82 provisions that would allow some retention of the complex monopoly provisions. The solution adopted, which came as a surprise to some, was to retain those parts of the FTA 1973 relating to monopoly investigations for both scale and complex monopolies.

The explanations given at the time the Bill was first published in August 1997 were set out in the attached consultation document, at paras 6.17–6.23. At para. 6.18 the argument is set out in relation to the complex monopoly provisions:

Although the prohibition of abuse of a dominant market position can deal with abuse by a single company, and the prohibition of anti-competitive agreements can deal with parallel behaviour resulting from agreement between the parties, the prohibitions are not capable of readily dealing with parallel behaviour in the absence of agreement between the parties. Reliance on the two prohibitions alone may therefore fail to deal with competition problems where the problem may be the structure and operation of the market. We therefore consider there is a case for retaining the complex monopoly provisions and propose to do so.

In taking this position the DTI maintained the view that there are situations in which intervention is justified even where they may not be an actual anti-competitive abuse by any one participant in that market. This view sits well with the tradition in the UK of exploiting competition law in pursuit of widely drawn policies. However, the argument made in favour of retention of the scale monopoly provisions is more tenuous. The argument set out in the consultation document at paras 6.22–6.23 is as follows:

A prohibition-based approach is, however, less able to deal with the situation where, for example, an individual abuse has been tackled but where there is a prospect that other abuses by the dominant company may continue in the future. In such a situation, structural remedies to reduce the dominant position of the firm concerned may be more appropriate than relying on the prohibition alone to deter future abuse. Taking action to reduce market power in this way would be possible under the scale monopoly provisions of the [FTA] but is not readily achievable under a prohibition-based approach. There is accordingly an argument that the scale monopoly provisions of the FTA should be retained for use in these limited circumstances.

We are therefore currently not persuaded that it would be right to repeal the scale monopoly provisions. However, we consider that there is a case for restricting the use of these provisions to exceptional circumstances. Therefore we believe that they should only be used where there has already been a proven abuse under the prohibition *and* the DGFT believes there is a real prospect of future different abuses by the same firm.

This is a surprising, and controversial, position. Unlike the complex monopoly argument it applies to situations in which the Chapter II prohibition would still be applicable, and therefore implies a lack of faith in the efficacy of that prohibition. It is likely that even the most recalcitrant company would be deterred by the prospect of fines of 10 per cent of turnover on a regular basis, and would know that recidivism would be unlikely to go undetected. It was confirmed at both the debate and Committee stages of the Bill's progress through the House of Lords that the scale monopoly provisions would be used only where the company in question had already breached the Chapter II prohibition. Thus, introducing the Bill, Lord Simon expressed the Government's view that 'with the introduction of the prohibition regime we believe that the use of the Fair Trading Act monopoly powers should in future be restricted to circumstances where there have been prior findings of dominance' (Hansard (HL) 30 October 1997, col. 1147).

Those arguing for the retention of this provision would be able to point with some conviction to the approach taken by the CC to the Milk Marque monopoly in July 1999 (*Milk: A report on the supply in Great Britain of raw cows' milk*, Cm. 4286, 2000). Here the CC examined the activities of the successor to the Milk Marketing Board, which was responsible for the collection of about 50 per cent of all milk collected from farms in Great Britain. The CC found that the company was able to increase the price of milk, and could use its power to enforce strong market discrimination. It recommended that the company be broken up (see para. 1.15) an option which was subsequently followed through. Such a solution would not have been available under art. 82, or the Chapter II prohibition.

Similarly the long-awaited report *New Cars: A report on the supply of new motor cars within the UK* (Cm 4660, 2000) may ultimtely have a significant impact on the prices applied in this sector. In mid-June 2000 the DTI entered into a consultation process designed to even the balance between individual and fleet purchasers of new cars following the finding of the CC that 'prices paid by UK private customers are currently likely to be, on average, about 10 per cent too high' (para. 1.17).

13

Monopoly anti-competitive practices

13.1 Introduction

Broadly, the approaches taken by different competition authorities to the same forms of anti-competitive conduct are similar, although this is not true in every case. Even before the enactment of the Competition Act 1998 there had been an element of cross-fertilization between the EC and UK in particular. This is more clearly noticeable in the impact Community membership has had on UK law, but domestic actions have been noted, and from time to time cited with approval, at the centre (see, e.g., *Napier Brown* v *British Sugar* 88/518 (1988) OJ L284/41, where the Commission relied in part on a MMC report). With an increasing convergence in Community and national law it is appropriate, therefore, to consider actions taken against specific forms of anti-competitive conduct in each regime alongside each other. Consideration of the practice in the United States and the principles of industrial economics may cast further light on the approaches likely to be taken in the UK and EC. The discussion that follows is focused on a range of pricing practices and refusals to deal, which together constitute the larger part of the anti-competitive and exploitative practices of dominant firms. It does not therefore give examples of all practices that may fall to be condemned in both jurisdictions.

13.2 Pricing policies

Price competition is one of the most visible forms of commercial rivalry and is often of short-term benefit to consumers who are unlikely to complain about 'price wars'. It is one of the inherent contradictions of competition law that firms may be attacked for pricing too high, which is a matter of exploiting a position of strength and may actually have the effect of promoting competition, pricing too low, termed 'predatory pricing—an extreme form of price competition, and for setting different prices for different customers. In the appropriate circumstances all of these actions may be of legitimate concern to competition authorities. In the context of art. 82 (see Chapter 11) it is clearly envisaged that the first and last of these are to fall within the meaning of abuse, as the examples set out in the article include: (a) 'directly or indirectly imposing unfair purchase or selling prices' and (b) 'applying dissimilar conditions to equivalent transactions'. Arguably predatory prices are 'unfair' and, as was the case in *ECS/AKZO—interim measures* 83/462 (1983) OJ L252/13, therefore also fall within (a); but even if they are not, their imposition may fall within the more general meaning of 'abuse'. All these practices have been condemned as falling within the Competition Act 1980, s. 2(1) or as being 'against the public interest' under the FTA 1973.

13.2.1 Predatory pricing

'Low prices or price reductions are normally seen as a benefit from and the success-ful result of the process of competition. Predatory behaviour constitutes a class of anti-competitive behaviour where prices are *too low*, to the extent that the competi-tive process itself is damaged' (Myers, G., *Predatory Behaviour in UK Competition Policy*, London, OFT (1994), para. 1.1). A good working explanation of the practice of predatory pricing is given by Hay and Morris (Hay, D. A., and Morris, D. J., *Industrial Economics and Organization Theory and Evidence*, Oxford, OUP (1991), p. 580):

A dominant firm reacts to competition in one of its markets, either a geographical or a product market, by cutting price so as to drive the competitor out of business. The competitor in question may be either a new entrant or a small firm that has been a passive 'follower' of the leadership of the dominant firm but has now begun to gain market share. The purpose of the dominant firm's price-cutting is to preserve its long-run monopoly by frightening off potentially serious competition. The dominant firm is therefore quite willing to accept losses in that particular market for the time being—losses which it can absorb since it is earning high profits in other markets. The losses are the price for establishing a tough reputation, which will protect its position in all its markets in the long term.

The primary concerns of competition authorities, then, are that predatory pricing acts either as a barrier to entry, or to drive firms out of a market; that this is achieved by making it unprofitable for entrants to compete with the incumbent, or by sending a false signal to the entrant as to the expected returns from the market; and that the intention behind such predation is to allow the incumbent to raise prices in the long term, once the short-term battle has been won. While any company could, in theory, choose to engage in predatory pricing, only a monopolist with access to significant capital reserves or to the capital market could do so with any hope of success.

Strong arguments are made, in particular by some members of the Chicago school, to the effect that predatory pricing should be of no concern to competition authorities as it can never be a successful strategy and is only ever of benefit to consumers (in particular see Bork, R. H., *The Antitrust Paradox*, New York, The Free Press (1993), pp. 144–55). A leading competition strategist, attempting to discourage firms from taking such action, argues that price competition may be 'highly unstable and quite likely to leave the entire industry worse off from the standpoint of profitability. Price cuts are quickly and easily matched by rivals, and once matched they lower revenues for all firms' (Porter, M. E., *Competitive Strategy*, New York, The Free Press (1980), p. 17). Following more recent economic developments, and analyses based on game theory, the better view appears to be that predatory pricing can be successful where 'the potential entrant is uncertain about the post-entry [equilibrium] because it does not have precise information about the nature of the incumbent' (Hay, D. A., and Morris, D. J., above, p. 580). In such a situation the entrant is facing the situation where its knowledge does not match that of the incumbent, and it cannot determine whether the action of the price cutter is a result of superior efficiency, in which case the entrant may predict losses following even a successful entrance, or of the desire of the incumbent to gain a reputation as a tough competitor. Further, it is argued by the consultancy firm London Economics that

the presumption that predation is not a rational strategy has been shown to be false in the recent literature . . . Rather, predatory behaviour can be part of a rational strategy under conditions in which there is no differential access to resources and each firm understands perfectly the incentives in the situation at hand.   (London Economics, *Barriers to Entry and Exit in UK Competition Policy*, London, OFT (1994), p. 21)

The first important case to consider the issue in the United States was *Standard Oil Co. of New Jersey v US* 221 U.S. 1 (1911), one of the earliest cases based on the Sherman Act 1890, s. 2 to reach the Supreme Court, and the case in which the 'rule of reason' was established (see Chapter 1). Standard Oil had been created in 1870 out of the various companies operating at different levels of the industry owned by, amongst others, the Rockefellers, and was one of the original 'trusts' against which the antitrust legislation had reacted. Within a period of just over 10 years the company controlled some 90 per cent of the oil industry in the United States. The Supreme Court found that one reason for this spectacular growth was that the company had engaged in predatory pricing, its practice having 'necessarily involved the intent to drive others from the field and to exclude them from their right to trade and thus accomplish the mastery which was the end in view'. In an influential analysis which has formed the basis of much of the subsequent literature in this area, McGee has argued that Standard Oil, on the evidence presented, did not act predatorially, and that had it tried to do so it would have failed (McGee, J. S., 'Predatory Price Cutting: The Standard Oil (NJ) Case' (1958) 1 *Journal of Law and Economics*, 137–69). *Standard Oil* was followed very quickly by *US v American Tobacco Co.* 221 US 106 (1911), in which the Supreme Court similarly found that the defendant had breached the Sherman Act in fighting price wars with smaller competitors to drive them out of the market.

By the 1970s the attitude of the US antitrust authorities to allegations of predatory pricing was one of varying degrees of scepticism, and the courts too showed an increasing tendency to dismiss private claims alleging predation. In *Matsushita Electric Industrial Co. v Zenith Radio Corp.* 475 US 574 (1986), the Supreme Court rejected a complaint made against 21 Japanese manufacturers by two US manufacturers of television sets. The American companies had argued that sets sold by the defendants in the USA were deliberately sold at a low price to weaken the ability of the American firms to compete in the global market. The Court referred with approval to the arguments made by Bork:

As [Bork] shows, the success of such schemes is inherently uncertain: the short-run loss is definite, but the long-run gain depends on successfully neutralising the competition . . . The success of any predatory scheme depends on *maintaining* monopoly power for long enough to recoup predator's losses and to harvest some additional gain. . . . For this reason, there is a consensus among commentators that predatory pricing schemes are rarely tried, and even more rarely successful. (p. 589)

That the consensus the majority opinion referred to is of doubtful provenance is clear even from the case itself in which four of the judges dissented. Only nine months after *Matsushita* the Supreme Court considered an allegation of predation again in *Cargill Inc.* v *Montfort of Colorado Inc.* 479 US 104 (1986). Here the Court held, by a majority of six to two, that 'there is ample evidence suggesting that the practice does occur' (p. 121). The leading American case is *Brooke Group Ltd* v *Brown & Williamson Tobacco Corp.* 113 S.Ct. 2578 (1993), where the Supreme Court took the opportunity to clarify the law, and in doing so recognized that predation might occur. However, the Court set a two-fold test to be applied that will prove difficult for plaintiffs. For an allegation of predation to be upheld it must now be shown, in the USA, that the prices are below an appropriate measure of cost, and that there exists the likelihood that the investment in predatory prices will be recouped in the future by the defendant.

A major contribution to the debate as to the appropriate standard (or, *per Brooke*, 'cost measure') by which to judge predation was published in 1975 when Areeda and Turner attempted to define a test that could be used by the courts (Areeda, P., and Turner, D. F., 'Predatory Pricing and Related Practices under Section 2 of the Sherman Act' (1975) 88 *Harvard Law Review* 697). Broadly, Areeda and Turner argued that predation occurs when prices are set below marginal cost (see Chapter 1 for definitions of the basic economic terms); but that as marginal cost can be difficult to determine, a proxy measurement of average variable cost, which is more easy to ascertain by standard cost-accounting techniques, would produce an acceptably close result. It is difficult to argue that below marginal cost pricing should be acceptable, as it is more profitable to produce nothing than it is to sell below marginal cost. This argument and those made following its publication are analysed in some detail in Scherer, F. M., and Ross, D., *Industrial Market Structure and Economic Performance*, 3rd edn, Boston, Houghton Mifflin (1990), pp. 472–9. While there are problems with what has now become known as the Areeda–Turner rule, it does at least have the benefit of simplicity, and found favour with the US Department of Justice and Federal Trades Commission.

An attempt was made in the leading European case of *ECS/AKZO* to persuade the EC authorities to adopt such a test (85/609 (1985) OJ L374/1; on appeal *AKZO Chemie BV* v *Commission* case C–62/86 [1993] 5 CMLR 215). The Commission had taken swift action following a complaint by an English firm, ECS, that a larger competitor, AKZO, was price cutting predatorially in ECS's traditional market. The product in question was benzoyl peroxide, which has uses both as a bleach in the flour market and as a catalyst in plastics manufacture. ECS had concentrated on the flour additive market in the UK and Ireland, and held a market share of 35 per cent, being heavily reliant on a single customer group, Allied Mills. In 1979 ECS began to expand its sales into the larger plastics markets, dominated by AKZO, and captured one of AKZO's larger customers, BASF, having offered a price significantly lower than that of AKZO. ECS then alleged that AKZO threatened to reduce prices in the UK flour sector, thereby threatening ECS's core operations. A memo prepared by an AKZO executive noted that it had been confirmed to ECS's managing director that 'aggressive commercial action would be taken on the milling side unless he refrained from selling his products to the plastics industry'. The Commission reacted to the complaint initially by ordering interim measures under which AKZO's UK arm was to stay within the profit levels that existed before ECS's competitive move (*ECS/AKZO—interim measures* 83/462 (1983) OJ L252/13). In its final decision in the matter (85/609 (1985) OJ L374/1) the Commission had to consider carefully the argument made by AKZO that its prices 'were not abusive since they always included an element of profit', by which, the Commission notes, AKZO was arguing that they covered average variable costs, and therefore would not fall foul of the Areeda–Turner test (para. 42). Apart from disputing the basis of the accounts on which these figures were derived, the Commission also turned to other evidence, such as the intent underpinning AKZO's conduct, and refused to apply a pure cost-accounting approach to the problem, pointing out that:

Article [82] does not prescribe any cost-based legal rule to define the precise stage at which price-cutting by a dominant firm may become abusive and indeed *the broad application of the concept of abuse to different forms of exclusionary behaviour would argue against such a narrow test.* (para. 75, emphasis added)

When the ECJ considered the appeal it appeared to be slightly less sceptical as to the basis of the figures on which AKZO made its arguments, but supported the EC Commission in rejecting the resolution of the issue by the exclusive application of any formal test. The ECJ did suggest, however, that prices below average variable costs would be considered abusive, and that prices set at higher levels than this, but below average total costs, might be considered abusive if other factors suggested a predatory intent.

In the more recent case of *Tetra Pak v Commission (No. 2)* case C–333/94P [1997] 4 CMLR 662, the ECJ indicated that prices set below average variable cost would be automatically held to be abusive, without the need to establish intent. However, it is likely that in such cases the undertaking pricing below average variable cost would be able to rebut the presumption of an abuse in some circumstances, such as where there is obvious over-capacity or over-supply in the market.

Where it can be established that a company is selling at a loss an allegation of predatory conduct will in most cases be sustained, although exceptions might be made where, for example, there has recently been a change in the market structure and the company is still adjusting to this. In *Napier Brown v British Sugar* 88/518

(1988) OJ L284/41, the Commission found that British Sugar was selling retail sugar at a price which did not reflect its own 'transformation costs'. It was making a loss on the retail sales, which it was able to subsidize by profits from its industrial sales. The effect of this, if sustained, would be that any company which could package and market sugar as efficiently as British Sugar, but which did not have its own source of industrial sugar, would leave the market. That being so, the allegation of predatory pricing made by Napier Brown was upheld by the Commission (see para. 66).

In 1997 the Commission considered allegations of predation in *Irish Sugar* 97/624 (1997) OJ L258/1, on appeal *Irish Sugar plc v Commission* case T–228/97 [1999] 5 CMLR 1300; upheld on appeal to ECJ, *Irish Sugar plc v Commission* case C–497/99 R [2001] 5 CMLR 29. In this case the undertaking targeted price cuts and discounts selectively so as to undermine imports. The case deals with both discriminatory pricing (considered further below) and exclusionary pricing, the effect of which may be indistinguishable from predation. In the case itself there is a muddying of the waters between predation and exclusion. The Commission, in condemning prices that lay above average variable cost, indicated that selective reductions would be regarded as strong evidence of intent to predate. The question arose as to the extent to which a company could cut prices in order to meet competition, a matter which critics of competition policy often point to as a failing of the system. The Commission's response was that 'There is no doubt that a firm in a dominant position is entitled to defend that position by competing with other firms in its market. However, the dominant firm must not deliberately attempt to effectively shut out competitors' (para. 134).

Where a smaller competitor would be shut out simply by the fact that the dominant firm is more efficient and has lower costs, it would not be abusive to rely on these advantages as long as the conduct was not introduced so as clearly to target a particular competitor, or was introduced as a specific response to a short-term competitive situation. It would not, for example, be abusive for a company enjoying substantial economies of scale to price consistently, and in a non-discriminatory manner, at a level lower than could be achieved by new entrants into the market.

In the guideline *Assessment of Individual Agreements and Conduct*, the OFT draws the following conclusions about the EC approach to predation (para. 4.4):

Price below average variable costs	Predation can be assumed
Price above average variable costs, but below average total costs	Evidence on costs may indicate predation, but the Director General would need to establish evidence that the dominant undertaking intended to eliminate a competitor before predation could be found
Price above average total costs	Evidence does not indicate predation

Even where prices are below average variable costs evidence to justify this will be considered under the Competition Act 1998. Such justifications might include: short-run promotions; inefficient entry (a situation where a company mistakenly enters a market in which there is no excess capacity, forcing all firms to cut prices); mistakes; and, in accordance with the expertise gained in the bus sector (discussed below), the fact that the undertaking is nevertheless making an incremental profit.

A long chain of cases relating to predation in the deregulated bus industry in the UK meant that the OFT gained a considerable expertise in this area. The broad views of the OFT relating to predation were set out in *Becton Dickinson* (*Becton Dickinson UK Ltd: The Supply of Hypodermic Syringes and Hypodermic Needles*, OFT, 1988): it would treat pricing below short-run marginal cost as *clearly* predatory, and pricing above this level *could* be predatory, depending on the presence of additional evidence. Myers summed up the position relating to this additional evidence:

There will be strong evidence of intent if the firm had no realistic expectation that a profit would be made . . . and, having incurred an incremental loss took no steps to alleviate it . . . Private statements (for example in a business plan) that a firm wishes to eliminate competitors would not usually be regarded as evidence of intent. Public statements to this effect could be seen as weak evidence of intent.   (Myers, G., above, paras 3.28–3.34)

In its first two adverse decisions under the Competition Act in relation to the Chapter II prohibition the OFT condemned predation. In *Napp* the core conduct attacked related to price discrimination, but the undertaking offered prices to one sector of the market place which were substantially below those offered to another sector, and, according to the decision, where it faced competition in the market for its product—sustained release morphine, or MST—Napp's 'prices to hospitals are below direct costs, where direct costs are defined, consistently with Napp's accounting system, as materials and direct labour' (*Napp Pharmaceutical Holdings Limited and Subsidiaries* CA98/2/2001 [2001] UKCLR 597, para. 189). Napp argued that its low prices were justified as sales to hospitals of the drug guaranteed that follow-on sales would be made through prescriptions continued by GPs, and that it was pricing across the entire usage of the drug, and therefore increasing its net revenue by pricing below cost in one sector. On appeal the CCAT rejected these arguments, and was scathing of the net revenue argument (*Napp Pharmaceutical Holdings Ltd and Subsidiaries* v *The Director General of Fair Trading* [2002] CompAR 13, paras. 231–66). At para. 225 the CCAT held that 'on the uncontested facts the situation that presents itself in this case is therefore that of a virtual monopolist that has been selling at prices well below direct cost'. Following *AKZO* the CCAT found that this behaviour would, absent an objective justification, constitute predation. As for the net revenue argument, which had been advanced by the undertaking's economic consultants, the CCAT held that it

provides no yardstick for distinguishing between what is legitimate, and what is abusive, behaviour on the part of a dominant undertaking. For instance, a monopolist driving away new entrants by predatory pricing is likely to maximise his net revenue by so doing, for example by avoiding the loss of market share and erosion of prices in the profitable market where he holds a monopoly. Yet plainly such behaviour does not cease to be abusive merely because it is profitable for the monopolist to engage in it.   (para. 259)

In *Predation by Aberdeen Journals Ltd* CA98/5/2001 [2001] UKCLR 856 predation was, as the title of the decision indicates, very much to the fore. In the decision the Director concluded that 'Aberdeen Journals failed to price above average variable costs regarding the *Herald & Post* in March, May and June of 2000' (para. 87). As well as conducting an analysis of the cost structure facing the undertaking, and its revenues, the OFT also relied on significant documentary evidence of intent. The undertaking argued that it was merely meeting competition, and that pricing levels were broadly equivalent between its title and that of the entrant. The OFT, however, found that the only reason for the similarity was that the entrant was being forced to meet the prices set by Aberdeen Journals. Aberdeen Journals, the OFT found, had 'initiated and sustained price cuts, and increased pagination and circulation, rather than simply responded to competition' (para. 79). The undertaking argued that the length of time over which the OFT was analysing the conduct was insufficient to fully take into account the dynamics of the market place, and the OFT accepted that there might well be circumstances in which undertakings 'might inadvertently price below average variable cost for a short period' (para. 109) but it did not accept that this was the situation in the present case. In para. 115 of the decision the Director held that:

Even if there were convincing evidence that Aberdeen Journals no longer intended to predate in March 2000 (which the Director is satisfied there is not), Aberdeen Journals' conduct from 1 March to 29 March 2000 would be predatory. These pricing levels were not inadvertent or caused by any external factor. They resulted directly from the sustained predatory campaign pursued by Aberdeen Journals against the *Independent* over the preceding four years, before the Act came into force. Aberdeen Journals' failure to take effective action to cease predating (even though it was subject to investigation by the Office) by reducing its costs or increasing its revenues was, at best, negligent, and continued to have the anticompetitive effect of potentially expelling its only rival from the relevant market. Consequently Aberdeen Journals' failure to cover its average variable costs until 29 March 2000 was not legitimate competitive conduct.

In *Aberdeen Journals Ltd v The Director General of Fair Trading* ([2002] CompAR 167) the CCAT set this Decision aside, remitting it to the Director for re-assessment. The CCAT did not consider the evidence relating to prediction as it found defects in the analysis of the relevant market. The OFT later announced its determination to continue to issue a new Decision.

Much time was taken up in the debates on the Competition Act 1998 as to whether a specific measure should be placed in the Act to address allegations of predatory pricing in the newspaper industry. This followed a campaign run by the *Independent* alleging predation on the part of *The Times*. The point was first raised in the debates by Lord Cocks (Hansard (HL) 30 October 1997, col. 1151), and was then returned to on several occasions. Although the matter was covered in the *Independent* on several occasions (see, e.g., 23 February 1998), the debate was an unnecessary one, predation being unlawful under the terms of the Act where coupled to the requisite market power, and being unlikely to succeed where not coupled with market power.

13.2.2 **Excessive pricing**

The popular, and not entirely accurate, view of monopoly behaviour is that it leads to 'rip-offs' and excessively high prices. As was demonstrated formally in Chapter 10, a monopolist is likely to price higher than a firm in a competitive market. While such situations can be of concern to competition authorities, there is again no standard formula by which excessive pricing may be identified. Excessive pricing is a dangerous strategy as the supernormal profits of which it is indicative are an invitation to other firms to enter the market (see, e.g., the comments made by the MMC in *Cross Solent Ferries*, Cm. 1825, 1992, at para. 7.71). Such a strategy is there-fore one that can be pursued successfully in the medium to long term only where there exist strong barriers to entry. These barriers might include a reputation for predation on behalf of the incumbent, so the situation can arise where, in a short space of time, a company prices first predatorially and then excessively.

A further problem in the analysis is to distinguish between excessive prices which lead to supernormal profits, and excessive prices which are the result of X-inefficiency, which might be the case where an incumbent is both inefficient and protected by high barriers to entry.

Where the EC Commission has acted against excessive pricing it often appears to have been on the basis of limited analysis and to have been inspired, as is often the case with EC actions, by concerns about divisions in the internal market. There has not been much case law in this area—a factor highlighted by the CCAT in its preliminary hearing in the *Napp* case (*Napp Pharmaceutical Holdings Limited and Subsidiaries* v *The Director General of Fair Trading* [2001] CompAR 1, para. 46).

The first decision to deal with the issue in detail in the EC was that of *General Motors Continental* 75/75 (1975) OJ L29/14. At the time the decision was taken cars sold in Belgium, or imported into Belgium for use, were required to satisfy technical standards laid down in law, and to carry an approval '*plaque d'identification*'. Either the manufacturer or a sole agent had to issue the certificate and confirm that the vehicle met the legal requirements. General Motors Continental was the sole authorized agent for the manufacturers belonging to the General Motors Group (GM). Where the approval certificate was being issued in respect of a car manu-factured and sold by a member of GM in Europe a fee of BF1,250 was charged. However, for private customers or dealers who brought cars into Belgium other than through the standard GM distribution channels ('parallel importers') the price for the certificate rose to between BF5,300 and BF30,000, the aim presumably being to encourage such customers to purchase only through approved GM distributors. It appeared to be the case that BF2,500 would be the maximum charged for such certificates by agents authorized in respect of other makes of vehicle. Pointing to the 'extraordinary disparity between actual costs incurred and prices actually charged' the Commission found that GM had 'abused its dominant position within the meaning of [art. 82] and applied unfair prices within the meaning of heading (a)'. Very similar facts arose in the case of *British Leyland* (BL) (84/379 (1984) OJ L207/11) where customers were buying BL-manufactured left-hand drive vehicles in continental Europe at prices substantially lower than the equivalent right-hand drive vehicle in the United Kingdom. BL's UK dealers responded to this situation by putting pressure on BL to curb the trade, and BL at first decided to refuse to grant the necessary 'national type-approval' certificates for the imported vehicles. Then, following public pressure and intervention in the House of Commons, it changed its policy, granting such certificates but at a price of £150. A Commission investigation found that BL was at the same time charging only £25 for the certificate in respect of imported right-hand drive vehicles. Whether a vehicle was right- or left-hand drive made no difference to the legal status of the certificates. BL was then condemned by the Commission for charging a fee that 'was both excessive and discriminatory' (para. 26).

An interesting variant on high pricing was considered in *Sabena* (*London European—Sabena* 88/589 (1988) OJ L317/47), where the primary concern was that pressure was being put on a smaller competitor to raise its prices. Following a complaint made by London European (LE), a small company operating a twice-daily air service on the Luton/Brussels and Luton/Amsterdam routes, the Commission found that Sabena, by refusing to grant LE access to its ticket reservation system, had the intention 'of placing indirect pressure on [LE] to fix a higher level of fares than, as an independent air carrier, it had planned . . . an artificial increase in fares [is] totally incompatible with a system of free competition' (para. 29).

In *United Brands* (*United Brands Co v Commission* case 27/76 [1978] 1 CMLR 429, paras 235–68) the ECJ dealt with the Commission arguments to the effect that UB had charged 'unfair' prices 'excessive in relation to the economic value of the product supplied'. The Commission had argued, taking prices charged in Ireland as a base, that a price reduction of some 15 per cent would be appropriate. The Court agreed that 'charging a price which is excessive because it has no reasonable relation to the economic value of the product supplied' is an abuse, and held that the question is one of whether 'the difference between the costs actually incurred and the price actually charged is excessive and, if the answer to this question is in the affirmative, to consider whether a price has been imposed which is either unfair in itself or when compared to competing products'. Unfortunately the Commission had failed to conduct any examination of the cost structures facing UB, and had based its claim of excessive pricing on a superficial comparison of prices based on a single exception to a trend, and on a solitary letter written by UB which was subsequently withdrawn by the undertaking. In respect of this claim, therefore, the Commission decision was in part struck down. Some care must be taken in applying this analysis elsewhere—the concept of 'economic value' is an interesting, but highly subjective one.

In *Duales System Deutschland AG* 2001/463 (2001) OJ L166/1 the Commission condemned what it termed 'unreasonable prices', which it said existed in cases in which 'the price charged for a service is clearly disproportionate to the cost of supplying it' (para. 111). In the case in question the undertaking, DSD, licensed the use of the Green Dot trade mark on packaging, and would in return look after the collection and recycling of such packaging. The Commission first announced that it was inclined to take a favourable view of the arrangement, but then received a number of complaints to the effect that DSD was abusing a dominant position on the German market. However, not all packaging bearing the mark would be dealt with by DSD, even though a licence fee would still be required for this. The Commission found that in these circumstances the fee was 'unfair' (para. 112). The Commission argued that 'as long as DSD makes the licence fee dependent solely on the use of the mark, it is imposing unfair prices and commercial terms on undertakings which do not use the exemption service' (para. 113). Again in Germany, in *Deutsche Post AG* 2001/892 (2001) OJ L331/40, the Commission dealt with a complaint from the British Post Office relating to various practices of its German counterpart. The practices complained of related to DPAG's approach to direct mail sent from the UK to addresses in Germany, but where the originating undertaking (the 'sender') had a connection in Germany. Such mail was on occasion delayed by DPAG, and a higher price was charged to the British Post Office for the onward transmission of this mail, than for deliveries that were entirely domestic in character. At paras 155–67 the Commission dealt with the arguments relating to excessive pricing, concluding that

the tariff charged by DPAG has no sufficient or reasonable relationship to real costs or to the real value of the service provided. Consequently DPAG's pricing exploits customers excessively and should therefore be regarded as an unfair selling price within the meaning of art. 82. In conclusion, the Commission finds that DPAG has abused its dominant position in the German market.

The EC approach is summarized in the OFT guideline *Assessment of Individual Agreements and Conduct*, and excessive pricing is dealt with at paras 2.1–2.23.

In the United Kingdom the OFT and MMC have often considered excessive pricing arising out of oligopolistic market structures. The treatment of these situations, where anti-competitive effects arise out of the very structure of the market rather than from specifically directed abusive practices, has been one of the strengths of the domestic regime. Rather than considering whether a particular company is pricing abusively, the UK authorities have been able to examine whether prices in a given industry have been against 'the public interest'. There are several instances in which the MMC has recommended price controls that have subsequently been subject to orders or undertakings. A high-profile example of the treatment of alleged excessive pricing arose in relation to the market for compact discs (CDs) (*The Supply of Recorded Music*, Cm. 2599, 1994). The reference was made by the DGFT in May 1993 following general expressions of dissatisfaction with CD prices and, in particular, a report by the National Heritage Committee (NHC) (*The price of compact discs*, HC 609, 1992–93). In its report the NHC condemned 'most strongly the pricing practices of the major record companies', arguing that 'it is now time for consumers to show they will no longer bear the prices currently charged for full-price [CDs]' (paras 42 and 43). The MMC concluded to general scepticism that in fact neither prices nor returns on capital were high in relation to those for similar consumer goods. As for arguments that prices were lower in the United States, the MMC's view, following a survey of some US prices, was that 'much of the apparent difference relates to different tax arrangements . . . record prices are displayed without sales tax in the USA, whereas shelf prices in the UK include VAT' (para. 1.5). As well as commissioning its own price surveys the MMC had the possibly doubtful 'benefit of a number of detailed price comparisons prepared by the record companies' to rely on (para. 2.63). An examination of the return on turnover (profitability) found that 'accounts prepared in accordance with generally accepted accounting standards do not reveal any evidence of excessive profits' (para. 2.110).

Elsewhere the MMC has not been so ready to dismiss concerns as to excessive prices. In 1996, for example, it found prices charged by Yellow Pages for classified directory advertisements to be excessive (*Classified directory advertising services*, Cm. 3171, 1996). Relying in part on the evidence that return on capital employed and return on sales would put Yellow Pages in the top 2 per cent of industrial and commercial companies in the UK (para. 2.43), and considering that there was little effective competition in the narrowly defined market, the MMC recommended that price constraints be imposed on Yellow Pages. Following the report an under-taking was negotiated that would restrict price rises to RPI—2 per cent for a period of some five years. It will be immediately clear that there are difficulties with such a solution. On the one hand a monopolist may be condemned for pricing too low, and on the other be required to set prices at levels significantly lower than had been the case across the industry for the years preceding the report. It may be presumed that one consequence of such an action is to make it harder for new entrants to join the market. In this case it appears that the MMC was of the view that the leading position held by Yellow Pages, which was considered to be largely the result of first-mover advantage and the esteem in which its trade mark and 'walking fingers' logo were held, would not be successfully assailed, and that therefore price con-straints would be the least bad option. It is perhaps not surprising that there was a dissenting view on the panel (by Catherine Blight, see pp. 33–4 of the report).

Generally it is the case that, where entry barriers are high (as in Yellow Pages), the MMC is more likely to be concerned about excessive pricing than where they are low (see, e.g., *Tampons*, Cmnd. 8049, 1981; and *Tambrands Ltd*, Cm. 3168, 1996). In *Soluble Coffee* (Cm. 1459, 1991) Nestlé was exonerated following concerns as to its profitability, in part because the MMC noted that competitors 'tended to speak highly of Nestlé's efficiency and reputation for fair business' (para. 7.63) and largely because over a dozen suppliers produced in excess of 200 brands of soluble coffee, suggesting that the company's actions were subject to reasonable market restraints.

Excessive pricing, which has been linked by the OFT with discriminatory pricing (see below) was attacked in *Napp Pharmaceutical Holdings Ltd* CA98/2/2001 [2001] UKCLR 597, on appeal *Napp Pharmaceuticals Holdings Ltd* v *The Director General of Fair Trading* [2002] CompAR 13. The Director argued that

The prices charged by Napp for MST in the community are excessive. The Director considers that a price is excessive and an abuse if it is above that which would exist in a competitive market and where it is clear that high profits will not stimulate successful new entry within a reasonable period. Therefore, to show that prices are excessive, it must be demonstrated that (i) prices are higher than would be expected in a competitive market, and (ii) there is no effective competitor pressure to bring them down to competitive levels, nor is there likely to be. (para. 203)

Price comparisons showed that Napp's prices were, to the relevant sector of the market, between 33 per cent and 67 per cent higher than those of the next nearest competitor (table 6). Napp argued that it was justified in charging higher prices because it was the innovator in the industry, and its product had a brand value. The Director however took the view that the product had lost its brand value (para. 211), and the Napp had been rewarded for its invention of the product during the period in which the patent for the product was in existence (para. 209). The Director found that it was inconsistent with normal market processes for Napp to maintain a market share of some 96 per cent at the same time as it charged prices that were so much higher than those of competing products. An analysis of the undertaking's profit margins was also carried out, but this raised problems as the situation in the industry was not symmetrical. Although Napp made a higher margin on sales than its competitors it was also the only undertaking that manufactured the product itself (para. 225). The Director therefore compared the average selling price of Napp's product, which was £15.47, with the average cost of the goods sold by its next most profitable competitor—which it should be emphasized was thought might be *higher* than the cost of production by Napp—which was £3.01. This would lead to a gross margin of 80.5 per cent, and for the next most profitable competitor the margin was less than 70 per cent (para. 228). On appeal the CCAT upheld the findings of the Director, and held that the fact that it is difficult to calculate whether a price is higher than that which would exist in a competitive market does not mean that the exercise should not be undertaken (para. 392). The comparisons that could be made in the case all suggested that the Director was correct to find that prices were excessive, and it did not matter that the Director had not specified by exactly how much the prices were excessive (paras 393–405).

13.2.3 Discriminatory pricing

Price discrimination may be defined as the supply of goods or services of the same contract description at different prices at the same time where the difference in price does not reflect cost differences (e.g., in transport or bulk supply). Whereas in a competitive market a producer is able usually to charge only one price for its product, in a monopolistic market the producer may be able to increase income and profits by charging a range of prices. In the extreme case of perfect differentiation the monopolist can charge each customer the maximum the customer is prepared to pay; more likely is the situation where various groups of customers are identified and prices set in relation to each group. The welfare effects of this practice depend on all the circumstances, and in some cases it can be clearly demonstrated that there is greater output as more customers are being satisfied than is the case where a single price maintains. Where there are objections to price discrimination it may be because the one certainty is that it results in a transfer of income from consumers to the monopolist. In the case of perfect differentiation the consumer surplus is transferred completely to the monopolist. Price discrimination can be successful only where the monopolist is able to control resale of the product, otherwise those who could purchase at low prices would resell to those who would be paying the monopolist higher prices, and is thus in itself sometimes taken as evidence of a degree of market power. Price discrimination may also play a part in predatory conduct: where a monopolist funds predatory prices by profits earned elsewhere an element of price discrimination is inevitable, unless the monopolist operates in more than one product or geographic market.

In the United States the Robinson–Patman Act of 1936—'the misshapen progeny of intolerable draftsmanship coupled to wholly mistaken economic theory' (Bork, R. H., *The Antitrust Paradox*, New York, The Free Press (1993), p. 382)—was drafted expressly to deal with the 'problem' of price discrimination. Bork aside, there has been much criticism both of the theory underlying the Act and of its application in practice, and even a report prepared for the US Department of Justice has recommended its repeal.

In the European Community the overriding objective of creating the single market (see Chapter 2) has resulted in greater focus being placed upon price discrimination than would be likely to be the case in purely national jurisdictions. If a monopolist is going to exercise a crude form of price discrimination and set different prices for groups of consumers an obvious division might be between the Member States.

This was the situation in *United Brands* (*United Brands Co.* v *Commission* case 27/76 [1978] 1 CMLR 429). In its decision taken in 1975 (*Chiquita* 76/353 (1976) OJ L95/1) the Commission had attacked United Brands for charging variations in prices to its customers which were 'not attributable to any differences in customs duties or transport costs, since these [were] borne by the distributor/ripeners'. At one point, according to the Commission's figures, Danish customers were paying 2.38 times the price charged to Irish customers. United Brands was able to achieve this in part by introducing contractual terms that prevented its customers from reselling green bananas to other retailers; once the bananas had ripened their perishability would mean that resale other than to the end consumer was not a practical possibility. The essence of the undertaking's defence was that the price differentials in the final markets were not of its making, being the result of historical factors. Whether United Brands charged these higher prices to some retailers would make little difference to the end consumer, for if United Brands did not take the monopoly profit the retailer would. One of the stronger points made tirelessly by Bork is that a monopoly price can be imposed only once—if there are monopolies at every step of a vertically integrated chain the price does not go on rising indefinitely as at some point the consumer's demand curve must still be faced. After conducting some particularly unconvincing economic analysis the ECJ found in the Commission's favour, in effect holding that United Brands had to bear some of the cost of the creation of the common market. It is unlikely that consumers benefited from the judgment, for if they were able to bear the higher prices these would be imposed by the retailers in place of United Brands.

Recital (c) of art. 82—'applying dissimilar conditions to equivalent transactions with other trading parties, thereby placing them at a competitive disadvantage'— suggests strongly that discriminatory pricing is to be considered an 'abuse', but the Commission does not generally wish to involve itself in pricing decisions. Consider, for instance, its approach in *HOV SVZ/MCN* 94/210 (1994) OJ L104/34. Here the Commission was reacting to a complaint about practices relating to the carriage by rail of sea-borne containers between Belgium, Germany, and The Netherlands. The Commission set out its general position thus:

> it is not part of the Commission's duties to assess as such the level of prices charged by an undertaking or to decide which criteria should govern the setting of such prices. On the other hand, where different prices are charged for equivalent transactions, *it is appropriate to assess whether such differences are justified by objective factors.*   (paras 158–9, emphasis added)

This is the general case under EC law, the position being that where a supplier can demonstrate that there are 'objective factors' that lead to the price differences, an allegation of abusive behaviour will not be sustained. Accordingly it will be a defence to an action if the supplier can demonstrate that discounts are given for bulk sales because it is cheaper for it to supply in bulk. Thus, for example, in *Tetra Pak II* 92/163 (1992) OJ L72/1—in which the Commission was considering the undertaking's position in relation to packaging machines and the packaging used by the machines—the Commission addressed Tetra Pak's 'selling prices for its cartons which vary considerably from one Member State to another', holding this practice to be 'discriminatory and constitut[ing] an abuse' (para. 154). The Commission was of the view that, particularly as raw materials (the prices of which were determined on the world market and did not therefore vary from Member State to Member State) accounted for 70 per cent of the cost of the cartons, and that given the relevant geographic market for the cartons had been found to be that of the Community as a whole, the 'price differences observed [could not] be explained in economic terms'. The price differences were found to be the result of the 'compartmentalisation policy which Tetra Pak managed artificially to maintain' (para. 154). In relation to the supply of the packaging machines themselves the Commission was even more emphatic, pointing out that 'the transport costs of machines are quite negligible in relation to the market value of the product' (para. 160). One of the requirements imposed on Tetra Pak was that it would 'ensure that any differences between the prices charged for its products in the various Member States result solely from specific market conditions . . . and shall not grant to any customer any form of discount on its products or more favourable payment terms not justified by an objective consideration' (arts 1, 2). Tetra Pak was fined ECU 75 million in respect of the infringements the Commission found (see Chapter 4).

The second Part of art. 82(c)—'thereby placing them at a competitive disadvantage'—is easily dealt with. In part, the use of 'thereby' suggests that it is presumed that a competitive disadvantage flows from the maintenance of 'dissimilar conditions'. On top of this, the ECJ held in *United Brands*, that a competitive disadvantage existed 'since compared with what it should have been competition had thereby been distorted' (para. 233). It should be recognized that drawing a comparison with what competition 'should have been' may not be a straightforward matter.

In the United Kingdom the issue of price discrimination has not been subject to the same scrutiny as it has in the EC and in the guideline the view is expressed that price discrimination will be an abuse 'only where there is evidence that prices were also excessive or that the discrimination was used to reduce competition significantly' (para. 3.2). As suggested above, there is a specific reason for the Commission to focus on the issue, and it is also the case that discrimination will be harder to maintain in a smaller market where customers can more easily respond. Nevertheless, price discrimination was dealt with in the *Napp* case (*Napp Pharmaceutical Holdings Ltd* CA98/2/2001 [2001] UKCLR 597, on appeal *Napp Pharmaceuticals Holdings Ltd* v *The Director General of Fair Trading* [2002] CompAR 13). In the decision price discrimination is dealt with at paras. 144–87, para. 144 stating that 'discounts will be an abuse if they serve to strengthen a dominant position in such a way that the degree of dominance reached substantially fetters competition'. Napp produced sustained release morphine tablets (MST), which were distributed to two sectors of the market, hospitals and the community sector. Hospital usage, which accounted for a relatively small share of the overall market, was a trigger for prescription by general practitioners in the community sector. Napp supplied MST to hospitals at a discount of over 90 per cent off the NHS list prices, and the OFT took the view that these discounts were targeted 'specifically at new competitors and hindered competition in the hospital segment of the market' (para. 145). The highest level of discounts were only offered on strengths of its own product line where it faced a direct rival (para. 182). Higher discounts were also offered to hospitals where Napp expected to be awarded a sole contract for a particular region (para. 183). The finding was upheld by the CCAT.

Where price discrimination has been attacked under the Fair Trading Act 1973 it has often been ancillary to charges of predation or exclusion. In *Contraceptive sheaths* (HCP (1974–75) 135), for example, the MMC was of the view that London Rubber Co., the monopoly manufacturer of condoms, was preventing access to the market by creating low-price brands so as to obstruct competitors from getting a foothold. As with EC law, the general position in the United Kingdom has been that price differentials may be justified by reference to objective cost factors (see, e.g., *Pest control services* (Cm. 302, 1988) and *Collective licensing* (Cm. 530, 1988)).

13.3 Refusal to deal or supply, and the essential facilities doctrine

13.3.1 Refusal to supply generally

A general presumption in the commercial world is that companies are free to choose with whom to have dealings. However, there are situations in which a positive obligation is placed on them to supply specific parties. In particular this is likely to be the case where refusals are: imposed to punish a customer who may have traded in more competitive fashion than the retailer wished; the result of the monopolist wishing to exclude others from directly competing with the monopolist in secondary markets; and an attempt to maintain high prices by dampening downstream competition, e.g., cases in which monopolists have refused to supply discount chains. A problem in requiring supplies to be made is that the competition authorities may also have to address issues such as the terms and conditions of supply and be prepared to be involved in an element of ongoing regulation.

In 1984 the Commission stated that '[a]s a general principle an objectively unjustifiable refusal to supply by an undertaking holding a dominant position on a market constitutes an infringement of Article [82]' (*Thirteenth Report on Competition Policy* (1984), point 157). The first case to deal substantially with the issue, *Commercial Solvents*, is one of the least satisfactory of all EC cases (*Istituto Chemioterapico Italiano SpA and Commercial Solvents Corp* v *Commission* cases 6–7/73 [1974] CMLR 309). Here Commercial Solvents (CSC), which manufactured aminobutanol, a raw material in the manufacture of drugs to combat tuberculosis, was required to resume supplies to the complainant Zoja. This followed the decision of CSC to expand into production of the final product itself and to cease supplies of the raw material. Even before that decision had been made Zoja had stopped taking supplies from CSC and had made attempts, which were eventually unsuccessful, to find a source of supplies elsewhere. Supporting the EC Commission the ECJ held that 'an undertaking in a dominant position as regards the production of raw material . . . cannot, just because it decides to start manufacturing [the derivative product] (in competition with its former customers) act in such a way as to eliminate their competition' (para. 25). The analysis of the welfare effects in this case is unsatisfactory. It is, for instance, likely that the vertically integrated CSC would be able to produce the end drug more efficiently than would be achieved by a combination of the two undertakings each engaged in one part of the manufacturing process only.

Similarly, Community law provides that a manufacturer is not allowed to foreclose competition in the market for the repair or service of its product by unreasonably denying spare parts to independent service companies (e.g., *Hugin Kassaregister AB and Hugin Cash Registers Ltd* v *Commission* case 22/78 [1979]

3 CMLR 345, and *Volvo AB* v *Erik Veng* case 238/87 [1989] 4 CMLR 122: see the discussion of both cases in Chapter 11).

In *United Brands (United Brands Co.* v *Commission* case 27/76 [1978] 1 CMLR 429) retailers that participated in advertising campaigns promoting rival products, or who resupplied green bananas, were threatened with having supplies cut off. Both actions were condemned by the Commission.

In *Boosey and Hawkes (BBI/Boosey & Hawkes: Interim measures* 87/500 (1987) OJ L286/36) the products in question were musical instruments for brass bands. BBI was established by two companies, GHH, a retailer of brass band instruments, and RCN, a repairer of the instruments, with the intention of manufacturing instruments in competition to *Boosey*, which was the only British manufacturer of brass instruments. Boosey responded to this move by, *inter alia*, withdrawing supplies of its instruments and spare parts from GHH and RCN. The Commission supported the claimants, holding (at para. 19) that:

A dominant undertaking may always take reasonable steps to protect its commercial interests, but such measures must be fair and proportional to the threat. The fact that a customer of a dominant producer becomes associated with a competitor of that manufacturer does not normally entitle the dominant producer to withdraw all supplies immediately or to take reprisals against that customer.

Under the decision adopted Boosey was 'required to meet within seven days of receipt any reasonable order . . . for musical instruments or spare parts' (art. 1).

Refusals to supply may be justified where, for instance, there is a general shortage and the supplier declines to supply new customers in favour of existing arrangements *(ABG Oil companies operating in the Netherlands* 77/327 (1977) OJ L117/1).

Consideration should also be given to the conditions under which producers may refuse to admit retailers to their distribution networks (see Chapter 7).

The approach to be taken under the Competition Act 1998 to both refusal to supply and essential facilities is dealt with in the guideline *Assessment of Individual Agreements and Conduct* at paras 7.1–7.5.

Prior to the enactment of the Competition Act 1998 the UK authorities received many complaints relating to refusals to supply. The first inquiry conducted under the Competition Act 1980 concerned a refusal to supply on the part of Raleigh, the large bicycle manufacturer *(Bicycles*, HC 67, 1981). Both this case and *Black and Decker* (Cm. 805, 1989) concerned situations in which manufacturers of leading brands refused to sell to a group of well-known retailers, including B&Q and Argos in the latter case, on the grounds that they were known for cutting prices to levels lower than those generally holding. The MMC made it clear that it would countenance restrictions only where they are related directly to the products in question. In *Black & Decker* the company (B&D) had relied in part upon the Resale Prices Act 1976, s. 13 which permitted a manufacturer to withhold supplies where the goods in question had been used as part of a loss-leading strategy by the retailer, the operation of which was criticized by the MMC. B&D also argued that its action, which it suggested had the effect of increasing the number of outlets selling the company's products, was pro-competitive and not restrictive. One of the key elements of the company's competitive strategy was to maximize volume 'on the basis of a uniform and equitable pricing structure' (para. 4.2). The MMC disagreed, holding that 'it is for the retailers to determine retail selling practices and prices and that a return, even in a limited way, to resale price maintenance would reduce competition' (para 1.3). In particular the MMC was concerned that a continuation of the practice would 'inevitably maintain and establish a minimum price [for the products in question] in all retail outlets . . . this effect of the practice runs counter to the continued development of an innovative and competitive retail sector' (para. 6.75). In its 1970 Report, *Refusal to Supply* (Cmnd 4372), the MMC had concluded that there are three situations in which refusal to supply may be against the public interest: where it involves refusal to supply known price cutters; where it is a response to a boycott threatened by other distributors; and where the supplier does not operate in a competitive environment. The first two of these were factors in *Black and Decker* and the first in *Raleigh*. The MMC also found that the third factor was present in both cases, but this conclusion has been criticized by Utton who argues that whilst the companies enjoyed large market share they did not enjoy great market power (Utton, M., 'Anti-competitive Practices and the Competition Act 1980' (1994) 39 *Antitrust Bulletin* 485).

Refusal to supply was also considered in *Fine Fragrances* (Cm 2380, 1993), in which the MMC accepted that, the reference products being marketed as luxury goods, 'the suppliers need to be able to control their distribution in order to protect the brand images which consumers evidently value' (para. 1.6). However, the refusal to supply retailers not meeting the criteria set by the fragrance houses was considered to constitute 'uncompetitive practices for the purpose of exploiting and maintaining the complex monopoly situation' (para. 8.63). If a company is to claim that a refusal to supply relates to the product's characteristics it will be expected to be able to justify thoroughly its position.

13.3.2 The essential facilities doctrine

An 'essential facility' is a facility or infrastructure without access to which competitors cannot provide services to their customers. 'The owner of an essential facility which uses its power in one market in order to protect or strengthen its position in another related market . . . imposing a competitive disadvantage on its competitor, infringes Article [82]' (*Sea Containers* v *Stena Sealink* 94/19 (1994) OJ L15/8, at para. 66). To date, in both the EC and the UK, the doctrine has been most prominent in decisions concerned with the operation of transport networks, although it is likely to have an increasing impact on the utilities and telecommunications sectors, especially in the context of deregulation.

Like many aspects of competition law the doctrine has its origins in American practice, and is traced to the case of *United States* v *Terminal Railroad Association* 224 US 383 (1912); USSCR 56 L Ed 810. In *Terminal Railroad* the 38 defendants, owners of a vital network of St Louis transport connections, denied non-owner railroads access to the facilities. Delivering the judgment of the court, Lurton MJ offered the defendants the option either of restructuring their mutual contracts so as to allow the admission of new firms into the network, or of dissolving the combination. While the court did not make explicit the creation of an essential facilities doctrine, it recognized the threat to competition posed by 'a unified system ... unless it is the impartial agent of all who [are compelled] to use its facilities' (at 405).

The operation of the doctrine was clarified by the court in *MCI Communications Corporation and MCI Telecommunications Corporation* v *American Telephone and Telegraph Company* 708 F.2d 1081 (1983). Here AT&T, a dominant telecommunications company, refused to interconnect MCI with the local distribution facilities of Bell operating companies, thus limiting the range of services that MCI could offer its customers. The court held that:

A monopolist's refusal to deal under these circumstances is governed by the so-called essential facilities doctrine. Such a refusal may be unlawful because a monopolist's control of an essential facility (sometimes called a 'bottleneck') can extend monopoly power from one stage of production to another, and from one market into another. Thus the antitrust laws have imposed on firms controlling an essential facility the obligation to make the facility available on non-discriminatory terms. (para. 31)

A four-fold test was put forward for the doctrine: '(1) control of the essential facility by a monopolist; (2) a competitor's inability practically or reasonably to duplicate the essential facility; (3) the denial of the use of the facility to a competitor; and (4) the feasibility of providing the facility' (para. 32). The focus on the denial of use means that the doctrine is better considered as a specific example of the wider category of cases in which there is a unilateral refusal to supply or deal.

The EC Commission has been keen to embrace the doctrine, which may be applicable under both arts 81 and 82 but is more likely to be of relevance to art. 82 cases as the holding of an essential facility is strong evidence of dominance.

In *British Midland/Aer Lingus* 92/213 (1992) OJ L96/34, the Commission found that those holding dominant positions should not 'withhold facilities which the industry traditionally provides to all other airlines'. Aer Lingus, the dominant undertaking in the market for the London/Dublin air route, was ordered to resume its interline facility with British Midland, having previously withdrawn it. Interlining is based on an agreement under which most of the world's airlines have authorized the others to sell their services, as a result of which travel agents can offer passengers a single ticket providing for transportation by different carriers. The Commission appeared to accept that such a facility could be withdrawn where the dominant airline could give an objective reason for its refusal to continue, such as, *inter alia*, concerns about creditworthiness (para. 26 of the decision), but in the present case no such reason could be advanced. At para. 30 of the decision the Commission's argument is crystallized:

Aer Lingus has not been able to point to efficiencies created by a refusal to interline nor to advance any other persuasive and legitimate business justification for its conduct. Its desire to avoid loss of market share, the circumstance that this is a route of vital importance to the company and that its operating margin is under pressure do not make this a legitimate response to new entry.

Similarities in approach to the American analysis are clear in this decision, as can be seen from a comparative examination of the case of *Otter Tail Power Company* v *United States* 410 US 366 (1973); USSCR 35 L Ed 2d 359.

In its *22nd Annual Report on Competition Policy* (1992, points 216–18) the Commission made it clear that the decision was taken with specific reference to a time period in which air transport was being liberalized, and argued that airlines making use of the new opportunities for competition should be given a fair chance to develop and sustain their challenge to established carriers. However, the duty on Aer Lingus was to be of a finite duration only, as new entrants should not be able to rely indefinitely on frequencies and services provided by their competitors.

A similar decision was taken by the Commission in *Port of Roscoff* (Commission Press Release IP (95) 492 of 16 May; [1995] 4 CMLR 677). Here the Morlaix Chamber of Commerce, in its capacity as port authority for Roscoff, denied Irish Continental Group (ICG) access to the port. The Commission required the authority to 'take the necessary steps to allow ICG access to the port'. In fact the parties had already reached an agreement subject to the resolution of certain technical requirements, governing access to the port, but the Commission clearly wished to establish strong precedents and guidelines in this area.

A step vital for the development of the essential facilities doctrine was made explicit in *B&I/Sealink, Holyhead* (*22nd Annual Report on Competition Policy* (1992), point 219). It will be recalled that for art. 82 to apply the allegedly dominant position must lie within 'a substantial part' of the EC. Some initial doubts were raised in relation to the doctrine on the grounds that a 'facility' could not constitute the requisite substantial part In *British Midland* the point was skirted, the Commission asserting merely that '[b]oth the UK and Ireland are substantial parts of the common market' (at para. 17). In *B&I* Sealink acted as port authority at Holyhead (the essential facility) in North Wales. The company instituted timetable changes which operated to the detriment of B&I and in favour of Sealink's own services. In particular, the loading and unloading of B&I services had to be interrupted to accommodate Sealink sailings. Indubitably Holyhead is *not* a substantial part of the common market. The Commission, recognizing that this was indeed the case, made clear that (emphasis added) 'it is important to stress that a port, an airport *or any other facility*, even if it is not itself a substantial part of the common market, may be considered as such in so far as reasonable access to the facility is indispensable for the exploitation of a transport route which is substantial'. Recognizing that this argument can extend to any infrastructure, and not merely to transport routes, the Commission stated that '[t]his consequence of Article [82] is of essential importance in the context of deregulation'.

It is important too that in both the American cases, such as *MCI* (above), and in *British Midland* it was considered significant that the offender's primary motivation for the exclusionary practice was the long-term detriment of the competitor. In *B&I* it would appear that while such a detriment was a *consequence* of Sealink's action there was little evidence that this was the primary *intention* of Sealink, which was rather to make the best use of its own resources. The requirement imposed in that case, that 'a company which both owns and uses an essential facility . . . should not grant its competitors access on terms less favourable than those which it gives its own services' (*22nd Annual Report on Competition Policy* (1992), point 219), is a stricter test both than that used in the American cases and than that suggested in *British Midland*.

Sealink also came to an arrangement with Sea Containers regarding access to Holyhead following Commission intervention. Subsequently the Commission instituted a formal proceeding, finding in favour of Sea Containers (*Sea Containers/ Stena Sealink* 94/19 (1994) OJ L15/8). The Commission expanded the doctrine further, suggesting that when a company 'is in a position such as that of Sealink in this case, it cannot normally expect to fulfil satisfactorily its duty to provide non-discriminatory access and to resolve its conflicts of interest unless it takes steps to separate its management of the essential facility from its use of it'. The point was not made as strongly as that in *Flughafen Frankfurt/Main AG* 98/190 (1998) OJ L72/31 although the Commission held that an undertaking that owned Frankfurt Airport could not use its property right in that airport and its physical infrastructure to exclude competitors in ancillary services such as baggage loading and cabin cleaning. In *Port of Rødby* 94/119 (1994) OJ L55/52 the principle was applied also to art. 86 EC.

Many of these Community cases could have been dealt with under the more general principles set out in other refusal to deal cases, and it thus appears, particularly in the light of comments in the annual competition reports, that the Commission took a conscious decision, in the face of moves towards deregulation, to introduce the essential facilities doctrine into Community law.

The leading case on the operation of the essential facilities doctrine is now that of *Oscar Bronner GmbH & Co. KG* v *Mediaprint Zeitungs-und-Zeitschriftenverlag GmbH & Co. KG* (case C–7/97 [1999] 4 CMLR 112). Here Advocate General Jacobs sounded a warning note about the expansion of the doctrine. In this case Bronner was the publisher in Austria of a daily newspaper, *der Standard*, with a market share of 3.6 per cent of circulation. Mediaprint was the publisher of papers with a combined market share of 46.8 per cent. Bronner argued that it could not feasibly develop its own home delivery service in view of its small market share, and that only such a delivery service would allow it to survive. It argued, in effect, that Mediaprint's delivery service constituted an 'essential facility' to which it should have access. Starting from the position that 'the right to choose one's trading partnersand freely to dispose of one's property are generally recognised principles in the laws of the Member States' and that 'incursions on those rights require careful justification' (para. 56) the Advocate General argued that 'intervention [under] an application of the essential facilities doctrine . . . can be justified in terms of competition policy only in cases in which the dominant undertaking has a genuine stranglehold on the related market' (para. 65). In this case the Advocate General's view was that Bronner had numerous, albeit less convenient, options open to it, and that to allow it to succeed in this case

would be to lead the Community and national authorities and courts into detailed regulation of the Community markets, entailing the fixing of prices and conditions for supply in large sections of the economy. Intervention on that scale would not only be unworkable but . . . also be anti-competitive in the longer term and indeed would scarcely be compatible with a free market economy.   (para. 69)

The Court followed this opinion in its judgment, holding in particular that 'it does not appear that there are any technical, legal or even economic obstacles capable of making it impossible, or even unreasonably difficult, for any other publishers of daily newspapers to establish, alone or in cooperation with other publishers, its own nationwide home delivery system' (para. 44).

The test that flows from the application of *Oscar Bronner* is in effect that set out by the Advocate General, commenting on a situation where a dominant company has a stranglehold on a related market. Such a situation, he suggested,

might be the case for example where duplication of the facility is impossible or extremely difficult owing to physical, geographical or legal constraints or is highly undesirable for reasons of public policy. It is not sufficient that the undertaking's control over a facility should give it a competitive advantage.

. . . the test in my view must be an objective one: in other words, in order for refusal of access to amount to an abuse, it must be extremely difficult not merely for the undertaking demanding access but for any other undertaking to compete. Thus if the cost of duplicating the facility alone is the barrier to entry, it must be such as to deter any prudent undertaking from entering the market. In that regard it seems to me that it will be necessary to consider all the circumstances, including the extent to which the dominant undertaking, having regard to the degree of amortisation of its investment and the cost of the upkeep must pass on investment or maintenance costs in the prices charged on the relevant market. (paras 65–6)

The key elements then are that: (1) access to the facility must be genuinely indispensable; (2) it is not possible practically to replicate the facility; (3) even by an undertaking of the same size and resources as the holder of the facility. It is not enough that without the facility the putative competitor would find it *difficult* to compete.

In *European Night Services* v *Commission* joined cases T–374/94, etc. [1998] ECR II–3141 the Court ruled that the Commission had taken too restrictive an approach in requiring that parties to a joint venture to 'supply services on their networks on the same technical and financial terms as they allow to [the joint venture]' (see *Night Services* 94/663 (1994) OJ L259/20). In particular the Court took the view that train crews could not constitute an essential facility. One of the more recent cases in which the Commission has been called upon to consider this area arose in 1999 in *Info-Lab/Ricoh* (*Competition Policy Newsletter* (1999) 1:35). Here the Commission, referring to the 'restrictive approach of the ECJ to the doctrine of "essential facilities" in [*Oscar Bronner*]', rejected a complaint by a provider of toner which had asked the Commission to oblige Ricoh to supply it with new empty toner cartridges which it could then fill in order to compete with Ricoh in the market for filled cartridges.

It is rare for the 'essential facilities' doctrine to be considered under general UK competition law, although it is fundamental to the 'special sector' regulation (and is a particular feature of the telecommunications licences), but one of the most significant reports produced by the OFT under the Competition Act 1980 was *Southern Vectis Omnibus Company Ltd* (OFT, 17 February 1988). This dealt with the refusal of the Southern Vectis Bus Company to allow its competitors access to Newport bus station, on the Isle of Wight, with the exception of those operators that had made such arrangements prior to October 1986. The bus station was of course a legacy of the highly controlled bus market prior to the deregulation initiative, which had been 'inherited' by Southern Vectis. In this case the barrier was one both of cost and of government action (exactly the sort of barrier of concern to the Chicago school). As the OFT noted:

A new bus operator ... will not wish to duplicate the facilities of a bus station owned and operated by a competitor since this is likely significantly to increase the costs of entry, and in any case may well be impractical in terms of planning permission and site availability. (para. 3.6)

Following its own survey and inquiries the OFT rejected the argument put forward by Southern Vectis that there was no capacity at the station that would permit the entry of other operators. The OFT was concerned that the effect of the policy would be permanently to exclude effective competition, the presence of which would likely switch revenue from the incumbent to the entrant. As regards the operation of bus stations, a distinction was drawn by the Transport Act 1985 between those which had been publicly owned and those in the private sector. The former were governed by s. 82 of the Act, which prohibited discrimination against any service; the latter were affected by s. 116(1) of the Act, which brought within the scope of general competition law all bus stations irrespective of ownership. In the 1984 White Paper on Buses (Cmnd. 9300, July 1984) the point was made that:

If competition is to flourish, no operator should be in control of a bus station of a size or strategic position which would allow him to gain an unfair advantage by excluding other operators. The Government believes that major bus stations should be operated whether in private or public ownership on a commercial basis under arrangements which will provide for all operators to have equal opportunity of gaining access to them. (para. 5.16)

In *Cross Solent Ferries* (MMC, 1992) a similar situation relating to access to ports was considered. Here the MMC noted that the relevant statutory regime served to set conditions under which access to certain classes of ports would be granted to operators (by virtue of the Harbour Docks and Pier Clauses Act 1847, s. 33 and the Harbours Act 1964, s. 27), but pointed to a successful recent entrant as evidence that even private ownership of such facilities by an incumbent did not create an absolute barrier to entry.

14

An introduction to the economics of merger control

14.1 Introduction

Even those commentators and analysts who would argue that competition law should be greatly curtailed on the grounds that its application causes more harm than good would in most cases support the existence of some form of merger control. However the economics of merger control is not a matter that has been subject to a great deal of scrutiny until recently (for general discussions about the economics of mergers see in particular the treatment in Neumann, M., *Competition Policy: History, Theory and Practice*, Cheltenham, Edward Elgar (2001), pp. 110–34, and Scherer, F. M., and Ross, D., *Industrial Market Structure and Economic Performance*, Boston, Houghton Mifflin (3rd edn, 1990), pp. 155–98). In this brief chapter we will deal with the key arguments that underpin the policy goals behind merger control. In essence these relate to two factors: first, the creation or extension of monopoly power, including the raising of barriers to entry for potential competitors; and secondly increasing the scope for collusion in a market which, post-merger, will be more oligopolistic and less competitive than was the market pre-merger. It will be noted that the first of these two factors is related to the control of dominant firm conduct, and that, as we have already seen, dominance itself is not condemned in either the EC or the UK. Nevertheless in merger control we find a situation where the attainment or extension of dominance may be condemned.

The greatest procedural difference between merger control and the control of dominance post-merger is that any analysis of a merger will usually be undertaken *ex ante*, and any assessment of dominant firm behaviour will always be made *ex post*. The assessment of individual mergers may therefore be particularly contentious as the undertakings concerned and the authorities are arguing on the basis of *anticipated*, rather than *actual*, results, and the scope of the transactions concerned are sometimes highly substantial.

For the present purposes the term 'merger' will be taken to refer to any situation in which the ownership of two or more undertakings is joined together. In the world of business the process that may lead to this joining of ownership may take many different forms, and may be either amicable and consensual, or unwelcome and hostile. In Community law the term used in preference to 'merger' is 'concentration' and a concentration is deemed to arise where 'two or more previously independent undertakings merge' (Regulation 4064/89, art. 3(1)(a)), or where an undertaking or person controlling an undertaking acquires control of another undertaking (art. 3(1)(b)). The law relating to these tests is dealt with in Chapter 15.

Mergers may take place either vertically or horizontally. The latter case, which will typically be of more concern to the competition authorities, arises where firms in the same industry, dealing in the same goods or services in the same geographical market, merge. A third type of merger, a conglomerate merger, may also be identified. A conglomerate merger is one in which firms produce products which are not in the same market, but which may to a greater or lesser extent be substitutes for each other. Although merger activity tends to fluctuate depending on the state of the economy and of the structure of particular industries the statistics show that the majority of mergers are horizontal ones, although in the 1960s there was in the United States a wave of conglomerate mergers in response to the harsh line being taken towards horizontal mergers by the antitrust authorities.

Mergers take place, like most business moves, primarily in order to increase profits. This may come about either because the effect of the merger is to reduce competition between the participants to the merger, or where the merger leads to cost savings through the gaining of efficiencies as a result of the joining of assets and fixed factors of production, allowing prices to be reduced and market shares to be increased. Increased concentration however will not inevitably lead to increased profits, and in some situations it may be demonstrated that the combined profits of a merged entity might be lower than the profits of the two independent undertakings were pre-merger. The argument whereby this result is achieved is a technical one.

A merger might have advantages over other forms of expansion (internal growth is an alternative to a merger). If an undertaking is seeking to increase its market share, the alternative to a merger is to expand production unilaterally. The result of this will be to lead to lower prices across the industry, and lower profit margins, and the ultimate impact on market shares will be uncertain *ex ante*. A merger may have particular advantages when an undertaking wishes to diversify into a market in which it is not presently based, overcoming barriers to entry, and again avoiding intense competition should the incumbent choose to defend its territory. Mergers also allow a much quicker, and certain response than does a strategy of internal growth. It might take only three months for a significant merger to yield results, but several years for the same results to be achieved by way of a 'competitive' process.

Mergers may also be undertaken for other reasons than merely to increase profits. In uncertain markets a merger may reflect differing views on future market performance among differing entrepreneurs. One owner may take a dim view of long-term market prospects, and another may anticipate brighter prospects. This might lead the former to be susceptible to offers from the latter. In some cases mergers might be driven by the desire of business leaders to manage a larger entity, and perhaps to operate at a global, rather than local, level. Even in this case however the rational entrepreneur would be presumed still to be making profit-maximizing decisions.

The fact that mergers take place for diverse reasons, and that the outcomes cannot be certain, suggests that a per se rule prohibiting mergers should be rejected, and that mergers should be assessed on a case-by-case basis. This is the process that exists in the EC and the UK, as well as the USA, although in the case of horizontal mergers there are some presumptions relating to the size of market shares pre- and post-merger which may come into play.

14.2 Horizontal mergers

Horizontal mergers may be substitutable for cartels, and Neumann points to the fact that 'in the US, after cartels were declared illegal by the Sherman Act, they were replaced by mergers which could more effectively be defended by invoking the rule of reason' (above, p. 113). The very fact that this is true suggests that horizontal mergers should be treated with some suspicion. However, the position is not a straightforward one. Cartels may self-destruct, but will in most cases be less efficient than mergers. Mergers are likely to be more efficient than cartels as they may generate economies of scale and of scope, but they are structurally embedded in a way that cartels are not. The key issue with horizontal mergers is that they may allow market power to be wielded, either by single-firm monopolists, or by collusive oligopolies.

14.2.1 The creation of a monopoly

The situation in which a merger creates a single-firm monopoly, or adds to the power of a single-firm monopoly, is relatively straightforward, and follows the relevant economic processes concerning monopoly conduct. Where the effect of a merger is to substantially lessen competition, or to create or strengthen a dominant position as a result of which competition will be impaired, the merger is likely to be blocked. As we have seen in relation to monopolies, and noted above, harm may be presumed to flow from the mere fact of the existence of a monopoly. However, as there are substantial harms in misapplying regulation or competition-law solutions to what may be later shown to have been efficient conduct, and as most monopolies will over time be eroded, the existence of monopoly itself is not condemned. However, in the case where it can be clearly demonstrated that a single, preventable, transaction will lead to the creation of a monopoly there are strong policy reasons why that transaction should be prevented. Of course the analysis needed to demonstrate that a monopoly will be created is not always straightforward, and the concept of market definition was first developed by the competition authorities to deal with the issue of whether a 'relevant market' was being monopolized as a result of a merger. These issues are best left to economics, and whilst the role of a legal team is likely to be of paramount importance in the process of any substantial merger, the role in relation to the substantive test of the merger's effect is likely to be marginal.

14.2.2 Oligopolistic coordination

The second area of concern, that a merger will lead to a more concentrated market in which oligopolistic collusion will be facilitated, is both theoretically and practically a difficult one. The basic danger is noted in the US DOJ *Horizontal Merger Guidelines* of 1992, s. 2.1:

A merger may diminish competition by enabling firms in the relevant market more likely, more successfully, or more completely to engage in coordinated interaction that harms consumers. Coordinated interaction is comprised of actions by a group of firms that are profitable for each of them only as a result of the accommodating reactions of the others. This behaviour includes tacit or express collusion, and may or may not be lawful in and of itself.

The economic issues that arise in these cases have been examined in a number of decisions taken in the EC. These are considered in the section on 'joint dominance' in the next chapter. The EC Commission has developed a 'checklist' of factors that it considers to be relevant to a finding of a situation in which an oligopoly can successfully coordinate action. In these cases, if the factors arise only following a merger, that merger is likely to be blocked. The factors highlighted are: concentration (probably up to a maximum of three firms), product homogeneity, symmetry of market shares and costs, transparency in pricing, the ease with which a firm may retaliate to another's competitive action, barriers to entry, inelastic demand, and absence of buyer power. It is also important that the market be relatively stable and mature. However, each of these factors should be considered carefully, as any industry is likely to show some of these features, and even if the majority of these factors are present an analysis sensitive to the particular conditions of the relevant market is necessary to determine if collusive conduct is likely to follow.

The collusion itself may take various forms. Most typically it would take the form of increasing prices, as was feared would be the case in the *Gencor/Lonhro* merger (97/26 (1997) OJ L11/30). Alternatively, as in *Airtours/First Choice* 2000/276 (2000) OJ L93/1 it may take the form of reducing capacity, or production, with the end result of increasing prices albeit in a competitive structure where price competition still existed; or it may take the form of market sharing. In each case different conditions must exist in order for such collusion to be effective. When analysing the possibility for collusion it is necessary to consider the problem in four stages. First, a plausible mechanism whereby collusion can take place must be identified. Secondly, the market must be analysed to determine whether it has within it characteristics or features which would support the suggested collusive mechanism. The third step is to identify whether those particular features exist in the particular case under consideration. The fourth step is to consider whether evidence of past conduct is suggestive that a collusive outcome might emerge in the new market situation. For example, in *Gencor/Lonhro* the Commission was concerned that there was evidence of previous collusive activity in the South African mining industry.

14.2.3 **The failing firm defence**

An argument is sometimes made that a merger which 'saves' a failing firm should not be blocked, on the grounds that were it not for the merger the market would both be more concentrated following the exit of the failing firm, and there would be social costs to this failure. Thus in the US DOJ *Horizontal Merger Guidelines* of 1992, s. 5.0 we find:

A merger is not likely to create or enhance market power or to facilitate its exercise, if imminent failure . . . of one of the merging firms would cause the assets of that firm to exit the relevant market. In such circumstances, post-merger performance in the relevant market may be no worse than market performance had the merger been blocked and the assets left the market.

This argument underlay the Competition Commission inquiry into the Air Canada and Canadian Airlines Corporation merger (Cm. 4838, August 2000). Here the Canadian Airlines Corporation would 'sooner or later run out of money' (report, para. 2.13) were it not saved by the merger. Although the Competition Commission was concerned about the reduction in competition on transatlantic routes from the UK to Canada following the merger it accepted that these were the result not directly of the merger, but of the fact that one of the parties was going out of business.

14.3 **Vertical mergers**

Vertical mergers generally give rise to less economic concern than do horizontal mergers, although

Vertical mergers can make entry more difficult by foreclosing rivals from previously independent firms at either the vertical level, by increasing capital requirements associated with entry and by promoting product differentiation. A vertically integrated oligopoly is insulated from competitive pressures that come from vertically related, competitive levels. This makes oligopolistic output coordination easier. (Martin, S., *Industrial Economics*, New York, Macmillan (2nd edn, 1994), p. 309)

Vertical mergers will not further concentrate a market, and the danger most often identified is that, as Martin suggests, they might foreclose a market to competition. For example, if a television broadcast network were to merge with a film production studio competing networks may find it more difficult to obtain product to transmit, and might therefore find it harder to compete for viewers. Where both of the relevant vertical markets are competitive there is likely to be no competitive harm from a vertical merger, and the presumption should instead be that the firms are merging as they have identified efficiencies of doing so that competition will force them to pass on to the consumer.

The process whereby oligopolistic collusion might be facilitated by vertical mergers is not immediately intuitive. However, the problem may be explained clearly by way of an example. Consider the situation where a four-firm oligopoly packages 85 per cent of the budget short-haul foreign package holidays sold to holiday-makers in a particular territory, but that these holidays are marketed by 20 independent chains of retailers, some of which have very large customer bases. Competition between these chains for custom, and the buying power that some of them are able to exercise, should compel the four firms producing the product to compete for their patronage, and should therefore dampen the adverse effects of there being a narrow oligopoly. If on the other hand each of the four firms bought four retail chains the position would be somewhat different, and it is likely that the oligopoly would be able more effectively to coordinate at all levels of the chain, raising prices to end consumers. Vertical integration may therefore be an essential condition for an oligopoly successfully to exploit its market power. However, such concerns will normally arise only where both markets, upstream and downstream, are concentrated, and where entry barriers are significant. The fact remains that the great majority of vertical mergers are not seriously challenged by the application of merger control procedures.

15

Merger control and joint ventures

15.1 Introduction

This chapter provides an outline of the application of competition law to mergers and joint ventures, and the basis for further study of these complex areas. The majority of competition law regimes give a prominent place to the control of mergers, which cannot be treated in the same way as other anti-competitive practices. The latter are normally dealt with once the practice has taken place, although there may be some situations in which prior notifications are made. Mergers are better dealt with prior to their occurring, as it can be very difficult, and tremendously costly, to disentangle a merger once it has taken place. Generally the approach is to require mergers above certain thresholds to be notified to the relevant authority, which then examines the likely impact of that merger in the light of the applicable criteria before determining whether the merger can proceed or not. It will often be the case that mergers will be cleared as long as certain conditions are met, which might include the offloading of certain parts of the newly combined enterprise, the selling of specific brands, or commitments as to price restraints. The approach to mergers in the European Community should take into consideration, in particular, the development of the single internal market. As the importance of national markets is reduced and the importance of the single market increased, one inevitable response has been an increase in mergers. A market of approximately 400 million consumers, and consisting of 15 states, cannot be approached by companies in the same way as much smaller national markets and companies need to be given the chance to restructure to meet the challenges. This fact informs much of the policy and application of the law at Community level, and is reflected in the preamble to the Merger Regulation (see below), which notes both that 'the dismantling of internal frontiers is resulting and will continue to result in major corporate reorganisations in the Community, particularly in the form of concentrations' (recital 3), and that 'it must be ensured that the process of reorganisation does not result in lasting damage to competition' (recital 5).

A joint venture is a form of arrangement between undertakings that is designed to facilitate long-term cooperation. Joint ventures are dealt with in this chapter because, at Community level, they are so closely related to merger control. At Community level a distinction is drawn between joint ventures which are 'concentrative' and fall to be dealt with under the merger regime, and those which fall within the direct framework of art. 81 EC. In the United Kingdom there is no specific legal entity recognized as a joint venture, although various vehicles are available to companies seeking to implement such an arrangement.

15.2 Merger control in the European Community

15.2.1 The application of articles 81 and 82

Articles 81 and 82 do not, explicitly, provide for the control of mergers, and for some time the general consensus was that they could not be so used. This view was given added weight by the fact that mergers were expressly dealt with in the earlier European Coal and Steel Community (ECSC) Treaty at art. 66. However, the application by the Commission of first art. 82 and then art. 81 to merger situations, and the approval of this action by the ECJ, confirmed that Community law could be applied to mergers.

The first such action, taken under art. 82, was in the *Continental Can* case (Europemballage Corp. and Continental Can Co. v *Commission* case 6/72 [1973] CMLR 199). The relevant facts were that Continental Can was a packaging company based in America with large interests in Europe. Continental Can was largely responsible for setting up another company, Europemballage, created for the purpose of bringing together a number of other European companies in the same market. Europemballage then made a takeover bid for Thomassen & Drijver Verblifa (TDV), which was accepted. Following the intervention of the Commission, which indicated to the parties that they might be in breach of art. 82, the deal nevertheless went ahead. The Commission, by a decision, found that the article had been breached and ordered that steps be taken to bring the infringement to an end (*Re Continental Can Co. Inc.* 72/21 (1972) OJ L7/25). Although the case was rejected by the ECJ on the grounds that the Commission had failed to define adequately the relevant market (see the discussion of this point in Chapter 11), the Court confirmed that the article could be applied to takeover, and thus by implication to merger, situations. The Court was not persuaded that the inclusion of an explicit merger provision in the ECSC Treaty and its non-inclusion in the EEC Treaty meant that mergers could not be reviewed under Community law. The Court adopted an expansive approach where it considered not only the explicit words of arts 81 and 82, but also the requirement set out in art. 3(g) that competition in the common market not be distorted. Such a distortion would indeed have arisen in this case, and the Commission's argument was that the takeover and consolidation of the market were facilitated by the dominant position held on the market by Continental Can. Coupled with the ability of the Commission to order interim measures within the ambit of the Court's judgment in *Camera Care Ltd* v *Commission* case 792/79R [1980] 1 CMLR 334, this gave the Commission the ostensible authority to order that contemplated mergers should not be completed until it had reviewed the situation. Such uncertainty often means the death of merger plans, and merger documents frequently incorporate a clause that provides that in the event of regulatory intervention the merger shall not proceed.

In *BAT Ltd and RJ Reynolds Industries Inc* v *Commission* cases 142 & 156/84 [1988] 4 CMLR 24, the Commission considered the application of art. 81 to an agreement between cigarette manufacturers including Rembrandt Group, which had a controlling interest in Rothmans, and Philip Morris which would have given Philip Morris a strong degree of control over the Rembrandt tobacco division. The two parties had notified their agreement to the Commission, which following negotiations and modification to reduce the level of control exercised by Philip Morris, met with the Commission's approval. The mere fact that the parties themselves had chosen to notify seeking an art. 81(3) exemption or negative clearance is evidence of the awareness of industry of the likely application of art. 81 to such situations. BAT and Reynolds, two large competing companies, brought an action before the ECJ on the basis of art. 230 to contest the Commission's decision. Although the Court rejected the argument made by the two applicants on the grounds that it could not be shown that the agreement carried the necessary restrictions on competition to fall within art. 81(1), the Court nevertheless held generally that agreements which lead to concentrations in the market could be reviewed in the light of art. 81 and could fall within the prohibition.

These developments led to a substantial degree of uncertainty for mergers taking place within the Community, and raised the prospect that a clearance by a national authority could be followed by condemnation by the EC Commission, with the serious consequences that that would entail. It was pointed out in particular that the application of art. 81(2) to any fully implemented merger could have disastrous and destructive consequences. Accordingly the EC Commission brought forward proposals to introduce a specific measure to clarify the position. This resulted in the enactment of Regulation 4064/89 on the Control of Concentrations Between Undertakings ((1989) OJ L395/1—because of a substantial number of errors in the original printed version the Regulation was reprinted at (1990) OJ L257/13), which entered into force on 21 September 1990; Regulation 4064/89 was amended by Regulation 1310/97 (1997) OJ L180/1. Any merger falling within the scope of the merger regulation cannot now be separately reviewed under either art. 81 or art. 82.

15.2.2 **Regulation 4064/89**

The primary purpose of the Regulation was to provide a 'one-stop shop', reducing the uncertainty facing companies contemplating mergers by requiring them to seek approval exclusively from the Commission where the merger took a 'Community dimension'. For the purposes of the Regulation mergers have a Community dimension where:

(a)   the combined aggregate worldwide turnover of all the undertakings concerned is more than ECU 5,000 million; and

(b)   the aggregate Community-wide turnover of each of at least two of the undertakings concerned is more than ECU 250 million, unless each of the undertakings concerned achieves more than two-thirds of its aggregate Community-wide turnover within one and the same Member State.   (art. 1(2))

The threshold criteria were significantly higher than those that had been sought by the Commission and were subsequently reviewed, with the Commission arguing for a reduction in the amounts. In 1996 the Commission issued a Green Paper which proposed that the thresholds be reduced to a world-wide turnover level of ECU 2bn, and a Community level of ECU 100m. Instead of adopting such a straightforward requirement the Council, led by the UK but with the active support of France and Germany, resisted this move. In the 1997 amendment the basic requirement was left intact, but additional jurisdiction was given to the Commission under a complicated formula in new art. 1(3). This is as follows:

For the purposes of this Regulation, a concentration that does not meet the thresholds laid down in paragraph 2 has a Community dimension where:

(a)   the combined aggregate worldwide turnover of all the undertakings concerned is more than ECU 2,500 million;

(b)   in each of at least three Member States, the combined aggregate turnover of all the undertakings concerned is more than ECU 100 million;

(c)   in each of at least three Member States included for the purpose of point (b), the aggregate turnover of each of at least two of the undertakings concerned is more than ECU 25 million; and

(d)   the aggregate Community-wide turnover of each of at least two of the undertakings concerned is more than ECU 100 million;

unless each of the undertakings concerned achieves more than two-thirds of its aggregate Community-wide turnover within one and the same Member State.

This new text is designed to bring within its ambit mergers that would have been faced with multiple notifications in the individual Member States, although at the time the amendment was introduced the Commission indicated that only 10 extra cases a year would fall within the new provision.

Because the formula is not an obviously easy one to apply, a simple example of its application is given here (Figure 15.1). Many other permutations to that following are possible.

This example is taken, with permission, from Cook, C. J., and Kerse, C. S., *EC Merger Control*, Sweet & Maxwell (3rd edn, 2000), p. 63, which is the leading practitioner text in this area, and should be referred to for further detail of the operation of the Merger Regulation.

The 'two-thirds' rule set out at (d) below is designed to leave to Member States those situations in which the effects of the merger will be very substantially felt within that state, even though these may also be situations in which the Community as a

Figure 15.1 Application of operation of Regulation 4064/89, as amended

Turnover (€ m)	A	B
Worldwide	3,500	2,000
Community-Wide	1,500	200
Germany	75	100
France	110	15
Italy	100	30
United Kingdom	1,200	30
Netherlands	15	25
Two-thirds earned in one MS	Yes, UK	No

The acquisition of undertaking B by undertaking A (the two undertakings concerned) would not fall within the original jurisdiction of the Commission because B does not earn 250 million euro turnover in the Community. The acquisition would, however, be caught by the additional thresholds since:

(a) A and B each earns more than 100 million euro from sales in the Community (art. 1(3)(d) is satisfied);

(b) the combined aggregate turnover of A and B exceeds 100 million euro in four Member States (France, Germany, Italy, and the United Kingdom) (art. 1(3)(b) is satisfied);

(c) the aggregate turnover of each of A and B is more than 25 million euro in Germany, Italy, and the United Kingdom (art. 1(3)(c) is satisfied); and

(d) the two-thirds proviso does not apply since B does not earn more than two-thirds of the Community turnover in the United Kingdom (or, indeed, any Member State) even though the acquirer A does.

Source: C. J. Cook and C. S. Kerse, *EC Merger Control*, Sweet & Maxwell (3rd edn, 2000), p. 63. Reproduced with permission.

whole is affected. However, the test can produce unwelcome results. This was most clearly demonstrated in 1992 when two companies, Lloyds, and the Hong Kong and Shanghai Banking Corporation (HSBC), were bidding for Midland Bank. The proposed takeover between Lloyds and Midland fell outside the Regulation, as in the case of both companies more than two-thirds of their turnover was in the UK; HSBC, on the other hand, did not have two-thirds of its turnover in the UK, and accordingly its bid fell to be considered by the Commission within the terms of the Regulation. When the Lloyds bid was referred to the MMC it collapsed, and in effect the Community consideration of the HSBC bid gave it a substantial advantage; having satisfied the Commission as to the nature of the concentration, it was this bid which was successful.

There is no territorial limit placed on the application of these criteria. The effect of this is that a merger between two American companies will fall within the scope of the Regulation as long as either of the thresholds is met. This was the case in *Boeing*; and in *Gencor/Lonhro* 97/26 (1997) OJ L11/30 the merger of two South African companies was subjected to scrutiny under the Regulation (see Chapter 18). Concentrations which have the Community dimension are removed from the jurisdiction of the individual Member States by virtue of art. 21(2) of the Regulation, which provides that 'No Member State shall apply its national legislation on competition to any concentration that has a Community dimension'. Exceptions are made for the protection of 'legitimate interests other than those taken into consideration' by the Regulation; such considerations include in particular 'public security' and 'plurality of the media' (art. 21(3)).

Concentrations falling within the Regulation are to be notified to the Commission on Form CO (see Commission Regulation 447/98 on the notifications, time limits, and hearings provided for in Council Regulation 4064/89, (1998) OJ L61/1)), 'not more than one week after the conclusion of the agreement, or the announcement of the public bid, or the acquisition of a controlling interest' (art. 4(1)). If the Commission finds that the concentration falls within the scope of the Regulation it shall make the notification public (art. 4(3)). 'Concentration' is defined in art. 3, which provides in part that:

1. A concentration shall be deemed to arise where:
    (a) two or more previously independent undertakings merge, or
    (b) one or more persons already controlling at least one undertaking, or one or more undertakings acquire, whether by purchase of securities or assets, by contract or by any other means, direct or indirect control of the whole or parts of one or more other undertakings.

The key power of the Commission is set out in art. 2 of the Regulation, the appropriate part of which is as follows:

1. Concentrations within the scope of this Regulation shall be appraised in accordance with the following provisions with a view to establishing whether or not they are compatible with the common market.
    In making this appraisal, the Commission shall take into account:
    (a) the need to maintain and develop effective competition within the common market in view of, among other things, the structure of all the markets concerned and the actual or potential competition from undertakings located either within or without the Community;
    (b) the market position of the undertakings concerned and their economic and financial power, the alternatives available to suppliers and users, their access to supplies or markets, any legal or other barriers to entry, supply and demand trends for the relevant goods and services, the interests of the intermediate and ultimate consumers, and the development of technical and economic progress provided that it is to consumers' advantage and does not form an obstacle to competition.

2. A concentration which does not create or strengthen a dominant position as a result of which effective competition would be significantly impeded in the common market or in a substantial part of it shall be declared compatible with the common market.

3. A concentration which creates or strengthens a dominant position as a result of which effective competition would be significantly impeded in the common market or in a substantial part of it shall be declared incompatible with the common market.

Article 2(4) makes special provision in respect of joint ventures and is discussed below.

Mergers that fall to be considered within the scope of the Regulation should not be consummated without being examined by the Commission. This is provided for in art. 7(1):

1. A concentration as defined in Article 1 shall not be put into effect either before its notification or until it has been declared compatible with the common market pursuant to a decision under Article 6(1)(b) or Article 8(2) or on the basis of a presumption according to Article 10(6).

An agreement or transaction which is carried out in contravention of this basic principle will be invalid if the Commission later rules against the concentration (art. 7(5)). It is unlikely that such a scenario would arise, given the adverse consequences that would flow from such a situation although there have been a small number of cases in which the Commission has imposed fines under art. 14 of the Regulation following failure to notify (see, e.g., *A. P. Møller* [1999] 4 CMLR 392). However, where companies are determined to press ahead, and can show good reason, the suspensory effect of the Regulation may be set aside on application to the Commission.

Initially the Commission may adopt one of three positions in relation to the notified concentration. These are:

(a) that it does not fall within the scope of the Regulation (art. 6(1)(a));

(b) that it falls within the scope of the Regulation but does not raise serious concerns and will not be opposed (art. 6(1)(b)); and

(c) that it both falls within the scope of the Regulation and raises serious concerns, and that the Commission intends to take open full proceedings (art. 6(1)(c)—these are generally known as 'Phase II Proceedings').

Obviously it is this last eventuality that will be of concern to notifying undertakings. However, if such a decision is taken it does not mean that the concentration will necessarily be condemned, as the Commission may go on to find that the concentration falls within art. 2(2), and may 'issue a decision declaring the concentration compatible with the common market' (art. 8(2)). Any decision taken under this article may have conditions attached to it. In the alternative, the Commission will issue a decision declaring that the concentration is incompatible with the common market (art. 8(3)). In these cases, if the concentration has already been implemented, the Commission may 'require the undertakings or assets brought together to be separated or the cessation of joint control or any other action that may be appropriate in order to restore conditions of effective competition' (art. 8(4)).

The Commission is required to act within strict time limits in its application of the Regulation. It must, for example, 'examine the notification as soon as it is received' (art. 6(1)), and must take the initial decision as to whether it intends to initiate proceedings under art. 6(1)(c) within one month of the notification (art. 10(1)), although this period may be extended to six weeks where a Member State intervenes under art. 9(2) (see below). Final decisions as to whether the concentration is compatible or incompatible with the common market must be taken 'within not more than four months of the date on which proceedings are initiated' (art. 10(3)). The Regulation removes concentrations falling within its scope from the application of Regulation 17 (art. 22(1)), and also provides (at art. 22(1)) that it 'alone shall apply to concentrations as defined in Article 3'. It is thus ensured that arts 81 and 82 of the EC Treaty will not be independently applied to any concentration falling within the scope of the Regulation. Simultaneously the Regulation establishes its own procedural provisions relating to investigations (arts 11–13) and penalties (arts 14–15), which in most significant details match those of Regulation 17.

In 2000 the Commission published its *Merger Control (Simplified Procedure) Notice* (2000) OJ L217/32 which aims to provide a streamlined procedure in respect of categories of mergers that do not normally raise any substantive doubts.

The Regulation has appeared to be successful, so much so that businesses appear keen to structure mergers deliberately so as to bring them within the scope of the Regulation, thus ensuring that they cease to become reviewable by all those states whose national authorities are charged with exercising merger control. A survey of businesses undertaken for the Commission found that industry was 'broadly in favour of lower thresholds', and the Commission itself reported in its *1993 Annual Report* that there have been 'many cases having a strong impact on competitive conditions in the Community but falling below the existing thresholds' (see points 43–73). Plans to reform the merger regime are dealt with below.

15.2.3 Joint dominance

The issue of joint dominance is dealt with here in relation to merger cases, and in Chapter 11 in relation to art. 82 cases, although there are strong links between the two threads.

It has been noted above that under the terms of art. 1 of the Merger Regulation, the test of a merger's acceptability is that of whether it 'creates or strengthens a dominant position as a result of which effective competition would be significantly impeded'. It is not necessary for this dominant position to be held by only one party, and in view of the fact that art. 82 makes explicit reference to a dominant position held by 'one or more undertakings', the EC Commission, assisted by the Court, has developed the law of 'joint', or 'collective' dominance. The economics of this area is briefly introduced in the preceeding Chapter (see 'Oligopolistic coordination'). The starting point in this respect is that of *Kali und Salz*, case IV/M080 (1994) OJ L186/38, on appeal *France v EC Commission* case C–68/94 and *Société Commerciale des Potasses et de l'Azote (SCPA) and Entreprise Minière et Chimique (EMC) v Commission* case C–30/95 [1998] 4 CMLR 829, in which a proposed joint venture was blocked on the grounds that it 'would lead to a situation of oligopolistic dominance'. This decision was affected by the fact that the products concerned were potash and rock salt (i.e., they were homogenous), and that the joint venture would be matched by only one other Community producer in the relevant geographic market. There were close links between the relevant undertakings already.

Although the decision was overturned by the CFI, the Court accepted the basic argument that the Regulation could extend to positions of joint dominance.

The difficulty left by this case was that the Commission had made explicit reference to the fact that there were 'economic links' between the various undertakings, and it left open the question of whether it was an essential feature of such a situation that there be these economic links. Joint dominance is also sometimes referred to as 'oligopolistic dominance', and this term gives a clearer indication of the problems that may be encountered in markets in which there are fewer players, and which tend towards conscious parallelism, even if not towards concerted practices. If the number of firms in a concentrated market is reduced by way of a merger, a possible effect is that such conscious parallelism becomes more likely. This will be the case, in particular, where the market is highly concentrated, where the product is homogenous, and where the market is a transparent one.

This problem was tackled by the EC Commission in *Gencor/Lonhro* 97/26 (1997) OJ L11/30 (on appeal *Gencor Ltd v Commission* case T–102/96 [1999] 4 CMLR 971). Here the Commission had argued that collective dominance

> can occur where a mere adaptation by members of the oligopoly to market conditions causes anti-competitive parallel behaviour whereby the oligopoly becomes dominant. Active collusion would therefore not be required for members of the oligopoly to become dominant and to behave to an appreciable extent independently of their remaining competitors, their customers and, ultimately, their consumers. (para. 140)

In this case the relevant market was that for platinum and rhodium, world-wide, and there were only three significant competitors, all based in South Africa. Following the merger there would be only two, and there was a history of parallelism in the South African market. The CFI agreed with the Commission that it was not necessary to demonstrate that there were any economic links between the undertakings, as long as there was economic interdependence. Thus the CFI held that

> there is no reason whatsoever in legal or economic terms to exclude from the notion of economic links the relationship of interdependence existing between the parties to a tight oligopoly within which, in a market with the appropriate characteristics, in particular in terms of market concentration, transparency and product homogeneity, those parties are in a strong position to anticipate one another's behaviour and are therefore strongly encouraged to align their conduct in the market, in particular in such a way as to maximise their joint profits by restricting production with a view to increasing prices. In such a context each trader is aware that highly competitive action on its part designed to increase its market share (for example, a price cut) would provoke identical action by the others, so that it would derive no benefit from its initiative. (paras 104–5)

In *Price Waterhouse/Coopers and Lybrand* 1999/152 (1999) OJ L50/27, the Commission recognized that some of the elements that had been at play in *Gencor/Lonhro* were factors in the accountancy market. However, it considered the possibility of joint dominance arising in a post-merger market of five, and held that 'collective dominance involving more than three or four suppliers is unlikely because of the complexity of the interrelationships involved, and the consequent temptation to deviate' (see paras 94–119).

A key, and to some surprising, decision in this context is that of *Airtours/ First Choice* 2000/276 (2000) OJ L93/1 in which the Commission blocked a merger between two companies operating in the UK market for short-haul foreign package holidays, travel agency services, and the supply to tour operators of seats on charter flights to short-haul destinations. The Commission set out the conditions that need to be in place for a finding of collective dominance to be sustained. These include: product homogeneity; low demand growth; low price sensitivity of demand; similar cost structures of the main suppliers; substantial entry barriers; and insignificant countervailing power (para. 87). In response to concerns raised by Airtours, the Commission went out of its way to emphasize that joint dominance does not require that there be any active collusion between the parties, indicating at para. 53 of the decision that 'active collusive conduct of any kind is not a prerequisite for collective dominance to occur. It is sufficient that adaptation to market conditions causes an anti-competitive outcome'. What is most surprising about this decision is that the market is a very dynamic one, into which entry would appear possible. In its regular newsletter the consultancy firm NERA noted:

the real element of surprise in the Airtours case concerns the nature of the industry involved. Unlike platinum or potash, package holidays are differentiated, branded consumer products. Furthermore, a brief look at the history of the industry indicates a market in which there has been a huge variability in supplier shares and profitability and in which high profile exits (such as the collapse of the industry number two ILG in the early 1990s) have been counterbalanced by instances of equally dramatic entry and growth.

Joint dominance was also discussed in the context of art. 82 in *Irish Sugar* 97/624 (1997) OJ L258/1, on appeal *Irish Sugar plc* v *Commission* case T–228/97 [1999] 5 CMLR 1300, paras 38–68. Here it was accepted by all that for joint dominance to exist 'there must be close links between the two entities, and that those links must be such as to be capable of leading to the adoption of the same conduct and policy on the market in question' (para. 45, citing *Almelo* v *Energiebedrijf Ijsselmij* case C–393/92 [1994] ECR I–1477, and *Compagnie Maritime Belge Transports* v *Commission* joined cases T24–26 & 28/93 [1997] 4 CMLR 273).

15.2.4 **Economic assessment of mergers**

The Commission has established a 'Merger Task Force' which operates alongside the other enforcement activities of the Competition Directorate, with its own staff and procedures. It has been noted by commentators that the quality of analysis undertaken in merger cases is more sophisticated than that in standard arts 81 and 82 cases, and is having the effect of improving the standard of assessment overall, although there are inevitably still inconsistencies across the cases. Initiatives such as the notice on market definition (see Chapter 11) have emerged in response to the experience gained in merger cases. In that notice it was recognized not only that the approach overall could be made more transparent, but that mergers and joint ventures required special consideration. Again this pressure is derived from the drive towards the creation of the single market:

Finally, the Commission also takes into account the continuing process of market integration in the European Union when defining geographic markets, in particular in the area of concentrations and structural joint ventures. The measures adopted in the internal market programme to remove barriers to trade and further integrate the community markets cannot be ignored when assessing the effects on competition of a concentration or a structural joint venture. The basic goal of increased economic efficiency of the internal market is to be realised through increased trade and a better allocation of resources. This process requires in certain cases structural reorganisations of companies which may take the form of concentrations that anticipate an emerging new competitive environment and have as their purpose to exploit fully possible economies of scale or scope.

A situation where national markets have been artificially isolated from each other because of the existence of legislative barriers that have now been removed, will generally lead to a cautious assessment of past evidence regarding prices, market shares or trade patterns. A process of market integration that would lead to wider geographic markets in the short term may therefore be taken into consideration when defining the geographic market for the purposes of assessing concentrations and joint ventures.

Although the basic tools of analysis are the same whether one is considering a merger, an agreement, or a monopoly situation, the position is more complex in the dynamic situation that a merger presents.

15.2.5 **Member States**

A strong argument may be made that merger control is one area that is best not left to the Member States in situations where, as is increasingly the case, the merger is likely to have an impact in more than one Member State. It is this consideration that led to the 1997 amendments. However, there remain tensions between the Commission and the Member States' national authorities, with the latter reluctant to cede power over matters which have a significant impact within their own territory. This is evident not only in the 'two-thirds' rule, but also in the amended art. 9. Article 9(2) provides that a Member State may inform the Commission where it is concerned that the proposed concentration threatens competition peculiarly within the state. Where the Commission agrees that such a threat is genuine it shall either deal with the case in such a way as to take these concerns fully into account (art. 9(3)(a)), or in the alternative refer the case back to the appropriate national authority (art. 9(3)(b)).

It is the fact that it provides the 'one-stop shop' that makes the Merger Regulation so attractive to business, and in art. 21(2) it is provided that no Member State can apply its own national merger control provisions to mergers which fall within the Community jurisdiction. There are, however, three exceptions to this broad principle, two of which are set out within the Regulation itself, and one of which stems from the Treaty. Article 9(2), which has been referred to above, and which was amended by Regulation 1310/97, provides that in some circumstances national authorities may request that mergers be referred back to their assessment. This is the case where:

(a) a concentration threatens to create or to strengthen a dominant position as a result of which effective competition will be significantly impeded on a market within that Member State, which presents all the characteristics of a distinct market, or

(b) a concentration affects competition on a market within that Member State, which presents all the characteristics of a distinct market and which does not constitute a substantial part of the common market.

Once these criteria are met, the Commission may, under art. 9(3), either deal with the case itself in such a way as to meet the Member State's concerns, or refer all or part of the case back to the Member State. The UK authorities have made requests under art. 9(3) of the Regulation on only a small number of occasions, and in at least one case have been subsequently satisfied when the Commission has not referred the case back, but has met the concerns in its own assessment (*Exxon Corpn/Mobil Corpn*, EC Case No IV/M. 1383; DTI Press release P/99/780, 29 September).

Article 21 provides a second exception in relation to 'legitimate interests' of the Member States. The three interests specifically referred to in this context are public security, the plurality of the media, and prudential rules which normally relate to companies in the financial services sector.

The third exception, found in the Treaty itself, is that at art. 298, which is in the following terms:

Any Member State may take such measures as it considers necessary for the protection of the essential interests of its security which are connected with the production of or trade in arms, munitions and war material; such measures shall not adversely affect the conditions of competition in the common market regarding products which are not intended for specifically military purposes.

In the so-called Dutch clause, of art. 22, Member States may ask that the Commission examine a concentration which falls within the Member State's jurisdiction, but lacks a Community dimension. This is rarely used, although in 2000 the Swedish authorities requested that the Commission consider a merger in the market for the supply of milk falling within the Swedish jurisdiction, and in 2002 the DTI asked the Commission to consider the UK competition aspects of the proposed merger between GE Engine Services and Unison Industries (DTI Press Release P/2002/134, 28 February 2002). Once art. 22 is invoked the national authorities referring the matter to the Commission lose control over the process, and cannot determine the scope of the Commission's review (*Endemol Entertainment Holding BV v Commission* case T–221/95 [1999] 5 CMLR 611, paras 37–47).

15.2.6 **Merger reform**

At the end of 2001 the EC Commission launched a major review of its merger control procedures (*Green Paper on the Review of Council Regulation (EEC) No. 4064/89* COM(2001) 745/6 final, 11 December 2001), designed in particular to open up discussion as to the extent to which the regime should move closer to that of the USA in an effort to avoid conflict (see also in this respect Chapter 18). Thus it opens up a debate as to whether the test of a merger's acceptance set out in art. 2—the 'dominance' test—should be replaced with a 'significant lessening of competition test' which is currently applied in the USA, Canada, and Australia. As the Commission recognizes, this would

facilitate merging parties' global assessment of possible competition issues arising from contemplated transactions, by obviating the current need to argue their case according to differently formulated tests. This would in turn provide competition agencies with a better basis on which to build effective cooperation in cases that are notified in several jurisdictions. (para. 160)

However, there are also drawbacks to such an approach, and one concern of the Commission is that until it had established a body of case law under any new test there would be considerable uncertainty as to how this would operate in practice.

The Commission has also made it clear repeatedly that it would like to lower the thresholds at which the regime operates in order to allow more mergers to be considered centrally under a single 'one-stop shop' procedure. This issue will become increasingly important as the number of states in the EU grows over the next few years. An interesting suggestion in this respect is that, alongside simplified thresholds, the Commission should be granted exclusive competence in respect of any merger which would be required to be notified in three or more Member States.

The Commission intends to adopt a proposal for a revision of the Merger Regulation late in 2002, although achieving consensus on what should happen may not be an easy task. As we have seen above there have in the past been strong disagreements between the Member States about the extent to which merger control should be surrendered to the EC Commission, and particular debate about the relevant thresholds at which this should happen.

Those interested in the merger reform process should read, with critical eyes, the *Green Paper* in its entirety, and review the progress towards reform set out on the Commission web site. Any reforms that do emerge will be dealt with fully in the next edition of this work.

15.3 **Merger control in the United Kingdom**

In the United Kingdom the merger control regime is that of the FTA 1973, ss. 63–75K, although for newspaper mergers (which are subject to a more rigorous regime and are not considered here) see ss. 52–62. These provisions were left intact by the

Competition Act 1998. The merger regime fully involves the tripartite structure: the DGFT decides whether to recommend to the Secretary of State whether a merger or anticipated merger justifies full investigation; the CC makes any such investigation as is required of it; and the Secretary of State determines to what extent any recommendations made by the CC will be followed. A merger situation is defined in the 1973 Act as being one in which it appears to the Secretary of State 'that two or more enterprises . . . of which one at least was carried on in the United Kingdom or by or under the control of a body corporate incorporated in the United Kingdom, have . . . ceased to be distinct enterprises' (s. 64(1)).

Section 65(1) provides that enterprises have ceased to be distinct in one of two situations:

(a) they are brought under common ownership or common control . . . or

(b) either of the enterprises ceases to be carried on at all and does so in consequence of any arrangements or transactions entered into to prevent competition between the enterprises.

The wide range of situations that may be encompassed within these sections means, *inter alia*, that the treatment of joint ventures under domestic law is not the same as under Community law, and in cases where joint ventures involve changing control or influence over an enterprise they may fall to be considered within the merger regime. Mergers will not fall within the scope of the 1973 Act where they have a Community dimension, and are thus brought within the scope of Regulation 4064/89, or where they are below the threshold criteria set out in the Act. These criteria are that the merger must either create or enlarge a 25 per cent share of the relevant market in the UK or a substantial part of it; or that the gross value of the assets taken over must exceed £70 million (s. 64(1)(a) and (b)).

Unlike the position at Community level, there is no requirement on companies to notify mergers to the OFT, although it will be in the interests of those operating in the UK to notify where they are contemplating a merger that is likely to fall within the scope of the FTA 1973. Companies are assisted at this stage by the fact that the OFT's 'merger panel' will, if requested, give confidential guidance as to whether, on the basis of the facts presented to it, a merger reference would be likely. If the advice is that a reference is indeed likely the parties will often abandon the merger: references are expensive, open the transaction up to unwelcome public inspection, and create legal and commercial uncertainty. The *City Code on Takeovers and Mergers* provides that bids made lapse in the case of a merger reference being made, unless the bid is an unconditional one.

References may be made under either s. 64 in the case of a merger that has already been implemented, or s. 75 in the case of a contemplated merger. If a reference is made, the role of the Commission is to investigate and report on the questions:

(a) whether a merger situation qualifying for investigation has been created, and

(b) if so, whether the creation of that situation operates, or may be expected to operate against the public interest. (s. 69(1))

The public interest test is that set out in s. 84 of the 1973 Act, and has been discussed in Chapter 12, as has the CC's approach to assessing competition. The CC must make its report within a period of three to six months (s. 70), and this is then submitted to the Secretary of State. The Secretary of State is bound by the finding of the CC, and if the CC finds that the merger does not, or will not, operate against the public interest, the Secretary of State is then unable to take any action. If the CC finds by a two-thirds majority that the merger is expected to operate against the public interest, the Secretary of State has the power to order that the merger should not proceed, or (in the unlikely case where the merger has already been implemented), to order that it be undone. In the event that the merger has proceeded, however, it is unlikely that an order for it to be demerged would be made. In practice the OFT would be asked to negotiate undertakings which would restore as far as possible the competitive position.

The Companies Act 1989 introduced ss. 75G–75K into the FTA 1973 which allow the Secretary of State to accept undertakings as to the divestiture of parts of the combined business as an alternative to making a merger reference. It is for the DGFT to identify the adverse effects of the merger and to negotiate the undertakings with the company, but for the Secretary of State to determine whether to accept undertakings or to proceed with the reference.

One problem that can arise is where there are competing bids tabled for a target company. Because the effect that the successful bid will have on the market will depend on the acquiring company as well as the target, it is not always going to be the case that all bids will be referred, although the OFT will at least try to deal with the initial stages of the process at the same time.

The level of political involvement in the system is subject to regular criticism, but this is one aspect of competition law that appears to have consistently united the two main political parties. Although decisions are likely to be criticized when they are made, neither party appears prepared to surrender this power to an independent agency. It is very evident that the rigour with which merger control is enforced depends in part on the agenda of the Minister. One of the first decisions made by Margaret Beckett following her appointment to the office was to refer to the CC a situation involving the purchase of two rail franchises, notwithstanding that the DGFT had advised against making the reference. This was the first time since 1990 that a reference had been made against the advice of the Director. Shortly after that, a referral was made against the advice of both the Director and the Electricity Supply regulator relating to the acquisition of The Energy Group plc by Pacificorp Acquisitions. The trend under the previous administration was, if anything, the reverse of this. In 1993, for example, the Secretary of State rejected the DGFT's view that a bid made for Owners Abroad by Airtours should be reviewed.

15.3.1 Merger reform

In the White Paper *Productivity and Enterprise: A World Class Competition Regime* (Cm. 5233, July 2001), the DTI indicated that 'the Government is committed to introducing a new merger regime—with final decisions taken by independent competition authorities on the basis of a competition test' (Chapter 5). The approach in the White Paper emerged following a discussion process begun in August 1999 with the publication of a discussion document *Mergers: A Consultation Document on Proposals for Reform*. The key planks of the proposed reforms are set out in para. 5.2 of the White Paper:

Firstly, decisions on the vast majority of mergers will be transferred from Ministers to the OFT and the Competition Commission. Secondly, the test against which mergers are assessed will be changed from a broad-based 'public interest' test to a new competition-based test. The Government is also committed to procedural and other improvements, such as the introduction of maximum statutory timetables for investigations, and building more transparency into the process.

While the plan is to remove the political aspect of merger control in almost all cases, a few will still invite ministerial involvement. This will be the case where there are 'exceptional public interest issues' (para 5.5), and such interests will be defined and set out in statutory instruments subject to approval by both Houses of Parliament.

The test to be adopted of a merger's acceptance will not be the dominance test currently favoured in the EC Merger Regulation, but will be the 'substantial lessening of competition test', in respect of which the EC Commission has invited discussion in its *Green Paper* (see above). In the view of the Government 'making competition the focus of the assessment will ensure that the underlying economic arguments can be brought to bear on the analysis of a merger in a clear and straightforward manner' (para. 5.8). In some circumstances it is suggested however that a merger which does substantially lessen competition may still be cleared where the effect is to bring an overall benefit to consumers. The problem here is to select an appropriate methodology to identify such benefits.

It is proposed in the White Paper that the threshold at which a merger should be reviewed is that of a turnover of the merging parties in excess of £45 million, instead of the current market share test (para. 5.12). An updated list of remedies available in the event that adverse consequences of mergers are identified will be created, and these will provide more flexibility than is currently available at present (paras 5.17–5.19). The organizations involved in the merger review process will be the OFT, making a preliminary assessment, and then the Competition Commission if the Director takes the decision that the merger needs a fuller examination. In all cases tight deadlines will be set.

The progress of the Enterprise Bill, which will include the provisions relating to reform of the merger regime, can be followed at **www.dti.gov.uk/enterprisebill.**

15.4 **Joint ventures in the European Community**

Although joint ventures may have anti-competitive effects they can also, by reducing individual risk, be important in facilitating innovation, penetration into new markets, and strengthening the ability of small and medium-sized firms to compete against larger competitors and in bigger markets. Accordingly the EC Commission has often made clear that it will seek to support any joint venture arrangement which improves the competitive position of the Community and reduces divisions in the market. The difficulty lies in distinguishing joint ventures having these positive effects from those which are primarily anti-competitive.

15.4.1 **The treatment of joint ventures under Regulation 4064/89**

The first question to be asked of any joint venture is whether it is concentrative. It is concentrative if it falls within the terms of Regulation 4064/89, and the rules set out above in relation to that Regulation will therefore apply equally to it as to other forms of concentration. Such joint ventures are termed 'full function', in that they have an autonomous existence and do more than merely act as a coordinating body for their parents' actions. This is explained in the Commission's notice on the notion of full-function joint ventures, which clarifies that application of art. 3 of Regulation 4064/89. To be regarded as a full-function joint venture the joint venture is expected to have its own management and 'access to sufficient resources including finance, staff and assets (tangible and intangible) in order to conduct on a lasting basis its business activities within the area provided for in the joint venture agreement' (para. 13).

A joint venture will not be regarded as being concentrative where it takes over only a specific function on behalf of its parents.

Joint ventures are specifically addressed in art. 3(2) of the Regulation: 'The creation of a joint venture performing on a lasting basis all the functions of an autonomous economic entity shall constitute a concentration'. This position is different from that which was initially the case, where a distinction was drawn between a 'cooperative' joint venture, which would not be subject to the terms of the Regulation, and a concentrative joint venture, which would be. The effect of the amendment has been to bring more joint ventures within the scope of the Regulation, but to reduce the inconsistencies in approach that the purely formulaic criteria could give rise to.

A response to the abandonment of this distinction was to lead to the introduction in the Regulation of a further test to be applied in relation to concentrative joint ventures. Article 2(4) provides that where a joint venture falling within art. 3

has as its object or effect the coordination of the competitive behaviour of undertakings that remain independent, such coordination shall be appraised in accordance with the criteria of Article [81(1)] and (3) of the Treaty, with a view to establishing whether or not the operation is compatible with the common market.

Satisfaction of this requirement is an additional obligation to that laid down in art. 2(1)–(3) (see above).

Where a joint venture falls outside the terms of Regulation 4064/89 the test for its acceptance becomes that of whether it falls within art. 81 EC. It is likely that many, if not most, joint ventures would fulfil the requirements of art. 81(1), assuming the jurisdictional threshold was fulfilled, and would therefore fall to be considered under art. 81(3). In many cases they are likely to be given the benefit of the exemption, either under one of the Block Exemption Regulations (see Chapter 8), or individually (see Chapter 7). There will also be entities that are described as joint ventures that do not fall within art. 81 on the grounds that they and their parents are all part of the same corporate group and therefore not subject to the article at all. In these cases the operation of the joint venture is purely a matter of internal organization that is not subject to Treaty rules unless the joint venture plays a part in conduct that breaches art. 82.

15.4.2 The treatment of joint ventures under article 81(3)

Cooperative joint ventures are horizontal agreements which fall to be considered within the terms of art. 81(3) where they do not have the concentrative aspects that bring them within the terms of Regulation 4064/89. The EC Commission *Guidelines on the Applicability of Article 81 to Horizontal Cooperation Agreements* replace an earlier 'Notice concerning the assessment of cooperative joint ventures pursuant to Article [81] EEC' ((1993) OJ C43/3), and are the most complete statement on the position. There is a welcome recognition in the new guidelines, in response to criticism made over the years from a number of quarters, that it is the fact of horizontal cooperation, and not its form, that should form the basis of analysis within the competition rules. Thus the guidelines recognize, at para. 7, that there is an 'enormous variety in types and combinations of horizontal cooperation and market circumstances in which they operate'. In effect, therefore, the separate treatment accorded to horizontal joint ventures under the old Notice has been replaced by a more economically driven and less formalistic approach. Research and development agreements, and specialization agreements which take the form of cooperative joint ventures, are to be analysed in accordance with the terms of the block exemptions discussed above where the market thresholds are below the levels required of the regulations. Other cooperative joint ventures should be analysed in accordance with the principles set out in Chapter 7, and the guidelines are discussed there in relation to horizontal cooperation.

15.5 Joint ventures in the United Kingdom

As was noted above, there is no specific recognition in UK domestic law of the concept of a 'joint venture'. Instead there is a variety of ways by which companies can put into place mechanisms to facilitate long-term cooperation. These can include the creation of a third company, legally a separate entity, in which the two partners play a joint role in terms of management and ownership, and putting into place contractual arrangements. Partnerships may also be used, but are not considered here (see generally the Partnership Act 1890 and commentaries on partnership law). The consideration of any such arrangement then falls to be conducted under the general competition law applicable in the United Kingdom.

16

The impact of Community law in the United Kingdom and the Member States

16.1 Introduction

The relationship between Community law and national law in any area where the two deal with the same subject matter is a complex one. In competition law the problems caused are highly visible, and have been a source of concern for business which is faced with demands that are not always the same.

16.2 The formal relationship between the two systems

There are two discernible trends in the developing interrelationship between national and Community competition law. One is conditioned by the need to avoid conflict in the operation of the law, and is visible through the development of case law and principles to resolve such positions. The other lies in the efforts taken by the EC Commission to devolve enforcement of Community law to the Member States and their courts so far as possible to increase the efficacy of Community competition law generally, and to ease its own burden particularly.

16.2.1 The resolution of conflicts between Community and national law

In any case where there is a conflict between Community law and national law, Community law takes precedence. This duty on Member States, which is not specifically set out in the Treaty, has been clarified by the ECJ in a number of cases, starting with *Costa v ENEL* case 6/64 [1964] CMLR 425, and is implicit in the concept of direct effect, which recognizes that duties are owed by Member States to their citizens on the basis of Community law. If the United Kingdom had needed this to be made any clearer the matter was resolved beyond all doubt in *R v Secretary of State for Transport, ex parte Factortame Ltd (Factortame II)* [1990] 3 CMLR 1, in which the ECJ confirmed, as in the light of its own previous case law it was bound to do, that the operation of even Acts of Parliament should be set aside where they would conflict with Community obligations. The judiciary have accepted that this means that 'the Treaty of Rome is the supreme law of this country, taking precedence over acts of parliament' (*Stoke-on-Trent City Council* v *B&Q plc* [1990] 3 CMLR 31, *per* Hoffmann LJ). This principle is applied particularly in the light of art. 10 EC, which has been widely interpreted by the Court and been used as the foundation for a range of duties imposed on the Member States and authorities which are emanations of the state. Article 10 provides that:

Member states shall take all appropriate measures, whether general or particular, to ensure fulfilment of the obligations arising out of this Treaty or resulting from action taken by the institutions of the Community. They shall facilitate the achievement of the Community's tasks.

They shall abstain from any measure which could jeopardise the attainment of the objectives of this Treaty.

The position taken under Community law is that Member States cannot apply national competition laws in any way that obstructs, directly or indirectly, the operation of the superior competition law of the Community. This does not, however, outlaw all differences in domestic and Community systems. In the landmark case of *Wilhelm* v *Bundeskartellamt* case 14/68 [1969] CMLR 100, the ECJ accepted the possibility of divergence, but held that 'parallel application of the national system should only be allowed in so far as it does not impinge upon the uniform application, throughout the Common Market, of the Community rules' (para. 6). This conclusion followed inevitably from the imperative force of Community law over national law, and from the application of art. 10: it would be incompatible with the Treaty to allow national laws to obstruct the aims of the Treaty. However, national authorities would be acting within their powers where they

intervene against an agreement, in application of their internal law, even when the examination of the position of that agreement with regard to the Community rules is pending before the Commission, subject, however, to the proviso that such application of the national law may not prejudice the full and uniform application of the Community law.   (para. 7)

A similar position was reached in *GB-INNO-BM NV* v *Vereniging van de Kleinhandelaars in Tabak* case 13/77 [1978] 1 CMLR 283, concerning the relationship of a provision of Belgian law with aspects of EC competition and trade rules. Here the Court held, *inter alia*, that the

Treaty imposes a duty on member-states not to adopt or maintain in force any measure which could deprive [art. 82] of its effectiveness . . . [and] Member States may not enact measures enabling private undertakings to escape from the constraints imposed by art. [81].   (paras 31 and 33)

There is no prohibition on the Member States examining a practice already dealt with under Community law, in the light of national law (*Procureur de la République* v *Bruno Giry and Guerlain SA* case 253/78 [1981] 2 CMLR 99). In practice the results of such conflicts will usually be clear. Where a practice has been condemned at Community level it cannot be allowed to continue on the grounds that it is not condemned under national law (see, e.g., *Vereniging van Samenwerkende Prijsregelende*

Organisaties in de Bouwnijverheid (SPO) v *Commission* case I–29/92, [1995] ECR–II 289, in which a cartel operating in the Dutch building industry was condemned by the Commission despite having been expressly approved by the Dutch Minister of Economic Affairs). Similarly, a condemnation at national law will not be over-ridden by acceptability under Community law. Thus companies face a double hurdle: to be permitted, any practice must be acceptable under both national and Community law. The one area of debate has centred around the application of exemptions granted under art. 81(3). The question has been asked whether these, being specifically addressed to undertakings and permitting conduct to be con-tinued, override national laws that would strike down the practice. The better view is that these exemptions, being permissive, are not prescriptive, and merely indi-cate that Community law will not be offended by the maintenance of the practice in question. This would not prevent the application of national law, even where a contrary result were reached. However, for a conflicting view see Galinsky, R., 'The Resolution of Conflicts between UK and Community Competition Law' [1994] *ECLR* 16. It is unlikely that any national authority would in fact condemn a practice that had been subject to such express authorization by the EC Commission, and the increased harmonization between national and Community law is further reducing the scope for such problems to arise.

In the case of *Masterfoods Ltd* v *HB Ice Cream Ltd; HB Ice Cream Ltd* v *Masterfoods Ltd* case C–344/98 [2001] 4 CMLR 14 the administrative relationship between the application of EC competition law by the Commission and by the national courts was explored in some detail. In this case, which arose out of challenges to ice cream freezer cabinet exclusivity in Ireland (see Chapter 12 for a discussion of some of the substantive issues raised in these cases), the Irish courts and the Commission were, independently, considering the same agreements in the light of the application of art. 81. The Irish High Court had found that the freezer exclusivity agreements were not restrictive of competition, and had injuncted another undertaking from placing its products in HB's freezers. The Commission, on the other hand, found that HB's agreements were in breach of art. 81(1) (in *Van den Bergh Foods Ltd* 98/531 (1998) OJ L246/1), although at the time at which the case was heard the operation of the Commission decision had been suspended by the Court of First Instance (*Van den Bergh Foods* v *Commission* case T–65/98R [1998] 5 CMLR 475). The fact that the Commission decision was contested before the CFI was clearly a factor that made the waters even more muddy than they were to begin with.

As Advocate General Cosmas recognized, the question of how to avoid inconsis-tent application of competition law between national courts and the EC institu-tions was 'the central issue' in the case (para. A14). The Advocate General first noted that the facts examined by the Commission and the national court were not the same, as they related to different time periods, and it was theoretically possible (although on a reading of the case unlikely) that the agreements could have not been restrictive of competition at one time, but been restrictive at another. In *Stergio Delimitis* v *Henninger Brau* case C–234/89 [1992] 5 CMLR 210 the Court had held that the handing down of conflicting decisions was contrary to the principle of legal certainty, and 'must therefore be avoided when national courts give decisions on agreements or practices which may subsequently be the subject of a decision by the Commission' (at para. 47). In the present case however, the *Delimitis* principles had already been breached as there was 'not merely a potential, but a clear and imminent, conflict between the decision of the first instance Irish court and a decision of the Commission that has already been adopted' (para. A25). The risk was that the Irish Supreme Court, from which the reference was taken, might also produce a decision that was in conflict with that of the Commission.

The Court held that,

> where a national court is ruling on an agreement or practice the compatibility of which with articles 81(1) and 82 of the Treaty is already the subject of a Commission decision, it cannot take a decision running counter to that of the Commission, even if the latter's decision conflicts with a decision given by a national court of first instance.   (para. 60)

A national court would not be obliged to stay proceedings before it in relation to a situation where a relevant Commission decision was under attack before the CFI or ECJ, but would be expected to do so in situations where, according to the Advocate General, 'the solution to the main dispute presupposes that the national court knows whether the decision at issue is valid or not' (para. A57).

16.2.2 The application of Community competition law by the Member States

The most important mechanism by which competition law is to be utilized other than through actions taken by the EC Commission lies in the operation of the principle of direct effect. This is considered in relation to third-party rights in Chapter 5, and in relation to the application of art. 81(2) in Chapter 7. However, it should be noted that the Commission has been keen to emphasize this route, and has published a notice designed to facilitate cooperation between itself and the national courts (*Notice on Cooperation between National Courts and the Commission* (1993) OJ C39/6). The evidence suggests that this initiative has not been entirely successful. Between August 1992 and July 1997, for example, the Commission appears to have dealt with only 15 questions from the courts of Member States. Only one of these came from the UK, when a Master of the Queen's Bench Division asked for various information regarding a case concerning the General Medical Council (see EC Commission, *Competition Policy Newsletter* (1998) 1, p. 47).

In some circumstances Member States themselves remain competent to enforce arts 81 and 82 directly. The only power that is exclusively reserved to the Commission in this respect is the granting of exemptions under art. 81(3) (see Chapter 7). The authority for this direct enforcement is found in art. 84 EC and art. 9(3) of Regulation 17. Article 84 provides:

> Until the entry into force of the provisions adopted in pursuance of Article [83], the authorities in Member States shall rule on the admissibility of agreements, decisions and concerted practices and on abuse of a dominant position in the common market in accordance with the

law of their country and with the provisions of Article [81], in particular paragraph 3, and of Article [82].

The phrase 'in accordance with the law of their country' does not mean that national competition law is to be applied to arts 81 and 82 type situations, but rather that national procedures, legal mechanisms, and guarantees should be applied to resolve matters in accordance with the two articles. Article 9(3), Regulation 17 is in the following terms:

As long as the Commission has not initiated any procedure under Articles 2, 3 or 6, the authorities of the Member States shall remain competent to apply Article [81(1)] and Article [82] in accordance with Article [84] of the Treaty.

The EC Commission would like all Member States to avail themselves of this power, and in the hope of facilitating this has published a notice 'on cooperation between national authorities and the Commission in handling cases falling within the scope of Articles [81] or [82] of the Treaty' ((1997) OJ C313/3). Research undertaken by the Commission in 1996 showed that in only seven of the 15 Member States did the relevant administrative authority directly apply the articles. The United Kingdom fell within the eight that did not, along with Austria, Denmark, Finland, Ireland, Luxembourg, The Netherlands, and Sweden. The Commission did not publish details of the vigour with which such enforcement takes place, and it is to be suspected that there is a void between the notional ability of the states to act in this way and the act of doing so. The notice calls upon those Member States that had not already done so to introduce the necessary mechanism into their national systems. This call, which was made in time to be incorporated into the Competition Act 1998, was clearly ignored in the United Kingdom.

In August 1996 the EC Competition Law (Articles 88 and 89) Enforcement Regulations 1996 (SI 1996/2199) entered into force. The Regulations provide for a limited form of direct application of arts 81 and 82 by the UK authorities. Under the Regulations the Secretary of State may request the DGFT to carry out a preliminary investigation, and may, following the investigation, refer the matter to the MMC. If the MMC concludes that there is a breach, the Secretary of State may determine the necessary remedial action. However, these Regulations relate only to very specific matters in respect of which no implementation has been made at Community level under art. 83 EC. These areas are those of air transport between the EC and non-Member States, and international maritime services. It cannot be coincidence that these measures were introduced at a time of a bitter debate about competition in the air transport industry, particularly relating to cross-Atlantic routes, and it is to be doubted whether the regulations will be applied in practice.

16.3 **Responses in the United Kingdom**

Over time there has been a significant change in attitude at government level to the reform of UK law so as to bring it into line with Community law. Compare these statements:

'the Government consider[s] that there may be benefit[s] in aligning this aspect of UK competition law with EC law' (*Abuse of Market Power*, Cm. 2100, 1992, para. 1.6);

'[the Government does not] see the need to ensure consistency with EC competition law as an objective in itself' (introductory notes attached to the August 1997 Draft Bill, para. 1.4);

'I cannot over-emphasise that the purpose of the Bill is to ensure as far as possible a consistency with EC approach and thereby to ease burdens for business' (Lord Haskel, Hansard (HL), 17 November 1997, col. 417).

It is the reforms of the Competition Act 1998 that are the most visible record of the pressure on the idiosyncratic domestic regime to align itself with that of the European Community. Quite simply, in the eyes of both industry and consumer groups, the national law had not been able to compete with Community law. Faced with the option of bringing an action on the basis of Community law, or national law, whether through the courts or via the administrative agencies, professional advisers in the UK would advocate the Community route every time. United Kingdom law was to be used as a 'stocking filler', or a fall-back position when all else failed. The cry from industry was for the certainty and simplified legal arena that would be provided by a 'one-stop shop', where even if two regimes were considering a practice they would do so on the basis of the same rules. The fact that Community law was taken as a given meant that the pressure to reform was placed on the national system. These pressures, coming from a range of sources, were made very clear in the Trade and Industry Committee Fifth Report, *UK Policy on Monopolies* (HC 249, 1995). The Committee found itself persuaded that the benefits of alignment, and steps already announced but not pursued by the government of the day, made it inevitable that alignment would follow.

This alignment has now been largely achieved, although as we have seen vestigial differences remain in relation to the application of the powers of the FTA 1973, and the domestic merger review process is not the same as that of Regulation 4064/89. A formal mechanism now exists in the Competition Act 1998 which is designed to ensure consistency in approach between domestic and Community law. Section 60 of the Act is of key importance, and is given here in its entirety.

60.—(1) The purpose of this section is to ensure that so far as is possible (having regard to any relevant differences between the provisions concerned), questions arising under this Part in relation to competition within the United Kingdom are dealt with in a manner which is consistent with the treatment of corresponding questions arising in Community law in relation to competition within the Community.

(2) At any time when the court determines a question arising under this Part, it must act (so far as is compatible with the provisions of this Part and whether or not it would

otherwise be required to do so) with a view to securing that there is no inconsistency between—
(a) the principles applied, and decision reached, by the court in determining that question; and
(b) the principles laid down by the Treaty and the European Court, and any relevant decision of that Court, as applicable at that time in determining any corresponding question arising in Community law.
(3) The court must, in addition, have regard to any relevant decision or statement of the Commission.
(4) Subsections (2) and (3) also apply to—
(a) the Director; and
(b) any person acting on behalf of the Director, in connection with any matter arising under this Part.
(5) In subsections (2) and (3), 'court' means any court or tribunal.
(6) In subsections (2)(b) and (3), 'decision' includes a decision as to—
(a) the interpretation of any provision of Community law,
(b) the civil liability of an undertaking for harm caused by its infringement of Community Law.

In the view of the Director General, 'relevant decision or statement of the Commission' (s. 60(3)) means:

decisions or statements which have the authority of the European Commission as a whole, such as, for example, decisions on individual cases under art. 81 and art. 82 of the Treaty. It would also include any clear statements which the European Commission has published about its policy approach in the *Annual Report on Competition Policy*. (See e.g., *The Chapter I Prohibition Guidelines*, para. 2.1.)

The approach taken to comfort letters has been discussed in Chapter 3.

The problem of distinguishing 'relevant differences' in relation to the substantive law has been discussed in Chapter 9.

16.4 Responses from other Member States

The majority of Member States, and in particular those without a strong independent tradition of competition law, have now modelled their competition laws on those of the Community. Thus, Austria, Belgium, Denmark, Finland, Greece, Ireland, Italy, Luxembourg, The Netherlands, Portugal, Spain, and Sweden maintain in place systems which are either expressly designed to mirror EC law, or likely in practice to achieve the same results as EC law. However, even in these states there are some specific differences from Community law. In Ireland, for example, the Competition Act 1991, which brought EC-style prohibitions into Irish law, allows 'aggrieved persons' to bring actions for remedies including exemplary damages. In Finland the Act on Restrictions of Competition of 1992 is not in the same language as that of the EC provisions, and various practices are prohibited outright, including resale price maintenance and price fixing.

France maintains a position which is a little different. The most important measure in France is the Ordinance of 1 December 1986, which relates to price fixing and competition. Article 7 however has effects similar to those of art. 81 EC, and art. 8 prohibits the abuse of a dominant position. The Ordinance also provides a mechanism for the control of mergers falling within the relevant thresholds.

In Germany the law relating to fair competition is laid down in the *Gesetz gegen den unlauteren Wettbewerb* (UWG), while the law relating to cartels, mergers and acquisitions, and market dominance is laid down in great detail in the *Gesetz gegen Wettbewerbsbeschraenkungen* (GWB), the literal translation of which is the 'law against restrictions of competition'. The last major reform of the GWB took place in 1998 to bring the German law closer to that of the EC. The GWB generally prohibits 'agreements between competing undertakings, decisions by associations of undertakings and concerted practices which have as their object or effect the prevention, restriction or distortion of competition' (s. 1 GWB), a formulation which is taken explicitly from art. 81 EC, but which was only added in the 1998 revision. Exemptions from this general prohibition are provided for in relation to arrangements between small and medium-sized enterprises (s. 4 GWB), and may also be granted in respect of situations similar to those falling to be encompassed within art. 81(3) EC (s. 7 GWB). There is no express enactment in the GWB of any provision mirroring art. 81(2) EC, and this result is achieved instead by an interaction of the GWB and the general rules of German civil law (s. 134 *Buergerliches Gesetzbuch*). Provisions which are similar to those of art. 82 are set out in s. 19 GWB, added in 1999, and a presumption of dominance will be raised where the market share of any undertaking is in excess of 33 per cent of the relevant market. In s. 33 of the GWB it is provided that in cases where there is a 'conscious' abuse of a dominant position, the offending undertaking can be forced to pay damages to any undertaking having suffered a competitive disadvantage. The competent authority in Germany is the *Bundeskartellamt* located in Berlin, although under the German federal system, if a case concerns only one *Land* of the Federation then the relevant authority will be the one located in that *Land*. There is little case law under the GWB, and most resolutions of disputes and procedures are administrative in nature.

17

The common law and competition

17.1 Introduction

While there is not a common law of competition as such, there are areas in which the operation of the common law impacts upon issues that are closely related to the public regulation of competition. As was seen in Chapter 1, the common law was originally important in this area, and at the time of its enactment the Sherman Act was viewed within the United States largely as a codification of existing common-law principles. The fact that common law now occupies only a residual role in relation to competition law generally may be attributed to several factors. One may be the apparent success of forms of public regulation, which have reduced the need for reliance on a common law. Another lies in the reluctance of the judiciary to venture into what is seen as a difficult and technical area; it was Fry LJ who commented in *Mogul Steamship* v *McGregor* (1889) 28 QBD 598 at 625, that 'to draw a line between fair and unfair competition . . . passes the power of the courts'. A related reason may be found in the reluctance of the judiciary to distinguish economic interests from those of personal liberty. The comment of Lord Atkinson in *H. Morris Ltd* v *Saxelby* [1916] 1 AC 688 at 700, HL is typical: 'no person has an abstract right to be protected against competition *per se* in his trade or business'. The most important area in which the common law continues to have relevance is the contract-based restraint of trade doctrine. Other areas where the common law may play a role are in the statutory tort lying in relation to breaches of arts 81 and 82, conspiracy, and a bundle of related 'economic torts'.

17.2 The restraint of trade doctrine

17.2.1 The development of the doctrine

The roots of the doctrine of restraint of trade are obscure. In *Chitty on Contracts* it is stated that 'cases go back to the second half of the sixteenth century' (Guest, A. G. (ed.), *Chitty on Contracts*, London, Sweet & Maxwell (27th edn, 1994), para. 16–066), although the first reported case appears to be *John Dyer's* case (1414)

YB 2 Hen 5, fo. 5, pl. 26. In this case, the defendant, a dyer, had given a bond to the plaintiff not to exercise his trade in the same town for six months. The bond was declared void by Hull J in no uncertain terms (technically the case was not one of 'restraint of trade', which was unknown then as a cause of action, but the case may be appropriately categorized as such at this distance).

The essence of the restraint of trade doctrine is that it is contrary to public policy to enforce contracts that are in unreasonable restraint of trade. It is generally considered to be the case that a contract in restraint of trade is void, unless that restraint can be shown to be a reasonable one. However, in *A. Schroeder Music Publishing Co. Ltd* v *Macaulay* [1974] 3 All ER 617, HL Lord Reid suggested that the contract in this case was 'unenforceable' (at 623), i.e., voidable, and whether such contracts are in fact void or voidable remains unclear. Whether a restraint is 'reasonable' is to be considered both in relation to the parties themselves, and in relation to the public interest.

Restraint of trade thus relates primarily to situations in which 'a party (the covenantor) agrees with any other party (the covenantee) to restrict his liberty in the future to carry on trade with other persons not parties to the contract in such manner as he chooses' (*Petrofina (Great Britain) Ltd* v *Martin* [1966] Ch 146, *per* Diplock LJ at 180).

All contracts restrain trade: if A agrees with B to sell B a car, then A cannot, without breaking that contract, sell that car to C. Clearly restraints of this nature are the essence of contractual relationships and will not, save in exceptional circumstances, be struck down. The difficulty with restraint of trade is to identify those situations in which the doctrine will apply, which is to say those in which the restraint is both unreasonable between the parties and against the public interest.

As is the case today, the doctrine, even in its earliest development, was determined by reference to the 'public interest', and public policy will also have an impact on the way in which the private interests of the parties are to be determined. This flexible criterion has meant that 'the law as to contracts in restraint of trade had, more than any other class of contracts, been moulded by changing ideas of public policy' (Holdsworth, W., *A History of English Law*, London, Methuen (1937), vol. 7, p. 6). The development of the doctrine became for a time inextricably linked with the resistance to the grants of monopoly by the Crown (see Chapter 1). In the reign of Elizabeth I, for example, all restraints were likely to be condemned as being contrary to public policy (*Colgate* v *Bacheler* (1602) Cro Eliz 872). By 1711, in the case of *Mitchell* v *Reynolds* (1711) 1 P. Wms 181, the courts had begun to distinguish between restraints which operated at the local level and those which purported to be countrywide. In *Mitchell* a countrywide restraint was criticized in the following terms: 'what does it signify to a tradesman in London what another does in Newcastle?' Even in the twentieth century *Mitchell* was referred to as 'among all the decisions, the most outstanding and helpful authority' (*H. Morris Ltd* v *Saxelby* [1916] 1 AC 688, HL, *per* Lord Shaw at 717). Public policy now recognizes that there is a broad interest in encouraging the sale and transfer of businesses, and mobility of employment. If an employer could not to a certain extent restrain the activities of an employee once he or she leaves the employment there might be less incentive to employ the worker in the first place. The same may be true of someone buying a business, who would be less attracted were the vendor immediately able to set up in competition to the new purchaser (see, e.g., Lord Watson in *Nordenfelt* v *Maxim Nordenfelt Guns and Ammunition Co. Ltd* [1984] AC 535 at 552).

The concept of 'reasonableness' appears to have entered into the application of the doctrine in the seventeenth century, and is usually traced to *Rogers* v *Parrey* (1613) 80 ER 1012. Here the judges, including Coke CJ, were called upon to determine the validity of a restraint under which the defendant had promised not to exercise his trade as a joiner 'in a shop, parcel of a house, to him demised in London, for 21 years'. Croke J expressed his concern as to the effect of the restraint: 'The doubt which at first troubled me, was, for the binding of one, that he should not use and exercise his trade, being his livelihood'. However, the fact that this was not the case here swayed the court, which unanimously agreed with Coke CJ that 'as this case here is, for a time certain, and in a place certain, a man may be well bound, and restrained from using his trade'. In *Broad* v *Jolyffe* (1620) Cro Jac 596, the court considered a case in which a trader selling his old stock to another had promised as part of the bargain that he would not trade in competition with the purchaser by keeping a shop in a particular place. When the plaintiff brought an action to enforce this term, the court was of the view that this was sustainable:

upon a valuable consideration one may restrain himself that he shall not use his trade in such a particular place; for he who gives that consideration expects the benefit of his customers; and it is usual here in London for one to let his shop and wares to his servant when he is out of his apprenticeship; as also to covenant that he shall not use his trade in such a shop or in such a street; so for a valuable consideration and voluntarily one may agree that he will not use his trade.

The extent to which the test of reasonableness could be reduced to clear criteria continued to exercise the courts through the eighteenth and nineteenth centuries. A problem facing the courts during this period was the rapid development in the patterns of commerce, and in particular the growth in transport and communications that would quickly render obsolete restrictive interpretations of the doctrine. In *Horner* v *Graves* (1831) 131 ER 284, the court refused to adopt a strict definition, holding instead (at 743) that

we do not see how a better test can be applied to the question whether reasonable or not, than by considering whether the restraint is such only as to afford a fair protection to the interests of the party in favour of whom it is given, and not so large as to interfere with the interests of the public. Whatever restraint is larger than the necessary protection of the party, can be of no benefit to either, it can only be oppressive; and if oppressive, it is, in the eyes of the law, unreasonable. Whatever is injurious to the interests of the public is void, on the grounds of public policy.

The test of reasonableness became the overriding consideration in *Nordenfelt* v *Maxim Nordenfelt Guns and Ammunition Co. Ltd* [1894] AC 535, and it was here that the modern test for determining the validity of any restraining contract was formulated by Lord Macnaghten, where he held (at 565):

The true view at the present time I think, is this: The public have an interest in every person's carrying on his trade freely: so has the individual. All interference with individual liberty of action in trading, and all restraints of trade of themselves, if there is nothing more, are contrary to public policy, and therefore void. That is the general rule. But there are exceptions: restraints of trade and interference with individual liberty of action may be justified by the special circumstances of a particular case. It is a sufficient justification, and indeed it is the only justification, if the restriction is reasonable—reasonable, that is, in reference to the interests of the parties concerned and reasonable in reference to the interests of the public, so framed and so guarded as to afford adequate protection to the party in whose favour it is imposed, while at the same time it is in no way injurious to the public.

In this case the flexibility of approach that Lord Macnaghten's summary of the position called for meant that a restriction unlimited geographically, and lasting for 25 years, was upheld. The restriction had been accepted by a manufacturer of guns who had sold his business and all the patents associated with it, and who had accepted a world-wide restriction on setting up a competing business. Given the nature of the arms trade, the court found that such a world-wide restriction served to protect the genuine commercial interest of the purchaser of the business and did not contain unreasonable restrictions. *Nordenfelt* may be contrasted with *Mason v Provident Clothing and Supply Co. Ltd* [1913] AC 724, in which a restriction on a salesman working for a cloth company, to the effect that he could not work within 25 miles of London for three years after leaving his job, was held to be too restrictive in relation to the interest being protected and the relevant circumstances. While it appears that the extent to which restraints are 'purchased' may be persuasive, the general principle is that the courts will not allow a party to 'buy' a restraint, and will not, in assessing whether a restraint is reasonable, consider the 'reward' given to the plaintiff in return for the acceptance of the restraint. To do so would raise the spectre of the courts assessing the adequacy of consideration, in this case for a single term in the contract, which is a matter that the courts generally avoid.

It has been suggested by Lever that:

Any idea that courts are inherently ill equipped to apply *any* sort of economic regulatory rules is readily dispelled when it is recalled that it was the English courts themselves that developed, without legislative assistance, the doctrine. (Lever, J., 'UK Economic Regulation: Use and Abuse of the Law' [1992] *ECLR* 55)

However, the interpretation given to 'reasonable', and in particular the restricted role assigned to the 'public interest', means that the doctrine serves a limited function, and the courts have very obviously rejected any scope for extending it so as to provide a more general protection to the competitive process itself.

17.2.2 The current operation of the doctrine

Restraint of trade concerns will not, save in exceptional circumstances, be raised in standard commercial contracts. There are two situations where the doctrine remains vibrant, both of which have obvious implications for the competitive market. The first concerns post-contract employment considerations, where an employee accepts restrictions on future conduct if he or she leaves that employment. Typically such restrictions might include a limitation on the time that must elapse before the employee works for a competing company, or sets up in direct competition himself. It is also common for a geographical area to be identified, within which the employee is, for a set period, not permitted to compete. The second common situation relates to the sale of businesses and the goodwill attached thereto, where the seller will agree to restrictions on its liberty to maintain a similar business. This was the position in *Broad v Jolyffe* (above), where the court recognized that there were often benefits accruing to the seller in accepting such a restriction, if, by doing so, the value of the business it is selling increases: a business is worth less if purchasers know that they are shortly going to be facing competition from the very person selling them that business. Both of these situations have important consequences for competition. For example, if a pop star covenants with his recording label not to record for another label for a certain period after the termination of his contract, that may reduce the ability of labels to compete with each other. If a business owner covenants not to set up in competition to the purchaser of his business, that may reduce the consumer choice in that area.

The position remains that there are three requirements for the operation of the doctrine:

(a) the restraint must protect a legitimate interest of the party in whose favour it operates;

(b) the restraint must be no wider than is necessary to protect this interest; and

(c) the restraint must be reasonable in relation to the public interest.

These last two requirements appear to be often conflated into an overall balancing act undertaken by the courts. Whether a restraint is reasonable or not is to be considered in the light of the circumstances at the time when the restraint was imposed (see, e.g., *Watson v Prager* [1991] 3 All ER 487).

It is for the party claiming the benefit of the restraint to show that it is reasonable and that there is a legitimate interest to protect. This was made clear in *H. Morris Ltd v Saxelby* [1916] 1 AC 688, HL, where Lord Atkinson held (at 700) that

the onus of establishing to the satisfaction of the judge who tries the case facts and circumstances which show that the restraint is of the reasonable character [between the parties] [rests] upon the person alleging that it is of that character, and the onus of showing that, notwithstanding that it is of that character, it is nevertheless injurious to the public and therefore void, [rests], in like manner, on the party alleging the latter.

This *dictum* has been used in support of the contention that the test of whether a restraint is reasonable between the parties is a private matter between them, and that only if the restriction is found to be reasonable should the public interest then be considered. However, such a clear division between the two factors is difficult to sustain. The point was made by Lord Pearce in *Esso Petroleum Co. Ltd v Harper's Garage (Stourport) Ltd* ([1968] AC 269 at 324:

> There is not, as some cases seem to suggest, a separation between what is reasonable on grounds of public policy and what is reasonable as between the parties. There is one broad question: is it in the interests of the community that this restraint should, as between the parties, be held to be reasonable and enforceable?

In the same case Lord Hodson gave further credence to the notion that the two factors tend to become conflated, when he noted (at 319) that 'the interests of the individual are much discussed in the cases on restraint of trade which seldom, if ever, have been expressly decided on public grounds'.

If the case does revolve around the public interest consideration, it is for the party claiming that the restriction is unreasonable to demonstrate that it is against the public interest (*Morris v Saxelby*, above). However, although this places a significant burden on the party challenging the restraint, the court is entitled to consider all surrounding aspects, and will be expected to achieve a balance between the private and public interest. There may be situations in which the defendant is expected to explain why a particular restraint is justifiable when, on the face of it, the restraint appears to be contrary to the public or private interest.

The consideration of public interest has caused some problems for the judiciary. The application of the doctrine to the economically important area of exclusive distribution contracts (or 'solus agreements' as they are sometimes referred to in the English cases) shows both the problems with applying a public interest test, and the application of the doctrine to areas central to competition law.

Esso Petroleum (above) was the first important case to consider this issue, and the case remains of fundamental importance to this area. This concerned a vertical distribution agreement under which the respondents agreed to buy petrol only from the appellant. The respondents owned two garages. In relation to the first the exclusive agreement was to last four years and five months, in return for which commitment the respondents were to be entitled to a discount on the petrol they obtained from the wholesaler. In relation to the second garage the respondents had accepted a £7,000 loan from the appellant, which was to be repaid as a mortgage over 21 years. The obligation to obtain petrol exclusively from the appellant was to continue for as long as the loan continued to be owed. Having decided that such a tie could fall to be considered within the restraint of trade doctrine, the court proceeded to consider whether either tie was in unreasonable restraint of trade. The first tie was considered to be in the interests of both the parties and was not found to be against the public interest. The longer tie was considered to be excessive in relation to the interest being protected, and was thus rendered unenforceable. The factors that were considered to be legitimate interests of the parties included the maintenance of the distribution system and the benefit of a stable flow of petrol to the market.

Their Lordships gave different reasons for the application of the doctrine to this situation, but the majority agreed on the formulation of what has been labelled the 'opening the door' test. Lord Reid set this out (at 298):

Restraint of trade appears to me to imply that a man contracts to give up some freedom which otherwise he would have had. A person buying or leasing land had no previous right to be there at all, let alone to trade there, and when he takes possession of that land subject to a negative restrictive covenant he gives up no right or freedom which he previously had.

Rightly, this formulation has come in for some criticism, notably, but not exclusively, by Valentine Korah ('Solus Agreements and Restraint of Trade' (1969) 32 *MLR* 323). While the approach has formal attractions, carrying as it does a degree of certainty, it takes little account of the realities of situations. The application of the test presumes that the surrendering of an existing freedom is somehow worse than entering a market for a first time carrying a restriction on freedom. In practice there may be little distinction between the two, particularly if it becomes apparent that the restricted entrant could have found much better terms and conditions elsewhere which would equally have facilitated entrance. Although the House devoted a lot of discussion to the concept of the public interest in the case, there is no point at which the public interest in the particular facts of the case itself are adequately resolved or discussed. It was also not made clear to what types of vertical restraints the doctrine would be applied. It was suggested, for example, that the traditional ties between landlords and breweries would not fall within the application of the doctrine as these were so much a part of accepted commercial practice (see too the comments of Lord Denning in *Petrofina (Great Britain) Ltd* v *Martin* [1966] Ch 146). If this is indeed the case, then it may be that over time the acceptance of solus ties will see a reduction in the scope of the application of the doctrine to these.

An example following *Esso* is that of *Texaco Ltd* v *Mulberry Filling Station Ltd* [1972] 1 All ER 513. The defendant, owner of a petrol filling station, had borrowed £36,000 from the plaintiff's agent, and accepted an obligation to buy petrol only from that supplier for a period of four years and seven months. The defendant subsequently broke this tie, and when he was sued under the contract sought to avoid the obligations on the basis of the restraint of trade doctrine. Ungoed-Thomas J accepted Lord Macnaghten's formulation of the doctrine from *Nordenfelt* (above), but was concerned that 'the doctrine has been much considered since, and has been the subject of observations which are by no means easy to reconcile' (at 521). In an effort to reconcile the authorities the judge took a very restricted view of the meaning of public interest, so as to exclude 'the interests of the public at large'. The judge's view (at 526) was that restraint of trade

is part of the doctrine of the common law and not of economics . . . if it refers to interests of the public at large, it might . . . involve balancing a mass of conflicting economic, social and other interests which a court of law might be ill-adapted to achieve; but, more important, interests of the public at large would lack sufficiently specific formulation to be capable of judicial as contrasted with unregulated personal decision and application—a decision varying, as Lord Eldon LC put it, like the length of the chancellor's foot.

Such a restrictive approach has not been taken since, but it is established law that the interests of the competitive economy are not part of the doctrine.

A final limitation of the doctrine arises from its place in contract law: the doctrine of privity means that only parties to the contract may invoke the doctrine, and third parties may not recover damages under it. There has, however, been a sprinkling of cases in which a more flexible approach has been taken, the most significant of which is *Eastham* v *Newcastle United Football Club Ltd* [1964] Ch 413. George Eastham was a distinguished inside forward for Newcastle United, but wished to transfer to another club. He was prevented from doing so by the rules of the Football Association (FA) and the League. These were binding on all the 92 league clubs. Under these rules a player could be retained by a club for the following season by the offer of a minimum wage acceptable to the League, which in this case was £418. Until the offer was accepted the player would not actually be under contract to the club and would not be playing. Only if players were able to persuade the FA that there were special grounds for allowing them to change their clubs could they move; and without such approval it would be virtually impossible to play professional football anywhere in the world, with the notable exception of Australia. That the agreement between the clubs and the FA operated in restraint of trade was evidently clear, and the justifications advanced for its continuance were rejected by the court. The fact that Eastham was not himself a party to the agreements was not held to be a bar to his action, given that his interests were so immediately affected by the agreement (see also *Greig* v *Insole* [1978] 1 WLR 302, relating to Test- and county-match bans on cricketers who had played for Kerry Packer, and *Watson* v *Prager* [1993] EMLR 275, relating to contracts between professional boxers and their managers). A similar approach was taken in *Pharmaceutical Society of Great Britain* v *Dickson* [1970] AC 403, where an individual chemist outlet was able to challenge a rule of the Pharmaceutical Society restricting the types of goods in which their members might deal; and in *Nagle* v *Feilden* [1966] 2 QB 633, the court held invalid a rule of the Jockey Club that prevented a woman from holding a trainer's licence. The issue of the 'right to work' considered in both this latter case and others raises further complexities that lie beyond the scope of this text.

The restraint of trade doctrine, for all its longevity, continues to play a vibrant part in domestic contract law, and to impact on competitive situations. For example, in *Hollis & Co* v *Mark Richard Stocks* [2000] UKCLR 658, the appellant was a solicitor employed by the respondent. A restraint in his contract of employment restricting him from working within a 10–mile radius of the respondent's office from the termination of his employment was found to be a reasonable one when it was challenged as being in restraint of trade. In *Lapthorne* v *Eurofi Ltd* [2001] UKCLR 996, on the other hand, the respondent was successful in challenging a post-termination clause in his contract which restricted his future employment. The relevant clause was too widely drawn, and hence fell within the restraint of trade doctrine and was unenforceable. Restraint of trade was a central argument in the case of *WWF – World Wide Fund for Nature (formerly World Wildlife Fund/and World Wildlife Fund Inc* v *World Wrestling Federation* ([2002] UKCLR 388) which related to the use of the initials 'WWF' by the defendant. In 1994 after a number of disputes the parties had entered into a contract under which the defendant would limit its use of the initials. In 1997 the Wrestling Federation set up a website making extensive use of the initials, and in 1998 it altered its logo so as to make it more obviously constitute the letters WWF. The fund objected, relying on the contract, and the defendant argued this was in restraint of trade. The court found that the federation 'gains no assistance . . . from the doctrine of restraint of trade' (para 66), holding that where parties enter into a contract to avoid litigation and settle a dispute 'the presumption is that the restraints, having been agreed between the two parties most involved, represent a reasonable division of their interests' (para 48).

17.2.3 Conclusion

The fact that restraint of trade can be applied to vertical commercial arrangements, and to the rules of professional associations, as well as to the classic sale of business or employee/employer relationships means that it continues to be relevant to competition law. In some situations the doctrine has been able to fill in gaps left by the statutory regulation. It is also becoming increasingly important in relation to ties between recording artists and their record companies, and to those between sportsmen and sportswomen and their managers or teams (see, e.g., Greenfield, S., and Osborn, G., *Contract and Control in the Entertainment Industry*, Dartmouth, Ashgate (1998)). The doctrine may also be examined as part of the wider class of illegal or unenforceable contracts, and may in particular be relevant to situations in which there are inequalities of bargaining power. Those interested in these aspects of restraint of trade should refer to a more detailed contract law text.

17.3 Economic torts

As early as 1410 it was clear that the mere act of competition could not be classed as tortious, even though the competition might have harmful effects for some parties (*The Schoolmasters of Gloucester Case* (1410) YB 11 Hen IV, fo 47, pl. 21). While the view persisted through the nineteenth century that it might be unlawful in some circumstances to deliberately act in such a way as to harm another's economic interests, judicial acceptance of this principle diminished, and the general position in English law was summed up by Bowen LJ in *Mogul Steamship* v *McGregor* (1889) 23 QBD 598, CA:

The substance of my view is this: that competition, however severe and egotistical, if unattended by circumstances of dishonesty, intimidation, molestation [or other illegalities] gives rise to no cause of action at common law. I myself should deem it to be a misfortune, if we were to attempt to prescribe to the business world how honest and peaceable trade was to be carried on in a case where no such illegal elements as I have mentioned exist, or were to adopt some standard of judicial 'reasonableness' or of 'normal' prices or 'fair freights' to which commercial adventurers, otherwise innocent, were bound to conform.

This view informs the various torts which relate to matters of competition. In each case, whether it be conspiracy, or inducement to break a contract, or interference with economic interests, the general rule is that an action which by itself is lawful does not become actionable if it results in adverse consequences for any particular trader. The courts are not well equipped to regulate competition, and in recognition of this fact will generally intervene only following an act that is itself recognized as unlawful.

17.3.1 Conspiracy

If there is an exception to the general principle set out above, and it has been recognized that 'the tensions in this history have, however, left their mark . . . there remains a penumbra of doubt' (Brazier, M. (ed.), *Clerk & Lindsell on Torts*, London, Sweet & Maxwell (17th edn, 1995), para. 23–04), it lies in the tort of 'conspiracy to injure'. Conspiracy in relation to economic torts has two arms, and a tort may also lie in situations in which there is a conspiracy to use unlawful means, which is related to the crime of conspiracy, although the unlawful means need not be criminal ones. The tort of conspiracy to injure may exist in situations in which there is a combination to harm another for no legitimate reason (see *Crofter Hand Woven Harris Tweed* v *Veitch* [1942] AC 435, HL).

The general proposition may be expressed thus:

(1) A combination of two or more persons wilfully to injure a man in his trade is unlawful and, if it results in damage to him is actionable. (2) If the real purpose of the combination is not to injure another, but to forward or defend the trade of those who enter into it, then no wrong is committed and no action will lie, although damage to another ensues. (*Sorrell* v *Smith* [1925] AC 700, *per* Lord Cave CJ)

Mogul Steamship v *McGregor* (1889) 23 QBD 598, CA; [1892] AC 25, HL is further authority for the proposition that it is quite legitimate, at common law, to conspire with others to improve a business position, even if harm to another is a direct consequence of this. In this case a group of ship owners formed an association to restrict access to routes, to raise prices and thence to increase the profits made. When the plaintiff company attempted to enter the market by undercutting the group's prices, the group acted in concert and reduced prices so as to drive out the entrant. The action was brought on the basis of both restraint of trade and conspiracy. Even had it been established that there was a restraint of trade issue, privity of contract would have prevented the plaintiff from recovering under this head.

There have been cases where the plaintiff has been successful in an action for damages following conspiracy. One such is *Quinn* v *Leathem* [1901] AC 495, in which a butcher employing a non-unionized work force lost custom when the union persuaded one of those being supplied meat by Leathem to cease to do business with him. Here there was no legitimate benefit to the union or to the customer in agreeing that the customer should cease to trade with Leathem, and the real object of the 'conspiracy' was to injure the plaintiff. In this, and other similar cases, it is necessary to establish, on the facts, that it is the intention to injure which is paramount. The House of Lords has labelled this tort 'anomalous' as

A is able to recover following B's otherwise lawful act that is made tortious only because it is committed as part of an agreement with C. However, the tort is 'too well established to be discarded, however anomalous it may seem' (*Lonhro Ltd* v *Shell Petroleum Co. (No. 2)* [1982] AC 173 at 189).

Although these principles remain good law, they have largely fallen into disuse, and it is unlikely that competition practitioners will have much recourse to the conspiracy doctrine when art. 81 EC and the Chapter I prohibition of the Competition Act 1998 are better able to provide a remedy in similar situations.

Where a conspiracy employs unlawful means and causes injury to a party a claim may also be upheld. This principle may extend to situations where the act complained of is not a criminal one, and in one case conspiracy was raised successfully when it was argued that the arrangement would, under the terms of the Restrictive Trade Practices Act 1956, be against the public interest (*Daily Mirror Newspapers Ltd* v *Gardner* [1968] 2 QB 762). It appeared briefly to be the case that intention to injure was also to be a determining factor in cases based on conspiracy using unlawful means, at which point the distinction between the two heads of conspiracy would be eroded. This was suggested in *Lonhro Ltd* v *Shell Petroleum Co. (No. 2)* [1982] AC 173, HL. In *Lonhro plc* v *Fayed* [1992] 1 AC 448, HL, the House of Lords retreated from this position, holding that it was necessary only to show that there had been an intent to injure, and not that this was to be the purpose of the conspiracy.

17.3.2 Unlawful interference with economic interests

Unlawful interference with economic interests will arise in situations in which a defendant commits an actionable wrong with the intention of harming the plaintiff. The tort is an independent one that is not dependent on conspiracy (see above), or inducement to breach a contract (see below).

In *Lonhro plc* v *Fayed* [1990] 2 QB 479, the plaintiff alleged that it had been tortiously deprived of the chance to bid for the share capital in the House of Fraser, which amongst other things owned Harrods, by virtue of the defendants misrepresenting their financial status. The plaintiff relied, in part, on the speech of Lord Watson in *Allen* v *Flood* [1898] AC 1, in which may be found the basis of a tort of *unlawful* interference with economic interests. This tort may apply where A intends damage to B, and achieves this by wrongful behaviour towards C (in *Lonhro*, a deceit), so that C's behaviour will damage B. A may then be liable to B. The Court accepted that such a tort existed, but, Dillon LJ argued, 'the detailed limits of [the tort] have yet to be refined' (at 489). It may be the case that there is little to distinguish *Allen* v *Flood* from *Mogul Steamship*, with the difference being that *Allen* v *Flood* relates to the actions of a single person and *Mogul Steamship* to conspiracy. Dillon LJ suggested, however, that it need not necessarily be the case that it was the predominant purpose of the tortfeasor to injure the victim rather than to pursue their own benefit (at 488–9), and that an action might lie on the basis merely that there had been wrongful conduct with respect to a third party, such as wrongful interference with a third party's contract, which caused harm to the plaintiff. The action complained of *must* be unlawful, and it was stressed in *Allen* v *Flood* that a lawfully exercised right cannot, in this context, become unlawful whatever the motive of the party.

17.3.3 **Unlawful interference with contractual relations and inducing a breach of contract**

It is a tort for C to induce B to breach a contract with A, to the detriment of A, without there being a reasonable justification. For example, in *Greig* v *Insole* [1978] 1 WLR 302 promoters of a cricket tournament brought an action against the English cricket authorities when the latter induced players contracted with the promoter to break those contracts. The application of this doctrine may be particularly pertinent to competitive situations, as it means that it may be tortious for one party to acquire another's customers by unlawfully inducing those customers to break contracts, or where existing contractual relationships are otherwise unlawfully interfered with (*DC Thomson and Co. Ltd* v *Deakin* [1952] Ch 646). It will not apply to situations in which A merely tries to persuade B's customers that A offers a better deal; B must show that A both knew of the existing contract and intended to interfere with it.

Although there have been some suggestions to the effect that a simple interference with a contract will lie within the tort (see, e.g., Lord Denning in *Torquay Hotel Co. Ltd* v *Cousins* [1969] 2 Ch 106), the better view remains that no action lies unless a full breach is induced.

17.3.4 **The tort of unfair competition**

The Paris Convention for the Protection of Industrial Property, art. 10*bis* requires that:

(1) The countries of the Union are bound to assure to nationals of such countries effective protection against unfair competition.

(2) Any act of competition contrary to honest practices in industrial or commercial matters constitutes an act of unfair competition.

The United Kingdom has not introduced specific instruments to ensure compliance with this principle, which relates primarily to intellectual property, and it is generally accepted that the obligations imposed by this article are met by the torts of passing off and injurious falsehood, and by the Trade Descriptions Act 1968. While these laws may indeed be invoked to protect economic interests 'it may be safely asserted that there is no tort of unfair competition in this country' (Adams, J., 'Is there a Tort of Unfair Competition?' [1985] *Journal of Business Law* 26, at p. 32). Because of its close relationship with intellectual property law, consideration of these issues belongs more properly to a text on intellectual property law. For a clear summary of the present position the reader is referred to Robertson, A., and Horton, A., 'Does the United Kingdom or the European Community Need an Unfair Competition Law?' [1995] *EIPR* 568.

17.3.5 **Statutory torts**

Because of the close relationship between the statutory torts based on breaches of arts 81 and 82, and those to be based on the Chapter I and II prohibitions of the Competition Act 1998, with the public regulation of competition this doctrine is dealt with in Chapter 5.

18

International issues and the globalization of competition law

18.1 Introduction

Competition law increasingly raises issues that cut across national and regional boundaries. Two cases from 1997 highlight the problems. In mid-1997, a trade war between the European Community and the United States was threatened when the EC Commission raised objections to the acquisition in the United States of McDonnell Douglas by Boeing (discussed further below). The United States' position was that this was a domestic matter and not one in which the EC should intervene; in the EC the concern was that competition in the global civil aviation market would be drastically reduced by the merger. After intense negotiations, which included the despatch of a US envoy to address the Commission, Boeing agreed to relax various exclusive arrangements, and the Commission withdrew its objections, although not before President Clinton had threatened that the matter could be taken to the World Trade Organisation (WTO) if the EC had carried out its threat to declare the merger illegal. The second major case concerned Microsoft, which found itself being challenged or investigated by the US Department of Justice, the EC Commission, and the Japanese Fair Trade Commission, as well as private parties in both the USA and Europe, and individual states inside the USA. Three years previously, in 1994, EC/US cooperation had worked effectively in dealing with another dispute concerning Microsoft's alleged anti-competitive practices (see below).

Within federal systems, such as the United States, or quasi-federal systems such as the EC, the conflicts that would arise between the component entities, states and countries respectively, are dealt with largely by the creation of the central rules which will generally take precedence over the state or national law (the relationship between Community law and the national law of the United Kingdom has been set out in Chapter 16). The creation of structures to manage conflicts between states that may lack a common interest, or to deal with, for example, activity that is permitted in one state but considered harmful in or to another, is more difficult. In its *1995 Annual Report on Competition Policy* the EC Commission noted that 'the increasing globalisation of the world economy and the changing pattern of modern trade makes international cooperation between competition authorities inevitable' (para. 12). The extent to which such cooperation is effective and the mechanisms by which such cooperation may be facilitated form the subject of this chapter.

There are several reasons why disparities in national laws are a cause of concern. First, they represent a cost to companies that increasingly operate in more than one state. These costs can relate both to learning the newly encountered law and to adapting a method of operation acceptable in one state to another state which may insist upon different commercial arrangements. Disparate laws may also lead to the erection of secondary import barriers by states that are, prima facie, committed to free market access and to the principles of the WTO which has assumed responsibility for the operation of the trade agreements concluded under the auspices of the General Agreement on Tariffs and Trade (the GATT). There is also a problem with the territorial effects of commercial decisions, which may impact upon more than one state with differing legal consequences in each state. This can lead to conflicts between national authorities competing for jurisdiction and, in the worst cases, either to multiple, conflicting actions taken against companies, or to companies avoiding actions altogether. Such a situation could lead also to the raising of the difficult problems posed by private international law, 'conflicts of laws'. If private litigants are involved this scenario is quite likely to arise, and it may also arise where a public authority proceeds on the basis of the 'effects' doctrine (discussed below). In this chapter a distinction will be drawn between public, institutional enforcement of competition law, which may raise issues of public international law, and private actions before national courts, which will be considered later.

The EC Commission has responded to the concerns raised by these issues by engaging in bilateral agreements with the United States; multilateral agreements with the European Economic Area; and by engaging in multilateral discussions via the WTO, the Organisation for Economic Cooperation and Development (OECD), and the United Nations Conference on Trade and Development (UNCTAD). In 1995 a group of experts convened by the Commissioner in charge of competition policy delivered its report, recommending that there should be an extension of the existing bilateral arrangements and a gradual move to multilateral forms of cooperation ('Competition Policy in the New Trade Order: Strengthening International Cooperation and Rules', COM(95) 395 final). In the United States the increasing focus on international enforcement in antitrust law has led to the appointment of a special Deputy Assistant Attorney General for International Affairs, and regular symposia are held between Japanese competition officials and their United States and Community counterparts. Other countries too are interested and involved in such dialogues and developments. Amongst others, Australia is very active, and Korea is also recognizing the international aspects of competition law enforcement. More recently the EC and USA have proposed the establishment of a 'Global Competition forum' (discussed below).

18.2 **Public enforcement**

In most competition regimes, whether in the major trading blocs or in developing countries, the enforcement of the law is largely left in the hands of the relevant public authorities. There will obviously be situations in which it will be in the interests of these bodies to cooperate with each other. Such cooperation might result, for example, in only one state taking action against a particular company where the result will remedy the wrongful conduct in all the affected states. It might lead also to the exchange of information gathered in one state that is needed to assist the relevant authority in another to press its case. It is equally possible to envisage, and find examples of, situations in which it is not obvious that it is in the authorities' interests to cooperate, or even where the authorities are in conflict. This will especially be the case where one country is seeking to protect a 'national champion', or is in no way harmed by activity undertaken by a company in its jurisdiction when that activity has effects only in another territory. A notorious example of such an approach applied generally is that of the Webb–Pomerene Export Trade Act of 1918 (15 U.S.C. ss. 61–65), which permits United States companies to implement export cartels 'provided such association, agreement, or act is not in restraint of trade within the United States, and is not in restraint of the export trade of any domestic competition of such association' (15 U.S.C. s. 62). The same Act, in s. 4, explicitly grants to the Federal Trade Commission jurisdiction over export practices outside the United States which constitute 'unfair methods of competition'. The 1982 Foreign Trade Antitrust Improvements Act (15 U.S.C. s. 6a) has provided additional emphasis to such claims. The hostility that these moves have led to abroad has inspired some countries to enact blocking statutes that are designed to frustrate the extraterritorial enforcement of US antitrust law (see Griffin, J. P., 'Foreign Governmental Reactions to U.S. Assertions of Extraterritorial Jurisdiction' [1998] *ECLR* 64).

Public enforcement of competition law will take place, typically, where a company based in a territory carries out acts which fall to be condemned under that territory's law. Such a situation will usually raise no issues that need addressing at the international level. Two other possible scenarios are more likely to lead to problems, however. The first arises where a company is based in several states, and is carrying out activities that are illegal in some states but not in others. If the company is attacked in those states where it is infringing, but its headquarters lie elsewhere, how will the state in which it is primarily based respond? The second situation arises where a company or companies based entirely in one state engage in behaviour that is condemned in another. This was the situation in the GE/Honeywell merger, where an act that was entirely legal in the USA was condemned in the EC (see below). Not all states recognize the validity of such actions, which are generally based on the 'effects' doctrine, and the United Kingdom in particular has been hostile to moves to base jurisdiction on 'effects'. The United States readily claims such jurisdiction, and the EC appears to do so, although the choice of words made by the Court of Justice in the leading case allows for some ambiguity.

18.2.1 The effects doctrine

The effects doctrine is a controversial part of international law, the position of which is not yet universally recognized. Under the doctrine a state may assume jurisdiction where an act that is committed in another state, by citizens or companies of other states, has effects in the former. This was accepted by the Permanent Court of International Justice in the *Lotus* case (*The SS Lotus (France* v *Turkey)* (1927) PCIJ ser. A, no. 10), although there continues to be strong debate amongst commentators about the exact scope of that judgment. If a group of Japanese and Korean businesses agreed to cooperate in raising prices for televisions in the EC, but were not based in the EC and sold into the EC only through agents who were themselves unconnected with the concerted action, the application of the effects doctrine might allow the EC Commission to take action against the companies, and the ECJ to uphold any fines imposed.

The United States has long applied the effects doctrine in the enforcement of antitrust law, the primary authority deriving from the case of *United States* v *Aluminum Co. of America ('ALCOA')* 148 E2d 416 (2d Cir. 1945). Both private claims, including those seeking treble damages, and public cases brought by the Department of Justice may be based on actions implemented in other countries that have a significant impact in the United States. This situation is explained clearly in the Antitrust Enforcement Guidelines for International Operations, issued by the US Department of Justice in April 1995:

SITUATION: A, B, C, and D are foreign companies that produce a product in various foreign countries. None has any US production, nor any US subsidiaries. They organize a cartel for the purpose of raising the price for the product in question. Collectively, the cartel members make substantial sales into the United States, both in absolute terms and relative to total US consumption.

DISCUSSION: These facts present the straightforward case of cartel participants selling products directly into the United States. In this situation, the transaction is unambiguously an import into the US market, and the sale is not complete until the goods reach the United States. Thus, US subject matter jurisdiction is clear under the general principles of antitrust law expressed most recently in *Hartford Fire* [see below for a discussion of some aspects of this case]. The facts presented here demonstrate actual and intended participation in US commerce.

There are restrictions on the operation of these principles. The 'act of state doctrine', the doctrine of 'foreign governmental compulsion', and the principle of comity all serve to limit the extraterritorial application of the law. The first of these is a general principle of public international law that provides that national courts cannot review the actions of sovereign states where that act takes place within the state. Thus a state body would not be found to be in breach of the Sherman Act were it to engage in activity that, if undertaken by a private party, would constitute a breach. Where a private party is *required* as a matter of national law to engage in activity that breaches United States antitrust law that law will also not be enforced (see, e.g., *American Banana Co.* v *United Fruit Co.* 213 U.S. 347 (1909)). The act of state doctrine has no place within intra-European Community relationships, where the Member States may themselves be liable if they encourage, or tacitly support, breaches of the law. This position flows from art. 10 EC, and was mentioned further in Chapter 2. The application of the principle of comity is discussed below.

In the Community legal order the most important case relating to the extra-territorial application of arts 81 and 82 is *Re Wood Pulp Cartel: A Ahlström Oy* v *Commission* (joined cases C 89, 104, 114, 116, 117, and 125–129/85 [1988] 4 CMLR 901; note that the ECJ dealt with this case twice—once on the issue of territorial jurisdiction and later on the issue of the substantive law of art. 81(1)). In this complex case (which is discussed in Chapter 7 in relation to the application of art. 81) the Commission had found that 41 producers of wood pulp, used in paper manufacture, and two trade associations had breached art. 81(1) (*Wood Pulp* 85/202 (1985) OJ L85/1). Thirty-six of these undertakings were based in either the United States or Canada, or Finland or Sweden, the latter two not being part of the Community at the time the Commission decision was taken. *Inter alia* the Commission held that the members of a trade association based in the United States had concerted on price announcements, had monitored any deviations from those prices, and had concerted on transaction prices. The Commission accepted an argument from these companies to the effect that they were unaware that their conduct breached the Treaty, since that conduct was expressly covered by the Webb–Pomerene Act (see above). The argument of the companies to the effect that the Act provided a total defence was rejected by the Commission and by Advocate General Marco Darmon, on the grounds that it did not actively *compel* the companies to organize their activity in this way, but merely exempted them from the application of US antitrust law. Similar charges were levelled against a Finnish trade association and Canadian producers.

The Commission argued in its decision that

Article [81] of the EEC Treaty applies to restrictive practices which may affect trade between Member States even if the undertakings and associations which are parties to the restrictive practices are established or have their headquarters outside the Community, and even if the restrictive practices in question also affect markets outside the EEC. (para. 79)

In its submission to the Court the Commission argued that the Community's jurisdiction 'is not in breach of any prohibitive rule of international law . . . in so far as its jurisdiction is based on the effects within the Community of conduct which occurred elsewhere' ([1988] 4 CMLR 901, at 915). Recognizing that 'the "effects doctrine" is still contested under international law' the Commission argued that 'the objections come primarily from the United Kingdom and not from the OECD or other countries' (pp. 915–16). Intervening in the case the United Kingdom asked the ECJ to resolve the issue by the application of territorial jurisdiction, that is, to find that the agreement had to the necessary extent been operated within the EC, rather than by any application of the effects doctrine. The Advocate General's view was that the Community should be able to assert extraterritorial jurisdiction where the 'effects of the conduct alleged ... were substantial, direct and foreseeable' (p. 938).

The judgment is sufficiently important to be quoted from at some length. The key paragraphs are as follows (pp. 941–2):

[16] It should be observed that an infringement of Article [81], such as the conclusion of an agreement which has had the effect of restricting competition within the Common Market, consists of conduct made up of two elements, the formation of the agreement, decision or concerted practice and the implementation thereof. If the applicability of prohibitions laid down under competition law were made to depend on the place where the agreement, decision or concerted practice was formed, the result would obviously be to give undertakings an easy means of evading those prohibitions. The decisive factor is therefore the place where it is implemented.

[17] The producers in this case implemented their pricing agreement within the Common Market. It is immaterial in that respect whether or not they had recourse to subsidiaries, agents, sub-agents, or branches within the Community in order to make their contacts with purchasers within the Community.

[18] Accordingly the Community's jurisdiction to apply its competition rules to such conduct is covered by the territoriality principle as universally recognised in public international law ...

[22] As regards the argument relating to disregard of international comity, it suffices to observe that it amounts to calling in question the Community's jurisdiction to apply its competition rules to conduct such as that found to exist in this case and that, as such, that argument has already been rejected.

In choosing to refer to the 'implementation' of the agreement instead of to the 'effect' of the agreement, the court may have been doing little more than applying an 'effects' doctrine in language that would be acceptable to the United Kingdom, and the application of the United States-style 'effects' doctrine and *Wood Pulp*'s 'implementation' may in practice produce equivalent results. However, this has left some uncertainty. What, for example, would be the position where there existed an anti-competitive agreement between Japanese producers with no direct selling arms in the EC? Would the agreement be said to be 'implemented' where EC customers placed orders for the products directly in Japan, under contracts governed by Japanese law? If there is a genuine distinction between 'implementation' and 'effect' it might be that in this hypothetical case there would be no jurisdiction under Community law, and that such jurisdiction might be assumed only where the Japanese companies were actively soliciting sales from the EC instead of passively responding to orders. A different situation could be one in which there is a market share agreement for a new product that has never been sold in the EC and that is not produced in the EC. It could be argued that this agreement would be implemented in situations either where a company will not sell the product into the EC when commercial sense would indicate that it should do so, or where it sells at an inflated price reflecting the action of the cartel. In such a case art. 81 might apply even though all participants are based entirely outside the EC.

The question of territorial jurisdiction was returned to in the case and decision relation to the *Gencor/Lonhro* merger (97/26 (1997) OJ L11/30), on appeal *Gencor Ltd v Commission* case T–102/96 [1999] 4 CMLR 971. In this case, which has been discussed in Chapter 15 in relation to merger control, the Commission blocked a merger between the South African interests of the two companies. The CFI was called upon to consider both the territorial scope of the Merger Regulation (at paras 78–88), and the compatibility of the decision with public international law (at paras 89–111). In determining the territorial scope, the CFI confirmed the position as being that jurisdiction does not exclude concentrations which, while relating to 'activities outside the Community, have the effect of creating or strengthening a dominant position as a result of which competition in the Common Market is significantly impeded' (para. 82).

When the undertakings attempted to rely on *Wood Pulp* in order to restrict the territorial application of the Regulation the CFI held that:

The applicant cannot, by reference to the judgment in *Wood pulp*, rely on the criterion as to the implementation of an agreement to support its interpretation of the territorial scope of the Regulation. Far from supporting the applicant's view, that criterion for assessing the link between an agreement and Community territory in fact precludes it. According to *Wood pulp*, the criterion as to the implementation of an agreement is satisfied by mere sale within the Community, irrespective of the location of the sources of supply and the production plant. It is not disputed that Gencor and Lonhro carried out sales in the Community before the concentration and would have continued to do so thereafter.   (para. 87)

The approach of the CFI was to introduce into the extraterritorial operation of the Merger Regulation a two-stage process. The first stage, to be answered by reference to *Wood Pulp* is that of whether there is territorial jurisdiction. The second stage is to determine whether, having exercised jurisdiction, the substantive tests set out in the Regulation should be applied so as to block a merger. In this respect the relevant parts of the judgment are, in part, as follows:

Application of the Regulation is justified under public international law when it is foreseeable that a proposed concentration will have an immediate and substantial *effect* in the Community.   (para. 90)

It is therefore necessary to verify the three criteria of immediate, substantial and foreseeable *effect* are satisfied in this case.   (para. 92)

And following a further discussion of these relevant factors the Court concludes this section of the judgment by holding that 'the arguments by which the applicant denies that the concentration would have a substantial *effect* in the Community must therefore be rejected' (para. 99, emphasis added).

In 1969 the United Kingdom vigorously protested at the application of EC competition law to a UK-based company, and appears in the Competition Act 1998 to have limited the application of domestic competition law to situations in which the practice condemned 'is, or is intended to be, *implemented* in the United Kingdom' (s. 2(3), emphasis added, which relates to the Chapter 1 prohibition; note that there is no need for a similar provision in relation to the Chapter II prohibition, which applies only where the dominant position is held *in* the UK, although the dominance may also extend *beyond* the UK). The position initially adopted was summed up in the 'statement of principles according to which, in the view of the United Kingdom Government, jurisdiction may be exercised over foreign corporations in antitrust matters', which was addressed to the EEC Commission, following its decision in relation to *Dyestuffs* (JO (1969) 24 July). Under this decision the EEC Commission had found that a number of undertakings in the dyestuffs industry had operated a cartel contrary to art. 81. Fines were imposed on, *inter alia*, ICI, which had its headquarters in the United Kingdom. Article 4 of the decision provided that the decision would be notified to ICI, and to Swiss undertakings that were similarly implicated, 'at the seat of one of their subsidiaries established in the Common Market'. Before the ECJ the issue was dealt with very simply, with the Court merely relying on the fact that, via its subsidiary, ICI *was* based in the EC (*ICI* v *Commission* case 48/69 [1972] CMLR 557). This has been termed the 'economic entity doctrine', which had been explicitly rejected by the UK courts in *Re Schweppes Ltd's Agreement* [1965] 1 All ER 195. Pointing to the conflicts arising between some of the Western European states and the United States in relation to the United States' assertion of jurisdiction over matters that fell outside its territory, the UK contested the 'fundamental point concerning the reach and extent of the jurisdiction exercisable by the Commission *vis-à-vis* undertakings which are neither incorporated in the territory of a Member State of the [EEC] nor carrying on business nor resident therein'. The stance taken at that time by the UK was that 'jurisdiction should be assumed only if the foreign company "carries on business" or "resides" within the territorial jurisdiction', and that 'on general principles substantive jurisdiction in antitrust matters should only be taken on the basis of either (a) the territorial principle, or (b) the nationality principle'. The *Dyestuffs* decision turned, in this respect, on the lack of distinction drawn under Community law between the various arms of an undertaking. For the UK the parent company, in this case ICI, should not have been considered to be carrying on business in the EEC by virtue of the fact that it had subsidiary companies there. Had the fine imposed by the EEC Commission been levied *only* on the subsidiaries that decision would probably not have been contested. However, this position has now changed. Intervening in the *Wood Pulp* case the United Kingdom took a more relaxed stance. The jurisdiction asserted over anti-competitive practices that have an impact in the United Kingdom under the Competition Act 1998 is intended to be an explicit and inflexible implementation of the *Wood Pulp* case law. In the passage of the Act Lord Simon explained that by 'copying out the test in *Wood Pulp* on the face of the Bill, we are also ensuring that in the event that EC jurisprudence develops and creates a pure effects-based doctrine, the application of the UK prohibitions will not follow suit' (Hansard (HL) 13 November 1997, col. 261).

Several forms of response have been made in relation to the problems raised by conflicts or potential conflicts in the application of competition law. Most loosely, the comity principle can be applied. More formally, bilateral and multilateral agreements can be concluded. Another possible solution would be the creation of a global competition order, similar to that of the trade order of the WTO. Were such a regime to be created it is likely that it would be under the auspices of the WTO, and preliminary discussions have already been held.

18.2.2 Comity and 'positive comity'

Standard international law texts are likely to draw a clear distinction between international law and international comity: the law is binding and comity is not. Thus comity has been defined as 'rules of goodwill and civility, founded on the moral right of each state to receive courtesy from others' (Shearer, I. A., *Starke's International Law*, London, Butterworths (1994), p. 18). This then is a principle of reciprocal courtesy, that may be of limited application in practice. In antitrust law comity has taken on a slightly different meaning and under the EC/US Agreement may have already generated enough law for it to be a recognition of a binding practice, akin to a legal principle.

The courts of the United States have, since the mid-1970s, turned to the doctrine of comity as a restraining factor in cases in which US antitrust law is applied to situations and parties outside the country's borders. For example, in *Laker Airways v Sabena, Belgian World Airlines* 731 F.2d 909, (1984) the court held that 'when possible, the decisions of foreign tribunals should be given effect in domestic courts, since recognition fosters international cooperation and encourages reciprocity, thereby promoting predictability and stability'. The approach of the courts has been to balance the interests arising out of the application of US antitrust law against the harm to comity that such an application may lead to. Four cases are of particular importance: *Timberlane Lumber Co. v Bank of America (Timberlane I)* 549 F.2d 597 (9th Cir. 1976); *Mannington Mills, Inc. v Congoleum Corp.* 595 F.2d 1287 (3d Cir. 1979); *Hartford Fire Ins. Co. v California* 113 S. Ct. 2891 (1993); and *United States v Nippon Paper Indus. Co.* 109 F.3d (1st Cir. 1997).

In *Timberlane*, which related to an alleged anti-competitive practice in Honduras, Judge Choy recognized that 'there is no doubt that American antitrust laws extend over some conduct in other nations' (p. 608), but expressed the concern that in many cases there was a danger that relatively weak interests of the United States could be asserted where it would be preferable to maintain good international relationships. He proposed a three-fold, cumulative test, by which to determine whether extraterritorial jurisdiction should be upheld (p. 615): (1) does the alleged restraint of competition affect, or was it intended to affect, the foreign trade of the USA; (2) would it fall within the Sherman Act; and (3) considering the principle of comity, should jurisdiction be asserted? These criteria were considered and refined in *Mannington Mills I* (pp. 1297–8) which concerned the allegedly anti-competitive enforcement and registration of patent rights by a United States company in 26 other countries to the detriment of Mannington Mills. The combined effect of these two cases was that the USA would assert jurisdiction where the alleged practice had direct and substantial effects, and that the courts would consider the 'balance of interests' to determine whether that jurisdiction should be upheld.

In *Hartford* the Supreme Court appears to have weakened the potency of the application of comity to antitrust cases. This case dealt with a situation in which 19 states and various private plaintiffs had complained that the defendants, which included both domestic and British companies, had conspired to restrict insurance terms in the United States. The British defendants, relying on *Timberlane*, argued that the effect of comity meant that any extraterritorial application of the Sherman Act should be struck down. At first instance this argument was successful. When the case eventually reached the Supreme Court it was held that the conduct fell within the Sherman Act, which could be applied extraterritorially where 'foreign conduct . . . was meant to produce and did in fact produce some substantial effect in the United States'. The *Hartford* judgment has been criticized both inside and outside the United States (see, e.g., Robertson, A., and Demetriou, M., ' "But that was in another country": The Extraterritorial Application of U.S. Antitrust Laws in the U.S. Supreme Court' (1994) 43 *International and Comparative Law Quarterly* 417). In *Nippon Paper* the Court of Appeals took a more hard-line approach. The claim was based on allegations that a Japanese cartel fixed the price of thermal fax paper in the United States. All the participants in the practice were Japanese; the meetings were held in Japan; and the sales to distributors were made in Japan. The Court held that the case should not, at first instance, have been dismissed, arguing that there was 'no tenable reason why principles of comity should shield [the Japanese companies] from prosecution'. The Court was swayed by the increasing amount of international commerce, and by that fact that the practice complained of would, if the allegations were sustained, be illegal in Japan as well as in the United States.

The level of court involvement in the antitrust process in the United States serves as a restraint on the application of the principle of comity. Even were the Department of Justice or the Federal Trade Commission to respect the interests and wishes of other states in the application of antitrust law, the courts are not obliged to follow their example should a case be brought by private litigants or by the individual states under their own antitrust law. It should be noted here too, that a US senate sub-committe is, at the time of writing, drafting a proposed amendment to the antitrust laws to allow actions to be taken against anti-competitive arrangements outside the USA, even where there is no proof that US consumers have been harmed. Such a proposal is, however, unlikely to become law.

The European Commission has shown that it is ready to embrace the principle of comity where it has the discretion to do so (see, e.g., *Boeing/McDonnell Douglas* 97/816 (1997) OJ L336/16, below).

The application of the Merger Regulation (see Chapter 15) raises particular problems with respect to the comity principle. The EC Commission does not appear to have discretion as to whether or not at least to consider any merger, wheresoever it is concluded, that falls within the threshold criteria set out in the Regulation. In some instances even such an examination is likely to be a matter of concern to other states.

There have been three important decisions which have related to mergers that would be carried out by companies whose production was entirely outside the EC.

In *Gencor/Lonhro* 97/26 (1997) OJ L11/30, on appeal *Gencor Ltd* v *Commission* case T–102/96 [1999] 4 CMLR 971, although both companies had substantial operations in the EC, and Lonhro was a UK company, the market in question was primarily that of platinum mined in South Africa. In this case the two undertakings jointly satisfied the thresholds set out in the merger regulation (see Chapter 15) and had sales into the EEA of over ECU 2bn at the time the concentrative joint venture was under consideration. Although the decision itself does not deal expressly with issues of jurisdiction other than to note that the thresholds were reached, it is clear that there was consideration of the South African position (see, e.g., paras 168–71). In its comment on the case in the *26th Annual Report on Competition Policy 1996*, the Commission found it 'worth underlining that, from the outset of the procedure, the South African authorities have been kept informed by the Commission of developments in this case and have attended the hearings organised in Brussels' (p. 184).

The *Boeing* case was particularly susceptible to charges of political interference in the regulatory process, although this was denied on both sides of the Atlantic. The merger between Boeing and McDonnell Douglas reduced the number of manufacturers of large commercial aircraft from three to two. As a result of this Airbus Industrie, based in Europe and part-owned by four European governments, was left facing a single dominant competitor. The Federal Trade Commission (FTC) publicly acknowledged that this level of structural restriction in the market was a problem, but then cleared the merger, holding in the process that there was no effective competition between the merging firms to be snuffed out by the merger. Notwithstanding reports in the United States press that emphasized the role of the new corporation as 'an American national champion' (e.g., *New York Times*, 17 December 1996), the FTC expressly denied that this was a consideration in its assessment of the merger. The EC Commission cleared the merger only after being given various assurances by Boeing relating to future commercial conduct. United States commentators, and Boeing's attorneys in particular, have argued that the concessions had little to do with the merger itself, but that the Commission was exploiting the situation to secure advantages for Airbus. Prior to the eleventh-hour settlement there had been speculation that if the merger proceeded contrary to Community law the severest of fines would be imposed and that Boeing planes landing in Europe might be seized. This was never a likely prospect, but the case is a perfect illustration of the problems that may arise in respect of such transactions and, notwithstanding the level of cooperation between the EC and the United States, 'diverging approaches of the competition authorities in Brussels and Washington made it impossible to reach commonly accepted solutions' (Schaub, A., 'International cooperation in antitrust matters: making the point in the wake of the Boeing/MDD proceedings', (1998) 1 *Competition Policy Newsletter*, p. 4). For further discussion and comment on this case see (1997) *Antitrust*, Fall issue, which features commentary and interviews with some of the leading players in the case.

Even more controversially, in July 2001 the EC Commission blocked the proposed merger between General Electric Inc (GE) and Honeywell Inc. In doing so, the Commission took a stance which was in direct opposition to that adopted by the US authorities, which had cleared the merger. It was noted in the Commission press release (IP/01/939, 3 July 2001) that

The European Commission and the US Department of Justice have worked in close cooperation during this investigation. It is unfortunate that, in the end, we reached different conclusions, but each authority has to perform its own assessment and the risk of dissenting views, although regrettable, can never be totally excluded. This does not mean that one authority is doing a technical analysis and the other pursuing a political goal, as some might pretend, but simply that we might interpret facts differently and forecast the effects of an operation in different ways. The GE/Honeywell is a rare case where the transatlantic competition authorities have disagreed.

The Commission was particularly disappointed in this case that offers of divestment and conduct remedies put forward to the merging parties were not accepted. Three articles in the Fall 2001 issue of *Antitrust* deal with this case with interesting perspectives.

It should be recognized that although the approach of the EC Commission in the Boeing and GE cases attracted considerable criticism within the United States, the latter's authorities have similarly examined mergers in situations where production has been outside the United States. This was the case, for example, with the Guinness/Grand Metropolitan merger leading to the creation of Diageo in 1998.

Where comity requires a country to respect another's interests in the application of its national law, 'positive comity' has greater force and might suggest, *inter alia*, that a country should enforce its own competition law in order to assist another country where it might not otherwise do so were it to consider purely national interests. This principle is prominent in the EC/USA cooperation agreements, discussed below, and has led to situations in which the EC is, on behalf of the USA, investigating anti-competitive conduct which is being pursued in the Community but which is of concern to the US authorities. One such complaint, for example, has been made about the European-wide airline reservation system, 'Amadeus', which the United States authorities believe has an adverse impact on United States' commercial interests (see below).

18.2.3 **Bilateral agreements**

Both the EC and the USA have concluded bilateral agreements relating to competition enforcement with a range of parties, and notably with each other. As well as its agreement with the EC the USA has also concluded agreements with Germany, which remain in force notwithstanding the links with the EC, Canada, and Australia.

In 1991 the Commission and the US authorities had reached a formal agreement on cooperation in the application of competition laws, but, following a challenge to the legal basis of the agreement by the French government, this was struck down by the ECJ on the basis of fundamental breaches in procedure (*France* v *Commission* case C–327/91 [1994] 5 CMLR 517). The Agreement, the purpose of which 'is to promote cooperation and coordination and lessen the possibility or impact of differences between the Parties in the application of their competition laws' (art. 1(1)) has now been readopted in its correct form on the basis of arts 83, 300(3), and 308 EC (95/145/EC, ECSC, (1995) OJ L95/45).

It is a primary requirement of the Agreement that the signatories will share information about the enforcement of antitrust activities. Article II(1) thus provides that 'each Party shall notify the other whenever its competition authorities become aware that their enforcement activities may affect important interests of the other'. This notification is to be far enough in advance of the taking of formal decisions 'to enable the other Party's views to be taken into account' (art. II(4)). Officials from the relevant authorities are to meet 'at least twice each year, unless otherwise agreed' to exchange information on a range of factors, and each is to provide the other with any information that comes to its attention that relates to anti-competitive activities of which the other should be aware (art. III). Article VIII provides that no Party is required to divulge information which it would otherwise be required to treat as confidential. Further, each Party is obliged, as far as possible, to treat as confidential any information given to it by the other Party.

To the extent compatible within each of the legal orders, the Parties will cooperate with each other in enforcement activity (art. IV) and in individual cases may coordinate their activities. Where they do so they shall act 'expeditiously and, insofar as possible, consistently with the enforcement objectives of the other Party' (art. IV(2)). This cooperation was tested for the first time in the approach taken to Microsoft in 1994. Microsoft, pursued simultaneously in both the United States by the Department of Justice and the EC by the Commission, appeared itself to be grateful for the cooperation between the authorities, which allowed the position to be resolved with the minimum of disruption to the company and with the benefit to Microsoft of a single solution satisfying both jurisdictions. So advantageous to the company was the procedure that it consented to the exchange between the authorities of information that would otherwise have remained confidential. The Commission was enthusiastic about the outcome of the case which, it claimed, 'serves as an important model for the future, as it shows how the two authorities can combine their efforts to deal effectively with giant multinational companies' (Press Release IP/94/653, 16 July 1994).

Article V of the Agreement is addressed to situations in which anti-competitive activities in the territory of one Party adversely affect the interests of the other. This introduces the 'positive comity' noted above. Articles V(2) and (3) are in the following terms:

2. If a Party believes that anti-competitive activities carried out on the territory of the other Party are adversely affecting its important interests, the first Party may notify the other Party and may request that the other Party's competition authorities initiate appropriate enforcement activities. The notification shall be as specific as possible about the nature of the anti-competitive activities and their effects on the interests of the notifying Party, and shall

include an offer of such further information and other cooperation as the notifying Party is able to provide.

3. Upon receipt of a notification under paragraph 2, and after such discussion between the Parties as may be appropriate and useful in the circumstances, the competition authorities of the notified Party will consider whether or not to initiate enforcement activities, or to expand ongoing enforcement activities, with respect to the anti-competitive activities identified in the notification.

The notified Party is not under an obligation to act (art. V(4)), but the principles of comity and goodwill suggest that it is likely at least to consider carefully any such notification. A general principle of comity is set out in art. VI, which deals with the 'avoidance of conflicts over enforcement activities'. This principle is sometimes referred to as 'negative comity'. Under this article 'each Party shall consider important interests of the other Party in decisions as to whether or not to initiate an investigation or proceeding, the scope of an investigation or proceeding, the nature of the remedies or penalties sought, and in other ways, as appropriate'. It would appear that this principle, which is clarified further in the article, is of a stronger and more generous nature than that recognized by the US Supreme Court in *Hartford Fire Ins. Co.* v *California* (above). This article was applied by both the EC and the United States in the Boeing case. Here the EC 'sought an appropriate way to take account of important national interests of the United States' and the Chairman of the FTC indicated that the body would 'take into account the expressed interests of the [EC] when reaching its decision' (97/816, para. 11). The two parties concluded a further Agreement, on positive comity alone, which was signed on 4 June 1998, the EU–USA Positive Comity Agreement 1998, 98/386 (1998) OJ L173/28. This agreement, from which mergers are excluded, creates a presumption that in some cases a Party will either suspend or defer its usual enforcement measures.

The core provision is art. III, which is in the following terms:

The competition authorities of a Requesting Party may request the competition authorities of a Requested Party to investigate and, if warranted, to remedy anti-competitive activities in accordance with the Requested Party's competition laws. Such a request may be made regardless of whether the activities also violate the Requesting Party's competition laws, and regardless of whether the competition authorities of the Requesting Party have commenced or contemplate taking enforcement activities under their own competition laws.

Even before the entry into force of this agreement, the Commission had acted under the positive comity provisions of the 1991 agreement. For example, in March 1999 it decided to open a formal procedure against Air France under art. 82 in relation to the information it made available to the Amadeus computerized reservation system, which was better than that given to a reservation system owned by American Airlines (IP(99)171, [1999] 4 CMLR 581).

The *Competition Laws Cooperation Agreement 1999 (EC/ECSC/Canada)* 1999/445 (1999) OJ L175 entered into force on 29 April 1999. It makes provision for consultation, coordination, and cooperation in the enforcement of competition law. It is, in essence, similar in approach to the agreement concluded with the United States, and takes the same approach towards comity (see art. VI).

In May 2000 the European Commission announced that it was seeking a mandate from the Council in order to negotiate with Japan an agreement similar to the ones with the USA and Canada (IP/00/495, 19 May 2000).

18.2.4 **Multilateral cooperation and globalisation**

18.2.4.1 *The European economic area*
There are several instances of multilateral cooperation in respect of competition policy. The most notable is that between the EU and the other members of the European Economic Area (EEA). The importance of the EEA is declining as its members assume full membership of the European Community. The EEA, concluded between the EC and the EFTA states, with the exception of Switzerland, entered into force on 1 January 1994 (1994) OJ L1/3). Liechtenstein acceded on 1 May 1995. As Austria, Finland, and Sweden have since joined the Community the non-EC contracting states are therefore Iceland, Norway, and Liechtenstein. Broadly the relevant law of the EEA mirrors that of the EC, arts 53 and 54 EEA reflecting arts 81 and 82 EC. Article 57 EEA essentially incorporates the Merger Regulation into the EEA.

18.2.4.2 *The North American free trade area*
In North America, Chapter 15 of the North American Free Trade Agreement (NAFTA, 32 ILM 605 (1993)) concluded between the USA, Canada, and Mexico, commits the parties to cooperation on antitrust matters. Amongst other provisions, each of the Parties is required, by virtue of the Agreement, to 'adopt or maintain measures to proscribe anti-competitive business conduct and take appropriate action with respect thereto' (art. 1501(1)). Primarily the provisions relate to the conduct and maintenance of state 'designated' monopolies, and they do not set new standards for the regulation of private anti-competitive conduct.

18.2.4.3 *The OECD*
The OECD has published a Recommendation which calls for countries to consult with each other in appropriate situations with the aim of promoting enforcement cooperation and minimizing differences that may arise (Revised Recommendation of the OECD Council Concerning Cooperation Between Member Countries on Restrictive Business Practices Affecting International Trade, OECD Doc. No. C(95)130 (Final), 28 July 1995). The preamble of this Recommendation suggests that 'if Member countries find it appropriate to enter into bilateral arrangements for cooperation in the enforcement of national competition laws, they should take into account' the Recommendation, and it would appear that the EC/USA Cooperation Agreement has been so influenced. Although the OECD has expressed an interest in competition law matters which is commensurate with its membership of industrialized nations, it has not taken formal steps towards harmonization, although a working group on international antitrust cooperation is trying to reach an agreement on a 'consensus recommendation' confirming members' hostility to hard-core cartels. This group is also examining ways of resolving jurisdictional problems in relation to

mergers having an international dimension. Early in 1998 a Recommendation on the prosecution of hard-core cartels was approved by the General Council.

18.2.4.4 *The WTO*

The WTO is primarily concerned with the free flow of trade, and with the elimination of trade barriers wherever possible. Its membership is nearly universal. A Draft International Antitrust Code was submitted to the members of GATT in July 1993, although no substantial progress was made in respect of this. More important was the failure of earlier efforts leading to the Havana Charter, which the United States refused to ratify. However, because of the increasingly close relationship between trade and competition policy the WTO established a working party following the 1996 Singapore conference, under the chairmanship of the French Vice President of the *Conseil de la Concurrence* (competition council), which was due to report on whether negotiations are advisable in this area in 1998. This followed a proposal from the EC Commission, which became an EU initiative, suggesting that it might be possible to reach international agreement in some key areas, such as the response to cartels (see Commission Press Release (1995) IP/95/752, 12 July). The prospects for success are uncertain. Neither the EC nor the USA envisages a globally binding agreement. Announcing the formation of an International Competition Policy Advisory Committee, Joel Klein of the Department of Justice, Antitrust Division set out the US position in words that do not suggest that the WTO group will succeed in creating a harmonized regime:

this working group can play an important educational role in demonstrating the important contributions of antitrust to efficient national markets and open international trade, and in fostering international cooperation. We are less persuaded that the time is ripe for the negotiation of global antitrust rules.   (24 November 1997)

Matters appeared to change somewhat following the change in Presidency with the election of George Bush in 2000. The future of the possibilities for international competition co-operation in the context of the WTO was discussed at the Doha Ministerial Conference, and parties signing up to the Doha declaration accepted that there was a valid case for the WTO to negotiate and conclude a multilateral Agreement on Trade and Competition. A key reason for this was a 'fundamental shift in the US position in July 2001' (see speech by Alexander Schaub, 4 April 2002). The areas that will be focussed on are the 'core principles of competition policy, such as transparency, non-discrimination and procedural fairness, commitment to outlaw hardcore cartels, [and] modalities for voluntary co-operation between antitrust authorities' (ibid.).

18.2.4.5 *ICPAC, the Global Competition Forum, and the International Competition Network*

On 28 February 2000 the International Competition Policy Advisory Committee, founded in 1997 by the US antitrust authorities, submitted its voluminous final report (this is available at **www.usdoj.gov/atr/icpac**—but is over 300 pages long).

Although the report was commissioned by the US authorities and prepared by US experts, it was well received internationally. The report made recommendations in relation to multijurisdictional merger review, cooperation in cartel enforcement, and the intersection of trade and competition policy.

Specifically the report argued that the steps to be taken in the future should first centre around the creation of further bilateral agreements, but that a multilateral approach is also needed. The ICPAC group suggested that the WTO was not the natural home for competition policy initiatives, and recommended instead the establishment of a new Global Competition Initiative for addressing the inter-national concerns relating to competition enforcement. This proposal met with approval within the EC, and in March 2001 Dr Alexander Schaub, then Director General for Competition, made a speech in favour of the establishment of a 'Global Competition Forum', which had been discussed by international experts at a meeting in February 2001. According to Dr Schaub, this GCF

should not be a new institution—it is not meant as an alternative to the involvement of the OECD or the WTO in competition policy. It should first and foremost be a competition authority forum, involving a minimum of permanent infrastructure, with support primarily provided by participating authorities and facilitators. However, it should draw together all interested parties—both public (e.g. other international organisations) and private (e.g. business, professional, consumer and academic bodies); these should be appropriately associated with the forum, as participants and/or facilitators.

In November 2001 the US DOJ and FTC, and the EC Commission became the founding members of the 'International Competition Network'. Six months after its launch some 50 competition authorities had joined the organisation, which will work flexibly on a project-by-project basis.

18.3 Private parties and the enforcement of judgments

18.3.1 Conflicts of laws

There are three issues that face any private party in a dispute which involves jurisdictional matters beyond the bounds of that party's state:

(a) Where should the action be brought?

(b) Under which law should the action be brought?

(c) How will any judgment be enforced?

In practice these issues can be highly complex. It would be possible to envisage a situation in which the courts of one state would hear the action and apply the law of another state, with the judgment being enforced in the courts of yet another state. These are complex matters that lie beyond the scope of this book, and the interested reader should refer to one of the specialist texts dealing with private international law or conflicts of laws.

18.3.2 **The World Trade Organisation**

The WTO agreement of 1994 is intended to be directed to the restrictive acts of governments. It appears, however, to have a limited potential for private antitrust litigants. In 1995 Eastman-Kodak filed a petition with the US authorities, based on s. 301 of the 1974 Trade Act (19 U.S.C. 2411), alleging that Fuji was hindering the distribution of Kodak film in Japan by operating an exclusionary distribution system that was blocked to Kodak, and that the Japanese Government was participating in limiting access to the Japanese markets. Kodak had alternative routes: it could, for example, have attempted to persuade the Japan Fair Trade Commission to take action based on violations of Articles 3, 8(1), and 19 of the Anti-Monopoly Law. The prospects for success would appear to be remote, however, and the Japanese authorities had already looked at the photographic film industry in 1974 without taking any significant remedial action. Kodak would also have had a private right of action through the Japanese courts, although art. 25 of the Anti-Monopoly Law provides that such relief becomes available only following certain formal action by the Fair Trade Commission, and again the prospect of success would be uncertain. The company could also have attempted to persuade the US Department of Justice to take action on the basis of an extended and aggressive effects-based approach to the application of US antitrust law. Again, such a step, although contemplated within the International Guidelines, would have been contentious and novel. In May 1995, therefore, Kodak filed a petition with the United States Trade Representative (USTR) inviting it to investigate the matter.

The USTR agreed to pursue the issue in July, and was prepared to do so not only on the basis of trade restrictions strictly interpreted, but also on the basis of the specific allegations of anti-competitive conduct made by Kodak. In the Summer of 1996 the USTR found that acts which restricted the sale of photographic materials by US exporters to Japan could be attributed to the Japanese Government. Section 301 of the 1974 Trade Act gives the USTR the discretion to take action when it finds that the actions of a foreign government are 'unreasonable or discriminatory'. The choice of approach is a wide one: at one extreme the United States government can take unilateral counter-measures. Such a step is, however, contentious and carries with it the risk of retaliation by the country against whose interests the steps are being taken. The United States authorities thus decided to turn to the binding dispute resolution procedure established in the WTO at the Uruguay Round. This procedure gives members of the WTO access to a dispute mechanism in the event of a conflict based on the trade laws of the GATT. A panel of three to five members is appointed to hear any dispute. The final complaint did not rely on the basis of the specific allegations made by Kodak, but was brought on the basis that 'Japan's laws, regulations and requirements affecting the distribution' of film treated importers 'less favourably', in breach of trade obligations. Only governments have access to this procedure; the hearings are closed to the public; private parties and counsel are, by custom, excluded; and governments are the only subjects of the proceedings. By seeking a ruling to the effect that the Japanese Government was impeding imports in its tacit support of anti-competitive industrial practices maintained in Japan the dispute moved to a new level, in which Kodak and Fuji ceased to act directly as litigants. The EC Commission also joined the panel as a third party due to its economic interest in the matter (see Press Release IP/98/122). Early in 1998 the WTO disputes settlement body rejected the United States' case on the merits, although it accepted that a similar route would remain open in the future (Panel Report *Japan—Measures Affecting Consumer Photographic Film and Paper*, WT/DS44/R, 31 March 1998; note that this has not been, as it could have, appealed). The panel also concluded that, in the appropriate circumstances, an action taken by a private party that has the effect of hindering trade may also be deemed to be governmental (para. 10.56). Such a procedure has clear advantages to the respective parties: although they are likely to be pressing their respective claims behind the scenes, they are not being required to invest heavily in the proceedings. The main drawback is that this procedure can be invoked only when it can be established that a government's action, or inaction, is involved as part of the original antitrust claim, and where the complainant can persuade its own government to bring the matter before the WTO. Although this is a somewhat tortuous route that will be beyond the reach of most companies and will require great patience, the position remains that lawyers

involved in international competition matters should keep in mind the possibility that the relevant trade agency might be convinced to bring a competition-related matter to the WTO for a resolution that might otherwise be unavailable in the antitrust system. (First, H., 'The Intersection of Trade and Antitrust Remedies' (1997) *Antitrust*, Fall, p. 21)

18.4 Conclusion

It is too early to envisage the creation of a global competition regime, with an international competition authority. The pattern at present is one of developing countries being encouraged to adopt competition laws, such as Zimbabwe's Competition Act 1996, and for expertise gained by states with developed competition regimes to be shared with the rest of the world. The ICN, and the WTO, appear to be the fora most engaged in this process.

Appendix

The Enterprise Bill

Introduction

In several of the preceding chapters it has already been noted that there are moves taking place aimed at substantial reforms of competition law in the UK. These took shape in late March 2002, when the Enterprise Bill was published on 26 March. The key areas affected by the Bill are:

- The institutional structure of the regime
- The carrying out of market investigations, which replace the scale and complex monopoly provisions of the Fair Trading Act 1973
- Merger control
- The criminalisation of certain cartel conduct

At the time of writing the Bill is at the Committee stage in the House of Commons, and the Government anticipates that the Bill will complete its passage in October 2002. It is not known when the various parts of the Act-to-be will take effect—some of the changes are substantial and it is likely that they will not bite on the date of Royal Assent. It has not been possible to incorporate a thorough discussion of the Bill throughout the preceding text, and this chapter therefore brings together in one place a discussion of the Bill, although the headings adopted here are intended to reflect those of the earlier chapters to allow for easy cross-referencing. It should be noted that the discussion here is based on the clause numbers as they stood at the time of the first publication of the Bill (Bill 115, 53/1), and it is certain that during its progress through Parliament these will be changed as some clauses are deleted, others added, and still others split. Not all of the Bill's clauses are dealt with here (neither are the more technical matters dealt with in the Schedules), and only the more salient points are set out. It should be possible to track further changes through the Government websites. In the next edition of this book the text will reflect fully the substantial impact that the Enterprise Act 2002 will have on the domestic competition law landscape.

The scope of the Bill is made clear in the preamble which describes it as a Bill to:

Establish and provide for the functions of the Office of Fair Trading and the Competition Appeal Tribunal; to make provision about mergers and market structures and conduct;

to establish the Competition Service; to amend the constitution and functions of the Competition Commission; to create an offence for those entering into certain anti-competitive agreements . . .

Clauses 239–60 make changes to the Insolvency regime and these are not dealt with here for obvious reasons. Clauses 1–200 deal specifically with competition law, and clauses 261–69 are also relevant in this context. Clauses 201–26 relate to a role of the OFT as they apply to the enforcement of certain consumer legislation, although this area lies outside the OFT's role as the primary enforcer of competition law in the UK. Clauses 227–38 relate to the disclosure of information by a public authority, and include provisions relating to 'competition information'.

The structure of the Bill is as follows:

Part 1 The Office of Fair Trading Clauses 1—11; Schedule 1
Part 2 The Competition Appeal Tribunal Clauses 12–19; Schedules 2, 3, 4
Part 3 Mergers Clauses 20–122; Schedules 6, 7, 9
Part 4 Market investigations Clauses 123–174
Part 5 The Competition Service and the Competition Commission Clauses 175–178; Schedules 10–12
Part 6 Cartel offence Clauses 179–193
Part 7 Miscellaneous competition provisions Clauses 194–200
Part 9 Information Clauses 227–238; Schedule 14

The regime (Chapter 2)

The Bill will make a number of changes to the roles played by the OFT and the Competition Commission, which also entails the repeal of parts of the FTA 1973 and the Competition Act 1998. In addition a new 'Competition Service' is to be created. Changes to the roles of the OFT are both set out in Part 1 of the Bill which deals specifically with institutional arrangements, and also elsewhere where changes will be necessary in order to accommodate new substantive responsibilities. For example, Part 6 of the Bill, which provides that cartelization may be a criminal offence, confers the power on the OFT to act as a prosecutor in these cases.

The most obvious immediate change in respect of the institutional structure made by the Bill is the abolition of the office of the Director General of Fair Trading ('the Director'), and his functions are to be transferred to the newly reconstituted OFT (cl. 2) which will be governed by a collegiate-style body (Sch. 1). The OFT is to carry out its functions on behalf of the Crown (cl. 1), and every year is to produce both an annual plan setting out a statement of its main objectives and priorities for the year (cl. 3) and a report on its activities for the previous year (cl. 4). Clauses 5–8 provide that the general function of the OFT includes the acquisition of information relating to its specific roles, the provision of certain information to the public and to Ministers. There are numerous minor amendments to the Competition Act

1998 to allow for the fact that the office of Director General of Fair Trading is abolished.

Clauses 12–14 relate to the role of the Competition Appeal Tribunal (CAT), which in effect is a reconstitution of the CCAT. As with the present constitution of the CCAT, the Tribunal shall be headed by a president, and appeals will be to the Court of Appeal. The CAT may hear appeals both under the Competition Act 1998, as at present, but also arising from the new merger control procedures, and from market investigations, although it is not to be involved in the new criminal offence relating to cartel conduct.

Part 5 of the Bill (cll. 175–178) deals with the new 'Competition Service' ('CS'), and the Competition Commission ('CC'). The purpose of the Competition Service is 'to fund, and provide support services to, the Competition Commission and the Competition Appeal Tribunal' (cl. 175(2)). The CS is required to make an annual report to the Secretary of State on its activities during the financial year (cl. 176(1)). Clauses 177 and 178 make necessary financial and procedural changes to the work of the CC in order to allow for the substantive changes made earlier in the Bill.

The Consumer Protection Advisory Committee, established under the FTA 1973 is to be abolished.

Investigation (Chapter 3)

There are some minor changes to the investigatory regime set out in the Competition Act 1998 made at cl. 194, which allow for other specified authorized persons to accompany the designated officer making an investigation under ss. 28, 62, and 63 of the Competition Act 1998. The position in relation to merger control, market investigations and the new criminal offence of cartel conduct are discussed below.

In Part 9 of the Bill cll. 227–238 relate to the control of information including 'competition information' relating to either 'the affairs of an individual' or 'any business of an undertaking'. Such information must not be disclosed unless the disclosure is expressly permitted under this Part of the Bill. Information is defined as competition information 'if it comes to a public authority' in connection with the application of the Enterprise Act, or of other specified legislation, although this does not include the Competition Act 1998, which contains its own rules relating to the protection of information (see Chapter 3). This part of the Bill does not prevent the disclosure of information if it is required by a Community law obligation (cl. 230), and in relation to other overseas authorities the OFT must issue criteria to be applied by a public authority in deciding whether to disclose information in accordance with cl. 233. Breach of the provisions relating to disclosure constitute an offence.

Penalties (Chapter 4)

There are no amendments to the penalty structure under the Competition Act 1998, although in some respects the regime is enhanced, as an amendment to the Company Directors Disqualification Act 1986 is amended by the insertion of new ss. 9A–9E to allow for a 'competition disqualification order' to be made against a director where:

(1) an undertaking which is a company of which he is a director commits a breach of competition law;

(2) the court considers that his conduct as a director makes him unfit to be concerned in the management of a company.

Breaches of two prohibitions of the Competition Act 1998, and arts 81 and 82 EC may give rise to such a disqualification. Other provisions allow for necessary investigations to be undertaken by the OFT to decide whether these provisions should be invoked.

The position in respect of penalties for breaches of the merger control provisions is discussed in the relevant section below. The most dramatic provisions in the Bill are those which give rise to criminal liability in the event of the committing of a 'cartel offence' (cll. 179–193). These provisions are dealt with below.

Third-party rights (Chapter 5)

The Bill makes a number of changes which are designed to make it easier for third parties to obtain remedies under the competition legislation, and in this respect it is clear that one aim of the reforms is to greatly facilitate the role that third parties play in the enforcement of competition law. In particular it is made much easier for an injured party to claim damages, adding to the likely payouts that infringing undertakings are going to be required to make.

The Bill makes provision, in cl. 11, for 'super-complaints', which relate primarily to the Chapter I Prohibition and Chapter II Prohibition of the Competition Act 1998. These arise where a 'designated consumer body' makes a complaint to the OFT relating to competition. Such complaints are given a privileged position in that the OFT will be obliged to respond to them within 90 days. The OFT is not required to pursue a complaint to the point of producing an adverse decision, but if no action is to be taken the OFT must explain why this is the case. Such a rejection of a super-complaint may be challenged before the CAT, as it will constitute a 'Decision'. It is for the Secretary of State to determine by order 'designated consumer bodies'. It is likely that at the first instance these would include both the National Consumer Council (NCC), and the Consumers Association (CA). The Secretary of State may by order provide that cl. 11 is to apply also to complaints made to specific regulators in regulated markets in the same way as it will apply generally to the OFT (cl. 196).

Section 47 of the Competition Act 1998 is to be replaced by a new s. 47 (cl. 15). Where the old s. 47 required third parties to make an application to the Director asking him to vary or withdraw a Decision, the new section allows for an appeal directly to the CAT. More importantly, a new s. 47A (cl. 16) makes provision for claims for damages to be brought directly before the CAT in any case in which either the OFT or the CAT have made a decision to the effect that the Chapter I Prohibition and Chapter II Prohibition have been infringed, or where a decision has been taken, either by the OFT, CAT, or the EC Commission to the effect that arts 81 and 82 EC have been infringed. This is a potent measure which, it is hoped, will greatly facilitate the prospects for third parties to claim for effective redress where they have been harmed by established anti-competitive conduct. Further, cl. 17 will insert into the Act new s. 47B which allows for class actions to be brought 'by a specified body on behalf of two or more individuals who have claims under that section as consumers and in respect of the same infringement'. This applies only in situations where claims would arise under s. 47A, and if successful damages may be awarded to the individuals named in the claim. These provisions do not affect the ability of third parties to bring actions in the civil courts in situations in which the OFT or the CAT have not made an infringement decision.

In respect of standard civil claims brought before the Courts on the basis of alleged infringements of the Competition Act 1998, a new s. 58A is added to the Competition Act 1998. This makes clearer the principles set out in s. 58, and provides that courts are bound by relevant decisions of the OFT. As with the new s. 47, specific mention is also made of findings to the effect that arts 81 and 82 EC have been breached, in anticipation of the new procedures to be adopted once the reform of the EC competition law system is completed, and more powers are given to the national authorities to implement EC law directly.

Third party rights are given in relation to the orders and undertakings entered into under the Bill in both relation to market investigations and to merger control (see below). Clause 159(3) provides that duties are owed to 'any person who may be affected by a contravention of the undertaking or (as the case may be) order' in relation to market investigations, and in relation to merger control the similar operative provision is cl. 90. In both cases any breach of an order or undertaking which gives rise to damage or loss shall be actionable by the aggrieved third party.

Agreements in the UK (Chapter 9)

Cartel offences

The most radical part of the Bill is that which makes certain cartel conduct a criminal offence. Thus, cl. 179(1) and (2) provide that:

(1) An individual is guilty of an offence if he dishonestly agrees with one or more other persons to make or implement, or cause to be made or implemented, arrangements of the following kind relating to at least two undertakings (A and B).

(2) The arrangements must be ones which, if operating as the parties to the agreement intend, would—

    (a)   directly or indirectly fix a price for the supply by A in the United Kingdom (otherwise than to B) of a product or service,

    (b)   limit or prevent supply by A in the United Kingdom of a product or service,

    (c)   limit or prevent production by A in the United Kingdom of a product,

    (d)   divide between A and B the supply in the United Kingdom of a product or service to a customer or customers,

    (e)   divide between A and B customers for the supply in the United Kingdom of a product or service, or

    (f)   be bid-rigging arrangements.

In all cases it is provided in cl. 180 that the criminal offence is created in situations in which the parties are, for the relevant act, at the same level in the supply chain—which is to say that the provision is concerned with horizontal restrictions only. The maximum penalty set in the Bill for a breach of this provision is a term of imprisonment not exceeding five years, or a fine, or both (cl. 181).

It has been noted already in the main body of the text of this book that there has been some debate as to whether the OFT or some other body—the Serious Fraud Office—is best placed to conduct criminal investigations. The decision has now been taken in the Bill that it is for the OFT to enforce this part of the Bill. Its powers of investigation are set out in cll. 183–193, and these stand apart from the powers of investigation under the Competition Act 1998, although they are clearly closely related to them. An investigation may be commenced where there 'are reasonable grounds for suspecting that an offence under [cl. 179] has been committed' (cl. 183). Clause 184 gives the OFT the power to, by way of notice in writing, require any person under investigation, or who it believes has relevant information, to provide that information, at which point the OFT may take copies or extracts of it. Clause 185 provides for powers of entry under warrant. A warrant may be applied for where the OFT reasonably believes that: (1) a person has failed to produce required material following the procedure set out in cl. 183; or (2) that it is not practicable to serve a notice under cl. 183; or (3) serving such a notice might seriously prejudice the investigation—because, for example, it might alert the relevant undertakings to the fact that an investigation is being conducted and give them time to destroy evidence, or agree on the way in which evidence would be presented. Once such a warrant has been granted the relevant officer(s) of the OFT have the power to enter and search premises, using reasonable force if it is necessary, to take copies or extracts of documents, and to require from relevant persons explanations of such documents, or information as to where they might be found.

One of the areas of concern raised by the authors of the report *Proposed Criminalisation of Cartels in the UK* ([2002] UKCLR 97), was that of the relationship between criminal actions and proceedings under the Competition Act 1998. This is an area which also raises some concerns in relation to the right to a fair trial under relevant human rights legislation. Clause 189 addresses some of these concerns, and provides in relation to statements made in the course of investigations under the Competition Act 1998 that:

30A Use of statements in prosecution

A statement made by a person in response to a requirement imposed by virtue of any of sections 26 to 28 may not be used in evidence against him on a prosecution for an offence under section 179 of the Enterprise Act 2002 unless, in the proceedings—

(a) in giving evidence, he makes a statement inconsistent with it, and

(b) evidence relating to it is adduced, or a question relating to it is asked, by him or on his behalf.

Various amendments made to legislation relating to criminal justice legislation necessary to effect proper investigations by the OFT in respect of cartel conduct, in particular to the Regulation of Investigatory Powers Act 2000 (see cl. 190).

Offences are created in respect of those who obstruct such investigations, make false or misleading statements, and falsify, destroy, or conceal evidence. Prison terms in these cases can range up to a maximum of seven years, depending on the seriousness of the offence.

Professional rules

As indicated in the main body of the text Schedule 4 of the Competition Act 1998 is to be repealed. This means that the general rules providing for the exclusion of the rules of professional bodies from the Chapter I Prohibition will cease to have effect. If professional rules are to be excluded this must now be done on a case-by-case basis analysing whether the requirements for individual negative clearance or exemption are met.

Single-firm conduct in the UK—Market investigations (Chapter 12)

Part 4 of the Bill relates to 'market investigations', which replace the provisions of the FTA 1973 relating to scale and complex monopoly investigations. It is to be regretted only that such a provision could not have been introduced at the same time as the Competition Act 1998. References in such cases are to be made by the OFT which, under cl. 123, may

make a reference to the Commission if the OFT has reasonable grounds for suspecting that any feature, or combination of features, of a market in the United Kingdom for goods or services prevents, restricts or distorts competition in connection with the supply or acquisition of any goods or services in the United Kingdom or a part of the United Kingdom.

Ministers are also given power to make references (cl. 124) where they are not satisfied in a situation where the OFT decides not to make a reference under cl. 123, or are not satisfied that the OFT will do so within a reasonable period of time. Relevant sectoral regulators are also given the power to make such references under the specific sectoral legislation.

It will be noted that this test, which adopts the wording of art. 81 EC and the Chapter I Prohibition, replaces that of the 'public interest' test currently set out in the FTA 1973. Clause 123(2) expressly provides that references may relate to structure—an issue which can still not readily be addressed under either art. 81 or 82 (or the two Competition Act 1998 prohibitions)—as well as to conduct. When it makes a reference the OFT is under a duty to give to the CC such information as it has in its possession which the CC may reasonably require, and to provide it with other reasonable assistance (cl. 162). As soon as is possible after the enactment of the legislation both the OFT and the CC shall produce general advice and information about the making of references under this part of the Act (cl. 163).

References are to be made to the CC, which is to decide both whether there is an adverse effect on competition (cl. 126(1), (2)), and whether it should recommend that remedial action be taken, in particular to address 'any detrimental effect on customers so far as it has resulted from, or may be expected to result from, the adverse effect on competition' (cl. 161(4)). A detrimental effect on customers is defined in cl. 126(5) as arising where there are:

(a) higher prices, lower quality or less choice of goods or services in any market in the United Kingdom (whether or not the market to which the feature or features relate); or

(b) less innovation in relation to such goods or services.

Commission reports into such market investigations will be published under the terms of cl. 128. The time period allowed for such reports to be completed is that of two years from the date on which the reference is made (cl. 129(1)), although the Secretary of State may by order amend this period, but only by lessening it.

Where the CC identifies adverse competition effects in any report it is under a duty to take such action as it considers practicable to amend or remedy these effects (cl. 130). This signifies a major difference to the regime under the FTA 1973 where, other than making recommendations, the CC had no role to play in remedying conduct against the public interest.

As with the position in relation to merger control (see below) the Secretary of State has the power to intervene in cases in which there is a 'public interest' (cll. 132–145). In such a case, no more than four months after a reference has been made, the Secretary of State may give an 'intervention notice' (cl. 131), which will state, *inter alia*, 'the public interest consideration or considerations which are, or may be, relevant to the case' (cl. 132(1)(c)). Under these references the final decision-making power following a CC report rests with the Secretary of State.

As with merger control the OFT may accept an undertaking or undertakings in lieu of making a reference under this Part of the Bill (cl. 146). Before accepting any such undertaking public notice of the procedure must be made (cl. 147). Once an undertaking has been accepted the OFT is precluded from making a reference in relation to the relevant market for at least one year unless the undertaking has been breached, or was based on false information provided by the person giving the undertaking (cl. 148). In certain circumstances, set out in cl. 149, interim undertakings may be made in order to prevent pre-emptive action, which is defined as 'action which might prejudice the market investigation reference concerned or impede the taking of any action [under other relevant clauses]' (cl. 149(6)). Following the conclusion of a reference the CC (or Secretary of State in the case of a 'public interest' reference) may accept final undertakings to remedy the harms identified (cl. 151), although in such cases it is for the OFT to enter into negotiations with the persons concerned to establish whether they are prepared to offer acceptable undertakings (cl. 155). Where such undertakings are not fulfilled it may be enforced by an order (cl. 152). It is the duty of the OFT to monitor undertakings and orders, and to ensure that they are complied with (cl. 154).

As well as being actionable by wronged third parties the relevant public authority may enforce compliance with an order or undertaking by way of proceedings brought for an injunction or for interdict or for any other appropriate relief or remedy (cl. 159(7)).

Clause 160 relates to market investigations in the regulated markets.

The powers of investigation and enforcement available to the OFT and the CC are the same as those set out in Part 3 of the Act relating to merger control (dealt with below), and offences are committed where, without reasonable excuse, persons fail to comply with the appropriate notices, or where evidence is destroyed, altered, or suppressed. Appeals under this Part of the Bill lie to the CAT (cl. 169).

Merger control (Chapter 15)

Part 3 of the Bill makes fundamental changes to the domestic merger control regime, and it is not possible here to deal with these in full detail given that at the time of writing the Bill is still being debated in Parliament. The structure of this Part is as follows:

Chapter 1: Duty to make references
1   *Duty to make references: completed mergers*
2   *Duty to make references: anticipated mergers*
3   *Determination of references*

In the FTA 1973, sections 63–76, will be repealed.

Under the new merger regime the role of the Secretary of State for Trade and Industry is largely eliminated, and the interaction is now almost exclusively between the OFT and the Competition Commission ('CC'), although in some 'public interest cases' the Secretary of State will continue to play a role. It is now for the OFT to make a reference to the CC in situations where (a) a relevant merger situation has been created; and (b):

the creation of that situation has resulted, or may be expected to result, in a substantial lessening of competition within any market or markets in the United Kingdom for goods or services (cl. 20(b)).

The substantial lessening of competition test (or 'SLC test') has been discussed briefly in Chapter 15 above. Two tests are set out for whether mergers fail to be considered. These are in the alternative. The first is that of a turnover threshold which as set out in the Bill at the time of writing is that the turnover of the enterprise being taken over in the UK exceeds £45 million (cl. 21(1)(b)). There is no reference to the turnover of the acquiring undertaking, and the test is therefore a straightforward one when compared, for example, to the thresholds applied in the EC merger control regulation (although a slight complication is raised in cl. 26 which sets out the turnover test in more detail). The second test is that the merger creates a situation, or arises in a situation, where at least 25% of the goods or services as defined are supplied by, or to, one and the same person (cl 21(1)(3)).

The new provisions make express allowance for an analysis of the beneficial effects of a merger, although these are couched in terms that are narrower than was the case when a less specific analysis could be conducted under the public interest test of the FTA 1973. Thus cl. 20 provides that a reference may not be made by the OFT in situations in which (a) the market concerned is not of sufficient importance to justify a reference, or when:

(b) any relevant customer benefits in relation to the creation of the relevant merger situation concerned outweigh any adverse effects of the substantial lessening of competition concerned.

This provision should be read in conjunction with that in cl. 28 which deals with the meaning of 'relevant customer benefits'. The factors to be taken into account are whether the merger may lead to 'lower prices, higher quality or greater choice of goods or services' (cl. 28(1)(a)(i)), or where it leads to 'greater innovation in relation to such goods or services' (cl. 28(1)(a)(ii)).

The provisions relating to anticipated mergers broadly mirror those in relation to completed mergers. It should be noted that in neither case is there an obligation on the part of the merging entities to notify their merger to the OFT, although powers are to be made available to the OFT to request information should it decide to investigate any particular merger.

In both cases the CC, to which references are to be made, is required to complete and publish its report into the merger situation within a period of 24 weeks, although this period may exceptionally be extended in 'special circumstances' (cl. 37). Where the CC identifies that there is an anti-competitive outcome arising out of the merger it has a duty to remedy these effects to the extent to which it is able to do so, and 'shall, in particular, have regard to the need to achieve as comprehensive a solution as is reasonable and practicable to the substantial lessening of competition and any adverse effects resulting from it' (cl. 39(4)).

In Chapter 2 of this part of the Bill reference is made to 'public interest cases' in which a vestigial role of the Secretary of State is set out. Under cl. 40(2) the Secretary of State may give an 'intervention notice' if he believes it to be the case that one or more public interest considerations are relevant to the merger situation. 'Public interest considerations' are those set out in cl. 56, or if not set out there, 'in the opinion of the Secretary of State ought to be so specified' (cl. 40(3)). The only specified consideration set out in cl. 56 is that of 'national security', which includes 'public security' and is taken to have the same meaning as in art. 21(3) of the EC Merger Regulation. Where an intervention notice is made the OFT shall report on the merger to the Secretary of State, and this report, as well as dealing with the standard legal and economic assessment required of the merger 'may, in particular, include advice and recommendations on any public interest consideration . . . which is or may be relevant to the Secretary of State's decision' (cl. 42(8)).

Following the report of the OFT the Secretary of State may himself make a reference to the CC. This might be the case either on the grounds that both a substantial lessening of competition and the public interest consideration raises issues that affect the public interest, or, in the alternative, that there is no substantial lessening of competition, but that the public interest consideration alone raises matters of concern (cl. 43). The CC's report will be presented to the Secretary of State within the same time limits as operate in relation to a reference made by the OFT. Following receipt of the report the Secretary of State 'shall decide whether to make an adverse public interest finding in relation to the relevant merger situation or whether to make no finding at all in the matter' (cl. 52(2)). The report of the CC will be binding on the Secretary of State to the extent to which it relates to (a) whether a relevant merger situation has been created; and (b) whether there is a substantial lessening of competition. However, the Secretary of State is not bound as regards the finding of the CC relating to the public interest (cl. 54).

Chapter 3 of this part of the Bill relates to 'special public interest cases', which may arise in situations in which 'special merger situations' are created. These are mergers which are not caught either by the £45 million, or the 25 per cent market share threshold. The OFT and CC have the same roles as above, although the CC is not required to deal with the question of whether the merger in question will lead to a substantial lessening of competition.

In the case of both of the public interest cases above, the Secretary of State may, following the report of the CC 'take such action . . . as he considers to be reasonable and practicable to remedy, mitigate or prevent any of the effects adverse to the public interest' (cll. 53(2) and 64(6)).

Chapter 4 deals with the enforcement procedures that are available in relation to merger control. This provides a self-contained mechanism that stands apart from that of the Competition Act 1998. The two primary mechanisms are those of 'undertakings' (by which is meant 'commitments' entered into by the enterprises in question) and enforcement orders. Undertakings may be entered into either to avoid 'pre-emptive action' where the OFT intends to make a reference in respect of a merger (cl. 67), or as an alternative to a reference (cl. 69). In the latter case the OFT is then prohibited from making a merger reference unless material facts were not made known to the OFT or were not public at the time at which the undertaking was made (cl. 70).

Enforcement orders may be made in a number of circumstances. Where undertakings made under cl. 69 are not being fulfilled the OFT has the power to make orders requiring that they be complied with (cl. 71). Where a merger has been put into effect, and a reference is contemplated, the OFT may make an 'initial enforcement order' in order to prevent pre-emptive action (cl. 68). Pre-emptive action is defined in cl. 67(8) as being

action which might prejudice the reference concerned and impede the taking of any action under this Part which may be justified by the Commission's decisions on the reference.

Various interim restrictions may be applied in cases where merger references have been made, but have not yet resulted in a completion of the appropriate procedure. Firstly, under cl. 73, the parties affected shall not take further steps to consummate the merger. Secondly, under cl. 74 where a reference has been made in respect of an anticipated merger no 'relevant person' shall acquire an interest in any company which is in the control of any company to which the reference relates. Interim undertakings and interim orders are further provided for in cll. 76 and 77. Both apply where a reference has been made but not yet determined.

Following the determination of the reference the CC may accept final undertakings (cl. 78) in order to remedy the adverse effects of anticipated or completed mergers. If such undertakings are made, but are not fulfilled the CC may make orders to deal with this under cl. 79, and where no undertakings are offered the Commission may make a final order to remedy adverse effects (cl. 80). In relation to public interest and special public interest cases the relevant instrument for enforcement is Sch. 6. Enforcement orders may, in certain circumstances, extend to conduct outside the UK, but only in situations in which the person in question is either (a) a UK national, (b) a UK company, or (c) carrying on business in the UK (cl. 82). A register of undertakings and orders is to be maintained by the OFT (cl. 87), and the OFT has a duty to keep under review and to monitor undertakings and orders (cl. 88). The rights of third parties to bring actions where undertakings or orders are breached, to their detriment, is discussed above.

Clauses 92–104 contain various supplementary provisions relating to mergers, which are largely of a technical nature. Of more general interest are the investigation powers set out in cll. 105–113. The CC may require any person to give evidence before it in relation to an investigation under a merger reference (cl. 105), and penalties may be imposed in the event of non-compliance (cll. 106 and 107). Such penalties may be either a fixed amount or a daily rate: in the former case the amount, which is to be set by an order made by the Secretary of State, may not exceed £30,000 and in the latter case not more than £15,000 per day (cl. 107(7)). At cl. 117 it is provided that where any offence is committed under this Part of the Bill by a body corporate, but is attributable to a specific senior officer of the company, that individual may be held liable to be proceeded against.

Decisions of the OFT and CC relating to mergers may, for the first time, be appealed, with cl. 114 providing that:

(1) Any person aggrieved by a decision of the OFT, the Secretary of State or the Commission under this Part in connection with a reference or possible reference in relation to a relevant merger situation or a special merger situation may apply to the Competition Appeal Tribunal for a review of that decision.

From the CAT an appeal on a point of law only may be made to the Court of Appeal (cl. 114(8)).

The impact of Community law in the UK (Chapter 16)

At various points throughout the Bill acknowledgement is made of the fact that it is anticipated that following the reform of EC competition law, the UK authorities will play a more active role in its enforcement. It has been noted above, for example, that third parties will be able to claim damages directly before the CAT in situations in which the OFT or CAT have reached adverse decisions relating to infringements of arts. 81 or 82 EC.

In cl. 200, the last clause of the Bill to deal specifically with competition law, a sweeping power is given to the Secretary of State in recognition that there may be a need to introduce further changes to the legislative framework following the EC changes. In particular it is provided that

The Secretary of State may by regulations make such modifications of the 1998 Act as he considers appropriate for the purpose of eliminating or reducing any differences between—

(a) the domestic provisions of the 1998 Act, and

(b) European Community competition law,

which result (or would otherwise result) from a relevant Community instrument made after the passing of this Act.

It is perhaps untimely that the Enterprise Bill was brought forward before the changes to the Community competition system became evident, but on the other hand the system, coupled to the potent effect of s. 60 of the Competition Act 1998, now allows for a swift domestic response to any such changes.

INDEX